"The Global Residence and Citizenship Handbook is the encyclopedia of residence and citizenship-by-investment programs. It is a most valuable comprehensive reference addressing all questions that may come up when planning residence or citizenship in another country, including the legal, the financial, the personal and the practical."

Ghada Alaltrash, Gulf News, Dubai

"Dr. Chris Kälin's book is the essential resource for anyone involved in the investment migration industry around the world. The world is truly 'on the move' in the 21st century, bringing with it opportunity that requires a global perspective epitomized by this must-have addition to your library."

Peter D. Joseph, Executive Director,
Association to Invest in the USA

"… a very helpful resource for guidance on residence and citizenship issues for the international client."

Marnin J. Michaels, Partner, Baker & McKenzie Zurich

Dr. Christian H. Kälin

Global Residence and Citizenship Handbook

Residence Planning • Alternative Citizenship
Passports • Visa Restrictions
Freedom of Movement • Tax Planning

6th Edition • Revised and Expanded

With contributions by
Dr. Marshall Langer, Professor Denis Kleinfeld and Simon Anholt

Foreword by
Tonio Fenech MP, former Minister of Finance,
Economy and Investment of Malta (2008-2013)

Introduction by
Julia Onslow-Cole
Global Head of Immigration, PwC

IDEOS
New York • London • Zurich • Hong Kong

For general information on our other products and services please visit: ideospublications.com

All books published by Ideos Publications are also available as e-books.

The CIP Catalogue record for this book is available from the British Library.

ISBN (Paperback): 978-0-9935866-2-0

ISBN (Hardback): 978-3-9524052-8-4

ISBN (eBook): 978-0-9935866-4-4

Where liberty dwells, there is my country.

Benjamin Franklin

Contents

About This Book   xi

Henley & Partners: The Global Leaders in Residence
and Citizenship Planning   xiii

Impact   xv

Acknowledgements   xvii

Foreword   xix

Introduction   xxi

Part I   RESIDENCE AND CITIZENSHIP PLANNING

1   Residence Planning   **3**

1.1   Why become resident in another country?   5

1.2   Residence and domicile   9

1.3   Change of tax residence   11

1.4   Factors to consider when choosing a new residence   13

1.5   Tax residence: considerations and implications   26

1.6   Financial planning and insurance   33

1.7   International health insurance   35

1.8   International residential real estate   38

2   Citizenship Planning   **47**

2.1   Why become a citizen of more than one country?   49

2.2   Who is interested in a second citizenship?   52

2.3   How to obtain a second citizenship   54

2.4   Criteria to consider when acquiring citizenship   59

3   Giving up US Citizenship or a US Green Card   **63**

4   The Identity and Brand of Nations   **75**

4.1   Can a nation's image be changed?   81

4.2   Measuring the Images of Nations   82

4.3   Measuring the Images of Cities   90

4.4   Looking to the future: "Governmental Social Responsibility"   94

Part II CITIZENSHIP, PASSPORTS AND VISAS

5	**Nationality and Citizenship**	**99**
6	**Freedom of Movement and Regional Arrangements**	**107**
	6.1 Introduction	109
	6.2 European Union	111
	6.3 European Free Trade Association and the European Economic Area Agreement	116
	6.4 The Schengen area	117
	6.5 Bilateral agreements with Switzerland	121
	6.6 Other regional arrangements and organizations	122
7	**Passports and Visas**	**129**
	7.1 Passports and other travel documents	132
	7.2 Visa requirements	138
	7.3 Health requirements	142
8	**Visa Restrictions Index**	**145**
	8.1 Definition of the Index	147
	8.2 2016 Highlights	148
	8.3 Methodology	150
9	**Quality of Nationality Index**	**157**
	9.1 Introduction	159
	9.2 QNI General Ranking	162
	9.3 The External Value of Nationality Ranking	165
	9.4 Settlement Freedom Ranking	166
	9.5 Travel Freedom Ranking	167
	9.6 Expert commentaries	168
	9.7 Concluding remarks	174

Part III THE WORLD'S PREMIER RESIDENCE OPTIONS

10	**Overview of Residence Options**	**177**
	10.1 The Global Residence Program Index	188
11	**Australia**	**191**
	11.1 Residence in Australia	194
	11.2 Requirements	194

11.3	Procedures and time frame	196
11.4	Taxation	197
11.5	Family law and inheritance aspects	198
11.6	Citizenship	199
11.7	Dual citizenship	200
11.8	Key advantages and disadvantages	200
11.9	General information	201
11.10	Climate	202
12	**Austria**	**203**
12.1	Residence in Austria	206
12.2	Requirements	208
12.3	Procedures and time frame	209
12.4	Taxation	209
12.5	Family law and inheritance aspects	210
12.6	Citizenship	211
12.7	Dual citizenship	212
12.8	Key advantages and disadvantages	212
12.9	General information	214
12.10	Climate	215
13	**Belgium**	**217**
13.1	Residence in Belgium	220
13.2	Requirements	222
13.3	Procedures and time frame	223
13.4	Taxation	224
13.5	Family law and inheritance aspects	226
13.6	Citizenship	226
13.7	Dual citizenship	227
13.8	Key advantages and disadvantages	227
13.9	General information	228
13.10	Climate	229
14	**Canada**	**231**
14.1	Residence in Canada	234
14.2	Requirements	235
14.3	Procedures and time frame	240
14.4	Taxation	241
14.5	Family law and inheritance aspects	242
14.6	Citizenship	242

	14.7	Dual citizenship	244
	14.8	Key advantages and disadvantages	244
	14.9	General information	245
	14.10	Climate	246

15	**Guernsey**		**247**
	15.1	Residence in Guernsey	250
	15.2	Requirements	253
	15.3	Procedures and time frame	254
	15.4	Taxation	255
	15.5	Family law and inheritance aspects	257
	15.6	Citizenship	257
	15.7	Dual citizenship	257
	15.8	Key advantages and disadvantages	257
	15.9	General information	259
	15.10	Climate	260

16	**Hong Kong**		**261**
	16.1	Residence in Hong Kong	264
	16.2	Requirements	267
	16.3	Procedures and time frame	268
	16.4	Taxation	270
	16.5	Family law and inheritance aspects	271
	16.6	Citizenship	271
	16.7	Dual citizenship	273
	16.8	Key advantages and disadvantages	273
	16.9	General information	274
	16.10	Climate	275

17	**Jersey**		**277**
	17.1	Residence in Jersey	280
	17.2	Requirements	282
	17.3	Procedures and time frame	284
	17.4	Taxation	286
	17.5	Family law and inheritance aspects	287
	17.6	Citizenship	288
	17.7	Dual citizenship	288
	17.8	Key advantages and disadvantages	288
	17.9	General information	289
	17.10	Climate	290

18   Malaysia   **291**

   18.1   Residence in Malaysia   293

   18.2   Requirements   295

   18.3   Procedures and time frame   296

   18.4   Taxation   296

   18.5   Family law and inheritance aspects   296

   18.6   Citizenship   297

   18.7   Dual citizenship   298

   18.8   Key advantages and disadvantages   298

   18.9   General information   299

   18.10 Climate   300

19   Malta   **301**

   19.1   Residence in Malta   304

   19.2   Requirements   304

   19.3   Procedures and time frame   305

   19.4   Taxation   305

   19.5   Family law and inheritance aspects   306

   19.6   Citizenship   307

   19.7   Dual citizenship   307

   19.8   Key advantages and disadvantages   307

   19.9   General information   309

   19.10 Climate   310

20   Monaco   **311**

   20.1   Residence in Monaco   314

   20.2   Requirements   314

   20.3   Procedures and time frame   316

   20.4   Taxation   316

   20.5   Family law and inheritance aspects   318

   20.6   Citizenship   319

   20.7   Dual citizenship   319

   20.8   Key advantages and disadvantages   320

   20.9   General information   321

   20.10 Climate   322

21   New Zealand   **323**

   21.1   Residence in New Zealand   325

   21.2   Requirements   326

   21.3   Procedures and time frame   327

21.4   Taxation 328

21.5   Family law and inheritance aspects 329

21.6   Citizenship 329

21.7   Dual citizenship 329

21.8   Key advantages and disadvantages 330

21.9   General information 331

21.10 Climate 332

22   Portugal **333**

22.1   Residence in Portugal 336

22.2   Requirements 338

22.3   Procedures and time frame 340

22.4   Taxation 340

22.5   Family law and inheritance aspects 341

22.6   Citizenship 342

22.7   Dual citizenship 343

22.8   Key advantages and disadvantages 343

22.9   General information 345

22.10 Climate 346

23   Singapore **347**

23.1   Residence in Singapore 350

23.2   Requirements 351

23.3   Procedures and time frame 354

23.4   Taxation 355

23.5   Family law and inheritance aspects 356

23.6   Citizenship 357

23.7   Dual citizenship 357

23.8   Key advantages and disadvantages 357

23.9   General information 359

23.10 Climate 360

24   Switzerland **361**

24.1   Residence in Switzerland 364

24.2   Requirements 365

24.3   Procedures and time frame 368

24.4   Taxation 368

24.5   Family law and inheritance aspects 371

24.6   Citizenship 372

24.7   Dual citizenship 373

24.8	Key advantages and disadvantages	373
24.9	General information	374
24.10	Climate	375

25 Thailand — **377**

25.1	Residence in Thailand	379
25.2	Requirements	380
25.3	Procedures and time frame	382
25.4	Taxation	382
25.5	Family law and inheritance aspects	383
25.6	Citizenship	384
25.7	Dual citizenship	384
25.8	Key advantages and disadvantages	384
25.9	General information	385
25.10	Climate	386

26 United Arab Emirates / Dubai — **387**

26.1	Residence in Dubai	390
26.2	Requirements	395
26.3	Procedures and time frame	396
26.4	Taxation	397
26.5	Family law and inheritance aspects	397
26.6	Citizenship	398
26.7	Dual citizenship	398
26.8	Key advantages and disadvantages	398
26.9	General information	399
26.10	Climate	400

27 United Kingdom — **401**

27.1	Residence in the United Kingdom	404
27.2	Requirements – Tier 1 Investor Category	408
27.3	Procedures and time frame	410
27.4	Taxation	411
27.5	Family law and inheritance aspects	415
27.6	Citizenship	416
27.7	Dual citizenship	417
27.8	Key advantages and disadvantages	417
27.9	General information	419
27.10	Climate	420

28   United States of America   **421**

   28.1   Permanent residence through the EB-5 Program   424

   28.2   Requirements   426

   28.3   Procedures and time frame   427

   28.4   Taxation   428

   28.5   Family law and inheritance aspects   429

   28.6   Citizenship   430

   28.7   Dual citizenship   430

   28.8   Advantages and disadvantages of EB-5   430

   28.9   General information   432

   28.10 Climate   433

Part IV   CITIZENSHIP-BY-INVESTMENT

29   Overview of Citizenship-By-Investment Options   **437**

   29.1   The Global Citizenship Program Index   466

30   Antigua and Barbuda   **467**

   30.1   Legal basis   469

   30.2   Requirements   470

   30.3   Procedures and time frame   472

   30.4   Grant of citizenship   473

   30.5   Dual citizenship   474

   30.6   Taxation   474

   30.7   Advantages of Antigua and Barbuda citizenship   475

   30.8   General information   476

   30.9   Climate   477

31   Austria   **479**

   31.1   Legal basis   481

   31.2   Requirements   481

   31.3   Procedures and time frame   482

   31.4   Grant of citizenship   483

   31.5   Dual citizenship   483

   31.6   Taxation   483

   31.7   Advantages of Austrian citizenship   483

   31.8   General information   485

   31.9   Climate   486

32   Cyprus   **487**

   32.1   Legal basis   488

   32.2   Requirements   489

   32.3   Procedures and time frame   490

   32.4   Grant of citizenship   490

   32.5   Dual citizenship   491

   32.6   Taxation   491

   32.7   Advantages of Cypriot citizenship   492

   32.8   General information   493

   32.9   Climate   494

33   Commonwealth of Dominica   **495**

   33.1   Legal basis   498

   33.2   Requirements   498

   33.3   Procedures and time frame   499

   33.4   Grant of citizenship   499

   33.5   Dual citizenship   500

   33.6   Taxation   500

   33.7   Advantages of Dominica citizenship   500

   33.8   General information   501

   33.9   Climate   502

34   Grenada   **503**

   34.1   Legal basis   505

   34.2   Requirements   506

   34.3   Procedures and time frame   507

   34.4   Grant of citizenship   508

   34.5   Dual citizenship   508

   34.6   Taxation   508

   34.7   Advantages of Grenadian citizenship   509

   34.8   General information   511

   34.9   Climate   512

35   Malta   **513**

   35.1   Legal basis   515

   35.2   Requirements   516

   35.3   Procedures and time frame   518

   35.4   Grant of citizenship   518

   35.5   Dual citizenship   519

   35.6   Taxation   519

35.7	Advantages of Maltese citizenship	520
35.8	General information	521
35.9	Climate	522

36   St. Kitts and Nevis   **523**

36.1	Legal basis	526
36.2	Requirements	527
36.3	Procedures and time frame	529
36.4	Grant of citizenship	530
36.5	Dual citizenship	530
36.6	Taxation	531
36.7	Advantages of St. Kitts and Nevis citizenship	531
36.8	General information	533
36.9	Climate	534

37   St. Lucia   **535**

37.1	Legal basis	538
37.2	Requirements	539
37.3	Procedures and time frame	540
37.4	Grant of citizenship	542
37.5	Dual citizenship	542
37.6	Taxation	542
37.7	Advantages of St. Lucia citizenship	543
37.8	General information	544
37.9	Climate	545

Useful Addresses and Websites	547
List of Abbreviations	561
Bibliography	565
Index	573

About This Book

This book, now in its 6th edition, presents in-depth yet practical information on the most important issues concerning residence and citizenship planning for private clients. It is designed as a guide for private client advisors such as law firms, tax consultants, private banks and family offices. It is also addressed directly to private individuals and families, business owners, entrepreneurs and investors who are interested in finding out more about the subject.

The use of concise and precise language reflects its character as a handbook and reference source. In particular, the author has endeavored to express the terms and concepts involved as transparently as possible in order to make them easily accessible even to those without a legal background. Footnotes are therefore avoided where possible for the sake of clarity.

This book can in no way substitute legal or other professional advice. The publisher and author therefore unreservedly exclude any liability for losses or damages of any kind – be these direct, indirect or consequential – which may result from the use of this book or the information it contains. Although the publisher and author have undertaken great care in preparing this book, they obviously cannot guarantee its correctness and completeness, and the explanations and strategies contained herein may not be suitable for your situation.

Any comments and suggestions, praise and criticism will be gratefully received. If you as the reader feel that a particular topic should be added to this volume, please let us know. We will be happy to recompense any useful information with a complimentary copy of the next edition of this book.

Dr. Christian H. Kälin is the Group Chairman of Henley & Partners. He is one of the pioneers and leading specialists in residence and citizenship programs and advises both private clients and governments.

Marshall J. Langer is Professor Emeritus at Thomas Jefferson School of Law and is recognized as the most experienced US tax attorney specialized in expatriation and international taxation.

Simon Anholt is the world's leading authority on measuring and managing national identity and reputation. He was Vice-Chairman of the UK Foreign & Commonwealth Office's Public Diplomacy Board, and has advised more than 50 national, regional and city governments worldwide.

Henley & Partners:
The Global Leaders in Residence and Citizenship Planning

The production of this book has been made possible by the generous sponsorship of Henley & Partners – the global leaders in residence and citizenship planning.

The concept of residence and citizenship planning was created by Henley & Partners in the 1990s, at a time when most international lawyers and wealth planning professionals did not consider the subject to be of much relevance.

Over the years, Henley & Partners has emerged as the world's leading firm specialized and focused in this particular area of practice. International residence and citizenship planning has itself become a major topic among the increasing number of internationally mobile entrepreneurs, as well as many wealthy individuals and families, who are interested in looking at alternative residence and citizenship solutions.

Lawyers such as Dr. Christian H. Kälin, as well as many others, further developed the discipline together with an entire group of specialists who now work at Henley & Partners. The firm's Chief Executive Officer, Eric G. Major, who formerly built the most important Canadian immigrant investor business at HSBC, is another guiding light in the area of global residence and citizenship planning.

Today, individual clients as well as advisors and law firms worldwide rely on Henley & Partners for specialized advice and assistance in this delicate area where its expertise and experience are second to none.

The firm's renowned Residence and Citizenship Practice Group advises private clients and their close advisors, as well as governments, on investor immigration and citizenship solutions. Henley & Partners works with the government authorities of all relevant countries and constantly monitors the worldwide situation. The firm also assists in designing, implementing and operating investor immigration programs and gives relevant advice to governments.

Two of the most recent mandates are from Antigua and Barbuda, where Henley & Partners act as a special advisor to design, implement and administer the citizenship-by-investment program for this country; and Malta, where Henley & Partners won a public call for services and was awarded a Public Services Concession for the design, implementation and international promotion of the Malta Individual Investor Programme.

Residence planning and related tax planning for private clients involves finding solutions for individuals and families who move internationally, own property in different countries and who often have complex international situations and requirements. In this regard, they work closely together with the firm's Trust and Tax Planning Group, and our combined services cover not only tax, immigration and citizenship law, but also international private law, real estate structuring and more.

For many years, Henley & Partners has organized the Global Residence and Citizenship Conference, which is the most important such event in the world. It is held annually in the first half of November in different locations each year. To check for the program of the next conference and to benefit from early registration discounts, please visit *henleyglobal.com/ events*. For more information about the firm please visit *henleyglobal.com*

Impact

Henley & Partners typically advises very wealthy individuals and families, successful entrepreneurs and investors, top-level managers, artists, and celebrities. Without a doubt, we and our clients are among the most privileged people in the world.

An important distinguishing feature of our firm is our substantial commitment to help those who are less fortunate. This commitment dates back to its roots and is today expressed mainly through the Henley & Partners Foundation. It operates quietly but very effectively.

While several of the firm's partners are themselves involved in important philanthropic work, for many years Henley & Partners as a firm has committed large parts of its yearly global profits to support humanitarian projects. This substantial commitment is further strengthened by the fact that all projects benefit directly from it and are administered by volunteers within the firm or associates in the countries where we operate. Furthermore, several of our clients have become important sponsors of our projects.

Most of the projects are focused on helping children in need. For example, more than 120 million children around the world are without any formal education or schooling, and many more have only very limited access to education. With rare exceptions, they never have the chance to improve their lives, and those children who are born poor tend to die poor. We therefore believe that one of the most significant contributions we can make to humankind is to help those who cannot help themselves, in particular underprivileged children.

We also fund other significant projects of local, national or international importance, such as youth entrepreneurship initiatives, reforestation, and our partnership with UNHCR. We support UNHCR's global refugee registration activities with a contribution of over USD 1 million and further advocacy to assist UNHCR's resource mobilization efforts.

If you would like to know more about our
humanitarian initiatives, or if you would like
to support them, please contact
foundation@henleyglobal.com

Acknowledgements

This work originally arose from my vision and the need for a first-rate, up-to-date and useful handbook on residence and citizenship options for private clients.

It was forward-thinking pioneers like US attorneys Marshall Langer and Stephen Gray who started to systematically plan for wealthy clients in terms of their residence and citizenship requirements, and have thus helped form the basis of this increasingly important field of private client advisory practice.

While there have been many different publications in the past, mainly information brochures, nothing of this kind, and in particular of this level of professional accuracy, has been attempted before. The publisher, Ideos Publications, concurred with this idea and together with the author, they are now pleased to present the 6th edition.

A great deal of specialist knowledge, work and effort has gone into this project, and it has certainly proved worthwhile. As an expression of its overall concept, this volume can unquestionably be seen as a pioneering achievement. The author and publisher hope that our readers share this viewpoint as well as our enthusiasm for the project.

Certainly this book will be useful for many lawyers, private bankers, immigration specialists, tax planners and other private client advisors, but also governments and government agencies – they all require first-hand information in this increasingly important field. We are convinced that with this book we continue to make an important contribution in the advancement of private wealth planning.

No great book is created without the contribution of a great team supporting it, and this book, though it may not be great, is no exception. At this point, I would like to thank all those who have contributed to and supported this book. Special thanks are due to my colleagues at

Henley & Partners and Ideos Publications, in particular Amanda Philp, Susanne Ferullo, Janine Droux, Elena Basheska, Cameron Stent and Karolina Laubscher, as well as many of my other colleagues at Henley & Partners in our various offices throughout the world, who made a tremendous effort to help me produce this book. Furthermore I also thank the reviewers and the publisher, as well as the main sponsor, Henley & Partners. Thanks to their valuable support, they have also contributed significantly to the successful and continued publication of this book.

Dr. Christian H. Kälin
London, September 2016

Foreword

They say the world is getting smaller and more interconnected every day. Indeed, the effects of globalization continue to expand and touch all aspects of our modern lives. In the age of the Internet, jet travel, free-flowing movement of capital and multinational companies, we have become both more interdependent and more mobile than at any time in human history. This poses interesting new challenges for governments, as the concepts of immigration, citizenship and even statehood are changing.

Malta introduced its first tax residence scheme more than twenty years ago. Around that time, it was Henley & Partners which started to focus on residence and citizenship planning when most international lawyers and wealth planning professionals were not considering the subject to be of great importance. Today, the world looks very different, and countries find themselves competing not only for international talent but also for investors, entrepreneurs and high net worth individuals and families.

Malta has risen to the challenge. Despite being a small country in the Mediterranean Sea, we are a globally networked nation with a vibrant multicultural population and a sizeable diaspora sprinkled across the globe. Being an outward-looking nation, we have always relied on trade and talent to channel our prosperity.

Our rich culture, beautiful climate and advanced standard of living are certainly an advantage, but we need to engage professionals who understand the investor immigration world and who can help us make the case that Malta is a prime destination of choice. One firm which we have had the pleasure of working with is Henley & Partners. Internationally recognized as the firm of choice for residence and citizenship planning, we sought their advice for the reform of our residence schemes and the development of new programs designed to attract foreign investors to settle in our country. Their knowledge and expertise in this area are truly unrivalled and they have imparted to us some very valuable advice.

Tonio Fenech MP
Minister of Finance, Economy and
Investment (2008-2013), Malta

Introduction

Since the 1ˢᵗ edition of this book was published, the world, and the Euro zone in particular, has been in the grip of unprecedented economic turmoil. Countries looking for new ways to generate growth are increasingly focused on the benefits of economic migration. However, governments are also under pressure to ensure that employers give priority to local workers when they are looking to fill vacancies. The global political climate is therefore one torn between the undeniable economic benefits of migration and the political need to be seen to be implementing protectionist measures to appease the concerns of the general public. This has led to a number of countries implementing immigration and citizenship laws designed to meet these twin aims, with varying degrees of success. While each country is eager to be seen to be making its own mark on the worldwide immigration environment, the global immigration landscape has become plagued with a plethora of inconsistencies and diverging rules.

The last twelve months has also been a time of significant political upheaval. As well as the uncertainty which has been a consequence of the "Arab Spring", there is an increasing sense that immigration itself is becoming a political battleground. With the rise in popularity of far right organizations, other, more mainstream, parties are having to rely on their support to form stable coalition governments. This has a knock-on effect on immigration policy in a number of countries which are now adopting a more protectionist approach. Furthermore, a number of countries are looking to increase their tax receipts by targeting high earning residents.

It is therefore clear that obtaining citizenship or residence rights in one or more countries, combined with the ability to quickly leave one country and settle in another, is becoming increasingly important, both politically and economically, for high net worth individuals.

In a mobile global economy, the reality is that key players live and conduct business on an international basis. For the ever growing number of these high profile and high net worth individuals, meeting the physical presence requirements for settlement or for naturalization in a country is becoming impractical. It is neither desirable for tax planning and wealth management purposes nor feasible if they are to take full advantage of international business opportunities across the globe.

For these individuals the option of a second or even third citizenship is enormously attractive. The freedom which is afforded them is unparalleled. When one considers the reality that, due to the nature of their business, many international entrepreneurs will not spend more than six months a year in any one country, the benefits of citizenship-by-investment become more apparent.

For individuals who hold passports of countries with fewer visa waiver agreements, a second passport can open up travel to countries previously restricted by time consuming visa application requirements and processes. Using their second passport means giving the individual and their business access to markets in countries previously beyond their reach. Greater access to new markets creates new opportunities for growth.

The economic crisis has brought this issue into stark relief. Nations are in greater need of ways in which to raise revenues and individuals are searching for more tax-effective means to structure their global lives. In exchange for a route to citizenship or residence, nations can incentivize high net worth individuals and their families to invest in and grow their economies.

In some sectors there remains a stigma attached to the practice of exchanging investment for residence or citizenship privileges. Some believe that in awarding permanent residence and citizenship to those making a significant investment into the local economy you are devaluing both. However, this outdated belief is no longer reflective of the true nature of investor immigration and citizenship-by-investment today. These fears stem from historical practices abandoned by modern governments.

There is no doubt that investor immigration and citizenship programs need to be properly monitored and administered in order to prevent abuse. These programs must be run in a manner which is legal and transparent and in keeping with the constitution of the nation offering citizenship. This not only prevents corruption but gives the individual obtaining permanent residence or citizenship a sound legal right to their new citizenship. This is a stark contrast to obtaining residence and citizenship illegally. Sadly, there are a large number of illegal schemes run predominantly on the internet through various agents which amount to immigration, citizenship and passport fraud.

When researching the options available in relation to investor immigration and citizenship for certain countries, much of the information is unclear and it can be very difficult to find real and accurate information. Furthermore, immigration laws are also increasingly being drafted "in a hurry" in response to the ever changing political environment. Legislation introduced in this way is inevitably going to contain errors and will not have been subject to sufficient consideration, resulting in certain scenarios not being covered. The publication of this 6th edition is, therefore, particularly timely, containing properly researched, up-to-date information on the immigration and citizenship options available today. Of course, it should never be seen as a substitute for proper legal advice obtained from an immigration specialist.

Most countries are currently able to offer investors citizenship or residence in return for economic investment. This is usually in the form of requiring substantial investment coupled with, amongst other things, compliance with residence and language requirements. Most countries are very selective in the type of investor they will allow to gain citizenship or residence. Many investors searching for permanent residence or citizenship will be motivated beyond money and looking to invest in countries more substantially from a family, social and cultural perspective.

Accordingly, investors are sought after individuals who contribute above and beyond their required investment. Investors who bring their families with them as dependents commonly contribute to the economy in a variety of ways ranging from paying for private school, real estate and the arts. They may extend their businesses to the country in question, further stimulating the economy and creating employment whilst also bringing cultural diversity, expanding the international network and increasing contacts to business.

Nations that do not offer an expedited route to citizenship may offer as an alternative an expedited route to permanent residence. The UK is a good example. It has the Tier 1 (Investor) program, which is a step in the process toward gaining citizenship. The UK government has always been adamant that investors are to be encouraged. While other migrant routes are being restricted in a desperate attempt to curb net migration figures, investors remain unaffected. It is perhaps unsurprising when one considers that Tier 1 (Investors) are required to invest into either the share capital of UK trading companies or UK government bonds thereby boosting inward investment to the UK as part of the eligibility and ongoing requirements of the route. The UK is open for business and willing to do what it can to attract international entrepreneurs.

In summary, we continue to live in a turbulent global economic and political climate plagued with uncertainty. Citizenship and permanent residence in another than one's home country can offer the stability and freedom which international high net worth individuals seek. The Global Residence and Citizenship Handbook aims to be a comprehensive guide to the investor immigration and citizenship programs of the world and to help the smart investors and their advisors make well-informed decisions when deciding which options would be best suited to their individual needs.

Julia Onslow-Cole
Global Head of Immigration
PwC Legal

PART I

Residence and Citizenship Planning

1

Residence Planning

Chapter Summary

Residence planning is the process of finding solutions to the complex range of considerations involved in moving your residence to another country, or obtaining residence rights in more than one country. This aspect of private wealth planning is growing in importance to optimize business and personal planning.

Improving your international tax situation is one of the key benefits of an alternative residence, alongside protecting your financial privacy and structuring matrimonial and inheritance interests in an advantageous manner. It also helps those who, due to political instability or other unfavorable elements, need to find a safe place to reside.

It is necessary to ensure that the country can accommodate all of your family, business, taxation and legal needs, and that the areas of infrastructure, physical environment, business and economy, and culture and lifestyle suit you.

Each country judges whether a person should be subject to taxation on a range of different factors. Residence planning can help you achieve a reduction in your tax burden, whilst ensuring that you meet the exact requirements for that country.

The move from one country to another can itself trigger tax implications, and all financial calculations must take into account exit taxes and extended income tax regimes. The timing of any move is also critical and can have a sizeable impact on taxation.

International health cover is one of the most important elements to have in place when thinking of moving abroad. Cover must be maintained both during the time of the move and upon settling in the new country.

When moving countries, one of the key factors will also be the selection of a new home. While an emotive decision, there are many important factors to consider when selecting property, besides the obvious question of location. The decision should also include analysis of whether it would be advantageous to use a holding structure such as a company for fiscal and succession planning.

The term residence planning was coined by Henley & Partners in the 1990s. At the time, most international lawyers did not consider it necessary for their clients to look at alternative residence solutions, or to conduct the relevant planning for their clients. Rather, obscure and often illegal structures were devised to essentially hide assets, which were then typically parked in "secure" jurisdictions such as the UK, the US, Switzerland, Luxembourg or many of the small island states and territories around the world.

Today the situation is different and many clients and advisors on all continents are working with this important aspect of private wealth planning. The political and legal climate means that the only sensible advice is to comply, or move out.

1.1   Why become resident in another country?

Whatever your situation, there are however many more reasons why you should consider becoming a resident of another country, or holding a residence permit from more than just one. However, anyone thinking seriously about moving their main residence abroad, or obtaining residence rights in more than one country, faces a series of questions which are not always easy to answer. Residence planning analyzes those questions, reasons and possibilities.

Historically, since the invention of agriculture led to more permanent settlements, it was not easy for people to move their place of residence, and immigration as we know it today was not possible. Generally only natives of the land had full rights, and various rules prevented the movement of people even from one district to another. Only wars, extraordinary abilities or contributions to society and other special factors enabled people to move within a societal structure, and across territorial borders.

In today's globalized world, moving from one's native country to another, possibly more attractive, country has become increasingly easy and commonplace. Although language differences continue to be a barrier, the global dominance of English provides a linguistic infrastructure that parallels the technological infrastructure of the cosmopolitan era we live in.[1] The advances in communications and computer technology have made it possible for "knowledge workers" to work and live almost anywhere, and for entrepreneurs and investors to operate and supervise their businesses and investments 24 hours a day from virtually anywhere in the world. In this borderless global economy, capital and to some extent also labor, has lost its link to individual countries.

Particularly for wealthy individuals and families, and business owners and investors with an international lifestyle, today's globalized world offers tremendous opportunity to optimize personal and business planning. This includes in particular tax and estate planning, increasing international freedom of travel, and diversification not just of business, but also on a personal level, by having multiple residences and possibly multiple citizenships.

Moving to a more attractive country of course means different things to different people: for refugees, this may mean bare survival, personal safety and escape from war, violence and starvation; for an economic migrant, more job opportunities; business opportunities for entrepreneurs who are looking beyond their country's borders; investment opportunities for international investors looking to diversify not only their assets but also their life and family ties geographically; or retirement and lifestyle options, combined ideally with tax and other benefits, for wealthy individuals and families with a global outlook. In Asia for example, since the 1960s, ethnic Chinese from Hong Kong and throughout Southeast Asia have sought residence rights in Western countries – in particular Canada, the US, Australia and the UK – to escape political discrimination and anticipated upheavals that could disrupt their businesses and threaten family security. With the rising affluence of Asian countries and the relative decline of the West, however, they increasingly found that economic opportunity and personal security are not both available in the same location, or even in the same part of the world.[2]

---

[1]   See Vertovec/Cohen (2008)
[2]   See Ong (1999)

An alternative residence is also an effective tool for international tax planning, and facilitates more privacy in investment and banking as many reporting and exchange of information requirements are based on (tax) residence. This can be very relevant for Europeans, who increasingly move their place of residence within Europe: wealthy families from the Netherlands move to Belgium, Germans move to Switzerland, French move to the UK and to Switzerland, British high-income earners move to Switzerland, Monaco and Portugal, and so on.

Depending on your current position, an alternative residence can also mean a better quality of life for your family, a good education for your children, and a safe haven in times of political instability in your home country. In fact, political instability in many countries now leads to a need for wealthy individuals and families to seek a safe place outside their home countries in which to establish an alternative residence for reasons of security and personal flexibility. Canada, Dubai, Singapore, Switzerland and the UK, for example, play an important role as bases for such wealthy people to establish a safe second residence, which may well become the primary residence for some family members.

In view of the increasingly aggressive fiscal and regulatory environment in some otherwise reasonably stable high-tax countries such as Canada, France, Germany, the Netherlands, the UK, the US and others, a move of residence to a country with a milder tax regime is an attractive option for many who feel they have to pay more than their fair share, and who do not like the constant erosion of their privacy.

In fact, often the only way to reduce the tax burden and regulatory restrictions legally and in a significant manner is to move.

In Germany, for example, the government has direct access to all bank accounts of all taxpayers. This intrusion in privacy is rather uncomfortable. Whenever there is access to information, such information is prone to leaks, to the information being sold to anyone interested and offering sufficient money in exchange for the information (for example kidnappers, who are already a serious problem in many countries around the world). The only way to avoid this is to move your residence to another country with a less invasive environment, providing more personal privacy.

In the US the erosion of privacy has reached even further, and especially if you are an entrepreneur and investor with international exposure, your tax return can become very complicated, to the point where you are never really sure whether you have complied with all the rules and regulations. You have to employ expensive tax lawyers to ensure you do not become a criminal merely by overlooking the filing of the right form.

In many countries, rules and regulations are mushrooming and so the legal environment is becoming increasingly vague, leaving lots of room for interpretation by the authorities and thereby leaving you vulnerable. This leads to a situation where effectively everyone is potentially a criminal because there are so many different tax laws, regulations and rules that it is practically impossible to comply with all of them. This is already the case in countries like Italy, where it is impossible to run a small business and comply with all the regulations imposed by the state because the burden and cost of compliance is so high. Therefore, practically all smaller and medium-sized businesses, and most large ones as well, operate in some kind of grey zone. This is hardly a good environment to thrive in.

However, you should never move for tax reasons alone. Even if the tax and other burdens are heavy, you should look at your overall life situation: where your friends are, the environment you feel comfortable with, etc. Therefore, it only makes sense to consider residence planning if you already have a sufficiently international situation, lifestyle and outlook.

If your life is already international, then of course a change of residence may not only reduce one's income-tax burden significantly, it usually also has a major impact on the inheritance tax situation.

Effective planning and advice is particularly important with regard to inheritance taxes, as in many countries the distinction between residence and domicile is relevant here. The person may well be tax resident in a jurisdiction which levies no inheritance tax, but upon their death their former country of residence (for example the UK) may claim that they were in fact domiciled in that country and consequently subject their worldwide estate to inheritance taxes. Furthermore, inheritance and gift taxes can also apply to heirs and beneficiaries of gifts (as in Germany), or to the property that is transferred (as almost always in the case of immovable property if not placed in an appropriate structure), and may thus be levied irrespective of the residence and domicile of the deceased. Trusts, foundations or life insurance structures may be used in such cases to mitigate adverse consequences.

A change of residence is a significant, very personal and multifaceted decision for any individual or family. Whilst this decision may have a direct impact on one's business interests, a range of social, political, economic and personal issues should also be considered to determine the best jurisdiction in which to reside or hold a residence permit for reasons of security or personal flexibility. Therefore it is imperative to understand the advantages of different options and how they best serve your specific needs.

1.2   Residence and domicile

The concepts of residence and domicile have far-reaching effects on a person's private life as they concern issues like marriage status, inheritance position in terms of applicable law and taxation, and tax status.

Residence simply refers to living in a particular place. Often expatriates who have moved to another country for work for a period of time are considered resident in that country. This is usually referred as habitual residence.

Domicile is an important concept in many countries where the legal system is based on the tradition of Anglo-Saxon common law. Domicile means to live in a place with the intention to make the place a fixed and permanent home – the person's 'real' home. Domicile is distinct from nationality or citizenship, although a person's nationality or citizenship may be a determining factor, too. A person can only have one domicile at any time, and the domicile may be a different place from the place of residence.

Ordinarily the country in which a person is domiciled will govern how the individuals' property is dealt with i.e. in case of divorce or upon death. It is imperative to determine one's status, especially if the person has more than one place of residence in different countries.

An individual will usually acquire the domicile of their parents, usually the father, at the time of birth. This will be the domicile of origin. Such can be changed to domicile of choice by taking up permanent residence in another country, with no intention of returning to the country of origin. However, an individual may still be considered domiciled in their previous country of residence and the country of domicile of origin, regardless of whether they have become resident in another country – this can have devastating effects, for example, on inheritance tax. Thus, there have been many cases where individual taxpayers left the UK years ago and lived abroad, were resident there continuously until their death, but their domicile was still considered the UK and therefore their estate became subject to UK inheritance tax.

Given that many people move from one country to another, it is essential to have a means of establishing which system of law applies to their situation, as each jurisdiction will have a different effect on their civil status (such as marriage and divorce) and some aspects of their property (such as applicable matrimonial property regimes and inheritance laws and taxation).

Although domicile is used as the fundamental connecting factor in the UK and most Commonwealth countries; in Brazil, Denmark, Ireland, Norway, the US and others, different connecting factors, and in particular habitual residence, are preferred.

Habitual residence, a concept used also in international (income) tax treaties based on the OECD (Organization for Economic Cooperation and Development) model treaty, is the generally accepted main factor to determine a person's tax residence, at least for income tax purposes, but also in many other cases and increasingly so for inheritance tax purposes. Critics argue that the connection is not strong enough to give sufficient weight to the individuals' civil rights and affairs in any given country, i.e. habitual residence as a concept can be problematic where a person is working or living abroad for a longer but essentially temporary period of time.

1.3   Change of tax residence

Even in countries which base their tax residence determination mainly or only on habitual residence, tax authorities begin to take note when (wealthy) taxpayers move abroad – or "arrive", i.e. start to spend a considerable amount of time in the country without necessarily declaring themselves as resident.

It can well be that even a change of residence abroad for two to three years may no longer be sufficient to "get rid" of the tax residence status if later on that taxpayer returns to the same country. Complicated and costly arguments can emerge with the tax authorities, during which the taxpayer often loses. Even if the facts are quite clear and in favor of the tax payer, and a tax lawyer may insist that they have a "good case", tax authorities, once on the case, often win simply because if it goes to court, in most cases the courts rule in their favor. With tax authorities in high-tax countries coming under increased pressure to collect more revenue, it is likely that they will scrutinize even more carefully cases worth their while.

For wealthy individuals moving their tax residence from one country to another, it is extremely important to plan a move carefully, and to anticipate possible issues later on depending on what the intention is in a few years' time. It is also critical that all laws and regulations are carefully observed, and that one's life can be properly organized around those rules without it being uncomfortable and impairing one's quality of life.

Besides tax residence, of course, other factors such as the impact on your matrimonial property regime, or the inheritance law applicable if you pass away, are important. Here, if habitual residence were the sole connecting factor, your matrimonial, property and inheritance rights would be subject only to the legal system of the country where you happen to be resident. In many instances, however, this is not the case: matrimonial property regimes may remain the same, either by law or by express choice (for example by a notarized marriage contract concluded between the spouses in order to establish the law applicable on their marriage and in particular their matrimonial property regime).

Due to the significant impact on a person's estate, it is essential to determine one's domicile, especially if the person is effectively connected to and resides in more than one country. Moreover, each country has its own tax laws and regulations which will establish the tax liability if considered a tax resident. Therefore, when a person wishes to change tax residence status, it is important to ascertain what will constitute domicile or habitual residence in the eyes of the particular jurisdiction.

Factors to take into consideration may include the number of days spent in the country, the location of the main family home, family and business connections, and nationality.

In some countries, having accommodation available for use in that country after moving abroad may deem you resident in that country. It is generally advisable not to have accommodation readily available in such jurisdictions, which include countries like Germany, Sweden and many others.

Tax liability always arises with the number of days spent in the jurisdiction, for example, 183 days a year or more spent in the UK makes a person resident for the purpose of tax. But very often, a much smaller number of days is sufficient (in Switzerland, for example, if you spend more than 30 days there in a year and are deemed to pursue an economic activity, you are considered resident for tax purposes unless a tax treaty applies and provides otherwise).

Small efforts such as cancelling licenses and memberships; amending the electoral register to show that one is voting abroad; transferring the main bank account outside the country; and moving any business operation out of the country will show the local authorities that the person has no intention of being resident in the country.

In the end, it is a combination of several hard factors (such as number of days spent in a country, availability of accommodation, etc.) and soft factors (memberships in clubs, social and business connections and activities) which will determine the successful outcome of your international residence planning. This can range from very clear situations where all relevant hard and soft factors are in your favor, to borderline situations with a considerable risk of being deemed tax resident in more than one country and having to engage in lengthy discussions and arguments with tax authorities in one or several countries.

1.4   Factors to consider when choosing a new residence

The decision to move to another country must not be taken lightly as there are many factors that will affect an individual and his family. It is recommended to undertake a thorough analysis of the country that you may consider as your new main place of residence and possibly your new domicile of choice.

There are significant aspects such as business environment and tax that must be considered but there are also seemingly minor aspects that one initially does not pay any attention to which may later become a source of discontent. It is important to distinguish between temporary stays such as vacationing in a country, visiting on business – and actually living there. Temporary visits can give a skewed perspective on a place. Each individual will have their own particular reason for changing residence; however, it is important to be mindful of the potential pitfalls when making the decision to change your residence and establish a new main base in your life.

Obtaining an alternative residence is a significant, very personal and multifaceted decision for any individual. Whilst this decision may have a direct impact on the applicant's personal situation and business interests, a range of social, political, economic and family issues should also be considered to determine the best jurisdiction in which to reside or hold a residence permit for reasons of security or personal flexibility. Therefore, it is important to understand the advantages of different options and how they best serve your needs. Some important criteria to consider when looking at an alternative country of residence include its geographical location and access via air, road, rail and sea; its political and economic stability as well as the stability of the region in which it is situated; its banking facilities and business environment; its legal system; its tax system and any double taxation treaties with your country of origin; if you are married or live with a partner, the implications for any (pre-)nuptial agreements or other arrangements and the impact on your matrimonial property regime; if you have school-age children, the education system and availability of private schools; visa-free travel possibilities as a residence permit holder; residence and other requirements for obtaining citizenship; and of course the overall cost of obtaining and maintaining a residence permit.

There are many different aspects which are relevant to consider. The following gives an overview of the most important of these aspects.

Personal situation

It is essential that your tax and estate planning follows your personal and business situation, and not vice-versa. You should never relocate mainly for tax reasons. Unless you are happy in the new environment from a personal, family and lifestyle point of view, experience shows that very often you would then act in a way that will sooner or later jeopardize the tax planning which made you change your residence in the first place. Nevertheless, there are many situations where a change of residence fits in well with an individual's personal, family or business situation, and in these cases a change of residence becomes a key element of international tax and estate planning. Indeed, the mobility made possible by modern technologies, logistics and efficient transport links means that persons of talent and wealth have an increased range of options with regard to where to reside and from where to conduct their business.

Education and schooling

An important personal aspect is the schooling of children. If you have children of school age, careful planning is required when you consider relocating to a new country. Besides the obvious priorities of whether the school environment is right for the child, language barriers, education systems, and a general idea about the education options available in the country need to be weighed up.

It can be traumatic for a child to move to a new country where everything is unfamiliar. Therefore it is paramount that one considers the education choices carefully.

International schools can be a good option as the curriculum is usually in English and based on an international standard, recognized worldwide. Children will often be integrated more easily as the school is geared towards foreigners. The downside is that your children will not integrate with the locals as much.

An alternative is to send your children to a boarding school in a country with exceptional educational institutions such as Switzerland, England or the US.

As each child will have different academic needs, the choice of school is a personal decision but it is important to consider the language and the credentials of the school. Is the curriculum recognized by international universities? Will the child easily adapt to the environment?

It is recommended to investigate the options in advance so that one has enough time for the application process. Also, it is important to settle prior to the school year beginning so the child feels more comfortable with his/her new surroundings.

Change of residence and domicile

Whereas residence simply means living in a particular place, domicile means living there with the intent to make it a fixed or permanent home. Legal domicile is an important concept in many countries with a legal system based on the tradition of Anglo-Saxon common law, with important implications in tax law. This is particularly relevant with regard to inheritance taxes. As explained herein, even after you have become resident in another country for income tax purposes, you may still be considered domiciled in your previous country of residence for purposes of inheritance tax. It may be desirable or necessary to acquire a domicile of choice, which in turn will be likely to require more planning and more robust indicators that your connection to the new country of choice goes beyond a simple residence.

Tax residence

Most countries use residence as the key criterion for subjecting you to personal income taxes and other taxes such as capital gains or net wealth taxes. Normally, various tests are applied to determine a person's tax residence, for example the number of days of physical presence in the relevant territory, having accommodation at your disposal, or your predominant personal and business interests. If an individual leaves a country and establishes bona fide residence in another country however, the former is generally no longer able to tax the emigrant's worldwide income.

Taxation based on citizenship

There is one important exception to the rule of taxation based on residence. Citizens and long term permanent residents (Green Card holders) of the US pay taxes there regardless of their place of residence, i.e. even if they move their residence outside the US. Therefore, the mere emigration of US citizens does not terminate their US tax liability. The only way for US citizens and long-term permanent residents to terminate their unlimited US tax liability is to relinquish their citizenship, i.e. to expatriate, or to give up their Green Card. The relinquishment of US citizenship or a Green Card usually trigger special taxes, and specialist US tax advice is required to ensure full compliance with the relatively complex rules[3] applying to expatriating from the US.

There are only a few other countries which have similar tax provisions. In the Netherlands, for example, inheritance tax applies for 10 years

---

[3] For an overview of these rules, see chapter 3

after leaving the country as long as one remains a Dutch citizen, and only the relinquishment of Dutch citizenship would end the extended inheritance tax liability before this 10-year period.

In early 2012, during the French presidential elections, Nicholas Sarkozy introduced proposals to base French tax laws on citizenship, in addition to a citizen's place of residence. Hence French citizens living abroad who pay less tax than they would do in France would have to pay the difference to the French government, or else give up French nationality. Since Sarkozy did not retain power, these proposals may have lost their immediacy, but it is unlikely that they will be forgotten. In the light of the global economic downturn, many governments will see this as a potential way to raise additional funds. This threat has already caused some French citizens to review their citizenship situation, and will continue to influence decisions before any such laws are passed.

Exit taxes

Although taxation based on citizenship and long-term residence is unique to the US (and a very small number of other countries), a growing number of countries have introduced specific measures to discourage the emigration of individuals through various forms of taxation. Such exit or emigration taxes may have considerable implications for the tax aspects of your relocation plans.

In coming years larger, high-tax countries with sovereign debt problems need to increase their tax revenue substantially; this is difficult to achieve beyond a certain point of tax burden on individuals and businesses. However, it is politically acceptable to tax wealthy people, and to prevent them or tax them even more if they try to leave the country. It can therefore be expected that countries will try to introduce different forms of exit taxes to prevent the exodus of good taxpayers. From this point of view, if you are contemplating a move to another country, you need to carefully observe the developments on that front so as to possibly pre-empt a move by the legislator by your move abroad sooner rather than later.

Family law and inheritance law

If you are married or live together with a partner, or if you have or plan to have children, you also need to concern yourself with the impact a change of residence may have with regard to family law. The UK, and in particular London, attracts many wealthy foreigners as a place of residence; however, many do not realize that London is also the divorce capital of the world. One reason for this is that it has a divorce law that favors the poorer partner in a marriage – often the woman. This can mean nasty surprises, particularly for rich foreign men whose wives file for divorce in Britain. Even marriage contracts or prenuptial agreements that were concluded before moving to London may simply be disregarded by English courts.

The impact on the matrimonial property regime applicable is also relevant if your marriage remains intact, as it can have considerable consequences in case of death of one of the spouses, up to the point of preventing common children from inheriting anything until the death of the remaining spouse.

On the other hand, the applicable inheritance law may also become an issue: in many countries, especially in continental Europe, forced heirship rules prevail and you may no longer be able to easily leave your property to whom you deem it most appropriate, but rather the law may dictate, for example, that each of your children as well as your spouse must inherit a certain portion of your wealth. This is also applicable on real estate in certain countries, for example in France, where, if you hold the property in your name, French inheritance law and forced heirship rules apply, and a choice of law is not possible – even if you live outside of France.

Inheritance taxes and estate planning

A change of residence may not only reduce one's income tax burden significantly, it usually also has a major impact on the inheritance tax situation. However, proper planning and advice is particularly important with regard to inheritance taxes, as in many countries the distinction between residence and domicile is relevant in this case. You may well be tax resident in a jurisdiction which levies no inheritance tax, but upon your death your former country of residence may claim that you were in fact still domiciled in that country and consequently may subject your worldwide estate to inheritance taxes. Furthermore, inheritance and gift taxes can also apply to heirs and beneficiaries of gifts (for example in Germany), or to the property that is transferred, and may thus be levied irrespective of the residence and domicile of the deceased. In the case of real estate, generally the country where the property is located will tax it. If you own US securities, however, the US imposes taxation upon the death of their owner even if there is no other connection to the US than the fact that the securities (the shares, bonds etc.) are issued by US entities. Trusts, foundations, companies or life insurance structures may be used in such cases to mitigate adverse exposure.

Tax treaties and tie-breaker rules

Tax treaties can be relevant in finding solutions to the various tax problems associated with moving from one country to another or with having multiple residences in different countries.

Nearly all tax treaties include tie-breaker rules that determine which country has the right to tax an individual who is deemed to be resident for tax purposes in two countries at the same time by their domestic rules. The tie-breaker tests are applied in stages in order to determine the country with which the individual has the closest connection and is therefore granted the right of taxation. The current version of the OECD model treaty makes the following provisions for an individual who is considered to be a tax resident in two countries with double tax treaties:

1. He shall be deemed to be a resident only of the country in which he has a permanent home available to him; if he has a permanent home available to him in both countries, he shall be deemed to be a resident only of the country with which his personal and economic relations are closer (center of vital interests)

2. If the country in which he has his center of vital interests cannot be determined, or if he does not have a permanent home available to

him in either country, he shall be deemed to be a resident only of the country in which he has a habitual residence

3. If he has a habitual residence in both countries, or in neither of them, he shall be deemed to be a resident only of the country of which he is a citizen

4. If he is a citizen of both countries or of neither of them, the competent authorities of both countries shall settle the question by mutual agreement

In reality, mutual settlements between countries are rare and a solution is usually found earlier, either with the tax authorities in the country where the dispute about tax residence has arisen, or in the courts of that country if no agreement could be reached with the tax authorities.

Acquisition of real estate

To acquire property in attractive locations and in particular in the new country of residence contributes to the quality of life, satisfies prestige needs, and to some extent also constitutes an investment. It is, however, a good idea to consider renting before purchasing a property as this is the best way to become familiar with an area before committing to a purchase. Obviously, there are many factors to take into account when acquiring property, besides tax and legal issues. It is usually advisable to appoint qualified professionals to assist with the acquisition and to navigate through the pitfalls of buying in a foreign country. Also, consideration needs to be given whether to own the property directly or through a structure, and how easy it may be to sell again in the future.

Although most countries, including Canada, the UK and the US, do not impose any restrictions on acquisition of real estate, there are countries such as Austria, Croatia, Greece and Switzerland[4] that restrict foreign persons from buying property there. It is imperative to check that there

---

[4]   With the sole exception of Andermatt, where foreign residents can buy without any restrictions whatsoever; see *www.henleyglobal.com/andermatt*

are no restrictions applicable that will pose a problem or that could affect resale.[5]

Timing

As generally in life, timing is important also in the context of tax and estate planning, and in particular regarding residence planning. Specifically, the discrepancies between the tax systems of different countries can sometimes be used in the course of changing residence. Indeed, an important element in cross-border planning is to synchronize the timing of the tax events and the taxpayer. For example, the tax treatment of income derived from activities performed before or after a person gives up his residence, and the different qualification of such income in different countries, may yield tax savings through the carefully chosen timing of a change of residence. The same goes for vesting of shares and share options, the receipt of commissions, proceeds from the sale of certain assets such as the main family home, where in many countries special tax exemptions apply, the date of signing of agreements which have significant value, the timing regarding the establishment of trusts and foundations, and so on.

Health insurance

Arranging adequate health insurance is an important element in international residence planning – yet it is often overlooked. If someone moves abroad, their current health insurance policy will normally expire. One is then usually left with a choice of finding another local insurer in the new country of residence or turning to an international health insurer. It is highly advisable to take out an appropriate health plan at a younger age and before the first signs of ill health manifest. Even if you are very wealthy and think you do not need health insurance at all, you need to think again: a private health policy with an internationally recognized insurer and arranged through a competent specialized consultant[6] which

---

[5]   A more detailed overview of this important aspect is given in section 1.9

[6]   e.g. Swiss Insurance Partners, see *www.sip.ch*

gives you access to a 24 hour assistance service and a kind of medical family office can be extremely useful. It can even be critical if you have an accident in a remote part of the world and if the closest adequate hospital needs to be found in an instant, or to help you find and select the best doctor or clinic for a particular medical problem. Indeed, one of the first steps in a planned change of residence should be to obtain worldwide health cover which ensures the necessary international flexibility.

Checklist: Moving to another country

The following table provides an overview of some of the questions to ask when moving to another country.

Infrastructure

Transport and accessibility	How good is general accessibility in the country including public transportation, train connections, domestic air travel, and condition of the roads?
	How good are the travel connections by road, air, rail or sea to other countries?
Utilities	Are the cost, access, quality and reliability of electricity, gas, water and waste services satisfactory?
	Is public water clean/safe to drink?
Telecommunications, IT, Internet	Are the telephone systems, mobile phone networks, broadband Internet access up to date? Are the quality and availability of IT-support services acceptable?
Access to services	How good is access to standard services such as local banks, post office, grocery stores, shopping malls, etc.?
Medical facilities	Are there reliable and modern hospital facilities?
	Is there free access to medical services? Are there any waiting times? What is the access to medical specialists? Are private medical facilities available and is access restricted?
Social security	Is there a mandatory social insurance scheme? What is the contribution level and is it in fact an additional tax? Is there a mandatory health insurance scheme?
Civic facilities	Are there civic facilities such as parks, playgrounds, city halls or public libraries available?

Infrastructure

Entertainment	What entertainment, cultural, sport and outdoor activities are available? Is there a good choice of cinemas, restaurants, bars, clubs etc.?
	Are there recreational options such as golf, sailing, polo and tennis clubs?
Education	What is the reputation of local schools and universities? Is private education readily available? Are there international schools? How do the education system and the schools rank globally?
Child care	Are there good public day nurseries/after-school care facilities? Are private nannies and au-pairs easily available?

Physical Environment

Geographic location	Is your new home centrally located in the region; is there a larger city in the vicinity? If your home is in a large city, are green spaces and recreational areas easily accessible? Are there any issues/problems with neighboring countries that could lead to conflict or war?
Climate	Is the climate to your liking? Number of sunshine hours per year? Average temperatures (summer/winter)? Is the area prone to winds and changeable weather?
Pollution	How clean is the environment and what are the levels of pollution of air, water, soil etc.?
Natural hazards	Is the place susceptible to flooding, hurricanes, tornadoes or other storms, earthquakes, heat waves, avalanches, landslides or heavy snow?
Industrial hazards	Are there any nuclear power or chemical plants in your area? Are there other factories or production sites that may affect you? (Industrial smells, dust, hazardous products etc.) Is your new home located in the flight paths of nearby airports?

Business and Economy

Currency and capital restrictions	Stability of local currency, exchange controls? Are there export-of-capital restrictions?
Government and political stability	Is there a stable government and political environment?
	What is the political culture like? Are there frequent protests? Strikes?
Cost of living	What is the cost of living? Are import duty exemptions possible?

Business and Economy

Banking and financial services	Are high-level banking services easily available? Can the local banking and financial services industry support your personal investment and business requirements?
Trade restrictions	Are there trade restrictions that could hamper international business dealings (i.e. repatriation of capital restrictions)?
Copyrights and patents	Is there a robust protection for copyrights and patents?
Company governance	Is it easy to incorporate and operate a company? Are corporate laws, regulations, taxes etc. mature and efficient? Are minority shareholders' rights protected?
Public and private corruption	Is there any public or private corruption? Is it difficult to do business legally without having to bribe or use other illegal means?

People, Culture and Lifestyle

Language	What is the local language? Do people speak English, or which other languages?
People	Are you moving to an open and liberal society? Are the people friendly and welcoming, non-discriminatory? Are there social tensions or harmony between different ethnic or other groups in the society?
Culture and religion	Is there uniformity or diversity in the community with regard to religion, ethnicity? Are there places of worship particular to your religion in the country? Is there discrimination against your own culture/religion?
Gender and minority issues	What is the status of women in society? Are there restrictions in public life for women or for people of certain ethnicity, religion, sexual orientation, etc.?
Civil rights and freedoms	Is there freedom of speech, religion, language, press, political expression, information etc.?
Quality of living	What is the overall quality of living in the main cities and the countryside? How do the main cities and the country compare globally in terms of quality of living?

Residence Permits

Application procedure	What are the minimum time and requirements to apply for a residence permit?
Ease	Is it easy to become a legal resident? Are there many steps required, interviews, visits to the country?
Physical presence	Are there any minimal physical presence requirements to maintain legal residence status?
Time to permanent residence status	What are the conditions and the minimum time required to obtain permanent resident status?
Cost	What is the cost to obtain and maintain the residence permit (including tax considerations)?
Visa-free travel	As a resident, are there any visa-free travel benefits irrespective of citizenship?
Status	Does residence in the country provide international social status benefits?
Revocation	Under what circumstances can residence permits be revoked/not renewed?

Citizenship

Time	What is the minimum time of residence required to apply for citizenship?
Ease	Is it easy to become a citizen or restrictive? Does the country traditionally welcome new citizens (e.g. Canada) or is it restrictive (e.g. UAE)?
Language	Are there strict language requirements?
Other restrictions	Are there other restrictions on becoming a citizen (e.g. sub-national restrictions, cultural, ethnic, etc.)?
Visa-free travel	Do citizens enjoy good visa-free travel?
Cost	What is the cost to obtain and maintain citizenship?
Obligations	Does citizenship come with burdensome obligations (e.g. military service, taxation)?
Status	Does citizenship provide national or international social status benefits?
Revocation	Under what circumstances can citizenship be revoked?

Legal and Tax

Taxation	What is the taxable base and rate of taxation of the following?
	Income and capital gains taxes
	Net wealth and property taxes
	Inheritance and gift taxes
	Are there good tax planning options?
Matrimonial and divorce law	Will pre-nuptial agreements be recognized in this country? What impact does residence in the country have on a possible divorce filing?
Real estate market	What is the state of the real estate markets (residential, commercial)? What is the availability of residential real estate for rent and purchase?
Real estate acquisition	Is it easy to acquire property? What are the transfer duties payable? Are there any restrictions on buying or selling?
Estate planning	Are there forced heirship rules?
	Can you use trusts or foundations?
	Do you need to adjust your will and other instruments of succession planning?
Licensing, business permits	How easy is it to set up a business? Are there license and permit rules that one must abide by, i.e. license for carrying out a profession, driver's license, boat license etc.?
Law enforcement and courts	How effective is the local law enforcement?
	Is there a reliable legal system?
	Can claims be effectively pursued in court?

1.5   Tax residence: considerations and implications

To determine if a person should be subject to taxation, countries generally use the following criteria:

- *Residence* – a country may tax the income of anyone who lives there, regardless of citizenship or whether the income was earned in that country or abroad

- *Source* – a country may tax any income generated there, regardless of whether the earner is a citizen, resident, or non-resident

- *Citizenship* – a country may tax the worldwide income of their citizens, regardless of whether they reside in that country or not

For the internationally mobile, the tax position across different countries will be an important concern. But the amount of tax they pay is also of interest to the relevant tax authorities. The simple rule is, the more you pay, the more interesting it becomes – for both sides.

Most countries use residence and/or source criteria when determining if a person should be subject to taxation. The US, and to a lesser extent some other countries,[7] are notable exceptions.

The place of residence for tax purposes or tax residence is therefore important in determining how you are taxed. If you have connections with, and spend long periods in, more than one country, there may be uncertainty about whether such connection or time spent in different jurisdictions does not make you tax resident in more than one place. The question of tax residence is very important for internationally active people, because getting it wrong can be expensive and time-consuming to resolve.

Other than the number of days spent in a country – which is perhaps the most important factor – a wide range of personal, business, property, economic and social connections must also be considered to determine 'tax residence'.

In many countries, the laws and regulations are ambiguous, except for minimum thresholds (i.e. below a certain number of days of presence in the country – with anywhere between 10 and 90 days a year, you are generally safe and would normally not be deemed resident for tax purposes, depending on the country), and there is generally no clear guidance on the relevant weight of each factor.

Factors that can play a role include:

- Where your spouse lives (if you are married)

- Where your children live (if you have children)

---

[7]   e.g. the Netherlands, with regard to extended inheritance tax for citizens even if they have already left the country and are residing abroad

- Where you have accommodation available for your use (i.e. where you own or rent homes)

- Whether or not you were tax resident in previous years

- Whether or not you carry out full-time work somewhere outside the country (i.e. you have a full-time job and workplace outside the country)

- Whether you are doing any work in the country (even if just a few days per year)

- Whether you spend more days in the country in any tax year than in any other single country

- What social ties you have in the country, memberships in clubs and societies etc.

By choosing a country with a mild tax climate for a main residence, a taxpayer can considerably reduce his burden legally and effectively without the need for complex tax planning. Belgium, Croatia, Hong Kong, Malta, Monaco, Singapore, St. Kitts and Nevis, Switzerland, and the UK, to name a few, are attractive destinations in this respect. So a change of residence may well be worthwhile not only as a lifestyle choice but also from the standpoint of taxation.

A move will either have tax advantages and tax savings or it can create a greater tax burden, depending on the jurisdiction. It is therefore imperative to establish the tax implications prior to changing residence. Interesting scenarios could arise that one would not ordinarily be aware of. Most sensibly, one should consult a tax advisor who is versed in the tax laws of both countries.

A trend which we see with tax authorities around the world is that they check not only how long you are resident in a particular country, but also whether you may be spending more days in their country than in any other single country. In other words, even if you spread out your presence globally across several jurisdictions, and say you are spending your year in six different countries with 80 days, 70 days, 60 days, 75 days, 10 days and 65 days in each, then it could be that the tax authorities of the country you spend 80 days could still deem you tax resident (in practice of course only if you have some other connection there), even if you are well below the normal threshold for that country but simply because you spent even less time elsewhere.

Day counting

If you spend more than 183 days in any country, you are normally tax resident in that country, unless the presence there is of a strictly limited, temporary nature. If you spend no time at all in a country, you cannot be deemed tax resident.

Between zero and 183 days lies a wide range of possibilities, although normally there are some minimum thresholds of number of days below which you are 'safe'.[8]

You also need to be aware of what constitutes a day spent in any particular country. Is it a full 24 hours? Is it just being present in any given day, even if just for half an hour in transit? Furthermore, the year in which the days are counted may correspond to a different period than the calendar year, depending on the country's tax year.

Some countries rely on a territorial (or source) based tax system[9] which has no impact on whether one is resident or non-resident as all income derived in that country is subject to tax, while income derived outside the country remains tax free.[10] Most countries, however, have taxation on world-wide income.

Therefore (tax) residence status becomes highly relevant as most countries use residence as the key criterion for subjecting one to personal income taxes and other taxes such as capital gains or net wealth taxes. Normally, various tests are applied to determine one's tax residence. In most countries this is determined by the number of days of physical presence in the country, in combination with other factors.

---

[8]   e.g. 10 days in the UK or 30 days in Switzerland
[9]   e.g. Hong Kong, Panama, Singapore
[10] For a good discussion of these issues, see Betten (1998)

The tax authorities will also establish whether the individual has accommodation readily available and family and business interests in the country. For former countries of residence, it is important for the individual to prove that he has left permanently to establish residence in another country as this confirms bona fide residence in the new jurisdiction so that the former country will no longer tax the emigrant's worldwide income. In some countries, this change of residence is confirmed by way of exit taxes.

The emigration of US citizens does not terminate their world-wide tax liability under Federal tax law, even if they are permanently resident in another jurisdiction. In such cases, the only way to legally relinquish US tax liability is to give up US citizenship and obtain an alternative citizenship.[11]

The discrepancies between the tax systems of different countries can also be used to one's advantage in the course of changing residence. Indeed, an important element in cross-border planning is to coordinate the timing of the tax events and the taxpayer. For example, the tax treatment of income derived from activities performed before or after a person gives up his residence, and the different qualification of such income in different countries, may lead to tax savings through carefully chosen timing of a change of residence.

Finally, it is important to be aware that a change of residence will not only have an impact on one's personal tax situation but that one's inheritance tax situation will also be affected. Even if one is not deemed tax resident in the jurisdiction, owning real estate in that jurisdiction may be a factor and in most countries where such taxes exist will still have local inheritance tax implications.

Exit taxes and extended income taxes

One problem with moving your tax domicile to another country, especially to one with low taxation, is that several high-tax countries have

---

[11]   See chapter 3

taken steps to discourage such moves, namely by introducing a form of exit tax or an extended income tax regime, or a combination thereof.

Exit taxes can be classified as general and limited taxes which are levied on income or capital gain that has accrued but not yet been realized; or as unlimited or limited extended income tax liability, which applies on income or capital gains arising after emigration.

Also, a claw back of tax deductions could be invoked – for example whereby a previously tax deductible accrual would be revoked.[12]

In Germany, for example, the extended limited tax liability can apply for a period of 10 years after emigration which can be very burdensome for the individual. More and more countries are drafting special tax rules to make moves abroad fiscally less attractive.[13]

Many high tax countries already impose such regimes to discourage fiscal emigration.[14] It is sometimes possible to mitigate – or in some cases even completely bypass – such taxation by appropriate structuring before, during and after a move abroad. However, this almost always requires the taxpayer to make a clean break with the former country of residence and to strictly avoid any links with it such as maintaining a second home there, making frequent visits or longer stays on its territory etc. These conditions can be tough for many expatriates and should be carefully weighed against the tax advantages such a radical change in one's life will bring.

Tax treaties

Bilateral agreements to avoid double taxation of persons resident in contractual states exist between many countries. Tax treaties delimit the tax-imposition rights between two countries and takes precedence over national legislation.

---

[12] Betten (1998)
[13] France has also recently introduced such a regime
[14] e.g. Australia, Austria, Canada, the Netherlands

Whereas ownership of real estate abroad usually implies limited tax liability as a result of ownership of this property in the foreign country, a move abroad always affects tax residence and has considerable consequences on tax liabilities. Therefore, tax treaties can play an important factor in limiting such tax exposure.

Inheritance and gift taxes, which depend primarily on the testator's last residence, may also be relevant. If a taxpayer who moves abroad has considerable income and assets, experience shows that the tax authorities concerned are particularly interested in the deceased's last tax residence, as this leads in most countries to unrestricted tax liability on his or her estate. However, relatively few tax treaties concern inheritance and gift taxes; when speaking about double tax treaties, these generally relate to income and possibly wealth taxes only.

It may happen that two countries – according to their respective tax laws – simultaneously consider a particular taxpayer as fiscally resident and unrestrictedly tax liable. This could result in him being taxed on his global income and possibly also on his assets by both countries on the basis of their domestic tax regimes. But if a double taxation agreement exists between the two countries, it will help to determine where the taxpayer is fiscally resident and thus liable to unrestricted taxation, and which country is to merely apply restricted taxation – namely on any assets or income located within its territory.

Residence in one of the two contractual states is normally the precondition for the application of the relevant double taxation treaty and all claims on its protection. The treaty formulates precise rules to determine in which of the two contractual countries a taxpayer is deemed to be fiscally resident. They are known as tie-breaker rules and in the majority of double taxation treaties they follow the OECD model treaty.

Accordingly, most double taxation agreements define the country of tax residence as the place where the taxpayer has his main permanent home. If he has homes in both countries, the crucial point is where his personal and/or economic activities are centered. His habitual place of living is then in third place, and citizenship is considered only in fourth place. If the tax residence cannot be determined on the basis of these criteria, it is decided by mutual agreement between the countries concerned.

Double taxation agreements can also be useful in terminating tax residence in the country of emigration more quickly. If someone no longer wishes to count as a UK tax resident, for instance to avoid paying capital gains tax, UK domestic law stipulates that certain taxes apply up to five years even after moving abroad. But if they move the tax residence to a country which has a suitable double taxation agreement with the UK, such as Belgium, they can bypass such domestic tax regulations and may be able to reduce the period during which certain UK taxes still apply after a change of residence.

In the absence of a double taxation agreement between the previous and new country of residence (such as when moving for example from the Netherlands to Monaco), only the respective domestic fiscal regulations apply. These are, as a rule, stricter – at least for high-tax countries – i.e. it is more difficult to terminate one's former tax residence if you directly move to a no-tax jurisdiction and there is no tax treaty. In order to avoid continuing to pay tax on one's global income and possibly assets too, often all links to one's former country of fiscal residence must be severed, and even then extended taxation may apply for some time after emigration.

1.6   Financial planning and insurance

For many wealthy people, an alternative residence is an effective tool for international tax planning, but it also increases the financial planning options and facilitates more privacy in investment and banking.

Anyone who is transferring their residence to another jurisdiction will certainly have to revisit their financial and estate planning. It is implicit that the various parameters of the financial aspects of one's estate will be affected. You may be familiar with the legal and fiscal situation and general framework conditions prevailing in your home country, but you must now become adept with a new framework.

It may make sense to retain investments in other currencies, for example if one moves from the US to Europe, where the local reference currency is the euro. As a rule, however, a move of a person's regular activities to a new currency area will also lead to different weighting of the currencies in their personal investment portfolio and will require a rethinking of their financial planning and asset management arrangements. It may be wise to consult a specialized investment advisor familiar with clients with cross-border issues.

It is also sensible to obtain advice from a tax advisor in the original jurisdiction, as there may be some interesting financial and tax planning options, or in a less favorable case, there may be exit taxes due that need to be calculated.

A move abroad also offers the opportunity for more flexible pension planning, as capital tied to government-regulated pension funds can often be released. Previous retirement provisions may have to be reorganized, liquidated or taken out prematurely (e.g. life insurance policies, pension claims, tied-up assurance funds etc.). It is particularly important to consider withholding taxes when receiving payouts from pension institutions and any tax concessions when drawing any benefits in the form of pensions or capital payouts. As a rule, different costs of living also change the provision requirement and usually make it necessary to adapt one's cash planning.

A move will also require careful examination of previous estate or succession planning (partnerships, foundations, trusts, family holding companies and the like). Here too, considerable scope may be available for optimization depending on one's destination. Thus, anyone moving, for example, to the Bahamas, Ireland, Malta, St. Kitts and Nevis or the UK can structure their assets by means of suitable succession structures so that they – or lifetime enjoyment thereof – are transferred without restrictions, and also often in tax-neutral form, to freely designated heirs. The situation will be quite different when moving to a country such as France or Spain, although here too various opportunities for optimization usually exist. In any case, existing estate-planning strategies should be checked and their adaptation to the new conditions and opportunities examined. Professional support is usually indispensable in this domain too.

It is also important to include the aspect of asset protection, especially in the US. In view of the peculiarities of the American legal system, which is characterized by a relatively low threshold of civil litigation, suitable measures to avoid excessive exposure of one's personal assets are indispensable. But when moving to other countries, it may also make sense to structure at least part of one's assets – perhaps including real estate – so that they are safe from seizure. Suitably designed asset protection trusts as well as specially structured Swiss annuities and life insurance policies are sensible options for this purpose.

1.7   International health insurance[15]

International health cover is a highly relevant topic for anyone thinking of moving abroad, and yet it is scarcely considered and hardly mentioned at all by advisors. Admittedly, it is not the job of a lawyer specializing in international inheritance law or an international tax advisor to know all about insurance as well – and especially about international health insurance. There is consequently relatively little specialist competence in this sector available to private clients. Most advisors and insurance brokers worldwide with such expertise merely represent a single insurer. Only very few offer more than a small number of products and are able to provide really comprehensive advice.

Trying to find ideal health cover is no easy task even without moving abroad, but it is of particular importance when moving to another country or even staying there for a limited period. The risks of sickness and accident must be covered comprehensively in an international context in order to avoid unpleasant surprises. A few important points must be considered in view of the wide choice of diverse solutions and different insurance products.

---

[15]   The author would like to thank Swiss Insurance Partners, Zurich/Dubai, for their valuable input in compiling this section

Anyone who lives or works abroad, runs a company or retires there should arrange insurance cover that is extensive and applicable around the world. Health insurance, in particular, should allow the patient to choose his preferred doctor and hospital with as few restrictions as possible, and ideally none at all.

A question of residence

In the event of a temporary stay abroad with no change of residence, basic state insurance usually assures at least minimum cover in emergencies. In addition, almost all local health insurers offer the option of comprehensive cover for sickness and accident via private supplementary policies, even for temporary stays abroad. Before moving abroad however, it is useful to check out the insurance options in detail, from free choice of doctor and hospital to medication cover. Previous health policies normally terminate with a move abroad, and continuing insurance cover must be assured during the actual process of moving.

Comprehensive cover with a free choice of doctor and hospital worldwide is strongly recommended in most cases. This is because, even in many developed countries, the public healthcare system satisfies only minimum requirements and it is essential to seek out private hospitals to ensure competent medical treatment. There is no alternative to comprehensive insurance cover for anyone thinking of moving to, say, the US or the Caribbean, or Eastern Europe, or to a developing country. Many countries have good local private health insurers, and some of them also offer international cover and a free choice of doctor and hospital. Although such a local insurer usually represents the least expensive solution, it is rarely the best one. It should be stressed that practically all insurers with a local or national scope of activity in the relevant country will only accept policyholders who are actually resident in the country. Anyone who leaves the country again will normally lose his insurance cover, which can become an insoluble problem with increasing age. It is also difficult to obtain a truly international and unrestricted free choice of doctor and hospital in many places. So the ideal insurance policy will be independent of residence and duration of stay and will also guarantee fully comprehensive cover as far as possible. Most local insurers offer only unsatisfactory solutions, if at all, and very few offer private health insurance which can be concluded or retained even when the policyholder lives abroad. So it is vital to check these important aspects, and in most cases it is worthwhile consulting an independent insurance advisor specializing in international health insurance.

Free choice of doctor and hospital, worldwide cover

Although an extensive choice of private health insurance schemes with an international scope is available worldwide, only very few can really be recommended. When comparing the various offers, it is important to not only to look at a specific insurance product but also at the financial soundness and reputation of the insurer as well as the latter's experience in international health insurance. The insurance product which best satisfies the individual requirements must then be considered.

Private health insurers are not obliged to accept you. So anyone who is over 55 years of age or is not perfectly healthy has little chance of obtaining private health insurance and still less comprehensive insurance with international cover. For this reason in particular, it is advisable to check out the insurance situation in detail before moving abroad. It may make sense to change over to an international health insurance scheme several years before a possible move abroad in order to be assured of the necessary flexibility later on. Even if no transfer of residence is planned, but one wishes to be optimally insured against sickness and accident, a detailed review of all options is worthwhile. It may even be of benefit to take out international health insurance in this case.

Anyone staying abroad frequently or planning to move to another country permanently should arrange insurance cover independently of residence and sojourn – i.e. inclusive of any subsequent moves or even a return to one's home country at a later stage. Such cover will ideally permit an unrestricted choice of doctor and hospital worldwide.

Checklist: International health insurance

In selecting suitable health insurance, care should be taken to consider the following points, which are listed below in the form of a brief checklist:

- Worldwide cover at reasonable premiums. It is also important to consider premiums in higher age brackets

- Free choice of physician and hospital worldwide without restrictions

- No restrictions on the policyholder's residence and duration of stay, even in the event of a later permanent return to the home country

- Guaranteed lifelong policy renewal, even in the event of a later change of residence, or illness of longer duration etc.

- Efficient processing in the event of a claim

- Multilingual emergency service manned around the clock throughout the year

- Insurance company that is well known and has a good reputation as well as broad experience in the domain of international health insurance

- Consult with an independent consultant who specializes in international health insurance

1.8   International residential real estate

One of the key factors when changing residence is the question of where one will physically reside. Ownership of real estate satisfies a basic human need, and to acquire a piece of property in an attractive location is equivalent to gaining a desired quality of life, and it is often also a sensible asset diversification.

However, it is recommended that initially you rent a comparable property in an area that could eventually be the location that you would settle. By renting, it gives you an opportunity to learn about the area before committing capital for the purchase.

Many countries allow foreign nationals to acquire real estate without restrictions. However, there are countries where permits are required to purchase property as a foreign national, or where property acquisition is limited to nationals of the country. The acquisition and ownership of real estate in a new country raises legal and tax issues that are often unsuspected by those concerned. Private acquisitions of real estate are frequently made without any accurate knowledge of the legal, tax and economic background particular to the country.

Value maintenance and capital growth will also play a vital role, so it is important to clarify these key factors before acquiring real estate in order to be protected from unexpected devaluation, legal and tax consequences. While this applies to real estate in general, it is particularly true for property located in a different jurisdiction, especially one with onerous legal systems and linguistic limitations.

It is generally an advisable risk-averse approach to appoint lawyers, tax experts, architects and trustworthy real estate agencies familiar with local expertise. The costs incurred will almost always be offset by the smooth and correct handling of the issues and procedures involved.

Other countries have different habits and different legal systems, especially in respect of real estate and tax law, which may assume very different forms in the various countries. So foreign acquirers of real estate should not let themselves be guided by their inherent feeling for what is right, but must inform themselves in an unprejudiced way about the circumstances prevailing locally. Still, the acquisition of real estate is safe in most countries as long as certain basic rules are observed.

Finding the right property

Although common knowledge, it is nevertheless worth remembering that location is the most important factor in the selection of any piece of real estate. Special care must also be taken to determine how the environment may change in the future. It is important to be aware of construction of projects for freeways, airfields, power lines, waste dumps or similar major developments that are planned in the area. One should also know in which construction zone the building plot and its surrounding plots are situated (might a neighbor add another level to his property and in doing so, obscure the marvelous lake view?).

The best way to gain certainty about these factors is to buy an existing property in surroundings which are already well developed and in which re-zoning is unlikely. If there are still many undeveloped plots of land around a property, it is hard to estimate how the surroundings and perhaps the entire appearance of the locality may change. Many location factors must be considered, above all the quality of the local municipality. The improvement of the location is critical for any future gain on the value of the property. Improvements to infrastructure such as transport links and shopping facilities will have a positive impact whereas construction of freeways will have a negative impact. In making an estimate of the future potential growth in value of a property, it is always worthwhile clarifying the planned and future development of the residential area in which it is located as well as any changes in local infrastructure prior to the purchase.

Also the quality of the location within the municipality where the property is situated is important as this will affect everyday life. Is the house located on a good street in a quiet area? Where are the nearest shops, banks, post offices, schools and kindergartens, high schools, location of evening classes, restaurants and sports facilities? Are there cultural facilities nearby? How easily can the property be reached by public transport? Where is the nearest national or international airport? Where is the nearest rail station? What are the connections like? How far is it to the nearest highway or freeway? How close is the nearest healthcare facility, and where are the nearest major hospitals?

Important aspects of the property itself are the size and shape of the plot, the orientation of the building and its exposure to sunlight, the view as well as the extent to which it is overlooked by neighbors. Tranquility is important – noise, especially from busy roads and airports, should not be underestimated. Intrusive odors also represent an important factor (proximity to paper factories, pig farms, food-processing establishments etc.). Exposure to wind plays a significant role in many areas (for example the

Mistral in southern France or the Bora in Dalmatia). A secluded outside patio can be very attractive, but excessive exposure to wind can make conditions quite disagreeable outside the house, on the patio or in the garden.

Furthermore, pollution levels must be considered such as the extent of emissions and pollution from fumes. Therefore it is important to be far away from filling stations, covered car parks and busy roads. Likewise, one should be sufficiently far away from high-tension lines and mobile phone network antennas.

Where buildings are constructed on a slope, excessive water pressure and thus damp masonry may be a problem. Any danger of natural hazards must also be clarified. Landslides, avalanches, earthquakes, forest fires as well as flooding, tidal waves and tornadoes may present considerable risks in certain areas. The situation and construction of the property must be carefully considered to estimate the real risks.

Certain special features must be considered in the case of rural and agricultural real estate as well as of historical properties and houses located by rivers, lakes and close to the sea.

The buyer must also consider factors such as access and access authorization – is there a public road leading to the property? If there is only a private road, the buyer must be fully apprised of authorization access to the property as well as issues such as snow clearance in winter.

Another factor that should not be overlooked is security. The buyer should enquire as to the frequency of burglaries in the area where the property is located. If the house is very isolated, the buyer must consider the precautions that should be taken, such as the installation of a burglar alarm or the hiring of a private surveillance service. Perhaps there are neighbors and trustworthy persons who can keep an eye on the house when the owner is absent.

The following aspects must be considered with regards to the actual building: the size and configuration of the rooms and ancillary premises, the number of bathrooms, potential for additional fittings and extensions, construction quality of the building, heating insulation, energy consumption, heating and cooling systems (i.e. is the oil tank located in an environmentally safe place such as in a cellar or protective trough?); and communication accessibility (telephone, Internet, ISDN/ADSL, cable TV connections, a satellite dish). Furthermore, the buyer should also carefully examine these various installations and technical equipment and check whether the installations have been regularly maintained.

It is important to ensure sufficient sound insulation especially in apartments/condominiums and duplex villas. The best way to investigate these premises is to spend several days in the building or, if that is not possible, to have the sound insulation inspected by an expert who can accurately measure it.

From a legal perspective, it is very important to check before every acquisition whether the property to be acquired is encumbered with any easements, servitudes, charges, restrictive covenants, liens or mortgages. Such rights may be significant and may often greatly restrict the enjoyment or use of the property. The existence of such encumbrances may also have considerable effects on its value and future appreciation. The various rights and restrictions will differ in each jurisdiction, therefore even though it is usually noted in a land or ownership register or in the title deeds, it is important to have a local legal advisor investigate this properly.

Finally, when searching for a property, one should ideally already apply criteria which will be significant to future buyers when it comes to a resale.

Real estate holding structures

In some situations, it is sensible to use a holding structure such as a company for fiscal and succession planning or to avoid restrictions or licensing requirements. There are also other factors which will dictate whether a property should be held in a holding structure. In many cases, the decision will be determined by the specific country in which the individual is purchasing the property as each country's specific regulations will have a different effect on their tax and succession planning.

In addition to tax and succession planning aspects, it is also desirable, for confidentiality and asset protection purposes, to hold real estate via the intermediary of a company rather than directly, as this prevents the effective owner from appearing in the ownership or land register.

The more expensive the real estate, the more sense it makes to use a holding structure rather than place the asset in the individual's name.

However, in some circumstances it is preferable to acquire the real estate directly in one's own name. Firstly, for example in France, comprehensive regulations aim to prevent acquisition via the intermediary of companies and thus make such procedures more complicated – with the notable exception of the domestic *SCI*.[16] Secondly, this can even have tax disadvantages, as companies are often liable to higher capital gains tax than directly owned properties at a resale. Furthermore, most companies (again perhaps with the exception of a French *SCI*) incur administrative costs. In many countries it therefore makes more sense to acquire properties in the lower to middle price range directly in one's own name. However, careful planning is of particular importance in such cases, and includes drawing up a suitable will or possibly also acquiring the property in the name of your children.

The use of a holding structure has differing effects in the various jurisdictions. Therefore it is important to understand the implications of the residence status and the local tax and succession laws. Often, companies are usually set up in countries where company taxes are nil or limited and annual maintenance costs are low. Such jurisdictions include Anguilla, the BVI, Luxembourg, Malta and Panama, where companies can be set up and maintained at low cost and with no or only limited local tax consequences. However, tax consequences may have to be taken into account depending on the country of residence of the company owner and the country from where the company is effectively managed. So it is essential to clarify all circumstances and tax consequences carefully – including in the country where the company owner is resident.

---

[16] Société Civile Immobilière

It is also worth noting that corporate and other holding structures (such as private foundations and trusts) are often recommended and also implemented despite failing to pass a thorough scrutiny by the relevant tax authorities – where such scrutiny takes place. Many countries have now extended their relevant tax laws with very extensive anti-abuse regulations. If more than 50% of a company's assets consist directly or indirectly of real estate, that company will often be taxed just like real estate. Thus the capital gain from the sale is also taxed on the same basis (and cannot simply accrue tax free in a zero tax country) when the responsible tax authorities discover the true nature of the transfer. Ultimately, many company structures are based on the transfer of company shares without the notification of the tax authorities. Although it is often highly unlikely that the tax authorities will ever find out about the transaction, it cannot form the basis of a legal arrangement and sound planning.

In 2012, new rules relating to dwellings worth over GBP 2 million held by corporate structures came into force in the UK, making it essential to take professional advice if you own, or are considering investing in, valuable real estate in the UK.

Real estate transactions

The buyer generally bears the greater transaction risk, as is fittingly expressed by a principle of Roman law: *Periculum est emptoris,*[17] or in other words: *Caveat emptor.*[18] That is why certain precautions and clarifications are needed prior to every purchase in order to minimize the risks. As a long-term investment which usually ties up greater capital, the acquisition of real estate should be planned and carried out in a careful and rational manner.

Once the buyer has identified the target property, there are a number of practical and legal criteria that the buyer should observe thereby ensuring full and proper title to the property. Besides restrictions imposed by the country, there may be problems with the seller's title, third party

---

[17] The purchaser runs the risk
[18] Buyer beware

claims and other onerous issues that are not immediately apparent. It is imperative that the buyer investigates the title thoroughly and carries out the necessary due diligence, ideally with the help of a legal advisor.

The seller must ensure that he can produce all authorizations (e.g. consent of his spouse) needed for the purchase, as failure to do so would delay the transaction.

In most countries the seller is obliged to inform the buyer of any defects. As a rule, the seller must also inform the buyer of the existence of any pre-emption rights. Often, the seller is liable to a comprehensive obligation for information and disclosure and bears corresponding liability to the buyer. Accordingly, it is essential for the seller to settle all questions of liability in the agreement in a detailed manner. In general, it is recommended wherever possible to exclude all liability by the seller from the agreement (this is also common practice for re-sale property in most countries). This liability exclusion should be comprehensive and expressly include liability for legal and material defects, error and damage compensation, as far as this is permissible on the basis of the local law. In any case, care must be taken to ensure that the sales agreement contains no guarantees which the seller is unable to satisfy. If the seller makes any representations and warranties, a carefully drafted sales agreement will limit the warranties and representations to the period of time the seller has owned the real estate and exclude the periods of ownership by previous owners.

The seller should also note who is responsible for which fees – for example taxes and lawyers' or notaries' fees. In many cases, notaries' fees and transfer taxes are divided on a fifty-fifty basis, but this division is ultimately a matter for negotiation. Lawyers' costs are usually borne by the party commissioning the lawyer. However, the seller is always responsible for paying capital gains tax.

In most cases, the seller is also liable to pay the broker's commission. This generally varies between 2% and 10% of the sale price in different countries and is usually subject to Value Added Tax (where such a tax exists).

The property acquisition taxes which are levied everywhere are as a rule borne by the buyer. However, if they cannot be collected from the buyer, they may in some countries be charged to the seller. This is particularly relevant when the seller remains resident in the same country. With regard to capital gains taxes it is exactly the reverse: they are payable by the seller but the buyer may be jointly liable if the seller doesn't pay them – and the tax authorities may be entitled to put a lien on the property.

When apartments or houses belonging to an owner's association (e.g. concerning the shared amenities of a condominium) are sold, the amount of any reserve or renovation fund must be determined, as this can have an effect on the sale price.

A property designed for private use should above all bring subjective pleasure to its users and not only maintain and increase its value in objective terms. Therefore, careful clarification of these factors is most important before closing the deal.

2

Citizenship Planning

Chapter Summary

Henley & Partners was the first and continues to be the leading firm to globally specialize in the field of citizenship planning. Today there are many reasons why you should consider becoming a citizen of more than one country.

There are a variety of different benefits to alternative citizenship. As citizenship may impact on your tax status, it could be a key factor in international tax planning. Alongside this, you may gain more privacy and security across your banking and investment portfolio. Frequent travelers, especially those who often require visas, find a second citizenship invaluable in ensuring flexibility and the ability to travel at short notice. Those who have the need to live in a safer country than their own, either now or in the future, can obtain that security through citizenship.

The most common factors in acquiring citizenship are by birth, by descent, by marriage or by grant. The US is an important example of the few countries that still grant citizenship by birth. Many people will be entitled to another passport by descent or by birth, and this may be easy to establish.

If birth, descent or marriage do not offer a solution, there are other options open to wealthy or skilled individuals. Eight countries offer citizenship-by-investment programs – Antigua and Barbuda, Austria, the Commonwealth of Dominica, Cyprus, Grenada, Malta, St. Kitts and Nevis and St. Lucia – and can give you a new passport swiftly and legally, which is of paramount importance, as illegal options are commonplace.

When considering any of these options, you must remember to take guidance on dual citizenship, as roughly only half of the world's countries allow this.

Finally, and of great importance, is the reputation of the country and its passport. The level of visa-free travel it affords you will be critical to the impact and benefits it has on your life.

In recent times, and especially since the dramatic events of 9/11, questions of citizenship, visa restrictions and freedom of movement have become more and more important for internationally active individuals and families, although the concept of citizenship planning was created by Henley & Partners about 20 years ago.

A main characteristic of the modern world system is that economy and trade increasingly take place on an international level, while people are still bound within nation-states by the instruments of citizenship and sovereignty.[19]

This new, transnational flexibility in business, production, labor and financial markets, travel and international family relations is increasingly being matched with flexible citizenship. This field can be described as the strategies and impacts of internationally mobile individuals and families seeking to optimize their situation in view of different nation-state regimes by selecting different sites for work, investments, leisure and family relocation.[20] Indeed, there are many reasons why all over the world more and more wealthy individuals consider becoming a citizen of more than just one country, and consequently holding more than one passport.[21]

2.1   Why become a citizen of more than one country?

Due to political or economic circumstances, citizens of many countries find it difficult to travel abroad and are confronted with strict visa requirements each time they want to enter a foreign country.[22]

Furthermore, nationals whose passports usually allow them easy access to most countries can find it impossible to obtain visas due to temporary travel restrictions during trade sanctions and other geopolitical disturbances; or due to their nationality may be overly exposed to terrorist threats and other hostility.[23]

---

[19]   Wallerstein (1974) and Zolberg (1981)
[20]   See Ong (1999)
[21]   See for example Torpey (2000), Lloyd (2005), Joppke (2010), Hokema (2002)
[22]   See the *Henley & Partners Visa Restrictions Index* (HVRI); *www.henleyglobal.com/hrvi*
[23]   This can happen even to citizens of small and generally neutral countries, as Danish citizens experienced following the publication of Mohammed cartoons in the *Jyllands-Posten* newspaper in Denmark on 30 September 2005

Moreover, even though the necessary visa may be granted to you, getting a visa is always a very tiresome procedure. During this time, the passport on which you are getting the visa is not available – and this can be a significant factor of delay for your travels. 18% of Chinese visitors to Europe, for instance, make it to the UK, but two-thirds visit France, a member of the Schengen travel zone where visas are easier to get.[24]

Visa-free travel can also be obtained via a residence permit, not only through a second passport. For example, residence in any of the Schengen countries will offer visa-free travel throughout the Schengen area. However, only the acquisition of a second citizenship and a second passport can guarantee the desired long-term visa-free travel, and only citizenship guarantees the long-term security of these privileges.[25]

If you cannot acquire or renew your passport in your home country, for example due to political instability, civil war, revolution or change of government, having another passport can be very useful, even critical. Even if you simply lose your passport, it may take some time until you can get a replacement.

There is a growing tendency in many countries to follow the US in taxing even non-resident citizens.[26] In fact, I believe that this will be an increasingly important issue in the future. As individual states are struggling to keep their tax base, both corporate and individual taxation systems will have to undergo substantial changes. For income taxation and other taxes on individuals, citizenship may become an increasingly important, if not decisive, factor. I anticipate that some countries will introduce similar legislation to that which the US currently has and will tax its citizens regardless of their place of residence. At the very least I can imagine that this would apply, for example, to all EU citizens resident within the EU. Therefore, having

---

[24] The Economist, 19 February 2013 *'Tourist visas: You're not welcome'*
[25] For a good discussion of the differences between residence and citizenship statuses, see Joppke (2010)
[26] See Betten (1998) and chapter 3 in this book

alternative citizenship options will become even more important for wealthy individuals who may want to plan around such new taxation rules. Being a citizen of more than one country, and ideally in more than one continent, will be the norm for the global entrepreneur and investor in the future.

Meanwhile, citizenship also plays a role in some countries to determine whether you may still be deemed tax resident or domiciled (including Germany, Sweden, the UK and others), and citizenship is one of the tie-breaker rules in most double tax treaties. Alternative citizenship is therefore becoming increasingly important as an effective tool for international tax planning.

If you wish to have the possibility to retire in a safe haven in the future you can only fully secure this option if you acquire either permanent residence or citizenship of that country. However, even a 'permanent' residence permit does not mean full security, as it may still be subject to renewal, revocation, or new conditions. Becoming a citizen is the only way to secure a life-long status and guarantees a secure and truly permanent alternative place to go to. This is also what the Hong Kong elite was aware of on the eve of the return of the colony from British to Chinese rule, as about 600,000 of Hong Kongers – about 10% of the population – held second passports as an insurance against mainland-Chinese rule. More than half the members of the transition preparatory committee carried foreign passports.[27]

Generally, as a citizen of two or more different states, you are in a privileged position compared to having just one citizenship, you have more planning options and more personal freedom. If you want to acquire real estate of a certain size in Italy for example, you can only do so if the country of your citizenship in return allows Italian citizens to buy property without restrictions. If that is not the case, you cannot buy in Italy, unless, of course, you are also a citizen of another country which may not have such restrictions in place.

---

[27]   See Ong (1999)

Most importantly, citizenship and a passport, particularly from a small, peaceful country, can save your life when travelling in times of political unrest, civil war, terrorism, and other difficult situations. Many international businesspeople and important people who are active worldwide actually consider an alternative passport to be the best life insurance money can buy.

In an unsettled, ever-changing world, acquiring a second citizenship is a wise decision and an investment for the future. When you acquire citizenship, your spouse and children, and sometimes parents,[28] may be included. Citizenship is for life and can be passed on to future generations.[29] Depending on the other country or countries of which you are a citizen, there is often no need to give up your present citizenship while you enjoy the benefits of a second citizenship and passport, as states increasingly allow multiple nationalities.[30]

2.2 Who is interested in a second citizenship?

People from all over the world and from a wide range of backgrounds are interested in multiple citizenships and consequently hold more than one passport.

Many of the wealthiest individuals and most internationally successful people hold more than one passport. In recent years, an increasing number of internationally forward-thinking entrepreneurs and investors have specifically acquired one or more additional citizenship(s) to diversify their personal exposure and options. They realize that not only their investment portfolio, but also their residence and citizenship portfolio needs to be diversified to reduce risk and increase international flexibility.

More than ever, wealthy citizens are becoming a target for kidnappings, terrorism, and in some countries politically motivated violence. Wealthy

---

[28] For example in St. Kitts and Nevis
[29] Although some countries, such as the UK and New Zealand, have introduced limits to the passing on of citizenship infinitely through blood line if not also remaining a resident
[30] See Hokema (2002) and Hansen/Weil (2001) on multiple citizenship

people are at risk in insecure countries where organized crime, in particular kidnapping, is widespread, as in many South American countries; but also where they may be part of an ethnic minority group and may face hostility within their own country or in regions with significant political upheaval, such as the Middle East in recent years, or where the future of their home country is uncertain.

Even if the home country is stable and personal security is not an issue, citizens of countries where the political and economic situation does not allow widespread visa-free travel for its passport holders are a further group where an alternative travel document offers great merits.

Persons who travel frequently to countries requiring visas also need an alternative citizenship and passport. They may need to travel at short notice while they are waiting for such visas to be issued on their current passports, and often passports have to be sent to the relevant embassies or consulates and remain there, sometimes for several weeks, before being sent back. This also includes the risk of one's passport being lost in the process and therefore having an alternative is critical if you wish to remain flexible with regard to international travel.

Citizens of countries with an uncertain future acquire alternative citizenship and passports to ensure that they will continue to be able to travel or have the option to relocate after possible political changes. Unfortunately, many countries fall into this category; citizens of these countries cannot be sure about the political future of their home. Alternative options need to be secured in good time.

Persons who value privacy when travelling, doing business or for banking and investment are concerned with protecting their interests and their personal data by using a different citizenship depending on where they operate and what they do. In times of widespread data abuse, identity theft and cyber-crime, it is increasingly important to be able to protect one's personal profile. Having more than one citizenship and passport can help achieve this.

Citizens who wish to have the option to renounce their current citizenship must first acquire another citizenship; otherwise they would become stateless, which is a status to avoid at all costs.[31] There are many reasons why one may wish to give up citizenship, for example to legally avoid otherwise compulsory military service requirements or taxation.

Persons who were rendered stateless by birth or through accidents of history need to acquire citizen status of at least one country, in order to have the freedom of travel and other rights that citizens can enjoy. They may not be able to acquire citizenship by naturalization in their country of residence[32] and thus may need to immigrate elsewhere or acquire citizenship-by-investment. If you have no citizenship, the situation can be extremely difficult.

Citizens of countries with high direct taxes may acquire alternative residence and citizenship as part of a strategy to reduce their tax liability. Citizenship may play a role in the determination of one's tax domicile, even though, of course, the main factor remains the place of residence and usually citizenship has only a very limited role to play.

Finally, anyone who wishes to have the possibility to retire in a safe country at any time in the future can secure this permanently by acquiring citizenship of that country.

2.3   How to obtain a second citizenship

The principal grounds for acquiring citizenship are birth within a certain territory, by descent, marriage to a citizen, and grant of citizenship or naturalization.

The conditions under which the privilege of citizenship by naturalization is granted vary from country to country, but essential factors are usually

---

[31]   Some countries do not even allow you to give up your citizenship unless you have another one. For a good discussion of statelessness, see Stiller (2011)

[32]   For example in China, Malaysia, the UAE and many other countries, there are minority groups which are resident there but are prevented from acquiring citizenship of the country they live in

family relationships or certain periods of residence, besides character, language and other requirements.[33]

Birth within a territory

Nowadays relatively few countries grant citizenship to anyone who is born within their territory. The US is the most important of those countries. The principle that citizenship is passed on by birth within a certain territory is called *ius soli* (law of the soil). In most countries which apply the *ius soli* principle, however, this is limited to second-generation immigrants and requires the parents to be legally resident for some time in order for the children born in the country to become citizens at birth.

If you know where you were born you can find out relatively easily whether you may have the right to another passport – or, in case of the US, whether you may actually be a US citizen (and possibly never filed tax returns and therefore need to consult urgently with a US tax lawyer).

You can plan your children's citizenship portfolio to a certain extent. If your children are born in a country that grants them citizenship either right away, or will make the acquisition easier later on, the right steps need to be taken prior to their birth. Some countries faced significant birth tourism[34] and adjusted their laws to make it more difficult to just fly in and give birth. Countries which did not adjust their laws, like the US and some Caribbean nations, are trying to be restrictive in granting visas to pregnant women.

Ancestry

Many people may not be aware that they are entitled to an alternative citizenship by virtue of their ancestry. The principle that citizenship is

---

[33] In some Swiss Cantons for example, you have to pass an "integration" test, which means that you may need to learn some Swiss history and other things deemed useful to qualify for the privilege of applying for Swiss citizenship. In some Asian countries, if you are not of a particular ethnic origin, your chances of ever being granted citizenship are close to zero. In most Muslim countries you need not apply if you are not Muslim

[34] Ireland, for example

passed on by descent is called *ius sanguinis* (law of the blood). Americans (and Argentineans, Australians, Canadians etc.) in most cases have traceable ancestry in Europe. If the ancestry is not too far back, it may be possible for them to re-acquire the citizenship of their ancestors. For example, many US citizens are entitled to Irish, Polish or Italian citizenship due to the mass immigration from these countries to the US in the early twentieth century. An Irish-born grandparent, or also a grandparent from Poland or Lithuania, may be the basis for a successful claim to Irish, Polish or Lithuanian citizenship and, as a result, to an EU passport. In Croatia, having proof of Croatian ancestry, no matter how far removed, is sufficient justification to reclaim citizenship.

Even though many countries have tightened their nationality laws, it is constructive to investigate the option, especially if one of your closer ancestors was born in another country. Dual or multiple citizenships offer numerous benefits beyond the possibility of taking up residence in the country of citizenship (and in case of citizenship of an EU country, to have the right of establishment throughout the EU).

Naturalization

For a person who cannot rely on the ancestral option there are residence and immigration options available to skilled people, investors and wealthy individuals in numerous countries:[35] Australia, the Bahamas, Canada, Hong Kong, Monaco, Singapore, Switzerland, and the UK are just a few examples of countries which offer residence to wealthy individuals and investors.

This book deals with the most attractive countries where residence permits are available to investors and wealthy individuals. Thus, the emphasis is not just on general quality of life, business and employment opportunities (in which case, for example, Australia or New Zealand would be among the immigration countries of choice), but specifically on factors concerning wealthy individuals, such as personal tax, privacy and

---

[35] For an extensive overview see Bauman (2009) and *www.henleyglobal.com*

personal security. The countries have also been selected with a view of citizenship planning and the possibility of acquiring an attractive alternative citizenship with relative ease. All these countries are welcoming foreign persons who are willing to invest.

Citizenship-by-Investment

There are currently only eight countries which offer citizenship programs that provide a direct route to citizenship based on investment and which have passed Henley & Partners' country due diligence.[36] These are Antigua and Barbuda, Austria, Cyprus, Dominica, Grenada, Malta, St. Kitts and Nevis, and St. Lucia. In 2014, Malta introduced a state-of-the-art program, which is the only such program that has the approval of the EU Commission. It held a public tender process for a public services concession to establish a citizenship-by-investment program, which is called the Malta Individual Investor Programme. It is the most attractive citizenship-by-investment program in the world today, featuring the highest standards of due diligence, an efficient application process, and a reasonable contribution requirement. Citizenship-by-investment offers the opportunity to legally acquire a new citizenship quickly and easily, without any disruptions to one's life.[37]

Apart from these seven countries, there are several others which have similar provisions in their laws to allow the granting of citizenship to substantial investors.[38] However, there is no established and clear practice in these countries; or the structures and processes involved are not transparent; or the conditions not clear and the decisions mostly arbitrary.[39] Also, in many countries there are suspicions that an element of corruption may be involved in the citizenship acquisitions. Therefore, if the intention is to acquire citizenship based on investment extreme care

---

[36] Henley & Partners constantly monitors and evaluates residence and citizenship programs around the world against a number of criteria

[37] For an in-depth discussion of these options see Part IV

[38] For example, Bulgaria, Cape Verde, Grenada, Nauru, the Seychelles, most South American countries, and others

[39] Montenegro, for example, granted citizenship to the controversial former Thai Prime Minister Thaksin Shinawatra on the basis of a mere promise to invest in the country

has to be exercised. In fact, in most cases it is not advisable unless a real, substantial investment is contemplated in the particular target country.

Some countries also have provisions to grant non-citizens passports[40] or honorary citizenships[41] which are legal but largely useless as no full citizenship status is acquired and thus the documents are often not recognized by other countries. Furthermore, as no citizen status is acquired, there is no protection and the documents can be revoked at any time just like residence permits, therefore not giving the kind of security that is desirable when acquiring an alternative citizenship.

Caveat emptor

With regard to the acquisition of alternative citizenship, it is important to always obtain proper advice from reputable legal advisors, and to check the citizenship laws and procedures of the relevant country. This is particularly important if citizenship is sought on the basis of an investment or other direct contribution to a country. Unfortunately there are many illegal activities and it is safe to assume that many offers are fraudulent. What makes matters worse is that sometimes even seemingly reputable professionals have been found to be involved in what turned out to be fraudulent offers. For example, between November 2010 and May 2011 a Canadian immigration lawyer and a private client lawyer based in Switzerland simultaneously offered citizenship in Iceland for a USD 400,000 investment in some private equity fund. Iceland's citizenship law requires the passing of a parliamentary bill in order to grant citizenship to a foreigner outside the normal naturalization procedures. A simple check of the Citizenship Act would have revealed this, yet the "marketing" activities of these lawyers made it necessary for the Icelandic Government to publish an unequivocal statement. The government statement underlined that Iceland has never had in the past and has no intention to establish any kind of citizenship-by-investment program.[42]

---

[40] Panama, under its retiree residence program
[41] Tonga and a couple of African countries
[42] For more information see the website of the Ministry of Interior of Iceland: *http://eng.innanrikisraduneyti.is/laws-and-regulations/english/citizenship/nr/27049*

Bulgaria has an investor immigration program that leads to permanent resident status if certain investments are made and conditions are met, which later on can lead to citizenship. However, Bulgaria does not have a citizenship-by-investment program as such (although provisions in its law would allow it, and are sometimes used to give citizenship to business people under unclear circumstances). Despite this, some agents mislead interested investors to make them believe that Bulgaria does in fact offer a formal citizenship-by-investment program.

Likewise, there are many companies now which provide services under legal programs (like St. Kitts and Nevis) but where either the company or persons involved have a questionable reputation or are linked to government officials, or real estate developments are being promoted which do not pass closer scrutiny.

2.4   Criteria to consider when acquiring citizenship

The most important criterion when acquiring alternative citizenship is that the acquisition is in accordance with the constitution and laws of the country, i.e. that it is legal. This seemingly obvious premise needs to be pointed out specifically in this context.

Citizenship documents and passports obtained by illegal means such as bribery are sadly not uncommon. In many countries it is possible to make (illegal) direct payments to corrupt government officials in return for passports and citizenship documents. Holders of such documents run a serious risk of exposure, arrest and deportation. Even in those countries where the law gives the President, Prime Minister or other government ministers relative discretion regarding the granting of citizenship, if any payments are involved, these are bribes – a crime in almost every country. Often the result is a revocation of previously granted citizenship and passports, for example after a change of government. Persons who have acquired documents this way are also frequently blackmailed and forced to pay further 'fees' later on.[43] It is therefore crucial that citizenship is

---

[43]   As has been the case in Costa Rica and other Latin American countries for many years

obtained based upon specific provisions in the law and clear, official procedures.

A related criterion is that the granting of citizenship and the passports issued in conjunction therewith have to be recognized by other countries. If full citizenship has been granted based on the legal provisions of a country, it will normally be recognized by other countries. However, if only non-citizens passports are granted, generally this is not a good option. One example is Panama where a (legal) non-citizens passport under the retiree residence program can be acquired.

Other important points to consider when intending to become a citizen of choice include the geographic location of the country, the official language, political and economic stability, the legal system, the banking and business environment, visa-free travel possibilities for passport holders of that country, the reputation of the country and the passport, and of course initial and future overall costs.

You will also need to consider restrictions on dual citizenship. Some countries do not allow you to hold any other citizenship besides theirs. About half of the world's countries allow dual nationality, and the other half does not allow you to be a citizen of another country at the same time. Among those countries which do not allow dual nationality, various degrees of strictness can be observed, but often the acquisition of another citizenship without first obtaining a formal permission (which may or may not be obtainable) leads to the automatic loss of one's current citizenship. Therefore, one needs to carefully check the legal situation in the home country with regard to dual citizenship, prior to taking any steps to acquire another citizenship.

The following is an overview of citizenship regulations in selected countries:[44]

---

[44]   The information is based on the author's own interpretation of citizenship legislation in the relevant countries; for a definitive assessment of the legal situation and possible exemptions, it is necessary to seek legal advice from a specialist in the relevant country

Selected countries which allow dual citizenship

Austria*	Cyprus	Germany**	Italy	New Zealand	Spain (only in certain cases)	United States
Australia	Denmark	Greece	Jordan	Pakistan***	Sri Lanka	Vietnam
Bangladesh	Dominica	Grenada	Latvia	Peru	St. Kitts and Nevis	Western Samoa
Belgium	Ecuador	Hungary	Lebanon	Philippines	Sweden	
Belize	Egypt	Iceland	Lithuania****	Poland	Switzerland	
Brazil	El Salvador	Iran	Macedonia	Portugal	Syria	
Canada	Fiji	Iraq	Malta	Romania	Thailand	
Chile	Finland	Ireland	Mexico	Russia	Turkey	
Colombia	France	Israel	Montenegro	Serbia	United Kingdom	

Source: KALIN (2016)

* Generally not allowed; except for persons who obtain two citizenships at the time they were born. The exceptions to this rule are stated in s 28 of the Austrian Citizenship Act; additionally Austria allows dual citizenship if Austrian citizenship is acquired under § 10 (6) of the Austrian Citizenship Act

** Dual citizenship is allowed in numerous circumstances (s 12 of the German Nationality Act) which have recently extended with the amendments of the German Nationality Act of 2014 (ss 25 and 29)

*** According to chapter 14, Annex J-Article 6* of 1951 Pakistani Nationality Law and the amendments 1952,1972,1973 and 2000, holding dual citizenship was not permitted. But now the government of Pakistan recognizes and allows its citizens to also hold citizenships of 16 countries, including Australia, Belgium, Canada, France, Iceland, New Zealand, Sweden, Switzerland, the UK, the US, and others

**** Only under limited circumstances, cf. *http://www.dualcitizenship.com/countries/lithuania.html; https://usa.mfa.lt/usa/en/travel-and-residence/consular-issues/ citizenship-of-lithuania*

On the other hand, countries which do not allow the acquisition of another citizenship include the following:

Selected countries which prohibit dual citizenship

Brunei	Kazhakstan	Malaysia	Netherlands	Singapore
China	Kenya	Mauritius	Norway	Solomon Islands
Indonesia	Kiribati	Myanmar	Papua New Guinea	Venezuela
Japan	Kuwait	Nepal	Saudi Arabia	

Source: KALIN (2016)

3

Giving up US Citizenship or a US Green Card

By Dr. Marshall J. Langer*
and Prof. Denis Kleinfeld**

*   Dr. Marshall Langer is Professor Emeritus at Thomas Jefferson School of Law and recognized as the most experienced US tax attorney specialized in expatriation and international taxation

**   Prof. Denis Kleinfeld is a noted lawyer, author and teacher. He is an Adjunct Professor at Texas A&M Law School's new LLM Program and known worldwide as an expert in international taxation, financial services, and expatriation

Chapter Summary

According to the Treasury Department there was a record number of US residents expatriating in 2015, up from 3,415 in 2014 to 4,279 in 2015. Prior to 2010, the recorded number of expatriates was always well below 1,000 persons.

Exit taxes are deliberately punitive, and have been designed specifically to prevent the highest taxpayers from leaving by removing virtually all of the financial benefit gained by doing so.

Giving up US citizenship is a complicated business, and a wide range of factors must be taken into account, including residence, domicile and citizenship, marital status and the status of beneficiaries, sources of income and location of assets, and the timing of any move. You must also acquire another citizenship to replace the one given up.

The exit taxes do not apply to everyone who gives up US citizenship; there are two key tests to determine whether you are caught by it. The first is based on income tax liability over the past five years and the second is based on your net worth. There are exclusions for certain items when calculating your net gain, and gains and allowable losses are taken into account.

Once you have relinquished or renounced US citizenship, and paid exit taxes if necessary, you must still take care not to fall back into the US tax pool by spending too many days there.

Depending on your new passport, you may need to obtain a visa to enter the US again. There is also a significant tax on gifts or bequests that you subsequently give to any other US taxpayer once you have left.

Taxation is not the only reason why Americans give up US citizenship or terminate long-term US residence, but it is frequently considered by wealthy individuals who are already living abroad or plan to do so permanently. Unlike citizens of France, Germany, Switzerland, the UK and other countries, US citizens remain almost fully subject to US income and death taxes even if they never intend to return to live in America. Despite tax treaties, they are often subject to at least some double taxation.

Thousands of wealthy British residents have already left Britain to avoid the maximum income tax rate which has been as high as 50% and is currently 45%. They have tried to escape British taxes by changing both their residence and their domicile. They can retain their British citizenship and their British passports which are also, for now at least, EU passports. Many wealthy Americans do not yet fully realize that they may now be facing combined federal and state income taxes that exceed the rates that have caused people to leave Britain. In some cases, the combined corporate and individual income taxes on dividends received from US corporations may exceed 60%.

The US applies all eight tentacles of the 'tax octopus'. To escape US income, gift and death taxes, you must consider each of the eight tax tentacles:

- *Residence* – you cannot have a green card, and you must avoid meeting the substantial presence test by spending too many days in the US

- *Domicile* – you must terminate your domicile in any US state or territory

- *Citizenship* – you cannot be a US citizen since the US taxes its citizens on a worldwide basis

- *Marital status* – you must take steps to eliminate the application of any "community property" rules under which each spouse is entitled to a half interest in most income and property acquired by the other spouse during the marriage

- *Source of income* – you must eliminate or minimize any taxable income from US sources

- *Location of assets* – you must eliminate or minimize holding any assets that would be subject to federal or state gift or death taxes

- *Timing* – the timing of various acts must be carefully considered (for example, you might sell your family home before you leave but try to postpone receipt of foreign-source income until after you go)

- *Status of beneficiaries* – several special factors must be considered if your spouse or any of your other intended beneficiaries will remain US citizens or residents

- While the percentage of the total population of US residents actually expatriating is quite small, the fact is that the reported numbers only reflect those officially listed by the Internal Revenue Service (IRS). This does not include residents who have merely left with no intention of returning but have not formally renounced their citizenship in the US. Many of those who have formally renounced their US citizenship or residence have done so since they were returning to a country in which they were born (such as South Korea) that does not permit them to retain another citizenship. Many countries permit dual citizenship, but some do not

If you expatriate, the new US exit tax law enacted in 2008 aims to make you promptly pay an exit tax on most of your previously untaxed worldwide gains and deferred income. In those cases where this tax is permitted to be postponed, the IRS makes sure that you cannot escape the exit tax or reduce it by using tax treaties. Finally, a nasty new special income tax is imposed on any US citizens or residents who receive gifts or bequests from you exceeding USD 14,000 a year at any time in the future. The bottom line: the new rules are designed to remove most or all of the tax benefits you might derive by leaving. The government wants to encourage you to stay and pay.

The US Congress didn't enact the first constitutional income tax on individuals until 1913. The US income tax rates in early years were generally quite low. The US Supreme Court decided in 1924 that it was okay to apply the income tax to US citizens living abroad as well as to everyone residing in the US. Despite the fact that the case involved less than

USD 1,000 and the result was questionable, it is almost inconceivable that either Congress or the courts will ever change it. Today, the US is the only developed country in the world that taxes not only its residents but also its citizens, even those who have never lived in the US or who have lived abroad for many years.

Having or acquiring another citizenship is a practical necessity for anyone seeking to reduce or eliminate US federal, state and local taxes that are becoming more confiscatory each year. Some Americans acquire a second citizenship through ancestry or by marriage; others do so through a citizenship program such as that of St. Kitts and Nevis. Dual citizenship does not eliminate US taxes if one of these is US citizenship.

Are you a US citizen? For many of those reading this the answer is obvious. They were born in the US or have been naturalized, and they have never done anything to lose their American citizenship. However, US citizenship is also acquired by birth abroad if at least one of your parents was a US citizen and has met minimum US residence requirements. These rules have been changed several times and your actual citizenship will normally depend on the law in effect at the time you were born.

A child born in the US to a mother who is an alien simply visiting the US at that time is a US citizen. A child born in the US whose parents are illegal aliens is also a US citizen. Anyone born in the US and "subject to its jurisdiction" is a US citizen by birth even if neither of his or her parents were US citizens or US residents. The only children born in the US who are not subject to its jurisdiction are the children of ambassadors or other representatives of foreign countries.

A child born abroad is a US citizen at birth if both parents are US citizens when the child was born and at least one of them had resided in the US sometime before the child's birth. If only one of the parents is a US citizen, the child born abroad is a US citizen if the citizen parent was physically present in the US for at least five years and at least two of those years were after they were 14 years old.

In the US 2010 Census, the government made every possible effort to count all individuals in the country, including illegal aliens. It did not count any US citizens who live abroad. Geneva-based American Citizens Abroad has estimated that there may be as many as seven million US citizens living abroad. No one, including the government, really knows. US citizens are not required to obtain identity papers nor are they required to have US passports. Most Americans living abroad do not register with a US Embassy; they are not required to do so.

A single (not married) US resident or citizen (including one living abroad) is not required to file an annual income tax return if they have less than USD 9,750 of gross income per year. The amount is less than USD 3,800 if they are married and filing separately.

A US citizen must relinquish (or renounce) his or her US citizenship in order to leave. If you do leave the US, you must also take into account the income and capital transfer taxes imposed by the US state and community in which you last lived or in which you own any property.

Until 1966, the US made no serious effort to keep Americans from giving up citizenship for tax reasons. The first US anti-expatriation rules enacted in 1966 were generally unenforceable, but they have been beefed up several times during the next four decades. Since 1995, most anti-expatriation rules have also applied to long-term resident aliens, those who have held green cards in eight of the last 15 years. The rules have never been applied to those who do not hold green cards, even those who have been fully subject to US income taxes for many years because they were deemed to be US residents under the substantial presence test (because they spent an average of more than four months a year in the US).

After more than a decade of unsuccessful attempts, Congress finally passed an exit tax in 2008. Anyone who gave up US citizenship or long-term residence before 17 June 2008 is covered by old rules. Most of these old rules have been replaced for persons covered by the new rules. Those who have expatriated after that date are covered by the new rules. They do not generally face continued US taxation or tax returns for ten years after expatriation. The new rules apply to US citizens who give up US citizenship and to departing aliens who have held a green card for eight of the last 15 years. Anyone who leaves after holding a green card even one day more than seven years risks becoming a covered expatriate subject to the exit tax and a new punitive death and gift tax regime.

The new US exit tax law is quite complex, and it contains numerous cross-references to other sections of the US tax law. This explanation is necessarily over-simplified. Anyone seriously interested in exploring possibly giving up US citizenship or a green card should obtain competent professional advice.

The new exit tax does not apply to everyone who expatriates. It applies to you if you meet either of two monetary tests, one of which can change each year because it is indexed for inflation. You must also certify to the IRS under penalties of perjury (on IRS Form 8854) that you have complied with all of your US tax obligations for the last five years. If you meet either an income tax test or a net worth test, or if you do not make the required certification, you are a covered expatriate and you are subject to all of the negative aspects of the new exit tax law.

If you expatriate during 2014, the income tax test will be based on the average of your US federal income tax liability after foreign tax credits for the five years 2009-2013. If your average net income tax liability during these years was more than USD 157,000 a year, you are a covered expatriate. This amount is indexed for inflation annually and will probably be increased in future years.

The other test is based on your net worth on the day immediately before your expatriation date. If your net worth is at least USD 2 million on that date you are a covered expatriate. That amount is not indexed for inflation.

If you don't meet either monetary test and you make the required certification, you are not a covered expatriate and you are not subject to the exit tax. If you are a covered expatriate, the next step is to calculate the amount of your exit tax.

Certain assets are excluded when you determine your net gain subject to the exit tax. These include your interests in non-grantor trusts and in eligible deferred compensation items such as qualified pension plans, profit sharing plans or qualified annuity plans. An alternative tax system applies to these properties. You will be required to send the payers of these items IRS Form W-8CE (Notice of Expatriation and Waiver of Treaty Benefits). The trustees or other payers must withhold 30% US income tax on any amounts they subsequently pay you that would have been taxable had you remained a US citizen or resident. You cannot reduce this tax under any tax treaty.

US real estate is covered by the exit tax. After you expatriate, each US real property interest will be covered by FIRPTA (the Foreign Investment in Real Property Tax Act), but its basis will be adjusted by the amount of gain to which the asset has been subjected to the exit tax.

If you have an IRA (individual retirement account) or some other specified tax-deferred account, you will be treated as receiving your entire interest in that account on the day preceding your expatriation date. You must pay tax thereon, but you will not be subject to a penalty for early withdrawal.

With respect to all of your other worldwide assets, you must determine the fair market value and the adjusted cost basis of each asset. Each of these assets must be marked-to-market as though you had sold it the day before your expatriation date.

Gains and allowable losses are taken into account. Tax is imposed on your net gain exceeding a set amount. The federal tax rate on long-term capital gains (those on most assets held more than a year) may now be as high as 23.8%. Most state and local governments impose additional taxes. One observation: many US taxpayers who sustained large capital losses during 2008 still have large capital loss carryovers and these can be taken into account in calculating their exit tax.

You can elect to defer paying the exit tax on some or all of your assets by making an irrevocable asset-by-asset election to do so until you die or dispose of the asset. You must provide adequate security to the IRS and maintain such security in force.

In a typical case, a US citizen's expatriation date is the date on which they sign a statement voluntarily relinquishing US nationality or an oath of renunciation before a US consular officer somewhere outside the US even though expatriation is not confirmed until some months later when they receive a CLN (Certificate of Loss of Nationality).

A typical long-term resident's expatriation date is the date on which they file a Department of Homeland Security Form I-407 with a US consular officer. You can't just cut up your green card.

If you pay any required exit tax (or you are not a covered expatriate) and you live overseas, you will be taxed as a non-resident alien individual provided you do not become a US resident under the substantial presence test by spending too many days in the US. That test generally permits you to spend an average of up to about 120 days a year in the US without being treated as a resident for US tax purposes. Since that test is based on a moving average of days (including partial days) you have spent in the US over a three-year period, you should obtain professional advice on how that test will apply to you.

You will also have to escape the other tentacles of the "tax octopus" and comply with all US immigration law requirements if you wish to visit the US. You must obtain a visa to enter the US unless your passport is issued by a country that is covered by the US visa waiver program.

If you are a covered expatriate, the nastiest part of the new law imposes a special new income tax or transfer tax on all covered gifts or bequests exceeding USD 14,000 per year that any US citizen, resident or trust receives from you either directly or indirectly at any time after you expatriate. The tax rate will be the highest rate of gift or estate tax imposed at the time of the gift or your death. For those dying after 2012, that rate is 40%. Exemptions apply for gifts or bequests received by your spouse (if they are a US citizen) or a qualifying charity. We are still awaiting regulations or other guidance from the IRS as to how this new tax on gifts or inheritances will work. The IRS has deferred the reporting and tax obligations with respect to this tax pending the issuance of guidance. The IRS has also stated that it will provide a reasonable period of time between the issuance of such guidance and the date it prescribes for filing the required reports and paying the tax.

The new law does not contain any immigration penalty. It is not a ground for denying you a visa or entry into the US. The 1996 Reed Amendment remains in effect but it has never been applied to bar any former US citizen who had expatriated from visiting the US.

You may still be subject to US Foreign Bank Account Reporting (FBAR) requirements even after you expatriate since these rules may apply to some non-Americans. The FBAR definitions and rules are different from the tax rules.

One of the unintended consequences of these rules is that some foreigners who might normally consider moving to the US to take long-term employment or start a business are having second thoughts and may decide to move elsewhere instead. A well-advised wealthy foreigner who does move to the US may now be advised to avoid trying to obtain a green card or becoming a US citizen and, if possible, to live in a tax-friendly state with a non-immigrant visa such as those available to a treaty investor or treaty trader.

Seven US states do not impose any state or local income taxes; they are Alaska, Florida, Nevada, South Dakota, Texas, Washington (the state, not DC), and Wyoming. The other 43 US states and many of their local governments do impose income taxes on top of those imposed by the federal government. The extra income taxes in at least 10 of these states can now exceed 10% and those imposed on residents of New York City can be as high as about 13%. Many states apply these high tax rates to both ordinary income and capital gains. About half of the states do not impose any extra death tax on top of the federal estate tax; the other half do.

Prior versions of US anti-expatriation legislation have been unsuccessful in raising meaningful amounts of revenue. The revenue estimates for this legislation are probably grossly overstated. Why then does the US Congress waste so much time and effort trying to pass these types of rules? The real aim of the exercise is apparently not to collect taxes from those who expatriate but to discourage you and others from leaving. Like most governments, the US wants to retain its best-paying 'customers'.

When a US exit tax was first proposed by President Clinton in 1995, the US Treasury Department issued a press release stating that the Clinton Administration aimed at "stopping US multimillionaires from escaping taxes by abandoning their citizenship."[45] It added that a few dozen of the 850 people who had relinquished their citizenship the previous year did so to avoid paying tax on the appreciation in value that their assets accumulated while they 'enjoyed the benefits of US citizenship'.[46]

Later that year, the staff of Congress' Joint Committee on Taxation issued a report that ran several hundred pages including eight lengthy appendices. I may be the only person outside of government that read the whole thing. I was fascinated by the following language excerpted from a lengthy letter near the end of Appendix G from Leslie B. Samuels, then Treasury's Assistant Secretary for Tax Policy, to Kenneth J. Kies, who was then Chief of Staff for Congress' Joint Committee on Taxation:

"A substantial revenue loss can occur if only one extremely wealthy taxpayer expatriates each year. Assume for purposes of illustration that: (i) absent the proposal a 70-year-old US citizen would expatriate, (ii) the taxpayer has been paying USD 40 million per year in income taxes, (iii) the taxpayer has assets worth USD 4 billion (USD 3 billion of which is accrued capital gains), and (iv) the taxpayer plans to leave half of his estate to charity. The revenue effect of this taxpayer staying in the United States for one additional year is approximately USD 73 million – USD 40 million in income taxes plus USD 33 million in estate taxes (USD 4 billion estate less USD 2 billion given to charity multiplied by the 55% estate

---

[45] Department of the Treasury, Treasury News, 'Clinton Offers Plan to Curb Offshore Tax Avoidance', RR-54 (6 February 1995)

[46] Ibid.

tax rate multiplied by the probability that he will die next year (about 3%)). If the proposal were to cause one additional individual who would otherwise have expatriated (or several individuals who cumulatively generate a similar amount of revenue) to remain in the United States each year, the six-year revenue effect for the total of six individuals affected during the six-year period would be USD 1.5 billion (USD 73 million in year one, USD 146 million in year two, USD 219 million in year three, USD 292 million in year four, USD 365 million in year five, USD 438 million in year six). Note that if the taxpayers in this illustration were to expatriate and pay the tax on expatriation, the revenue effect over six years would be about USD 5 billion (USD 840 million each year for six years)."

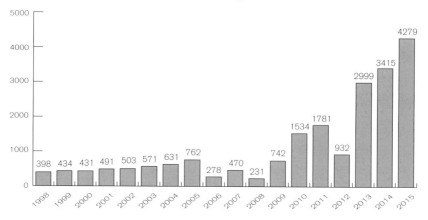

Number of Published Expatriates Per Year

I wonder how many people realized that some revenue estimates used to support the exit tax legislation were predicated on counting not only expected continued income tax revenues but also an accrued sum each year based on the possibility that you will die that year and your estate will have to pay a high death tax if they can keep you from expatriating.

It is fairly obvious that the rules concerning expatriation are complex and that anyone considering giving up US citizenship or a green card needs professional assistance. Hopefully, this book will assist you in asking the lawyers and accountants supporting you the right questions.

4

The Identity and Brand of Nations

By Simon Anholt*

* Simon Anholt is the world's leading authority on measuring and managing national identity and reputation. He was Vice-Chairman of the UK Foreign & Commonwealth Office's Public Diplomacy Board, and has advised more than 50 national, regional and city governments worldwide

Chapter Summary

Nation Brand encapsulates the idea that the reputations of countries and cities are as important as the reputations of corporate entities. These reputations are critical to the country's or city's appeal to tourists, investors, and the media, and form a key role in attracting new residents.

There are, of course, a range of obvious factors usually considered critical in terms of considering where to live, such as infrastructure, political stability, fiscal policy, transport links, government incentives and climate. Other factors however, related to the brand or image of the destination, may play as important a part in decision making. Every individual will be influenced by the reputation of the city or country and its level of prestige.

The incoming residents also play a part in the development of the reputation of the country. High-profile immigrants and investors bring and share their own brand or reputation, which in turn is altered by the destination – meaning that the identity of a new country is as important as the more tangible factors in choosing a new location to live or invest.

However, each individual's image of a destination is, by its very nature, subjective. Reputation is key, but reputations are frequently distorted, usually outdated, and always over-simplified. It is therefore incumbent upon government and administrations to take seriously the value, development and management of the identity of the country, city or region. This does not call for clever marketing campaigns, but rather, solid communication of the ideas, products and policies which define the place.

The Anholt-GfK Roper Nation Brands Index[SM] measures the image and reputation of 50 nations, across six key areas: exports, governance, culture, people, tourism, and immigration and investment. Alongside this, the Anholt-GfK Roper City Brands Index[SM] examines the appeal of 50 cities under the headings of presence, place, prerequisites, people, pulse and potential.

I first wrote about an idea I called 'nation brand' in 1998, and claimed that the reputations of countries, cities and regions are just as critical to their progress and prosperity as the brand images of products are to the companies that own them. A powerful, positive national image makes it relatively cheap and easy to attract wealthy and talented individuals, tourists, investors, positive media coverage, and to export products, services, ideas and culture. A weak or negative image usually means spending more to achieve less.

For individuals going through the difficult, time-consuming and often bewildering process of selecting a new or additional home base, the image and reputation of the country they finally choose are closely tied up with these questions.

As the financier J. P. Morgan famously observed, "A man always buys something for two reasons: a good reason, and the *real reason*". High net worth individuals and their advisors tend for obvious reasons to focus on the 'good reasons' for choosing their domicile, but, as analysts have increasingly come to recognize, the 'real reasons' – what are sometimes misleadingly referred to as 'soft factors' – are unquestionably major and often determining factors in the equation.

From the viewpoint of business investors, entrepreneurs and persons of independent means, the image and reputation of the destination country is one of the 'real reasons' why one place is preferred over another. Even if prospective residents or investors appear to be thinking mainly of practical issues like infrastructure, political stability, fiscal policy, transport links, government incentives and climate, they cannot fail to be swayed by the considerable impact their choice of residence will have on their personal or corporate "brand image" and on the morale of their family, friends, staff and other stakeholders. Some locations are universally regarded as a badge of success for those that move there or acquire citizenship rights; other places might give out more complex and nuanced messages about the individual's world view. Certain destinations are perceived as upmarket in some circles and downmarket in others. Some are strongly associated in the public imagination with media celebrity, or great wealth earned in certain sectors; others with inherited wealth or a quieter sort of success. For some people, the well-known and widely recognized aspirational destinations remain the most desirable; for others, a 'new' or less well known (and possibly less crowded) destination suggests a more refined taste and presents a more exclusive image.

And if the country is successful in attracting significant numbers of new residents, especially if they are prominent or particularly wealthy, this will play a part in altering the image of the country itself. This effect is very similar to what in the commercial sector is known as "co-branding": the combination of the incoming residents' own image, the image of their country of origin, and the image of their new country of choice, will bring about changes to the image of each. The image of a developing economy, for example, can be enhanced by the presence of well-known investors or individuals from wealthier countries: public opinion places trust in the decisions made by such individuals and organizations (partly, in turn, because of the esteem in which their own country of origin is held), and consequently accepts the decision to relocate there as a reliable token of confidence in the destination. Conversely, when an individual from a poorer country relocates to a richer country, this can add significant equity to their personal or corporate brand.

So both the incoming resident and the destination are affected by their own and each other's images during the decision-making process, and in turn, the images of both are affected by the outcome of the decision. For these reasons, the question of image and reputation simply cannot be separated from the business of relocation and citizenship – as well as foreign investments of other kinds – or excluded from any serious consideration of the topic.

Of course, national image and reputation affect, and are affected by, many other factors. A nation or region or city's international standing adds a measurable premium, or a measurable discount, to every transaction made with the rest of the world, whether that transaction is political, social, cultural, legal or commercial. The things that people believe about other places may be biased, utterly misconceived, weirdly distorted, unfairly negative, sometimes undeservedly positive, often outdated and always ludicrously simplified, but that doesn't mean we can ignore them.

Relocation decisions tend to be as much about human capital as about infrastructure or tax conditions, and they are thus profoundly affected by the 'brand image' of the country's population. An investor or prospective resident can easily find statistical data relating to a population's educational level and standards of living, but where does one get information about the population's intelligence, honesty, loyalty or even good humor? All these factors matter – indeed, they can make the difference between the success or failure of the move – yet we only have our own perceptions, anecdotal evidence, and often limited personal experience to rely on. Once again, everything hinges on reputation.

In the busy and crowded marketplace which forms the modern world, most people and organizations don't have time to learn about what other places or their populations are really like. We all navigate through the complexity of our world armed with a few simple clichés, and they form the background of our opinions, even if we aren't fully aware of this and don't always admit it to ourselves: Paris is about style, Japan about technology, Switzerland about wealth, precision, integrity and efficiency, Rio de Janeiro about carnival and football, Tuscany about the good life, and most African nations about poverty, corruption, war, famine and disease. Most of us are much too busy worrying about ourselves and our own countries to spend too long trying to form complete, balanced, and informed views about six billion other people and nearly two hundred other countries. When you haven't got time to read a book, you judge it by its cover.

These clichés and stereotypes – whether they are positive or negative, true or untrue – fundamentally affect our behavior towards other places and their people and products. It may seem unfair, but there's nothing anybody can do to change this. It's very hard for a country to persuade people in other parts of the world to go beyond these simple images and start to understand the rich complexity that lies behind them.

Some quite progressive countries don't get nearly as much attention, visitors, business or investment as they need because their reputation is weak or negative, while others are still trading on a good image that they acquired decades or even centuries ago, and today do relatively little to deserve.

The same is true of cities and regions: all the places with good, powerful and positive reputations find that almost everything they undertake on the international stage is easier; and the places with poor reputations find that almost everything is difficult, and some things seem virtually impossible.

Perhaps it's not so surprising that such a big part is played by 'mere image' or 'mere reputation' in even the hardest of decisions, those relating to personal residence, family life, and personal financial security: as the economist Maurice Allais showed in 1953, the more important and consequential a decision becomes, the more likely people are to rely on their feelings and intuition rather than logic to make the decision.

For these and for many other reasons, all responsible governments, on behalf of their people, their institutions and their companies, need to measure and monitor the world's perception of their nation, and to develop a strategy for managing it. Whether or not attracting high net worth individuals is a part of their growth strategy, it is a key part of their job to try to earn a reputation that is fair, true, powerful, attractive, genuinely useful to their economic, political and social aims, and honestly reflects the spirit, the genius and the will of the people. This huge task has become one of the primary skills of administrations in the twenty-first century, and it is one of the critical underpinning factors in attracting foreign capital and talent.

Equally, prospective residents need to be familiar with the dynamics of country, city and region image – their own and those of their shortlisted destinations – and to understand how these factors impact their decisions as well as the consequences of those decisions.

4.1   Can a nation's image be changed?

Unfortunately, the phrase I coined back in 1998, *nation brand*, soon became distorted, mainly by a combination of naïve (or perhaps lazy) governments and ambitious consulting firms, into *nation branding:* a dangerously misleading phrase which seems to contain a promise that the images of countries can be directly manipulated using the techniques of commercial marketing communications, and an ignored or less desirable country magically transformed into the destination of choice almost overnight.

Yet despite repeatedly calling for it over the last 15 years, I have never seen a shred of evidence to suggest that this is possible: no case studies, no research, and not even any very persuasive arguments. I conclude that countries are judged by what they do, not by what they say, as they have always been; yet the notion that a country can simply advertise its way into a better reputation has proved to be a pernicious and surprisingly resilient one.

The message is clear: if a country is serious about enhancing its international image, it should concentrate on the "product" rather than chase after the chimera of "branding". There are no short cuts. Only a consistent, coordinated and unbroken stream of useful, noticeable, world-class and, above all, relevant ideas, products and policies can gradually enhance the reputation of the country that produces them.

Of course, sectoral promotion is a different matter, and much confusion is created by the conflation of sectoral promotion with national image. The confusion isn't helped by the fact that people who are responsible for marketing places as investment, relocation, study or tourism destinations often describe their work as 'branding'. However, the distinction is really quite clear: when you're selling a mass-market product or service (such as holidays, investment opportunities, exported goods or even – at a stretch – culture) then of course advertising and marketing are legitimate and necessary. Each country's competitors are doing it, and consumers accept it: the underlying message (buy this, it's good) is fundamentally honest and straightforward. Nation branding, on the other hand, has nothing to sell, and the underlying message (please change your mind about my country) is government propaganda, which investors, high net worth individuals and indeed most other people rightly ignore.

Having made this distinction, however, it is important to stress that relocation and citizenship are in a rather different sub-category from tourism or cultural promotion, since they are targeted at a highly specialized audience, whereas tourism and culture are predominantly mass-market consumer matters. For this reason I have always been skeptical about the use of mass-marketing techniques, such as print or broadcast advertising campaigns, to promote foreign direct investment, citizenship or residence. The target audience is, after all, a small and easily defined one, and in such circumstances it's difficult to justify the expense of mass-media exposure. Experience suggests that the administrations which focus their expenditure on a world-class sales operation rather than spending huge sums on consumer-style marketing, achieve better return on investment in the long run.

4.2 Measuring the Images of Nations

I launched the Anholt Nation Brands Index^{SM} in 2005 as a way to measure the image and reputation of the world's nations, to track their profiles as they rise or fall, and, if possible, to link these changes to the country's performance in attracting foreign investment, significant individuals, tourism, major events and skilled workers or students, to its success in promoting exports, culture and ideas, and to its profile in the international media.

The study was originally carried out every three months and measured the images of between 10 and 30 countries. Since 2008, in partnership with GfK Roper Public Affairs & Media in New York City, the survey – now known as the Anholt-GfK Roper Nation Brands Index^{SM} – takes place annually and has been expanded to measure the image of 50 nations. Each NBI^{SM} survey is conducted in Argentina, Australia, Brazil, Canada, China, Egypt, France, Germany, India, Italy, Japan,

Mexico, Poland, Russia, South Africa, South Korea, Sweden, Turkey, the UK and the US. Around 20,939 interviews are conducted with approximately 1,050 interviews per country. Using the most up-to-date online population parameters, the achieved sample in each country has been weighted to reflect key demographic characteristics such as age, gender, and education of the online population in that country. In all, the sample used for the NBI[SM] represents approximately 60% of the world's population and 77% of global GDP.

The Anholt-GfK Roper Nation Brands Index[SM] measures the power and appeal of each country's brand image by examining six dimensions of perceived national competence. Together, these dimensions make up the Nation Brand Hexagon®. The 'points of the hexagon' are the following:

Exports. This is what marketers call the 'country of origin effect' whether knowing where the product is made increases or decreases people's likelihood of purchasing it, and whether a country has particular strengths in science and technology, and has creative energy. Perceived associations with particular industries round out that country's image in this space.

Governance. This aspect incorporates perceived competency and honesty of government, respect for citizens' rights and fair treatment, as well as global behavior in the areas of international peace and security, environmental protection, and world poverty reduction. Respondents also select one adjective that best describes the government in each country.

Culture. Cultural aspects measured are perceptions of a country's heritage, its contemporary cultural 'vibes' from music, films, art and literature, as well as the country's excellence in sports. Various cultural activities are presented to respondents to gauge their strongest images of a country's cultural 'product'. Culture is one of the strongest indicators of perceived quality of life, and is generally associated with a rich, intelligent, sophisticated, self-respecting society.

People. The general assessment of a people's friendliness is measured by whether respondents would feel welcome when visiting the country.

Additionally, we measure the appeal of the people on a personal level – whether respondents want to have a close friend from that country – as well as human resources on a professional level, that is, how willing respondents would be to hire a well-qualified person from that country. Respondents are also asked to select adjectives out of a list to describe the predominant images they have of the people in each country.

Tourism. Respondents rate a country's tourism appeal in three major areas: natural beauty, historic buildings and monuments, and vibrant city life and urban attractions. Tourism potential is also asked: how likely they would be to visit a country if money is no object and the likely experience represented by adjectives such as romantic, stressful, spiritual, etc.

Immigration and Investment. Lastly, but most significantly in the area of residence and citizenship, a country's power to attract talent and capital is measured not only by whether people would consider studying, working and living in that country but also by the country's economic prosperity, equal opportunity, and ultimately the perception that it is a place with a high quality of life. The country's economic and business conditions – whether stagnant, declining, developing or forward-thinking – complete the measurement in this space. Questions are asked which aim to distinguish clearly between those countries which are considered desirable for a short stay (such as tourism or business visits) and for a longer period of work, study or residence.

The rankings for the overall top 10 countries in the 2013 Anholt-GfK Roper Nation Brands Index^{SM}, plus a selection of the countries featured in this Handbook which rank below this level, are shown in the tables below. Each table shows the countries' average global rankings for each of the six categories described in the previous paragraphs.

EXPORTS	Rank	GOVERNANCE	Rank	PEOPLE	Rank
United States	1	Canada	1	Canada	1
Japan	2	Switzerland	2	United States	2
Germany	3	Germany	3	Australia	3
United Kingdom	4	Sweden	4	United Kingdom	4
France	5	Australia	5	Italy	5
Switzerland	6	United Kingdom	6	Germany	6
Canada	7	Holland	7	Switzerland	7
Sweden	8	Denmark	8	Sweden	8
Italy	9	Finland	9	Japan	9
Australia	10	France	10	France	10
Austria	17	Austria	12	Austria	19
Belgium	19	Belgium	14	Belgium	20
Singapore	22	Singapore	22	Singapore	23

CULTURE	Rank	TOURISM	Rank	INVESTMENT & IMMIGRATION	Rank
United States	1	Italy	1	United States	1
France	2	France	2	Canada	2
Italy	3	United States	3	Germany	3
United Kingdom	4	United Kingdom	4	United Kingdom	4
Germany	5	Spain	5	Switzerland	5
Spain	6	Greece	6	France	6
Japan	7	Australia	7	Australia	7
China	8	Canada	8	Sweden	8
Russia	9	Germany	9	Japan	9
Brazil	10	Switzerland	10	Italy	10
Canada	13	Austria	16	Denmark	12
Austria	17	Egypt	19	Austria	14

CULTURE	Rank	TOURISM	Rank	INVESTMENT & IMMIGRATION	Rank
Switzerland	19	Belgium	28	Belgium	18
Belgium	26	Singapore	31	Singapore	20
Singapore	38	Malaysia	37		

NBI TOTAL	Rank	NBI TOTAL	Rank
United States	1	Switzerland	8
Germany	2	Australia	9
United Kingdom	3	Sweden	10
France	4	Austria	13
Canada	5	Belgium	19
Japan	6	Singapore	25
Italy	7		

All data and associated methodology © Simon Anholt 2001-2013. All rights reserved. Not to be reproduced in part or in full without express written permission of the copyright holder.

Countries in which the research is conducted (panel countries)

	Passport Question	Total	Argentina	Australia	Brazil	Canada	China	Egypt	France
Countries which respondents selected	United Kingdom	2	6	1	4	2	5	9	6
	Switzerland	3	4	5	6	3	1	5	3
	Canada	4	5	4	6	■	4	5	1
	Austria	18	11	10	-	14	-	-	18
	Singapore	18	-	10	-	-	1	-	-
	Belgium	-	-	-	-	14	-	-	13

Countries in which the research is conducted (panel countries)

Marriage Question		Total	Argentina	Australia	Brazil	Canada	China	Egypt	France
Countries which respondents selected	United Kingdom	2	16	1	12	4	4	9	12
	Canada	5	16	4	8	▪	10	7	1
	Switzerland	9	5	9	8	8	8	10	6
	Singapore	14	-	9	-	17	1	-	-
	Austria	21	16	15	15	-	12	-	20
	Belgium	-	-	20	-	17	-	-	7

Countries in which the research is conducted (panel countries)

Quality of Life Question		Total	Argentina	Australia	Brazil	Canada	China	Egypt	France
Countries which respondents selected	Switzerland	1	1	4	1	3	1	2	3
	Canada	2	3	2	3	1	6	10	2
	United Kingdom	7	8	5	14	4	9	7	11
	Austria	13	14	15	17	16	13	12	16
	Belgium	17	17	19	13	17	21	16	9
	Singapore	21	32	20	40	21	4	32	25

A dash (-) indicates that the country has not attracted sufficient marks to achieve a ranking. Grey squares occur because respondents may not rank their own countries.

Countries in which the research is conducted (panel countries)

Germany	India	Italy	Japan	Mexico	Poland	Russia	South Africa	South Korea	Sweden	Turkey	UK	US
10	2	4	2	6	2	3	2	6	3	11	■	1
1	3	2	3	6	3	1	3	2	4	5	6	8
2	4	5	3	2	5	6	5	3	6	5	3	2
3	-	-	9	-	18	9	14	10	-	-	-	17
-	4	-	9	-	-	-	-	15	-	18	11	17
-	-	-	-	-	18	18	-	-	-	-	-	-

Countries in which the research is conducted (panel countries)

Germany	India	Italy	Japan	Mexico	Poland	Russia	South Africa	South Korea	Sweden	Turkey	UK	US
7	2	8	2	7	10	5	1	2	4	12	■	1
13	10	11	8	5	6	2	6	5	11	9	5	1
1	3	5	6	8	11	5	10	4	19	20	16	10
-	6	17	17	-	16	-	15	16	19	-	-	-
1	16	11	17	-	16	16	-	9	19	20	-	-
-	16	-	-	-	-	21	-	16	-	-	-	-

Countries in which the research is conducted (panel countries)

Germany	India	Italy	Japan	Mexico	Poland	Russia	South Africa	South Korea	Sweden	Turkey	UK	US
1	2	1	7	3	1	2	2	1	5	1	5	5
6	7	4	7	1	7	9	3	2	2	6	1	2
10	3	3	2	9	4	4	6	4	9	19	7	4
3	19	14	15	15	11	8	14	16	13	14	15	17
12	22	16	16	14	12	16	13	20	19	12	19	19
21	4	21	16	30	25	25	21	15	20	30	21	24

In addition, we even ask people certain penetrating questions such as "if your lost passport were accidentally replaced with one from the wrong country, which country would you prefer this to be?". This question is particularly good at isolating the attraction of citizenship and the perceived benefits it confers on the individual and his or her family. We also ask people which country they would most and least prefer an imaginary wife or husband to come from, if they had to marry a foreigner: this question is very useful for checking how countries rank in people's emotional rather than practical perceptions.

The table above shows the data collected from these two questions for six of the countries featured in this Handbook (Austria, Belgium, Canada, Singapore, Switzerland and the UK). To use the table, select one of the countries where the research is conducted from the top row – the panel countries – and follow its column down to find how respondents in that country ranked each of the six target countries listed in the first column. For example, to find out how highly people in South Africa rate the value of a Swiss passport, find where the "South Africa" column intersects with the "Switzerland" row; the figure 3 indicates that a Swiss passport is the average third choice of South Africans. Similarly, to find out how Chinese people rate other nationalities as spouses, follow the 'China' column and see where it intersects with each target country – thus, the highest-ranked nationality for Chinese respondents out of the six target countries shown is Singapore (first), and the lowest is Belgium (not chosen by any respondents).

Perhaps the most significant 'soft' factor when selecting a new country of residence is the perception of quality of life – a concept which conveniently embraces economic, social, human, political, cultural and climatic factors. The table below shows how respondents in each of the 20 panel countries rank six of the countries featured in this Handbook in response to the simple question: 'Please state how far you agree with the following sentence: "This country is a place with a high quality of life."' The table is read in the same way as Table 2 above.

It is important to emphasize that the NBI[SM] is not a survey of professional investors, wealthy individuals or corporate decision-makers, but a general population survey. There are numerous other studies that measure investment and relocation intentions, but the NBI[SM] is unique in that it was the first and is by a considerable margin still the largest and most thorough study for measuring the opinions, prejudices and beliefs of a broad cross-section of the general global population. Obviously, there is significant overlap with the views of investors and other "élite" audiences (who are, after all, members of the general population in their spare time). It is the differences between élite opinion as measured in most investor surveys, and mass opinion as measured in the NBI[SM], which have the most interesting tale to tell.

Nonetheless, since the NBI[SM] questionnaire also contains numerous demographic questions (such as age, sex, educational level attained, income bracket, urban/rural dweller, occupation type), it is a simple matter to weight the NBI[SM] data towards the segments with higher economic and educational worth.

4.3   Measuring the Images of Cities

The Anholt City Brands Index[SM] was launched in 2006, following the Nation Brands Index (NBI)[SM], and like the NBI[SM] was updated and expanded in partnership with GfK Roper Public Affairs & Media in 2009. In the Anholt-GfK Roper Nation Brands Index[SM], nation brands are presented as a complex mixture of global perceptions of a country's people, its government policies and behavior, products, culture and heritage, opportunities for employment and study and tourism potential. Cities, clearly, are rather different: they aren't usually famous for producing particular products; the tourism emphasis is often as much on conventions as on leisure visitors; the apparatus of government is usually more technocratic than political; and the city's culture isn't always easy to distinguish from the culture of the country as a whole.

Consequently, the Anholt-GfK Roper City Brands Index[SM] measures the power and appeal of each city's brand image by examining the following six rather different dimensions:

The Presence. This point of the City Brands Hexagon is about the city's international status and standing. In this section, we ask how familiar people are with each of the 50 cities in the survey and whether each city has made an important contribution to the world in culture, science, or in the way cities are governed, during the last 30 years.

The Place. Here, we explore people's perceptions about the physical aspect of each city: how pleasant or unpleasant they imagine it is to be outdoors and to travel around the city, how attractive it is, and what the climate is like.

The Prerequisites. This is the section where we ask people about their basic requirements of a city: how easy they think it would be to find satisfactory, affordable accommodation, and what they believe the general standard of public amenities is like – schools, hospitals, public transport, sports facilities, and so on.

The People. The people make the city, and in this point of the hexagon we ask whether our respondents think the inhabitants would be warm and friendly, or cold and prejudiced against outsiders. We ask whether they think it would be easy for them to find and fit into a community which shares their language and culture. Finally, and very importantly, we ask how safe our respondents think they would feel in the city.

The Pulse. The appeal of a vibrant urban lifestyle is an important part of each city's brand image. In this section, we ask how easy people think it would be to find interesting things to do, both as a short term visitor and as a long term resident.

The Potential. This point of the City Brand Hexagon considers the economic and educational opportunities that each city is believed to offer businesses, immigrants and students. We ask our panels how easy they think it would be to find a job in the city, and, if they had a business, how good a place they think it would be to do business in. Finally, we ask whether each city would be a good place for them or other family members to get a higher educational qualification.

The CBI[SM] survey is conducted in the same 20 major developed and developing countries as the NBI[SM], and measures the image of 50 cities.

The rankings for the overall top 10 cities in the 2013 Anholt-GfK Roper City Brands Index[SM], plus some of the cities featured in this Handbook which rank below this level, are shown in the tables below. Each table shows the cities' average global rankings for each of the six categories described in the previous paragraphs.

CBI TOTAL	Rank
London	1
Sydney	2
Paris	3
New York	4
Rome	5
Washington D.C.	6
Los Angeles	7
Toronto	8
Vienna	9
Melbourne	10
Barcelona	13
Geneva	14
Singapore	22
Hong Kong	25
Brussels	26
Edinburgh	30

PRESENCE	Rank	PLACE	Rank	PREREQUISITES	Rank
London	1	Sydney	1	Sydney	1
Paris	2	Paris	2	Toronto	2
New York	3	Rome	3	London	3
Washington D.C.	4	Vienna	4	Berlin	4
Rome	5	Barcelona	5	Washington D.C.	4
Los Angeles	6	Geneva	6	Amsterdam	6
Sydney	7	Melbourne	7	Melbourne	7
Berlin	8	Milan	8	Montreal	8
Beijing	9	Madrid	9	Boston	9
Hong Kong	10	Los Angeles	10	Copenhagen	10
Singapore	14	London	12	Geneva	13
Geneva	19	Toronto	14	Vienna	16
Vienna	22	Singapore	21	Brussels	21
Toronto	26	Brussels	25	Edinburgh	24
Brussels	30	Edinburgh	31	Singapore	30
Edinburgh	41	Hong Kong	37	Hong Kong	33

PEOPLE	Rank	PULSE	Rank	POTENTIAL	Rank
Sydney	1	Paris	1	London	1
London	2	New York	2	New York	2
Toronto	3	London	3	Sydney	3
Melbourne	4	Rome	4	Los Angeles	4

PEOPLE	Rank	PULSE	Rank	POTENTIAL	Rank
Vienna	5	Sydney	5	Washington D.C.	5
Montreal	6	Los Angeles	6	Paris	6
Geneva	7	Tokyo	7	Toronto	7
Amsterdam	8	Barcelona	8	Boston	8
Rome	9	Vienna	9	Melbourne	9
Stockholm	10	Madrid	10	Berlin	10
Barcelona	12	Amsterdam	11	Geneva	14
Edinburgh	16	Hong Kong	15	Vienna	18
Madrid	18	Singapore	19	Brussels	22
Brussels	22	Geneva	28	Hong Kong	24
Singapore	30	Edinburgh	35	Edinburgh	26
Hong Kong	33	Brussels	36	Singapore	29

4.4 Looking to the future: "Governmental Social Responsibility"

One thing is abundantly clear from the mass of data generated by the Anholt-GfK Roper Nation Brands Index[SM] and the Anholt-GfK Roper City Brands Index[SM] over the last six years, and equally from my experience of advising more than 40 governments on their countries' and cities' international standing and attractiveness: if a country, city or region wants to be admired, it must be relevant, and in order to become relevant, it must participate usefully, productively and imaginatively in the global "conversations" on the topics that matter to people elsewhere and everywhere.

The list of those topics is a long one: climate change, poverty, famine, narcotics, migration, economic stability, human rights, women's rights, indigenous people's rights, children's rights, religious and cultural tolerance, nuclear proliferation, water, education, corruption, terrorism, crime, war and arms control are just a few of the most obvious ones. It's hard to imagine any country that couldn't pick at least one item on this list with a special relevance to its own needs or resources, and find a way to make a prominent, thoughtful, meaningful and memorable contribution to the debate and to the global effort.

There is a strong precedent for this kind of behavior in the commercial world. For the past twenty years or so, it has become more and more evident that corporations which fail to demonstrate and maintain high ethical standards, transparency and social responsibility will soon lose the trust and respect of their consumers. Corporations are at last being forced to treat their social responsibilities as a matter for the board rather than for the PR agency.

What a revolution it would be if countries, cities and regions, nowadays as obsessed with the value of their reputations as companies are, were to follow the same principles.

It is already clear from the NBI^{SM} data that more and more people in more and more countries feel unable to admire or respect countries or governments that pollute the planet, practice or permit corruption, trample human rights or flout the rule of law: in other words, it's the same audience, starting to apply the same standards to countries as they apply to companies.

In just a few decades, consumer power has changed the rules of business and transformed the behavior of corporations almost beyond recognition. It doesn't seem unreasonable to hope that consumer power might achieve a similar transformation in the way that countries, cities and regions are run in the years to come.

These matters are of direct relevance to countries wishing to promote residence and citizenship to high net worth individuals. Quite clearly, a favorable tax regime, a pleasant climate and good connections are no longer enough: a country also needs a good name. Responsible prominent individuals who value their own reputation – and it is rare to find successful people who don't see their reputation as their primary asset

– will only want to be associated with countries whose international image enhances and reflects their own. Moving oneself, one's family and one's business interests to another country is the most public and most emphatic endorsement of that country's status, values, principles, governance, population and prospects: nobody will do so unless they are thoroughly satisfied that the country will repay that trust and commitment.

In 2006 I wrote, "*if the world's governments placed even half the value which most wise corporations have learned to place on their good names, the world would be a safer and quieter place than it is today.*" This lesson has a strong resonance for all countries wishing to attract capital, tourists, consumers, investment, aid, and perhaps most particularly wealthy individuals looking for a new or additional country of residence.

PART II

Citizenship, Passports and Visas

5

Nationality and Citizenship

Chapter Summary

Citizenship is a legal status which involves responsibility from both citizen to state and state to citizen. It is a particular form of nationality and determines an individual's relationship with their country. Nationality, in contrast, describes your national identity, and is also used in relation to other entities such as corporations, ships, and aircraft.

Each state has the right to determine its own citizenship and nationality laws. Citizenship has little day-to-day impact on many people, but others may face challenges or discrimination due to their citizenship, especially when travelling. Statelessness is unjust and undesirable, and citizenship is a universal right of every human being, enshrined in the Universal Declaration of Human Rights.

There are four common ways in which a person can acquire citizenship: by birth; descent; marriage; or naturalization. Naturalization may occur due to marriage, religion, legal residence or exceptional circumstances, and may come with conditions such as language or amount of time residing in that country.

It is sometimes necessary to renounce citizenship, either because the country does not permit dual residence, or to escape duties such as national service. Renunciation of citizenship must be accepted by the state to be valid, and is sometimes dependent on certain conditions.

Citizenship is defined as the relationship between an individual and a sovereign state. It is defined by the laws of that state and carries corresponding rights, duties and privileges.[56] Citizenship also implies the status of freedom with accompanying responsibilities and obligations.

Although often used as if interchangeable, citizenship is different from nationality, as citizenship concerns the various rights, duties and opportunities that define one's place and conduct in society. Citizenship is the relationship between an individual and a country and affords the individual a membership to the heritage, culture and values of the country. Citizenship is not a private but a legal status that confers a responsibility on the citizen including duties such as paying tax, voting and military service. Additionally the citizen may have certain rights and the country provides protection and benefits to its citizens. The citizen is ordained with the quality of belonging to a community.

In many ways, citizenship is the most privileged form of nationality. In international law the concept is used in broader terms to denote all persons a state is entitled to protect. In the same context, nationality is one's international identity as belonging to a sovereign state, which may be evidenced by a passport. Nationality also serves to denote the relationship between a state and entities other than individuals such as corporations, ships, and aircraft – these entities also possess a nationality.

However, some legal systems and treaties consistently use the term nationality,[57] whereas others use the term citizenship[58] as interchangeable concepts.

Citizenship or nationality law is the branch of law that governs how citizenship is conferred upon its citizens, and how it may be lost. In most cases, this is clearly determined by statutory law and case law. A sovereign state is, in principle, free to decide in its legislation how and to whom its citizenship may be granted. This doctrine of

---

[56] For a concise overview of the principles of nationality and citizenship, see Fransman (2011)
[57] E.g. the European Convention on Nationality of 1997
[58] E.g. in Eastern and Central Europe

general freedom of states in matters of citizenship is well established in public international law.[59] However, it is also generally established that this freedom should be "consistent with international conventions, international custom and the principles of law generally recognized with regard to nationality".[60] This is a very open provision and leaves a lot of room for interpretation. Many countries have granted citizenship or similar rights in a manner of which it is questionable whether it is in line with international custom and principles of law generally recognized with regard to nationality. For example, the British Protected Person status granted by the British government would appear to be in violation of these "principles", and likewise, the grant of citizenship to a foreign soccer player at short notice to include him in the national soccer team seems questionable, but has so far not led to any country not recognizing such a grant of citizenship. This is also important when looking at the concept of granting citizenship for important contributions to the state, including economic contributions, as this is sometimes frowned upon. However, throughout history countries have granted citizenship for extraordinary achievements and in special cases, and similarly to the cases involving sportsmen, no cases of refusal to recognize such citizenship by other countries are known.

Many people take their citizenship for granted without giving a second thought to rights and duties conferred on them by virtue of their citizenship. However, for other individuals, the reality of their citizenship may often be a great burden especially when moving across borders and facing visa restrictions and other discrimination, based on the passport they hold.

This personal relationship that an individual shares with a particular state has important implications. Without a nationality, an individual is stateless and effectively does not belong anywhere in a legal sense. The international community agrees that statelessness, by accidents of

---

[59] Certainly since the often cited Nottebohm case (ICJ Reports 4, 1955)
[60] The Hague Convention on Certain Questions Relating to the Conflict of Nationality Laws of 12 April 1930

history or otherwise, is unjust, and therefore the right to a nationality is enshrined in Article 15 of the Universal Declaration of Human Rights[61] as a universal right:

1. Everyone has the right to a nationality

2. No one shall be arbitrarily deprived of his nationality nor denied the right to change nationality

The issue of having a right to a nationality arises in case of newly independent states or succession of states: which nationality will the persons affected by such events of history obtain or retain?

Interestingly, the concept of citizenship was first recorded in Ancient Greece and Rome and was developed in order to determine who belonged to the community and who was to be excluded. "Citizen Status" entitled the member of the particular political community privileged rights within the community. It also conferred on the member certain obligations and duties to the community. In Roman times, the codified law did not distinguish between private and public law as practiced today, and it determined every aspect of the citizens' lives from economic to political to domestic and religious.[62]

Modern concepts of citizenship were established in the 18th century during the American and French revolutions, during which the term citizen came to suggest the possession of certain liberties.

Every country has a right to determine who its citizens are, and each country will formulate its own policy and rules to determine and confer citizenship on its citizens.

Generally, citizenship can be acquired by birth *(ius soli)* or by descent *(ius sanguinis)*; by marriage *(ius matrimonii)*; or by naturalization (or registration in case of Commonwealth Citizens).

---

[61] Universal Declaration of Human Rights (adopted 10 December 1948) UNGA Res 217 A(III)
[62] Magnette / Long (2005)

In a few special cases, citizenship can even be acquired automatically upon a change in civil status such as adoption, legitimization, or affiliation to a national of that state.

Citizenship acquired by descent is based on ethnicity or ancestry of the parent(s) at the time of a person's birth and at the time of acquisition. *Ius sanguinis* directly translated from Latin means "right of blood". This form of citizenship came about largely due to the split of empires in Europe in the past century, leaving some citizens stateless, therefore the best way to confer a status was to acquire the nationality of the person's parents.

Nowadays, citizenship by descent is the preferred policy for most countries as it provides a flexibility for families that have moved abroad to still pass on their citizenship to their children. In some countries, citizenship can only be acquired if both parents are citizens. In most cases though, it does not matter whether it is the mother or the father who has the citizenship, unless the parents are not married, in which case the child may not have a right to the father's citizenship.

Citizenship by birth is the grant of citizenship to anyone born in the territory of the state. The US is a good example of this practice as it is enshrined in the US Constitution that any person born on the soil of the US will automatically become a US citizen.

It has become common for states to restrict citizenship by birth especially in respect of persons who are illegally in the country or are only in the country temporarily. However, even though citizenship by birth is not favored generally, many countries have introduced a hybrid form of the policy whereby the country will grant citizenship to children of migrants if the parents have resided in the country for a certain period of time.

There was a well-known case in Ireland[63] that changed the citizenship laws of the country. A Chinese woman resident in the UK, visited Ireland,

---

[63]   European Court of Justice judgment: Case C-200/02: Chen and Others

ostensibly to have her baby there, thereby automatically conferring Irish citizenship on the child. This case led to a country wide referendum which restricted the rule of *ius soli* to only non-Irish persons possessing a valid residence permit.

In countries that recognize the rule of *ius soli*, there is one exception to the rule, with regard to children of diplomats or officials in foreign countries on government business. Children born to these officials will not acquire the nationality of the state where they are born.[64]

A person can also obtain citizenship of a country by way of naturalization through a formal act of granting nationality to a legal alien.

An individual may be naturalized based on the person's ancestry, by marriage, religion, legal residence or because of exceptional circumstances. In addition, collective naturalizations are possible in cases of annexation of territories by sovereign states, and similar situations.

The most common forms of naturalization are by marriage or based on certain years of residence and may be conditional upon language skills or other "integration" factors. In most countries a person may acquire citizenship by marriage but is required to reside in the country for a number of years before they may be naturalized. The years of required residence before an application for naturalization may be lodged may range from a mere two years[65] to 12 years[66] or more.

In some cases, especially when an individual acquires citizenship by way of exceptional means (e.g. a large investment in the country or by way of exceptional talent) the government may confer citizenship at discretion within the powers given by the law or constitution, which may or may not require a certain period of residence in the country.

It is also important to understand the process of giving up citizenship, as in some countries a person is not permitted to hold citizenship of

---

[64] This is applicable to diplomats and officials covered by the Vienna Convention
[65] E.g. Singapore
[66] E.g. Switzerland

more than one country, and in others it may be necessary to give up citizenship if you legally wish to avoid certain duties such as national service,[67] military draft[68] or taxation.[69] In this case, the individual will be required to renounce the citizenship. The loss of citizenship usually occurs by voluntary declaration of renunciation, or automatically where provided by law if certain actions are performed such as taking an oath of allegiance to a foreign country.[70] If citizenship is not lost automatically upon taking up a foreign nationality,[71] citizenship cannot merely be renounced by tearing up the passport. The individual must obtain the acceptance of the state in order for the renunciation to be valid. In some countries, renunciation of citizenship can only be accepted if certain conditions have been met, such as paying taxes or performing military service, or other duties expected from a citizen.

---

[67] E.g. Israel, Singapore, Turkey
[68] Mostly in countries which are at war or have civil conflict
[69] In particular the US
[70] Taking an Oath of Allegiance, or making a similar declaration, is however very often part of the naturalization procedure
[71] In many countries where dual citizenship is prohibited, citizenship is lost automatically if a foreign citizenship is acquired voluntarily

6

Freedom of Movement and Regional Arrangements

Chapter Summary

Every citizen has the fundamental right to freedom of movement within the country of which they are a citizen. In response to the growth of the global economy, regional arrangements have been developed to enable free trade and movement across borders. These regional arrangements in turn shape political and economic relationships across regions and across the world.

The European Union (EU) is foremost among these arrangements and gives every citizen of a member state the right of EU citizenship. In general, this means they can freely move to another member state and be equally treated with regard to employment, pay and access to education as domestic citizens.[72]

The European Free Trade Association (EFTA) promotes free trade and economic integration to the benefit of its four member states: Iceland, Liechtenstein, Norway and Switzerland. Relations with the EU are at the core of EFTA activities. The European Economic Area brings the EU member states and the three EEA EFTA states (Iceland, Liechtenstein, and Norway) into an Internal Market governed by the same basic rules.

Also within Europe, and part of EU law, the Schengen Agreement has abolished internal border and passport checks between participating states. The UK and Ireland are not full members but do cooperate in police and judicial matters. The core features of the agreement allow for the removal of checks on persons at internal national borders, common rules applying to external border crossings, management entry rules and visas, and improved police and judicial cooperation. Furthermore, a central database has been established to manage public security and external border controls.

Beyond Europe, there are other regional arrangements across the world that support the free or easier movement of people. These include: the Asia-Pacific Economic Cooperation, the Andean Community, the Caribbean Community, the Commonwealth of Independent States, the Economic Community of West African States, the Gulf Cooperation Council, the Nordic Passport Union, the Trans-Tasman Travel Arrangement and the UK-Ireland Common Travel Area.

---

[72] An exception to the right to employment applies to citizens of Croatia due to the transitional period of up to seven years. The following EU Member States still apply restrictions in this respect to citizens of Croatia: Austria; Malta; the Netherlands; Slovenia; the UK

6.1   Introduction

The right to freedom of movement is a fundamental right preserved in the laws and constitutions of most countries. The establishment of the United Nations entrenched the right to freedom of movement, as evidenced in documents such as the Universal Declaration of Human Rights[73] and the International Covenant on Civil and Political Rights.[74] However, the right to freedom of movement is limited to the borders of the country within which a person holds citizenship or lawful resident status.

During the last two decades, many countries have become conscious of the rapidly growing global economy. In response to this, throughout the world countries have established regional arrangements to promote free trade, free movement of capital, labor and people. The focus of this chapter is the freedom of movement of persons within the various countries that have established regional arrangements.

Most notable is the EU, the embodiment of a supranational[75] union that promotes the concept of free movement and establishment between EU

---

[73] Article 13 of the Universal Declaration of Human Rights, reads:

(1) Everyone has the right to freedom of movement and residence within the borders of each State

(2) Everyone has the right to leave any country, including his own, and to return to his country

[74] Article 12 of the International Covenant on Civil and Political Rights (adopted 16 December 1966, in force 23 March 1976) 999 UNTS 171, incorporates this right into treaty law:

(1) Everyone lawfully within the territory of a State shall, within that territory, have the right to liberty of movement and freedom to choose his residence

(2) Everyone shall be free to leave any country, including his own

(3) The above-mentioned rights shall not be subject to any restrictions except those which are provided by law, are necessary to protect national security, public order (*ordre public*), public health or morals or the rights and freedoms of others, and are consistent with the other rights recognized in the present Covenant

(4) No one shall be arbitrarily deprived of the right to enter his own country

[75] Supranational pertains to an international organization, or union, whereby member states transcend national boundaries or interests to share in the decision-making and vote on issues pertaining to the wider grouping. This term is often loosely used to denote other inter-regional arrangements between countries but technically, the EU is the only union that correctly fits the definition

member states. Citizens of each EU member state are also considered citizens of the EU, and as such, are entitled to move to and establish freely in other EU member states.

The exclusion of free movement of citizens in regional organizations, which is in many cases inseparable from the concept of free movement of labor, can be understood in a socio-political context evident in countries such as South Africa. South Africa is a member of the South African Development Community (SADC) – a regional organization for the development of Sub-Saharan African countries. However, this arrangement does not extend to free movement of labor. The steadfast position of the South African government is to protect the local workforce from foreign nationals that may take employment opportunities away from locals[76] and consequently create higher levels of unemployment amongst the South African nationals.

A significant benefit for citizens of member states in a regional organization is easier access for travel between the states. Some regions have even abolished internal border checks (UK-Ireland Common Travel Area, Schengen area, Nordic Passport Union). There is also a growing trend to electronically process regional passengers via immigration check points to further enhance the travel experience of nationals and residents of the member states of the particular organizations (e.g. APEC Travel Card).

It is virtually impossible for a country to ignore the effects of such regional integration. The development of regional organizations has helped shape many political and economic relationships globally which largely contribute to a more stable and safer world.

This chapter explains the regional arrangements currently in existence, which permit freedom of movement between the regions' member states. Particular focus is given to the European framework as it is a unique and noteworthy system with the EU as a strong foundation leading the way in this sphere of international relations.

---

[76] South African Department of Home Affairs Immigration Policy

6.2   European Union

The EU currently consists of 28 member states: Austria, Belgium, Bulgaria, Croatia, Cyprus, Czech Republic, Denmark, Estonia, Finland, France, Germany, Greece, Hungary, Ireland, Italy, Latvia, Lithuania, Luxembourg, Malta, Netherlands, Poland, Portugal, Romania, Slovakia, Slovenia, Spain, Sweden and the UK. The UK has recently announced its intention to leave the EU, but the process may take some years.

EU citizens

The EU, in its judicial and legislative form as known today, was established by the Treaty on European Union[77] which was signed in Maastricht on 7 February 1992 and officially came into force on 1 November 1993. Since then, the Maastricht Treaty has been amended by the treaties of Amsterdam (signed 2 October 1997, entered into force on 1 May 1999), Nice (signed 26 February 2001, entered into force on 1 February 2003), and Lisbon (3 December 2007, entered into force on 1 December 2009).

The Maastricht Treaty introduced the concept of citizenship of the EU. Article 20 TFEU (former Article 17 TEC replacing Article 8 TEC) confers the right of EU citizenship on every person holding nationality of a member state. EU citizenship complements and does not replace national citizenship. Article 21(1) TFEU (former Article 18(1) TEC) enshrines the right of every EU citizen to move and reside freely within the territory of the member states, subject to the limitations laid down in the Treaty. Article 18 TFEU (former Article 12 TEC) further protects EU nationals from discrimination or prejudice on the grounds of the EU citizen's nationality.[78]

From a historical perspective, it is important to note that the free movement of persons had in fact existed since the foundation of the European Community in 1957. The right was extended to workers as part of the goal to create a common market with free movement of labor, capital, goods and services. However, the directives adopted in the 1990s developed the concept further by guaranteeing the rights of citizens other than employees or service providers.

In summary, a citizen of an EU member state may move and reside within another member state on similar terms as nationals of that member state. The person moving must observe certain regulations and

---

[77] Treaty on European Union (Maastricht Treaty) OJ C191 (as amended)
[78] See also in this respect Directive 2004/38/EC of the European Parliament and of the Council of 29 April 2004 on the right of citizens of the Union and their family members to move and reside freely within the territory of the Member States [2004] OJ L 158/77

the right to reside within another member state is also dependent on the period of time and the purpose of the move.

Right to move and right of residence within the EU for up to three months

All EU citizens have the right to enter and right to stay[79] in another member state by virtue of possessing an identity card or a valid passport.[80] For a stay longer than three months, the EU citizen should:

- Be engaged in economic activity (on an employed or self-employed basis). A resident permit will be issued upon presenting an identity document and proof of employment or self-employment; or

- Provide proof of sufficient resources to sustain themselves and their family if they are of independent means and do not wish to exercise any gainful economic activity in the host member state; or

- The applicant must have or be following vocational training as a student and have sufficient resources to ensure that they do not become a burden on the social services of the host country; or

- Family members, irrespective of their nationality, have a right to accompany and establish themselves with EU citizens who fall into one of the above categories. Non-EU family members may be required to obtain, free of charge, an entry visa from the member state where they intend to reside. Family members may include the spouse, minor dependent children under the age of 21, and dependent parents

Family members who do not hold the nationality of an EU member state enjoy the same rights as the EU citizen whom they accompany. They may be subject to a short-stay visa requirement, but a valid residence permit from the EU citizen's country is deemed equivalent to a short-stay visa. Other from this, it is mandatory for family members who are not EU nationals to apply for a residence permit. These permits are valid for five years from the date of issue. Certain conditions such as the death of

---

[79] *http://europa.eu/legislation_summaries*
[80] EC Directive 2004/38/EC, chapter III, Article 6 (1)

the EU citizen, his/her departure from the host member state, divorce, annulment of marriage or a termination of partnership do not affect the right of family members who are not EU nationals; they can continue residing in the member state in question.

Equal treatment

An EU citizen residing in a host member state is entitled to the same benefits and treatment when it comes to employment, pay and access to education as a national of the host country. Even family members, irrespective of nationality, are entitled to work in the host country. Under certain circumstances, an individual may not be entitled to social security benefits if the period of residence in the host country is less than three months. Student grants or loans are only available to permanent residents. Such financial aid is only available for the individual and his family if they are permanent residents of the host country.

Permanent residence

The right of permanent residence entitles a person to reside in a member state permanently, without any restrictions. The right of permanent residence in a host member state can be acquired after a five-year period of uninterrupted lawful residence. This rule also extends to family members of an EU citizen who have lived with the EU citizen in the host country for five years. The right of permanent residence is lost only in the event of two successive years' absence from the host member state. Once the individual has achieved permanent residence status, they are entitled to the same rights, benefits and advantages as the nationals of the member state.

Restriction on right of entry

Restrictions on right of entry can be imposed on EU citizens or members of their family in particular circumstances. An EU citizen or family member may be expelled from a host member state on grounds of public policy, public security or public health but not on economic grounds.

The decision to expel an individual will be based exclusively on the personal conduct of that individual. It must also be shown that the conduct represents a sufficiently serious and present threat which affects the fundamental interests of the state. Previous criminal convictions and expired entry documents will not automatically justify expulsion. Lastly, persons affected by an expulsion order can apply for a review of the order after three years.

Transitional provisions for the new member states

In 2004, 2007, and 2013 respectively, the following became members of the EU: Czech Republic, Estonia, Hungary, Latvia, Lithuania, Poland, Slovakia, Slovenia, Malta and Cyprus in 2004; Bulgaria and Romania in 2007; and Croatia in 2013.

In principle the provisions of the EU Treaties in relation to freedom of movement also apply to the new member states. However, the new member states are subject to transitional arrangements that include some restrictions on the right of freedom of movement. These transitional provisions mean that the original, pre-May-2004 member states have certain rights to limit free movement of the new member states for up to seven years after they joined the EU.

Such restrictions to free movement apply to employment of the new EU-nationals (but are not applicable to self-employed persons and persons of independent means). The restrictions exclude nationals who wish to reside in existing member state for purpose of study or as a retiree.

However, as of 30 April 2011, there has been complete freedom of movement for citizens of the member states that joined in 2004.

The transitional arrangements for Bulgaria and Romania were also subject to restrictions. This right to apply restrictions on freedom of movement was given to all the existing member states including the 10 which joined in 2004. From 2014, complete freedom of movement to citizens from Bulgaria and Romania applies. The transitional period still applies to citizens of Croatia (which joined the EU in 2013) in five EU member states: Austria; Malta; the Netherlands; Slovenia; and the UK. All restrictions must end on 1 July 2020 at the latest.

6.3 European Free Trade Association and the European Economic Area Agreement

The European Free Trade Association (EFTA) - an intergovernmental organization, came into force in 1960. It was set up to promote free trade and economic integration for the benefit of its member states.[81]

Member states include the following countries: Iceland, Liechtenstein, Norway and Switzerland.

The EEA Agreement, which entered into force on 1 January 1994, brings together the EU Member States and the three EEA EFTA States — Iceland, Liechtenstein and Norway — in a single market. The agreement provides for the free movement of goods, services, capital and people within the EU and EEA EFTA member states[82] and secures the free movement of workers[83] in the EU and EEA EFTA states. An EU/EEA EFTA national may enter an EEA member state as a worker, self-employed person or service provider. However, EU/EFTA nationals are restricted from being employed in public service.[84]

Switzerland is not part of the EEA Agreement, but has its own bilateral agreements in place with the EU[85] that governs the free movement of persons.

---

[81] *www.efta.int*
[82] There are currently 31 member states under the EEA: all EU member states; Iceland; Liechtenstein; and Norway
[83] Part III, Chapter 1, Article 28 EEA
[84] Article 28(4) EEA
[85] Bilateral Agreements I of 1999

6.4   The Schengen area

The Schengen member states currently include Austria, Belgium, Czech Republic, Denmark, Estonia, Finland, France, Germany, Greece, Hungary, Iceland, Italy, Latvia, Lithuania, Luxembourg, Malta, the Netherlands, Norway, Poland, Portugal, Slovakia, Slovenia, Spain, Sweden and Switzerland.

The establishment of the *Schengen acquis*

The Schengen Agreement emerged outside the framework of the EU. On 14 June 1985 the governments of Belgium, France, Germany, Luxembourg and the Netherlands signed the Schengen Agreement to gradually abolish border controls to facilitate the freedom of movement of persons, goods and services amongst the signatory countries.

The Schengen Agreement was later supplemented with the Schengen Convention of 19 June 1990 in order to implement the provisions of the Schengen Agreement.[86] Together, the Schengen Agreement and the Schengen Convention form the *Schengen acquis*.

The *Schengen acquis* was absorbed into EU law by a protocol[87] attached to the Treaty of Amsterdam.[88] The Schengen area is now within the legal and institutional framework of the EU. Thus, it comes under parliamentary and judicial scrutiny, and attains the objective of free movement of persons, while also ensuring democratic parliamentary control and giving citizens accessible legal remedies when their rights in respect of the *Schengen acquis* are challenged (Court of Justice and/or national courts, depending on the area of law).

Gradually other countries in Europe have joined the Schengen agreement. Italy signed the agreement in 1990, Spain and Portugal joined

---

[86] Introduction to the Convention implementing the Schengen Agreement of 1985

[87] Article 4 of the Protocol annexed to the Treaty on the European Union and to the Amsterdam Treaty integrates the Schengen acquis

[88] The Treaty of Amsterdam was signed on 2 October 1997 and came into force on 1 May 1999. It made substantial changes to the Treaty of the European Union and incorporated the Schengen Agreement into mainstream European Law

in 1991, Greece followed in 1992, then Austria in 1995 and Denmark, Finland and Sweden in 1996.[89]

The Czech Republic, Estonia, Hungary, Latvia, Lithuania, Malta, Poland, Slovenia and Slovakia joined in 2007. Bulgaria, Croatia, Cyprus and Romania are not yet fully-fledged members of the Schengen area and border controls between them and the Schengen area are maintained until the EU Council decides that the conditions for abolishing internal border controls have been met. A protocol on the participation of Liechtenstein in the Schengen area was signed on 28 February 2008.[90]

Norway and Iceland, although not EU member states, joined the Schengen area in 1996 to preserve the Nordic Passport Union with Finland, Sweden, and Denmark. Switzerland, also not an EU member state, joined the *Schengen acquis* at the end of 2008.

The UK and Ireland opted out of the agreement, for fear of terrorism. However, in May 2000 and February 2002 respectively, the UK and Ireland requested to partly cooperate with the Schengen framework. They now partake in a police and judicial cooperation in criminal matters, the fight against drugs and the Schengen Information System. The cooperation was duly approved by the EU Council.

The Schengen framework

The purpose of the *Schengen acquis* was to abolish internal borders and passport checks between the participating states. The agreements also deal with visa and border checks, movement of persons and the granting of visas by the participating states. The idea was to create a borderless region known as the Schengen area. This arrangement has changed the procedures for entering or connecting in all of the Schengen states, as well as travelling between them.

---

[89] *http://europa.eu*
[90] *http://europa.eu*

There are certain measures adopted within the Schengen framework that each participating state must guarantee. These rules adopted generally include:

- Abolition of checks on persons at internal national borders within the Schengen area (but, in order to compensate, more stringent checks on the Schengen area's external borders)

- A common set of rules applying to people crossing the external borders of the EU member states/Schengen states

- Management of the conditions of entry and of the rules on visas for short stays

- Improved police cooperation (including rights of cross-border surveillance and hot pursuit)

- Stronger judicial cooperation through a faster extradition system and transferable enforcement of criminal judgments

- Establishment and development of the Schengen Information System

As entry into one Schengen state results in visa-free access to all the others,[91] the immigration procedures have been standardized and have overall become stricter than in the past. Schengen states can now issue visas on behalf of the others, and as a consequence the procedure for issuance has become complicated. For example, visas can no longer be issued by Honorary Consuls.

An important practical consequence of this system is that if an applicant receives a visa refusal from a particular Schengen state, the applicant is blocked from applying for a Schengen visa at any other Schengen state until the visa refusal has been cleared from the system. This can have significant practical implications as visas can be refused without reason and it is difficult and time-consuming to appeal. It is therefore important that Schengen visa applications are carefully prepared and lodged with the Schengen state with which the applicant has the closest connection

---

[91]   It is also possible however for a Schengen state to issue a visa that is restricted to give access only to the territory of the issuing country

and the best reason to apply. Questions on how to obtain a visa should be addressed to the competent embassy of that Schengen state.

Third-country nationals who are in possession of a valid residence permit issued by a Schengen member state can travel within the Schengen area by presenting the residence permit and do not need to apply for a visa. Contrarily, third-country nationals travelling to EU member states that are not in the Schengen area will still require a visa for the member state they intend to visit.[92]

In addition, third-country nationals who live in an EU member state that participates in the Schengen Agreement have the right of free movement after a minimum of five years of legal residence upon acquiring permanent residence status.[93]

The Schengen Information System

The Schengen Information System (SIS) was set up in and has been operational since 1995. It allows national border control and judicial authorities to obtain information regarding certain categories of persons and property. Member states supply information to the SIS through national networks connected to a central system.

In Europe, the SIS is the largest shared database dedicated to maintain public security, support police and judicial cooperation and manage external border control. Participating states provide entries, so called "alerts", on wanted and missing persons, lost and stolen property and entry bans. It is immediately and directly accessible by all police officers at street level and other law enforcement officials and authorities who need the information to carry out their roles in protecting law and order and fighting crime. A second generation Schengen Information System (SIS II) replaced the SIS I in April 2013. The SIS II will continue to play a crucial role in facilitating the free movement of people within the Schengen area. It replaced the previous system, with a more up-to date system offering additional

---

[92] Council Regulation (EC) No. 539/2001
[93] Council Directive 109/2003/EC

functionalities. The SIS II allows for easy information exchanges between national border control, customs and police authorities, and ensures that crossing borders can take place in a safe environment.

Data protection

A directive[94] provides for the protection of personal data and an independent body monitors the lawfulness of the data processing.

A person has the right to access their information contained in the SIS. Furthermore, the person has the right to demand deletion or correction of incorrect data if stored unlawfully. This means that when encountering problems during a visa application or when arriving at a Schengen border, if a person wants to view the data stored in the SIS, this person has the right to contact a Schengen state of choice to obtain the data. The national authority in charge of the SIS data must provide the person with the data that has been processed. The person is also entitled to access the details about the authority that had stored the data, all possible recipients of this data and the purpose of the use of the data. However, it can be very cumbersome to apply for and request this information, and the request can be refused if it is not deemed in the public interest to release the information.

6.5   Bilateral agreements with Switzerland

Since 2002, it has become significantly easier for citizens of EU and EFTA member states to become resident in Switzerland,[95] irrespective of whether they are gainfully occupied or not. One purpose of the bilateral agreements on the free movement of persons which came into force on 1 June 2002 (between Switzerland and the EU as well as between the individual EU member states) was to gradually introduce free movement for both working and non-working persons.

Since 1 June 2007, for citizens of all member states that joined the EU before 1 May 2004, as well as for citizens of Cyprus, Malta, and the

---

[94]   Directive 95/46/EC
[95]   A good overview of the applicable rules in the law concerning foreign nationals may be found at *www.auslaender.ch*

EFTA member states, the free movement of persons agreement has come into force without any restrictions (with exception of citizens of Liechtenstein who already enjoyed this right in 2005). For other member states from the 2004 expansion the restrictions were moved in 2011, and for Bulgaria and Romania restrictions were moved in 2016. Since 1 April 2015, citizens of the 27 EU member states (all but Croatia) or EFTA States who are looking for work in Switzerland are only granted a residence permit if they have sufficient financial means to cover their living expenses. However, special rules apply to Croatia to which the agreement on the free movement of persons will not be extended due to adoption of mass immigration initiative (following the popular vote of 9 February 2014). Instead, as from 9 February 2014, Croatian nationals are subject to separate quotas (outside quotas for third country nationals), which consist of 50 one-year "B" permits and 450 short-term "L" permits.

The EU/EFTA nationals may acquire real estate without prior authorization if their main residence is in Switzerland. Even if they give up their residence at a later stage, they may nevertheless retain their Swiss real estate.

6.6 Other regional arrangements and organizations

There are several regional arrangements beyond the European context that provide for free movement of people, especially with regard to the liberalization of labor movement. These regional arrangements extend from Asia and Australia across the oceans to the Americas. For the purpose of this book, only the regional arrangements and organizations that also provide for the free or easier movement of persons are dealt with in this section.

Asia-Pacific Economic Cooperation

Asia-Pacific Economic Cooperation (APEC)[96] is an organization aimed at liberalizing trade and investment, facilitating business and promoting economic and technical cooperation in the Asia-Pacific region.

---

[96] www.apec.org

The APEC Business Travel Card (ABTC) scheme commenced in 1997 and is an initiative that facilitates the movement of accredited business people across the Asia-Pacific region. The ABTC is valid for up to three years and provides multiple short term entries (maximum of two months stay) without a visa. The ABTC also provides access to streamlined immigration airport lanes on arrival and departure.

Card holders travelling to the US or Canada can use the special service or fast-track lanes for passenger clearance at all major international airports. However, ABTC holders are still subject to the usual immigration clearance process as applicable to other travelers, such as presenting valid passports and where applicable, valid visas for entry into the US or Canada.

The current APEC member countries include: Australia, Brunei Darussalam, Canada, Chile, China (People's Rep.), Hong Kong (SAR), Indonesia, Japan, Republic of Korea, Malaysia, Mexico, New Zealand, Papua New Guinea, Peru, Philippines, Russia, Singapore, Republic of China (Taiwan), Thailand, the US and Vietnam.

Andean Community

The current member states of the Andean Community include: Bolivia, Colombia, Ecuador and Peru.

The Andean Community[97] is an organization of four[98] South American countries joined together for the purpose of the development and integration of the Andean region.

The Andean Community Labor Migration Instrument (Decision 545) provides freedom of movement and temporary residence for employment purposes among the participating states. This provision is specifically created for migrant workers who need to obtain temporary residence in the sub region as wage workers.[99]

---

[97] www.comunidadandina.org
[98] Venezuela was a member but withdrew from the Andean Community in 2006
[99] Article 1 of the Andean Community Labour Migration Instrument (Decision 545)

Caribbean Community

The Caribbean Community (CARICOM)[100] is an organization established in 1972, when Commonwealth Caribbean leaders decided to transform the Caribbean Free Trade Association (CARIFTA) into a common market with free movement of persons.

CARICOM has introduced recently a Regional Travel Card system known as CARIPASS.[101] This entitles current holders of passports issued by CARICOM member states and legal residents of any of the member states, who are 16 years and over, to become part of a trusted traveler regime once they have been deemed eligible. CARIPASS holders will in the future be expeditiously processed through special self-service gates at airports and sea ports which entitle them to proceed directly to baggage arrival and customs. The card is an alternative travel document for regional travel and is valid for periods of one or three years. The travel card is issued by national passport and immigration authorities and will help the frequent regional traveler avoid immigration lines at the airport.

Current member countries of CARICOM include Antigua and Barbuda, Bahamas, Barbados, Belize, Dominica, Grenada, Guyana, Haiti, Jamaica, Montserrat, St. Kitts and Nevis, St. Lucia, St. Vincent and the Grenadines, Suriname, and Trinidad and Tobago.

Commonwealth of Independent States

The Commonwealth of Independent States[102] (CIS) was established in 1991 following the collapse of the Soviet Union. It consists of the nations that made up the former Soviet Union except Georgia. The CIS member states signed an agreement to create an economic union that would promote, among others, the free movement of labor.

---

[100] *www.caricom.org*
[101] *www.caripass.org*
[102] *www.cisstat.com/eng/cis.htm*

Current CIS member countries include: Armenia, Azerbaijan, Belarus, Kazakhstan, Kyrgyzstan, Moldova, Russia, Tajikistan, Turkmenistan, Ukraine and Uzbekistan.

Economic Community of West African States

The Economic Community of West African States (ECOWAS)[103] is a regional group of fifteen countries, founded in 1975. Its mission is to promote integration in all fields of economic activity.

Citizens of the ECOWAS member states do not require passports when traveling within the Community. Article 59 of the ECOWAS Treaty provides that "citizens of the community shall have the right of entry, residence and establishment".

The member states include: Benin, Burkina Faso, Cape Verde, Côte d'Ivoire, Gambia, Ghana, Guinea, Guinea Bissau, Mali, Niger, Nigeria, Senegal, Sierra Leone, and Togo.

Gulf Cooperation Council

The Gulf Cooperation Council (GCC)[104] is a political and economic union involving the six Arab states of the Persian Gulf with many economic and social objectives, including easier travel within the borders of the GCC member states.

The leaders of the six states launched the framework in 1981 in order to achieve unity by strengthening the relations, links and areas of cooperation among their citizens.

The GCC member countries currently include: Bahrain, Kuwait, Oman, Qatar, Saudi Arabia and the United Arab Emirates.

---

[103] *www.ecowas.int*
[104] *www.gccsg.org*

Nordic Passport Union

Denmark[105], Finland, Iceland, Norway and Sweden belong to the Nordic Passport Union, a protocol that has abolished internal border checks between the member states. Citizens of these Nordic states can enjoy passport-free travel and reside in the other member states without a special residence permit.

The 1954 protocol abolishes the need of nationals of Denmark, Finland, Norway and Sweden to have a passport or residence permit while resident in a Scandinavian country other than their own.

Trans-Tasman Travel Arrangement

The Trans-Tasman Travel Arrangement (TTTA)[106] is a set of policies between Australia and New Zealand and allows nationals of either country to live and work in the other country indefinitely. Citizens of New Zealand require a Special Category Visa due to Australia's stricter border security,[107] but Australian citizens do not require a visa to travel or reside in New Zealand.

UK-Ireland Common Travel Area

The United Kingdom of Great Britain and Northern Ireland (UK), the Channel Islands, the Isle of Man and the Republic of Ireland collectively form a common travel area. A person who has been checked at immigration at the point of entry into the common travel area does generally not need to apply again for leave to enter while moving within the travel area. No separate entry clearances have to be issued if a person is going to transit through or remain for a while in one part of the Common Travel Area before travelling to another part. The entry clearance should be issued for the sole purpose of the journey. However certain people, described in Paragraph 15 of the UK Immigration Rules, who enter the

---

[105] Including the Faroe Islands
[106] *www.gccsg.org*
[107] An outcome from the negotiation of the Australia-New Zealand Closer Economic Relations Trade Agreement (ANZCERTA)

UK through the Republic of Ireland do require leave to enter, as well as a visa, if they are citizens subject to visa requirements.[108]

The Common Travel Area has no formal legal status as a multilateral agreement but is a shared understanding between the UK, the Republic of Ireland and the authorities in Jersey, Guernsey and the Isle of Man, which they reflect separately for themselves in their separate immigration regulations. The UK has power to change its arrangements in relation to the Common Travel Area unilaterally but as a matter of good practice, it consults its Common Travel Area partners before doing so.

---

[108] *www.ukvisas.gov.uk*

7

Passports and Visas

Chapter Summary

Passports are issued by governments both as a way of certifying their citizens' identity and to enable international travel. It also represents confirmation of citizenship.

It is possible to hold more than one passport or other travel documents. An individual may travel on any valid travel document that they possess, as long as the destination country will accept it. Where possible, using an identity card will normally be more efficient and quicker than using a passport. There are some regions where, to travel freely, it is necessary to hold more than one passport.

The International Civil Aviation Organization regulates all passports. They also manage standards for machine-readable passports and biometric passports, and prescribe the formats that passports should follow and the minimum information and security features that they must contain.

While most passports follow their country's standard format, there are a range of special passports for use in certain circumstances. These include alien (or non-citizen) passports, children's identity cards, diplomatic or consular passports, official, special or service passports, International Red Cross passports, family passports and temporary and emergency passports.

While passports allow international travel, visa regulations impose restrictions on travel. Visas are often required in addition to your passport and confirm that you have been approved to enter the country you are visiting. There are generally two main categories of visa – non-immigrant visas and immigrant visas. Each will have certain conditions and it is critical to comply with the terms under which the visa is issued to avoid serious consequences.

The increasing numbers of international travelers every year mean an increased risk and spread of disease. Alongside ensuring that your passport is valid and you have the appropriate visas, you must also check that you comply with any health requirements of the country you are visiting.

Today, international travel almost always requires a passport or other form of identification. This has not always been the case.

The modern system of passports and border controls only fully emerged after 1918 because of the significant number of World War I refugees.[109] However, the concept of a travel document dates back much further, to at least 450 BC.[110] In medieval Europe, passports were issued to travelers by local authorities, and generally contained a list of towns and cities which the document holder was allowed to enter.

In addition to its function as a travel document, a passport also represents *prima facie* documentary evidence that shows the belonging of a person to a state, normally indicating that the holder is a citizen of the country that issued the passport.

In addition to a valid passport, often a visa must be obtained before you are able to travel to other countries. A visa is an entry in a passport or other travel document made by a consular official to indicate that the bearer has been vetted and granted permission to enter or re-enter the country concerned.

Visa restrictions are an important form of border control and an effective foreign policy instrument. Whether as a citizen of a particular country you will need a visa to visit another country depends on a number of factors, but not least on the international standing and relationships of the relevant countries. Thus citizens of certain countries find that they can travel to many other countries without the need for a visa, while others require visas more often and are therefore faced with considerable restrictions in their international mobility.[111]

Applying for a visa normally means that you have to send your passport to the consulate or embassy of the country you want to travel to, and

---

[109] For a detailed analysis of the history of the passport see Torpey (2000), and Lloyd (2005)

[110] A reference was found in the Hebrew Bible that dates back to the Persian Empire around 450BC

[111] For an overview of the state of the world in terms of visa restrictions, Henley & Partners publishes the *Henley & Partners Visa Restrictions Index* (HVRI). See *www.henleyglobal. com/hrvi* and the relevant chapter in this book

during the time it takes to process your visa application – sometimes two weeks or more – you are not in possession of your passport. This is one of many reasons why it is very useful to have a second passport at hand in case you need to travel unexpectedly.

7.1 Passports and other travel documents

A passport is an official document issued by a competent public authority to citizens or to alien residents of the issuing country.

The document is issued for international travel to certify the travelers' personal identity. Furthermore, a passport also represents some documentary evidence that shows the belonging of a person to a state, normally indicating that the holder is a citizen of the country that issued the passport.

However, a country with complex nationality laws such as the UK may issue various passports which are similar in appearance but are representative of differing national statuses. The different classes of passports and relationships cause foreign governments to subject holders of different UK passports to different entry requirements.

The passport does not entitle the person to enter into other countries but does normally provide the right to return to the country that issued the passport.

A passport issued to a citizen represents the exercise of citizenship and gives the individual civil status[112] within a specific country.

The fact that passports are issued by governments, not least to document their bearer's citizenship, indicates the immense importance of citizenship in a world of nation-states.[113]

However, as the scholar Mark Salter aptly says, "'the passport offers only two guarantees (both of which are limited): identification of the bearer, and the place of repatriation".[114]

---

[112] Noiriel (2001)
[113] Fahrmeir (2001)
[114] Salter (2003)

The permission to enter a country without a visa is normally based on the citizenship of the individual, and not on the country which issued the travel document. Therefore, passports issued to non-citizens are often of limited use as fewer and fewer countries recognize them as valid for entry.

Issuance of a visa is however considered an acceptance of the passport's validity.

A person may be a citizen of two (or more) countries and may therefore hold more than one passport or other travel documents such as identity cards. This person is entitled to travel on any of these documents, provided the travel document will be accepted by the country of destination. The visa requirements will depend on the passport (or other document) used in each case.

Although it is perfectly legal to hold more than one passport or other travel document when crossing borders, it is advisable for practical reasons to decide beforehand which one to use. It may confuse border guards if you show several passports, which can lead to delays.

If you have the choice of using either a passport or an identity card for border crossings, normally using the identity card is preferable as checks are quicker. Often the officer at the border will require more time looking at a passport than a simple plastic card. Also, passports may reveal previous trips, which depending on the countries you have travelled to and the country which you now wish to enter, may look suspicious and may raise unnecessary questions.

In some situations, you may need two different passports as you may not always be able to travel with the same passport. This is the case, for example, if you travel to Israel and also to certain Arabic countries, where entry is categorically refused if your passport shows evidence of a visit to Israel.

Passports also play an increasingly important role in monitoring the movements of individuals internationally. Australia, for example, monitors every border crossing electronically. However, in some areas such as within the EU, a passport is not required for travel between the various states. This poses questions of uncontrolled movement which can threaten overall national and international security. In the case of the EU, there are very strict security policies in place[115] to mitigate such risks.

The International Civil Aviation Organization (ICAO), a specialized agency of the United Nations, has regulated the standards of passports since 1974. The ICAO later on introduced the 'one person, one passport' policy, resulting in the creation of children's passports. Children under the age of 16 may no longer travel on their parent's passport, but require their own passport instead, regardless of age. Nowadays, therefore, even babies can have their own passports, although these are normally issued with a validity of only three years or less.

The ICAO also issued standards for machine-readable passports. Every machine-readable passport has an area where most of the information contained in the identification page of the passport is also printed in a manner suitable for optical character recognition (OCR). The OCR field can be swept through reading devices at immigration checkpoints and thus facilitates efficient immigration clearance at the border.

The regulation of biometric passports is also developed and administered by the ICAO. All countries are urged to produce biometric passports (or e-passports) for their nationals. The biometric passport has been introduced to reduce passport fraud. The enhanced passport has a microprocessor chip embedded in a plastic inlay that can be read by special scanners at immigration checkpoints. The microchip stores personal details including the portrait picture, fingerprints and/or iris recognition.

An ongoing debate has developed whether biometric information systems are an infringement on privacy. Of course, biometric information is not only a policing tool for immigration officials but has in some cases been useful in respect of international law enforcement.[116]

---

[115] See chapter on Freedom of Movement and Regional Arrangements
[116] See Zureiak and Salter (2005)

Regardless of the privacy issues debated, the biometric passport can assist in the alleviation of passport fraud which in turn may curb international crime and terrorism.

Most countries now issue biometric passports, and more and more often a biometric passport is becoming a prerequisite for visa-free entry. For instance, to enter the US under the visa-waiver program as a citizen of one of the countries that are part of this arrangement, you must use a biometric passport or else you will still require a visa. The EU also has plans to introduced a similar regime, and citizens from Albania, Bosnia and Herzegovina, Macedonia and Serbia can enter the EU without a visa only if they have biometric passports. It is therefore advisable to obtain a biometric passport if you can.

The ICAO standards also require that all passports follow a uniform format and should include at least certain defined information such as the person's name, citizenship, date of birth and signature. It also prescribes a certain minimum of security features, even for those passports that are not yet biometric.

Passports are often produced by private companies specialized in security printing rather than the government issuing the passport. There are only a handful of companies worldwide that produce passports for almost all the world's governments.[117]

The international status of a person's passport will determine the travel freedom available to that individual. Despite visa free travel for some countries, there will always be restrictions of entry for other countries. The majority of OECD countries for example require citizens from most developing countries to obtain visitor visas. On the other hand, passport holders from most countries must obtain a visitor visa for countries such as China, Russia and India, regardless of their nationality. Many countries also impose visa restrictions on most visitors in order to collect visa fees; Egypt,

---

[117] These include De La Rue in the UK, the US Government Printing Office in the US, Canadian Bank Note Company in Canada, Oberthur in France, Giesecke & Devrient in Germany and Orell Füssli in Switzerland

for example, a popular tourist destination, requires a visa for virtually all its visitors. The Egyptian tourist visa is nonetheless easily obtainable for a fee. Australia, on the other hand, has an elaborate system of border control in place, which is the reason for its also virtually universal visa requirement with the exception of New Zealand citizens. For many foreign citizens visiting Australia, a visa is easily obtainable and is often even organized by the travel agent. One of the main purposes of this Australian visa system is to monitor border crossings and curb illegal overstays.

Types of passports

Most countries issue a standard passport to its citizens. However, it is possible to obtain a special passport under certain conditions and for certain persons. Among these are the following types:

- *Alien (or non-citizen) passports* – issued to alien residents who are not citizens of the issuing country

- *Children's identity cards* – issued to minors instead of a passport (e.g. the German *Kinderausweis*)

- *Diplomatic or consular passports* – issued to diplomatic, consular and other government officials on missions entitling the bearer to diplomatic or consular status under international law and custom

- *Official, special or service passports* – issued to government officials or other persons on government missions

- International Red Cross passport, Laissez-Passer issued by the United Nations

- Joint passports (family passports) which are no longer in circulation in most countries

- Temporary and emergency passports issued in emergency cases by a country's government to its own citizens. These passports have the same legal effect as normal passports, unless otherwise stated, but are usually only issued for a limited period of time and limited purpose. Also, in many cases they cannot be used like normal passports as for example visas by other countries will not, as a rule, be issued in a temporary or emergency passport. Emergency passports are issued for example by your country's embassy or consulate if you are in a foreign country and your passport was stolen

A camouflage passport on the other hand is a document that appears to be a regular passport but is actually in the name of a country that no longer exists, never existed, or that has changed its name. Companies that sell camouflage passports claim that in the event of a hijacking they could be shown to terrorists to help escape. Because a camouflage passport is not issued in the name of a real country, it is not a counterfeit and is not illegal per se to have. However, attempting to use it to actually cross an international border is illegal in most countries.

Alien residence cards or residence permits can also be used for cross-border travel. Alien residents are citizens who have taken up official residence (either permanent or temporary) in a country of which they are not a citizen. Proof of alien residence may appear in the form of a stamp in the national passport, a separate document or an identity card. In some countries even passports are issued to alien residents.[118]

For example, anyone who is a legal alien resident in any of the Schengen states is able to travel visa-free to any other Schengen state on the basis of his or her residence status.

There are also other travel documents which may not always have the same legal effect as passports and are valid only for limited countries and purposes. Such travel documents include identification cards, travel certificates, special travel cards issued to registered persons to facilitate visa-free travel (such as the NEXUS[119] card or APEC travel card), military identification cards, seaman discharge books and records.

Most countries accept passports of other countries as valid for international travel and valid for entry. There are exceptions, such as when a

---

[118] Panama, for example, issues non-citizen passports to certain categories of residents who retire in the country. Often such non-citizen passports are however no longer recognized by other countries and are therefore of limited use for international travel

[119] The NEXUS card allows border-crossing between the US and Canada

country does not recognize the passport-issuing country as a sovereign state.[120] Likewise, the passport-issuing country may also place restrictions on the passports of its citizens not to go to certain countries due to poor or non-existent foreign relations,[121] or security or health risks. Some countries do not accept temporary passports or provisional passports from specific countries.[122]

Finally, in some countries, there are immigration checks and passport controls even for travel within the country, and consequently passports or other travel documents are required to travel within the country. This is true for travel between the Special Administrative Regions (SAR) Hong Kong, Macau and mainland China, or for travel between Peninsular Malaysia and Eastern Malaysia. Internal passport systems also exist in Russia, amongst others.

7.2   Visa requirements

While the passport opens up possibilities of international movement, visa regulations impose restrictions to curb this free movement.

A visa is an entry in a passport or other travel document made by a consular official of a government to indicate that the bearer has been granted authority to enter or re-enter the country concerned.

Generally a country has full sovereignty and control over who enters the country. In some cases, however this control may be diminished by an international treaty like the Schengen Agreement. Switzerland, for example, had a very liberal visa policy, and by giving up some of its

---

[120] Due to the special political status of Taiwan, neither the People's Republic of China (PRC) nor the Republic of China (ROC) recognizes the passports issued by the other and neither party considers travel between mainland China and Taiwan as formal international travel. The Taiwan Compatriot Entry Permit is therefore issued as the travel document for Taiwan residents to enter mainland China. Its counterpart for citizens of mainland China is the Entry Permit of Mainland Residents to the Taiwan Area

[121] E.g. many Muslim countries endorse their passport "valid for all countries except Israel" or similar

[122] Canada, for example, will not accept any passport claiming to have been issued by Somalia, non-machine readable passports issued by the Czech Republic, temporary passports issued by the Republic of South Africa, and provisional passports issued by Venezuela

sovereignty when it became part of the Schengen area, now has to adhere to the EU's visa policy, which is more restrictive.

Visa requirements (or visa restrictions) divide the world into two classes of citizens: those from mostly middle-income and rich countries who can travel visa-free to many other countries, and those from generally poorer or geopolitically isolated countries who require a visa for most travel. Henley & Partners constantly monitors the global situation regarding visa restrictions and produces the annually updated Henley & Partners Visa Restrictions Index in cooperation with IATA. This index consists of a ranking of countries and territories according to how many other countries/territories allow visa-free travel for a particular country's passport holder. The ranking consists of a score that each country achieves in terms of numbers of other countries to which visa-free access is possible.[123]

Special rules apply to certain categories of citizens including diplomats, employees of international organizations, visiting forces, or seamen and aircrews. Generally the same visa requirements apply on all passports issued by a certain country or organization, but bilateral or multilateral agreements may provide that holders of diplomatic passports, for instance, can be exempt from the visa requirements while holders of ordinary passports still require a visa.

However, a visa, transit visa or visa exemption for a country does not guarantee admission to that country. The final decision always rests with the competent authorities at the port of entry in the country concerned.

For example, in some Muslim countries including Egypt, Saudi Arabia, Iran and Jordan, passport holders who had an Israeli visa or stamp affixed in their passport are generally refused entry into the country. Or if you arrive in the US with a visitor's visa but the immigration officer questioning you comes to the conclusion that you have "immigrant intent", you may be refused entry even though you have a valid (tourist) visa.

---

[123] For more information see *www.visaindex.com* and the relevant chapter in this book

In a number of countries "transit without visa" permission is given to citizens and passport holders of certain countries and under specific conditions. Passport holders of qualifying countries who comply with these conditions do not require a (transit) visa for the country concerned if they only travel via that country to an onward destination.

The US Visa Waiver Program allows citizens from certain countries[124] to travel to the US for business or pleasure, for stays of 90 days or less without obtaining a visa. Travelers admitted under the Visa Waiver Program must agree to waive their rights to review or appeal.

International visitors who are travelling to the US under the Visa Waiver Program are now subject to enhanced security requirements. All eligible travelers who wish to travel under the Visa Waiver Program must apply for authorization using the Electronic System for Travel Authorization[125] at least 72 hours before starting their journey. If you do not have an ESTA authorization you will not be allowed to board a plane to the US.

It can be useful to avail yourself of visa expediting services, which are provided by specialized companies such as CIBT[126] and other visa service providers, immigration consultants and travel agents.

Applying for a visa often means that you have to send your passport to the consulate or embassy of the country you want to travel to, and during the time it takes to process the visa application you do not have your passport – sometimes that can take two or even more weeks. A second passport, in such cases, may be extremely useful in the event that you need to travel urgently.

---

[124] The following countries currently participate in the Visa Waiver Program of the US: Andorra, Australia, Austria, Belgium, Brunei, Czech Republic, Denmark, Estonia, Finland, France, Germany, Greece, Hungary, Iceland, Ireland, Italy, Japan, Latvia, Liechtenstein, Lithuania, Luxembourg, Malta, Monaco, the Netherlands, New Zealand, Norway, Portugal, San Marino, Singapore, Slovakia, Slovenia, South Korea, Spain, Sweden, Switzerland, and the UK

[125] *www.esta.cbp.dhs.gov*

[126] *www.cibt.com*

Types of Visas

There are generally two main categories of visa – non-immigrant visas and immigrant visas.

A non-immigrant visa is applicable to a person that requires entry to a country for a short stay (usually under three months) for business, tourism, studies, press work or government work, and similar reasons. An immigrant visa is most commonly issued to give the person residence status for a period of six months to five years depending on the nature and purpose of residence. Most residence visas will be issued on the basis of family connection, employment, study or investment. An immigrant visa is essentially the same as a residence permit, although the immigrant visa also refers to the specific visa issued for the initial entry to a country for the purpose of taking up residence.

It has become popular to allow economic migration into countries by way of highly skilled workers or financially independent persons who do not need to work but instead invest in the country or who may simply be interested in retirement. The purpose is to create value from allowing foreigners into the target country on this basis.

Every country has a separate set of criteria that the visa applicant must fulfill. Usually in terms of short-stay visa for business or tourism, the country requests an invitation from a company (business visa) or travel arrangements such as hotel bookings (tourism visa). Often the person is required to show a return ticket back to his country of residence to satisfy the issuing authority and border control that the person does not intend to stay in the country.

Before applying for a visa, it is important that you check carefully the requirements and prepare a proper application with all supporting documentation to avoid unnecessary delays or possibly rejection by the visa issuing authority. The rejection of a visa application or visa refusal should be avoided at all costs, since whenever you are applying for another visa you will normally be asked on the application form whether you have ever been refused a visa. It is better if you can then still tick the box "no".

For the same reason it is important that you always strictly adhere to the conditions under which the visa has been granted to you, otherwise, once in the country, you may find yourself in more serious trouble and may be deported. This could happen, for example, if you overstay your visa.

Breach of Visa Conditions and Overstays

A visa is always issued for a particular purpose of entry (e.g. tourism, immigration, journalism, etc.) and for a particular time frame. Furthermore, visas are usually either issued as single-entry visas or multiple entry visas. It is very important that you strictly obey the conditions under which the visa is given. If you breach the visa conditions, for example by entering a country on a tourist visa when in fact you intend to immigrate, this can have serious consequences including deportation, fines or imprisonment. Likewise, it is important that you do not overstay the term for which the visa has been granted to you – or the term during which you qualify to stay without the need for a visa. For example in the US, if you qualify to enter under the US Visa Waiver Program, when you enter the US you fill in a form in which you confirm that you will stay for no longer than 90 days and that you waive all rights to appeal etc. In other words, you really need to leave at the latest after 90 days, or otherwise you are in breach of US immigration law, which has serious consequences.

7.3   Health requirements

The number of people travelling internationally is increasing every year. According to statistics from the United Nations World Tourism Organization (UNWTO), international tourist arrivals are expected to reach 1.6 billion by 2020. This leads to an increasing risk of spreading diseases and is a challenge for health authorities in many countries. In many parts of the world health regulations exists for persons crossing borders. Therefore, besides visa requirements, it is also important to check the requisite health requirements for the destination country, transit countries and even, in some cases, the country of departure as there may be prescribed health regulations upon return to the country.

The World Health Organization (WHO) has an interactive travel and health map[127] on its website that provides information for each country and includes information on requirements for mandatory yellow fever vaccination, recommendation for malaria prevention and the risk of malaria as well as for rabies.

The health requirements of the various countries officially sent to the WHO are published in its *International Travel and Health* book. Unfortunately, this official information does not always reflect actual practice at a point of entry in a country. It is hence advisable to check not only the WHO information but also with the relevant countries of transit, destination and return before travelling. The IATA Travel Centre[128] also provides up-to-date information on health travel requirements.

---

[127] *www.who.int*
[128] *www.iatatravelcentre.com*

8

Visa Restrictions Index

Chapter Summary

Since the First World War, governments have generally tightened the entry requirements for foreign nationals to visit their countries. Visa restrictions now play an important role in controlling the movement of foreign nationals across borders. Many countries now require visitor visas from certain non-nationals who wish to enter their territory. Visa requirements are also an expression of the relationships between individual nations, and generally reflect the relations and status of a country within the international community.

The *Henley & Partners Visa Restrictions Index* (HVRI) is a global ranking of countries according to the travel freedom their citizens enjoy. Henley & Partners has analyzed the visa regulations of all countries and territories in the world and has created an index which ranks countries according to the visa-free access its citizens enjoy to other countries. This is the only global ranking that shows the international travel freedom of the citizens of the various countries, and thereby the international relations and status of individual countries relative to others in this regard.

For most of the 20th century, governments have increased entry restrictions for foreigners wishing to visit their countries, and visa restrictions and requirements continue to play an important role in controlling the movement of individuals across borders. Visa requirements are also an expression of the relationships between individual nations, and generally reflect the relations and status of a country within the international community.

The HVRI is produced by Henley & Partners in cooperation with the International Air Transport Association (IATA), which maintains the world's largest database of travel information. In compiling the index, the unique global ranking methodology developed by Henley & Partners is applied to data provided by IATA's Timatic passport and visa information database.

The index is updated on an annual basis and has been produced every year since 2006, providing an interesting view of the way in which the relationships within the international community of nations has developed during that time. This year's Index, along with the unique cumulative data from the last ten years, gives an unprecedented and inimitable insight into the development of visa policies over this time.

8.1   Definition of the Index

The Index consists of a ranking of countries/territories according to how many other countries/territories one can travel to visa-free on a particular country or territory's passport. The ranking is made according to the score each country achieves in terms of numbers of other countries to which visa-free access is possible.

The basis of the data consists of all countries and territories covered in the IATA database.

Since not all territories issue passports there are fewer countries/territories to be ranked than destination countries/territories against which queries are made.

8.2   2016 Highlights

Comparing the 2016 Index to previous years shows many interesting results.

Germany has retained its position in the top spot, with visa-free access to 177 countries out of a total of 218, while Sweden remained in second place with a ranking of 176. The UK meanwhile, dropped from first to third place this year, after three consecutive years in first place. A larger group of countries sit in third place, with Finland, France, Italy, Spain and the UK all having visa-free access to 175 countries.

The United Arab Emirates (UAE) has been catapulted into the spotlight as the biggest climber with its dramatic addition of 37 countries and improvement in rank from 55 to 40. It is also the biggest climber over the ten years of the Visa Restrictions Index, and one of only 22 to have moved up in the rankings over the last year.

Looking at movement over the last decade throws up other interesting patterns. European countries are notable for their stability over this time - Belgium, France, Italy, Luxembourg, Spain and Sweden all remain in exactly the same position as 10 years before. The top 10 positions are almost identical, with 30 countries in 2015, compared to 26 ten years before. While Liechtenstein dropped, the Czech Republic, Finland, Hungary, Malta, Slovakia and South Korea all made it into the top 10. Albania, UAE, Bosnia and Serbia all moved up more than 20 places in the Index over the last ten years, while the biggest drops were experienced by Guinea (-32), Liberia (-33), Sierra Leone (-35) and Bolivia (-37).

Generally, there was significant movement across the board with only 21 of the 199 countries listed remaining in the same rank. No country however, dropped more than three positions, indicating that overall, visa-free access is improving around the world. Four countries in partic-ular made huge gains: Tonga rising 16 spots, Palau by 20, Colombia by 25 and Timor Leste, a Southeast Asian nation, being the highest climber with an increase of 33 ranks.

Somalia, Iraq, Pakistan and Afghanistan meanwhile, continue to hold the bottom four positions on the Index, and thus have again been labelled the worst passports in the world.

The number of countries in the 'Top 10' remained static in this year's Index at 28 countries, with Hungary joining the category after one year of being pushed out, and Malaysia dropping to 12th position after three years in the premier group.

The Importance of Investment Migration

The growing importance of investment migration can be seen in steady growth of those countries offering residence and citizenship-by-investment programs. Those countries with relevant programs continue to perform strongly and all now feature in the top 30 of the Index.

Malta, the EU member country which runs the world's most successful citizenship-by-investment program with over EUR 1 billion in capital raised since its launch in 2014, has gained visa-free access to another two countries since 2015, making it the 8th most powerful passport in the world. The other key location of citizenship-by-investment in Europe, the Mediterranean island nation of Cyprus, also added two countries to its basket, ranking 17th on the Index with visa-free access to 159 countries. The leading Caribbean citizenship-by-investment location, Antigua and Barbuda, ranked 30th and its passport-holders may now travel to 134 countries visa-free.

Portugal, which holds the most attractive residence-by-investment program through its Golden Visa Program, has taken 6th position in the 2016 Index, gaining two countries to total 172 countries its citizens may travel to visa-free.

The continued development of these countries demonstrates the critical nature of good visa-free access to countries offering investor migration programs. In turn, this speaks of the importance of due diligence in such programs, since the reputation of a country's passport and its relationship with other countries is only as good as its newest citizens.

Henley & Partners' powerful insight and experience continues to lead the industry, supporting both governments to create and manage the top immigration programs in the world, and individuals to improve their lives by achieving alternative residence or citizenship.

To view the *Henley & Partners Visa Restrictions Index 2016*, containing the detailed scores and rankings, please visit *visaindex.com*

8.3   Methodology

To determine the score for each country/territory, the IATA database is queried in the following way:

1. Each country/territory (passport holder's country) for which the score is to be determined is checked against every country/territory (destination) for which travel restriction information exists in the IATA database

2. Each query is made on the following conditions, i.e. it is assumed that the following conditions are met by the passport holder who wishes to enter the destination:

   a. The passport is issued in the country of nationality

   b. The passport is valid

   c. The passport holder is a citizen of the country which issued the passport

   d. The passport holder is an adult

   e. Entry is sought for a tourism or business visit

   f. Duration of stay is three days

3. Further conditions:

   a. The queries are only made for holders of normal passports (requirements for diplomatic or service passports and other travel documents, including identity cards, non-citizens passports, merchant seamen, etc. are disregarded)

b. Complex requirements regarding passports (such as translations or empty pages) are disregarded, i.e. as if such requirements do not exist

c. Requirements by the destination country/territory regarding a particular length of validity of passports are disregarded, i.e. it is assumed that all that is required is a valid passport at the time of entry

d. Countries with restrictions on female travelers are disregarded, i.e. as if such restrictions do not exist

e. Any health requirements, requirements of sufficient funds or return tickets are disregarded, i.e. as if such restrictions do not exist

f. Advance passenger information and advance approval to board are not considered to be a visa requirement or travel restriction, neither is the requirement to pay airport tax at arrival or embarkation, and these are therefore disregarded, i.e. as if such requirements do not exist

g. Queries are made based on direct travel to destination only (i.e. excluding transit points)

4. If no visa is required for passport holders from a country/territory for which the score is to be determined to enter the destination under the above conditions, then a score (value = 1) is made for the passport holder's country/territory

After all queries have been made, the total score for each country/territory is equal to the number of destination countries/territories for which the outcome is "no visa required" under the conditions defined herein

Henley & Partners Visa Restriction Index – Global Ranking 2016

Rank	Citizenship/Passport	Score	Rank	Citizenship/Passport	Score
1	Germany	177	15	Poland	161
2	Sweden	176	16	Monaco	160
3	Finland	175	17	Cyprus	159
	France		18	San Marino	156
	Italy		19	Chile	155
	Spain		20	Hong Kong (SAR China)	154
	United Kingdom		21	Brazil	153
4	Belgium	174		Bulgaria	
	Denmark			Romania	
	Netherlands		22	Andorra	152
	United States			Argentina	
5	Austria	173	23	Brunei Darussalam	151
	Japan		24	Croatia	149
	Singapore		25	Israel	147
6	Canada	172	26	Barbados	141
	Ireland (Republic of)		27	Bahamas	140
	Korea (Republic of, South)		28	Mexico	139
	Luxembourg		29	Uruguay	137
	Norway			Taiwan	
	Portugal		30	Antigua and Barbuda	134
	Switzerland			Vatican City	
7	Greece New Zealand	171	31	Seychelles	133
8	Australia	169	32	St. Kitts and Nevis	132
9	Malta	168		Venezuela	
10	Hungary	167	33	Costa Rica	131
	Czech Republic		34	Trinidad and Tobago	130
	Iceland		35	Mauritius	128
11	Slovakia	165	36	Panama	127
12	Liechtenstein	164	37	Paraguay	125
	Malaysia			St. Lucia	
	Slovenia			St. Vincent and the Grenadines	
13	Latvia	163	38	United Arab Emirates	122
14	Estonia	162	39	Grenada	121
	Lithuania		40	Macao (SAR China)	120

Rank	Citizenship/Passport	Score
41	Dominica	119
	Honduras	
42	Guatemala	116
43	El Salvador	115
	Serbia	
44	Samoa	112
45	Macedonia (FYROM)	111
46	Nicaragua	110
	Tonga	
	Vanuatu	
47	Montenegro	107
48	Russian Federation	105
49	Palau	104
50	Colombia	103
51	Turkey	102
52	Bosnia Herzegovina	101
	Moldova	
53	Albania	98
54	South Africa	97
55	Belize	94
56	Peru	86
	Solomon Islands	
57	Guyana	82
	Kuwait	
	Timor-Leste	
	Tuvalu	
58	Ecuador	81
	Fiji	
	Ukraine	
59	Maldives	80
	Nauru	
60	Kiribati	79
	Marshall Islands	
	Qatar	
61	Jamaica	78
62	Papua New Guinea	77

Rank	Citizenship/Passport	Score
63	Micronesia (Federated States of)	75
64	Suriname	74
65	Bahrain	73
66	Bolivia	72
	Botswana	
67	Oman	71
	Thailand	
68	Namibia	70
69	Lesotho	69
	Saudi Arabia	
70	Kenya	68
71	Belarus	67
72	Tanzania	65
	Gambia	
	Georgia	
	Kazakhstan	
	Malawi	
	Swaziland	
	Tunisia	
73	Ghana	64
74	Zambia	63
75	Azerbaijan	62
76	Cape Verde	61
	Philippines	
77	Uganda	60
78	Benin	59
	Cuba	
	Morocco	
	Zimbabwe	
79	Indonesia	58
	Kyrgyzstan	
80	Armenia	57
81	Burkina Faso	56
	Cote d'Ivoire	
	Mongolia	

Rank	Citizenship/Passport	Score
82	Mauritania	55
	Niger	
	Senegal	
	Togo	
83	Dominican Republic Sao Tome and Principe	54
84	Tajikistan	53
85	India	52
	Mali	
	Uzbekistan	
86	Bhutan	51
	Guinea-Bissau	
	Mozambique	
	Sierra Leone	
87	Cambodia	50
	China	
88	Chad	49
	Egypt	
88	Gabon	49
	Turkmenistan	
89	Algeria	48
	Central African Republic	
	Haiti	
	Madagascar	
	Rwanda	
90	Comoros	47
	Jordan	
	Laos	
	Vietnam	
91	Guinea	46
92	Angola	45
	Cameroon	
	Equatorial Guinea	
	Nigeria	

Rank	Citizenship/Passport	Score
93	Congo (Republic of)	44
	Djibouti	
94	Liberia	43
95	Burundi	42
	Korea (Democratic People's Republic of, North)	
	Myanmar	
96	Bangladesh	39
	Congo (Democratic Republic of)	
	Lebanon	
	Sri Lanka	
97	Kosovo	38
	South Sudan	
	Yemen	
98	Eritrea	37
	Ethiopia	
	Iran	
	Nepal	
	Palestinian Territory	
	Sudan	
99	Libya	36
100	Syria	32
101	Somalia	31
102	Iraq	30
103	Pakistan	29
104	Afghanistan	25

Underlying assumptions

The *Henley & Partners Visa Restrictions Index* was created with visa regulations effective on 1 January 2016, including any temporary visa regulations applicable on that date. The Index contains the following assumptions:

- All passports evaluated are assumed to be biometric (ICAO 9303 compliant)

- There are 219 destination countries (territories) in total. The maximum attainable score is 218 (points are not assigned for a national traveling to their own country)

- The number of nationalities (passports) evaluated is 199. These are:
  - The 193 member states of the United Nations
  - Taiwan
  - Kosovo
  - Palestinian Territory
  - Vatican City
  - Hong Kong (SAR China)
  - Macao (SAR China)

- E-visas are treated in the same way as visas on arrival. Where the conditions for obtaining an e-visa are straightforward (fee, return ticket, hotel reservation), a point was assigned. Where there are additional conditions (e.g. invitation letter, consular approval), a point was not assigned

- Countries that do not enforce their own visa restrictions are considered as a nationality, but not as a destination:
  - Andorra
  - Liechtenstein
  - Monaco
  - Palestinian Territory
  - San Marino
  - Vatican City

- Countries that enforce their own visa restrictions but issue passports under the authority of a governing country are considered as a destination, but not as a nationality:
  - Aruba
  - Anguilla
  - Bermuda
  - Bonaire, St. Eustatius and Saba
  - Cayman Islands
  - Curacao
  - Cook Islands
  - Falkland Islands
  - French Guiana
  - French Polynesia
  - French West Indies
  - Gibraltar
  - Guam
  - Mayotte
  - Montserrat
  - New Caledonia
  - Niue
  - Norfolk Island
  - Northern Mariana Islands
  - Puerto Rico
  - Reunion
  - Samoa (American)
  - St. Maarten
  - Turks and Caicos Islands
  - Virgin Islands (British)
  - Virgin Islands (US)

9

Quality of Nationality Index

Chapter Summary

A new index unveiled in Zurich on 2 June 2016 is the first to ever objectively rank the quality of nationalities worldwide. *The Henley & Partners – Kochenov Quality of Nationality Index* (QNI) explores both internal factors (such as the scale of the economy, human development, and peace and stability) and external factors (including visa-free travel and the ability to settle and work abroad without cumbersome formalities) that make one nationality better than another in terms of legal status in which to develop one's talents and business.

Based on the above factors and using a new method of assessment for external value of nationalities to take into account both diversity and weight of accessible countries, the QNI ranks nationalities of states, regions, blocs and international organizations into four categories: very high quality, high quality, medium quality, and low quality nationalities. This new method allows for a realistic assessment of the value of nationalities rather than merely counting destinations to which citizens of individual states might have visa-free access to.

The QNI provides valuable expert commentaries on nationalities of different states, blocs and regions, as well as on the concept of acquisition of citizenship by investment as effectively applied by a number of states. Citizenship of the EU is particularly interesting one as it provides a wide range of rights to citizens of all member states. Furthermore, the EU nationalities derive particular value from their unmatched settlement freedom, thereby boosting the continent's overall value. Finally, the analysis of the concept of citizenship-by-investment in the light of the QNI ranking of states is particularly important. Such analysis does not only point to programs offered by states, but also gives indications as to what might be the "best value for money" for those who decide to undergo the procedure.

9.1   Introduction

Various indexes measuring quality of life in different countries are now made available by many different sources. These take into account a number of indicators which make life more desirable in some countries than in others – income, jobs, education, health, safety, and work-life balance, to name a few.

However, unlike what has been seen so far, a new index, entitled *The Henley & Partners – Kochenov Quality of Nationality Index* (QNI), has been most recently released by Ideos Publications.[47] The QNI largely contributes to the existing citizenship literature by being the first index to objectively rank the quality of nationalities worldwide. In particular, the QNI ranks nationalities – the legal statuses of attachment to states – rather than states *per se*, taking into account the increase in world migration flows as well as the lack of a correlation between the nationality held by a growing number of active individuals and the countries where their businesses are established and their lives are lived.

This chapter summarises some of the most important and interesting findings of the QNI.

Why is the QNI important?

The QNI uses an array of objective sources to present the opportunities and limitations that each nationality gives its owners – the World Bank, the International Air Transport Association, the Institute for Economics and Peace, to name a few, blends into a transparent measurement tool that divides world nationalities of the world into tiers based on quality, giving a clear picture of the standing of each nationality at a glance. As noted by Dr. Christian Kälin, a leading specialist on international immigration and citizenship law and policy, and Chairman of Henley & Partners, "What makes the QNI so unique is that for the first time ever … the internal and external values of each nationality [have been

---

[47]   *The Henley & Partners – Kochenov Quality of Nationality Index*, edited by Dimitry Kochenov (Ideos, New York/London/Zurich/Hong Kong 2016), unveiled in Zurich on 2 June 2016

combined] to create a true perspective of our globalized world."[48] As for the practical use of the QNI, Kälin further emphasizes that it "is relevant to both individuals interested in the mobility, the possibilities and the limitations of their nationality, and governments focused on improving the local, regional and global opportunities inherent in their passports."[49] In particular, "The QNI is a vital resource for financially independent individuals who wish to acquire the benefits of dual citizenship, as it provides assistance in selecting the most valuable second nationality for themselves and their families."[50] Kochenov, a leading constitutional law professor with a long-standing interest in European and comparative citizenship law, and the editor of the QNI, is clear about this: "Just as with the states, the nationalities themselves differ too. Importantly, there is no direct correlation between the power of the state and the quality of its nationality. Nationality plays a significant part in determining our opportunities and aspirations, and the QNI allows us, for the first time, to analyze this objectively."[51]

Content and structure

The QNI consists of three parts, the first of which describes the methodology used and the use of both internal and external factors. In other words, the QNI measures both the internal value of nationality, which refers to the quality of life within a nationality's country of origin, and the external value of nationality, which identifies the diversity and quality of opportunities that nationalities allow us to pursue outside our countries of origin.

The second part of the QNI, which is divided into four equally important sections, discusses quality of world nationalities (2011–2015), comparing regions and trends in travel freedom, providing general statistics and values for quality of nationalities of individual states, and analyzing

---

[48] Washington Examiner, 2 June 2016 '*U.S. ranks 28th in world "quality" index, behind Greece, Poland*'

[49] Statement available at: *www.henleyglobal.com/press-articles-details/first-global-index-to-rank-quality-of-nationalities/*

[50] Ibid.

[51] Ibid.

nationalities of states belonging to different regions and member states of different international organizations and blocs.

The third and final part of the QNI is dedicated to expert analysis of a number of citizenships including the US citizenship, EU citizenship, citizenships of the Commonwealth of Independent States Region, citizenships of South America, citizenships of the Gulf Cooperation Council states, citizenships of the Pacific Region states, citizenships of China and India, citizenship of Georgia, as well as to the legal status of "non-citizens" of Latvia and to the concept of acquisition of citizenship by investment in general.

Ranking quality of nationalities: relevant internal and external factors

Internal value relates to the practical value of a legal status for all nationals of a particular state or territory, including those who "stay at home" all of their lives. Such value, which comprises 40% of the score, is calculated on the basis of three sub-elements:

- The economic strength of the country granting nationality, measured by Gross Domestic Product (GDP): 15%

- The scale of human development, as expressed by the United Nations Human Development Index (HDI): 15%

- The level of peace and stability, according to the Global Peace Index (GPI): 10%

The external value of nationalities, which accounts for 60% of the ranking score, represents the extent to which holders of a particular nationality can genuinely enjoy the benefits of a globalized world and an increasingly transnational life. To calculate the external value of each nationality, the QNI takes into account four sub-elements:

- The diversity of settlement freedom, which considers the number of "full access" countries, i.e. countries where the holders of a given nationality can work, live and settle freely with either no or merely minimal formalities: 15%

- The weight of settlement freedom, which measures the aggregate value of the full access countries based on their economic strength and level of human development: 15%

- The diversity of travel freedom, which measures the extent to which holders of a particular nationality can freely travel without extensive administrative hassles and time-consuming preparation: 15%

- The weight of travel freedom, which measures the actual quality of the countries and territories, which a particular nationality allows to be visited visa-free or with a visa on arrival: 15%

Based on the above internal and external factors, the QNI offers four rankings that measure various combinations of the sub-elements:

- QNI General Ranking, which comprises all seven sub-elements described above

- External Value of Nationality Ranking, based on the four sub-elements measuring external value of nationalities

- Settlement Freedom Ranking, which measures the diversity and weight of settlement freedom specifically

- Travel Freedom Ranking, which is concerned with the diversity and weight of travel freedom

All in all, the four QNI rankings give a comprehensive indication of the value, constraints and freedom of having a particular nationality.

9.2   QNI General Ranking

The QNI General Ranking comprises internal value (40%) and external value (60%) of nationality. Based on the above internal and external factors, the resulting QNI General Ranking presents all nationalities on a 0% to 100% scale.

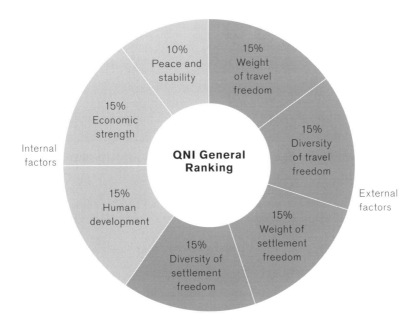

Moreover, nationalities are categorized in four tiers:

- *Very high quality* – nationalities with a value of 50.0% and above

- *High quality* – nationalities with a value of between 35.0% and 49.9%

- *Medium quality* – nationalities with a value of between 20.0% and 34.9%

- *Low quality* – nationalities with a value of 19.9% and less

In 2015, 42 nationalities had a very high quality (above 50.0%). Nationalities of all the EU member states (apart from that of non-citizens of Latvia) and EEA countries, as well as Switzerland, are categorized under the first group, with the German nationality at the top of the list with a score of 83.1%. Other nationalities belonging to this group include: the EU nationality itself;[52] the US; Japan; New Zealand; Canada; Australia; Chile; Singapore; Republic of Korea; and Argentina.

---

[52]   See Kochenov's expert commentary later in this chapter

Furthermore, 30 nationalities scored a high quality, 93 nationalities were in the medium quality tier, and 21 nationalities had a low quality, with the nationality of the Democratic Republic of Congo sitting at the bottom of the index on 14.3%.

Unlike nationalities of EU member states, values of nationalities of states of regional and international organizations differ. Thus, the quality of G20 nationalities, which consists of the 20 most important economies in the world, varies tremendously, from top 10 nationalities such as Germany and France, to medium scoring nationalities below 30% like India and Indonesia. Members of the OECD are all developed countries. Apart from Liechtenstein, the entire top 20 of the QNI General Ranking are also members of the OECD. In comparison to the other OECD members, Israeli, Mexican and Turkish nationalities have particularly low value. Comparable is the value of nationalities of NATO Members. Apart from Turkish and Albanian nationalities, and the Latvian non-citizen status, all NATO nationalities are in the very high quality tier of the QNI. Somewhat in contrast stands the value of BRICS nationalities which is below average. Not a single one of them is of very high quality in QNI terms, in spite of the significant influence of the members of this association on regional and global developments – both political and economic. Nationalities of countries affiliated to other associations have also different values: CIS nationalities are in the medium quality tier of the QNI, with Russia standing out in the lower range of the high quality tier; MERCOSUR countries are in the high to very high quality tier of the QNI; ECOWAS nationalities are in the medium quality tier of the QNI; ASEAN nationalities vary widely in quality, ranging from very high to low quality nationalities; nationalities of the Arab League are predominantly in the medium to low quality tiers of the QNI with the Gulf Cooperation Council nationalities, which have a high to medium quality of nationality, clearly standing out in quality.

As far as regions are concerned, the quality of European nationalities far exceeds the global average. Most prominent are the nationalities of the EU member states. Passport holders of any of the EU member states enjoy an unprecedented external value of nationality. The non-EU European nationalities have considerably lower external value, which is directly visible in their overall values. The nationalities of North America remain fairly stable and follow the EU member states in the very high quality tier of the QNI. The nationalities of Central America and the Caribbean are invariably in the medium to high quality tiers of the QNI. There exist quite substantial differences between the top-ranked nationalities of the region, which are in the top 60 of the QNI General Ranking, and the less valued nationalities, falling outside the top 100. Among the South American nationalities, full members of MERCOSUR outperform other nationalities of the continent as a result of their higher level of economic integration and stronger economic development. The Middle East and North Africa largely consist of medium to low valued nationalities. The Sub-Saharan African nationalities on average have the second to lowest value just above South Asia. The Asian and Pacific regions sit quite far below the global mean. However, Asian nationalities occupy positions in the entire spectrum of the QNI, from the very high quality tier to the low quality tier, while the majority of Asian nationalities have a medium quality.

9.3   The External Value of Nationality Ranking

The External Value of Nationality Ranking is based on the all sub-elements related to external value of nationality. This ranking reflects the degree to which each nationality grants its holders global possibilities and opportunities, taking equally into account both the diversity and weight of travel freedom and those of settlement freedom. On each sub-element, the highest scoring nationality on the respective index is attributed a full score of 25%, the other nationalities receive a proportionate score.

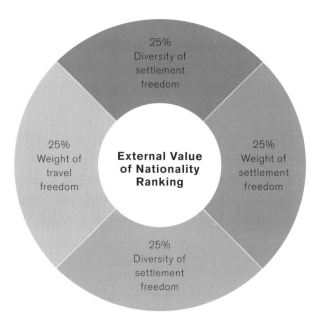

The normalized scores for the External Value of Nationality Ranking are calculated using the same principles as the QNI General Ranking – only the weights attributed to the sub-elements differ so that each ranking is based on a 0%–100% scale. On each sub-element, the highest scoring nationality on the respective index is attributed a full score of 25%, the other nationalities receive a proportionate score.

As with the QNI General Ranking, the EU and EEA member states, as well as Switzerland, are on the top of the External Value of Nationality Ranking list. The above countries with lowest value nationality in terms of the QNI General Ranking are also listed towards the bottom of the External Value of Nationality Ranking with a highest value of Mozambique (11.3%) and lowest value of Afghanistan (6%).

9.4 Settlement Freedom Ranking

The Settlement Freedom Ranking specifically focuses on the global opportunities and life chances nationalities can provide – reflecting individual freedom beyond borders. For that purpose, the Settlement Freedom Ranking is composed of the diversity and weight of settlement freedom of nationalities. The Settlement Freedom Ranking is based on a scale from 0% to 100%. Diversity and weight are valued equally:

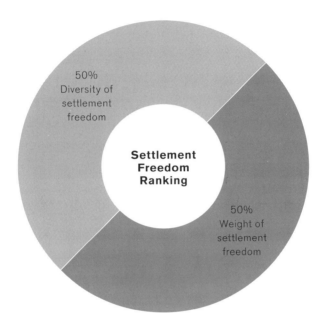

The EU and EEA member states, as well as Switzerland, are on the top of the Settlement Freedom Ranking list with four nationalities having the highest value of 100%: Slovakia; Latvia; Liechtenstein; and Hungary. Croatian nationality has the lowest value (52.3%) compared to other nationalities of this group. On the very bottom of the ranking list are over 100 nationalities with no Settlement Freedom possibilities (i.e. value of Settlement Freedom = 0%).

9.5 Travel Freedom Ranking

The Travel Freedom Ranking is based on both the diversity and weight of travel freedom, and describes one's freedom to look beyond national borders and experience the world. By taking into account both diversity and weight, the Travel Freedom Ranking intends to combine the quantity and quality of travel destinations as accurately as possible. Diversity and weight are valued equally:

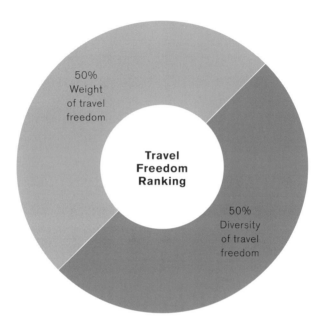

The nationality with the highest value in terms of Travel Freedom Ranking is that of Singapore (98.2%), followed by the nationality of Japan (98.1%), while the nationality with the lowest value in this respect is that of Afghanistan (11.9%). Among the nationalities of EU member states, the one of Finland has the highest value (96.9%), while the nationality of Croatia has a lowest value (74.2%). On the bottom of the Travel Freedom Ranking list is the nationality of Afghanistan (11.9%).

9.6   Expert commentaries

As noted in the introductory part of this chapter, the third and final part of the QNI is dedicated to expert analysis of a number of citizenships enumerated above, as well as to the concept of citizenship-by-investment in general. For the purposes of this chapter most of two expert commentaries have been presented: a) the expert commentary on the citizenship of the European Union;[53] and b) the expert commentary on the citizenship-by-investment concept and its application.[54] The first commentary has been chosen given the specificity of EU citizenship and the opportunities it gives to the citizens of each EU member state to move and settle freely on the territory of other member states. The second commentary has been chosen due to the increased importance and widespread of the concept of acquisition of citizenship through investment, and also because, in the light of the QNI ranking of nationalities, such analysis gives valuable information to all those who might be interested in acquiring citizenship through the existing programs of different states.

Citizenship of the European Union

Although the EU is not a state, it boasts a citizenship like many others, established more than 20 years ago by the Treaty of Maastricht. This citizenship allows the Union to distinguish between "European citizens" and foreigners, called "third-country nationals" in contemporary Eurospeak. By law, every national of each of the EU's 28 member states is also a citizen of the Union. EU citizens enjoy an array of important rights, including residence, work and non-discrimination, in the territory of the Union, as well as some political rights, including in European Parliament elections and municipal elections. As the biggest economy in the world and boasting very high levels of human development, the EU can legitimately be expected to be the site of one of the best nationalities in the world – and it is. EU citizenship has steadily occupied one of the leading places among the nationalities of very high quality in the QNI ranking, placed just above US citizenship and thus also above those of Australia, Canada and Japan. Indeed, should the individual EU nationalities be excluded from the QNI, EU citizenship would then end up in the top five, right under Norway, Iceland, Switzerland and Liechtenstein and just above the US, steadily occupying the 5th or 6th place in the world.

---

[53] Expert commentary of Dimitry Kochenov
[54] Expert commentary of Dr. Christian H Kälin

European Union

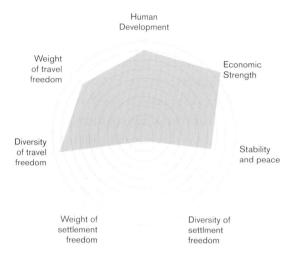

EU citizenship is a legal construct mostly for the internal consumption within the EU. The only exception from this rule is the right which EU citizens enjoy outside the EU to receive protection and services from the consulates of any EU member state in the countries where their own Union member state of nationality is not represented. Yet, since the classical legal orthodoxy connects nationalities with states recognized as such by the international community, all EU citizens become nationals, uniquely, of their particular states as they travel. This allows foreign countries to treat EU citizens holding the nationalities of different member states differently. In one example, while the absolute majority of EU citizens can travel to the US visa-free, EU citizens whose Union status derives from the nationalities of Bulgaria, Croatia, Cyprus, Poland, Romania do not enjoy this possibility. To reflect this reality, the QNI looks at the average values of the weight and diversity of travel freedom enjoyed by all the nationalities of the EU to come up with the figure for the nationality of the Union. This explains why EU nationality actually occupies a lower place on the QNI rankings than the nationalities of many of the individual member states of the Union, such as German, Estonian and Finnish, for instance.

All in all, the QNI makes it absolutely clear that the quality of EU and US nationalities has consistently remained at a relatively similar, very high level. Importantly, while being attached to extremely important economies, both nationalities enjoy a high level of preferential treatment around the world through asymmetrical travel access for short term tourist and business travel: just like Americans, Europeans are not required to obtain visas in advance to visit the absolute majority of the countries in the world, even if here some discrepancies exist between the two nationalities: US citizens need visas to travel to Iran and Brazil, for instance, while these destinations are visa-free for the Europeans. The EU and the US are similar in that plenty of countries around the world whose own citizens cannot visit the US or the Schengen area without a visa do not apply reciprocity to EU and US citizens, reflecting the power balance in the contemporary world.

Citizenship-by-Investment

The acquisition of citizenship-by-investment is an accelerating global trend. Rather than through lengthy stays of residence, language tests and other requirements that are typically part of naturalization procedures, countries increasingly offer foreign individuals the option to become citizens if they make a significant direct investment in the country. A few countries have permitted citizenship-by-investment for many years, including Austria and St. Kitts and Nevis, and in recent years more and more countries have started to introduce such options. The following chart looks at how such countries are positioned in the QNI.

Malta

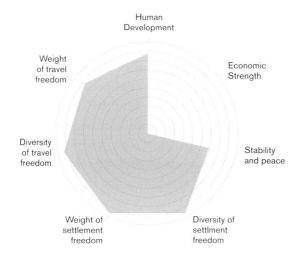

St. Kitts and Nevis

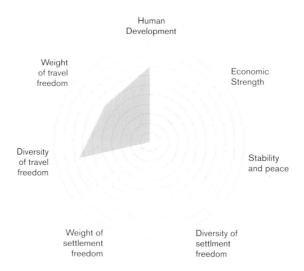

As expected, the European countries – Austria, Cyprus and Malta – come out very high, both in the overall ranking as well as in the very relevant Settlement Freedom Ranking. In every year, Austria is in the top 10 countries, while all three are in the top 10 in the Settlement Freedom ranking. This is no surprise as EU citizenship, as noted above, is exceptionally strong. Accordingly, these three countries also ask the highest price: in Austria, no specific amount is set in law or by regulation, but current practice requires several million Euros in the form of a donation for public purposes or investments that create employment. Malta requires a donation to its National Development and Social Fund of at least EUR 650,000, plus investments in government bonds of EUR 150,000 and real estate of EUR 350,000 or the rental of an equivalent property for at least five years. The least expensive option in Europe is currently Cyprus, which requires a recoverable real estate investment of EUR 2.5 million.

There are now five Caribbean countries which run citizenship-by-investment programs: Antigua and Barbuda, Dominica, Grenada, St. Lucia and St. Kitts and Nevis. They are all part of the Caribbean Community (CARICOM), which provides conditional freedom of movement.[55] This is why the individual CARICOM countries relevant here are ranked much lower in the Settlement Freedom category.

On the QNI General Ranking, the Caribbean countries are well positioned: Antigua and Barbuda ranked high at 58th (38%), just above St. Kitts and Nevis, also ranked high at 59th position (37.7%), and both well above St. Lucia (30.3%), Grenada (29.8%) and Dominica (29.3%), all ranked in the medium band at 86th, 91st and 93rd respectively. Panama, which does not have a citizenship-by-investment program but a residence program that comes with a non-citizens passport, ranks high and comes in just above Antigua and Barbuda in 57th place. A Caribbean passport can be acquired through contributions to national development funds or the treasury (ranging from USD 100,000 to USD 250,000 for a single applicant, more if dependents are included) or through real estate

---

[55] As a CARICOM citizen, you also need a skills certificate together with your passport to avail yourself of the freedom of movement. Nationality alone does not qualify

acquisition (starting at USD 300,000) and is thus one of the best options in the world in terms of "value for money".

Other countries with citizenship-by-investment provisions in their law, such as the Comoros (19.5%), Montenegro (34,6%) and Seychelles (38.3%), are spread across the QNI. In the Comoros you can acquire economic citizenship (with some limitations to the ordinary citizenship) for as little as USD 45,000, making this currently the cheapest nationality in the world that you can officially acquire through investment. Montenegro and Seychelles both have provisions in the law but are very restrictive in its application, although Montenegro has indicated that it wishes to expand its program. As a country on the path to NATO and EU membership, and already quite well positioned in the 2015 QNI, Montenegro has the highest potential of improvement of all citizenship-by-investment countries: once Montenegro joins the EU, it will catapult its position to the top tier alongside other EU countries.

9.7 Concluding remarks

Nationalities diverge strongly in their practical value – and this value is not always reflected in basic characteristics like economic strength or the level of development of the countries with which such nationalities are associated. Economically strong countries can have relatively unattractive nationalities, and micro-states can offer nationalities of great value. It is not a secret that our nationalities have a direct impact on our lifestyles, freedom to think independently, do business, and live longer, healthier, and more rewarding lives. While the extremes are well-known – a child in Somalia or the Democratic Republic of Congo is 50 times more likely not to survive the first five years of life than a child in Japan or Finland; or Liberians and North Koreans are infinitely less likely to experience Paris, New York or Moscow than, say, Singaporeans and Argentineans – a single source that ranks the worth of nationalities was missing. The QNI provides that single source. Being updated annually, it is a source of a dynamic understanding of the quality of world nationalities measured based on a set of clear and transparent criteria.

PART III

The World's Premier Residence Options

10

Overview of
Residence Options

Eighteen countries make our list of the world's premier residence options: Australia, Austria, Belgium, Canada, Guernsey, Hong Kong, Jersey, Malaysia, Malta, Monaco, New Zealand, Portugal, Singapore, Switzerland, Thailand, the UAE/Dubai, the UK and the US. All of these countries are open to foreign nationals and offer residence or citizenship options and are reviewed in the following chapters on how easy it is to attain those, and other key criteria. Of course there are other countries and territories that are of interest to entrepreneurs and wealthy clients in terms of residence and citizenship planning, however if you weigh in all criteria which are really relevant, you end up with just a handful of what we describe as the premier residence options.

All these countries are attractive and viable, but of course vary within those parameters. Some may offer a wonderful and safe way of life for families and children, but it may be difficult to become a citizen; while others may be very easy to settle in, but then demand onerous numbers of days in the country to meet residence requirements.

Taxation will always be a key factor, and is one of the most widely varying criteria, not only in terms of tax rates but also in terms of reporting and planning requirements.

Each of these options will appeal more or less depending on your personal situation. There is no such thing as the perfect location, just the one that suits you, your family, and business and personal requirements best. Your long term aims and needs are very relevant, particularly if you desire to take up a new citizenship either now or in the future.

OVERVIEW OF RESIDENCE OPTIONS

	Australia	Austria
Visa type	Investor Stream	Private Residence
Time frame	6-8 months	5-12 months
Requirements	Under the age of 55 years, net assets of AUD 2.25 million, meet the points test pass mark; have at least 3 years' experience of direct involvement in eligible investment	Proof of financial funds to finance daily life without working income; health insurance; accommodation in Austria; clean criminal record
Minimum investment	AUD 1.5 million	None
Taxation	Progressive tax rates on worldwide income of up to 47%; corporate tax is a flat 30%	No wealth, net worth, gift or IHT tax; flat-rate income tax of 25% on most interest payments received from banks, on dividends received from shares and on most capital gains; other income subject to max. tax rate of 50%
Years to qualify for citizenship	5 years. One may apply for citizenship if during a 5 year period, permanent residence status was held for at least the 12 months immediately prior to the application. In addition, during the 4 years prior to submitting the application, one must not have been absent for more than 12 months in total	6-10 years residence
Language for citizenship	Yes	No
Permanent residence	Yes, after 4 years and subject to having lived in Australia for at least 2 years in the last 4 years	n/a
Other requirements	Applicants must pass the Australian Citizenship Test, which focuses on Australia's values, history, and traditional and national symbols	None
Dual citizenship	Yes	Only if via citizenship-by-investment

	Belgium	Canada
Visa type	Residence Permit	Start Up Visa
Time frame	1-3 months	6 months
Requirements	Employment by a Belgian company, self-employed or foreign executive employment	Minimum personal net worth CAD 1 million; business ownership experience or senior management position
Minimum investment	Investment in business set-up / minimum salary requirements per year may apply	CAD 350,000 or more, depending on the proposed venture
Taxation	Taxation on personal worldwide income; no tax on capital gains, no wealth/net worth tax, max. withholding tax of 25% on all interest payments, max. tax on dividend income for individuals 25%, 0-3% taxation of gifts, income subject to max. tax rate of 50% (plus additional community tax 0-8%)	Federal taxation on personal worldwide income in addition to provincial income tax, combined rates up to approx. 54%. No inheritance, wealth or gift tax, capital gains tax applies instead at point of transfer
Years to qualify for citizenship	5 years residence allows application for citizenship	4 years in the last 6
Language for citizenship	Yes, with exceptions	Yes
Permanent residence	Yes	PR Card with 5 years expiry, (min. 2 years out of 5 years residence to extend)
Other requirements	Several ties with Belgium	Physical presence required
Dual citizenship	Yes	Yes

	Guernsey	Hong Kong
Visa type	Investor Stream	Investment as Entrepreneurs
Time frame	2-8 weeks	4 weeks
Requirements	Minimum investment of GBP 1 million; make Guernsey your "Main Home"	A substantial contribution to the economy of the HKSAR, with other requirements including a business plan, business turnover, financial resources, investment sum, number of jobs created locally and introduction of new technology or skills
Minimum investment	GBP 1 million	No specified min.
Taxation	Basic rate of income tax is 20%; standard rate company of tax is 0%, although some financial services are taxed at 10%; no capital gains, inheritance or wealth taxes and no VAT	Territorial tax regime, income from outside HK not taxed if not remitted; max. tax rate for local source income is 17%
Years to qualify for citizenship	5 years, residence, of which max. 450 days out of the country and max 90 days out of the country in the 12 months preceding the application	7 years of ordinary residence
Language for citizenship	Yes	No
Permanent residence	Yes, after 5 years	Yes
Other requirements	Able to support yourself and your family financially. Spend more time there than elsewhere else	None
Dual citizenship	Yes	No

	Jersey	Malaysia
Visa type	2(1)e Category High Value Residence Scheme	My Second Home (MM2H)
Time frame	1 month	3-4 months
Requirements	Substantial net worth; min. annual tax payment of JEP 125,000	Applicants < 50 years' old: Proof of liquid assets of a minimum of MYR 500,000; and offshore monthly income of a minimum of MYR 10,000 Applicants of 50 years old and above: Proof of liquid assets of a minimum of MYR 350,000; and offshore monthly income of a minimum of MYR 10,000 (approx. USD 2,500)
Minimum investment	JEP 125,000 tax contribution paid annually	Applicants under the age of 50: Fixed deposit of MYR 300,000 Applicants of 50 years old and above: Fixed deposit of MYR 150,000
Taxation	Max. income tax rate of 20%, special provisions for 2 (1) e residents; no net wealth, capital gains or inheritance taxes	Territorial taxation system. Residents are only taxed on Malaysian sourced income and the progressive tax rate on chargeable income reaches a maximum of 25%
Years to qualify for citizenship	5-6 years	Not available
Language for citizenship	Yes	No
Permanent residence	Yes	No
Other requirements	None	Open a local bank account; obtain a medical report; purchase local medical insurance
Dual citizenship	Yes	No

	Malta	Monaco
Visa type	The Malta Residence and Visa Programme	Long stay private residence (for non-EEA nationals)
Time frame	6 months	6 weeks – 6 months
Requirements	Acquire property in Malta with one of the following criteria: purchase a property for minimum value EUR 320,000 if in Malta (or EUR 270,000 if the property is in the South of Malta or in Gozo), or rent a property for a minimum of EUR 12,000 annually (or EUR 10,000 if in the South of Malta or in Gozo); an investment in government bonds of EUR 250,000 to be retained for a minimum period of five years; a non-refundable government contribution of EUR 30,000; valid EU health insurance worth EUR 30,000	Proof of sufficient funds: confirmation by a local bank which will require a minimum balance to be deposited, employment or business setup; proof of accommodation; no criminal record
Minimum investment	Requirements as above	None
Taxation	Individuals who are resident but not domiciled in Malta pay tax on (a) income arising in Malta and (b) on income (excluding capital gains) remitted to Malta that arises outside the island (i.e. 'remittance basis')	No income or capital gains tax (for non-French residents), no inheritance tax in direct line, low rates in general
Years to qualify for citizenship	N/A	10 years but not easy to obtain
Language for citizenship	No	No
Permanent residence	Indefinite	Yes
Other requirements	None	None
Dual citizenship	Yes	No

	New Zealand	Portugal
Visa type	Investor Visa	Golden Residence Permit
Time frame	4-5 months	3-8 months
Requirements	Age limit of 65 years or younger, at least 3 years business experience, English speaking background or competent user of English, health and character test	Capital investment of EUR 1,000,000 in specified options, or of EUR 500,000 in SMEs, or of EUR 350,000 in national scientific and technological research, or EUR 250,000 in national cultural heritage
		Property acquisition of a minimum of EUR 500,000, or of EUR 350,000 for the refurbishment of properties older than 30 years or in specific areas
		Business investment leading to the creation of a minimum of 10 new jobs
Minimum investment	NZD 1.5 million	EUR 250,000 investment; or EUR 350,000 real estate, or creation of 10 new jobs
Taxation	Progressive tax rates on worldwide income of up to 33%; Corporate tax is a flat 33%	Non-habitual resident scheme for professional categories at 20% on local income only, for a 10-year period. NHR scheme exempts income derived from a foreign source; no wealth or inheritance tax
Years to qualify for citizenship	5 years	6 years, residence
Language for citizenship	Yes	Yes
Permanent residence	Yes	Yes
Other requirements	Minimum physical presence of 146 days in each of the last 3 years	None
Dual citizenship	Yes	Yes

	Singapore	Switzerland
Visa type	Global Investor Program	Private residence (for non-EEA nationals)
Time frame	8-10 months	2-6 months
Requirements	At least three years of entrepreneurial experience and a track record of successful business practice. Investors must own at least 30% equity of a company (or collection of companies) which has a turnover of at least SGD 50 million per annum	Payment of a min. yearly flat-rate tax of at least CHF 250,000 – 500,000 (minimum amounts depend on the canton of residence and other factors)
Minimum investment	SGD 2.5 million	None
Taxation	Territorial tax system; income sourced outside Singapore is tax free, even if remitted to Singapore; no net wealth or capital gains tax; no inheritance or gift taxes	Flat-rate (*forfait*) tax available at minimum of CHF 250,000 – 500,000 per year regardless of worldwide income (min. tax depends on canton and other factors); not available in Zurich, Basel-Stadt, Basel-Landschaft, Schaffhausen or Appenzell Ausserrhoden
Years to qualify for citizenship	Minimum 2 years residence	Minimum 12 years, residence; between the ages of 10 and 20 the years count double
Language for citizenship	No	Yes
Permanent residence	Yes	Integration requirement
Other requirements	Set up a business in Singapore with 5 or more Singaporean employees and have incurred at least SGD 1 million in total business spend in a year	Integration requirement
Dual citizenship	No	Yes

	Thailand	UAE
Visa type	Investment Category	Residence Permit
Time frame	12 months	1-2 months after company set-up
Requirements	Have been granted a non-immigrant visa and permitted to stay in Thailand on the basis of 1 year visa extensions for a total of at least three consecutive years up to the date of the submission of the application; provide proof of investment both before and after permanent residence is granted	Ownership, partnership, investment or employment in a UAE company
Minimum investment	THB 10 million	None
Taxation	Income tax is levied on an individual's net assessable income at progressive rates up to a maximum of 35%	No income, property, capital gains or net worth taxes. No corporate income taxes for most businesses. A small % of income to social security
Years to qualify for citizenship	10 consecutive years holding permanent residence	Not available
Language for citizenship	Yes	No
Permanent residence	Yes	No
Other requirements	Investment must be made into a limited or public company, state-issued security, state enterprise's security or the stock market	None
Dual citizenship	No	No

	UK	US
Visa type	Tier 1 (Investor) Visa	EB-5 Green Card
Time frame	1-2 months	12 – 24 months
Requirements	Min. investment of GBP 2 million for 5 years, GBP 5 million for 3 years, or GBP 10 million for 2 years in UK government bonds, share capital or loan capital in UK companies	Minimum investment of USD 500,000 in a pre-approved "regional center" in a targeted employment area, or the individual can invest a minimum amount of USD 1 million in a new business
Minimum investment	GBP 2 million	USD 500,000 – USD 1 million
Taxation	The tax system is immigration-friendly. Currently, as a 'Non Dom', only income arising in the UK or remitted to the UK is taxable. After 7 years charges will apply depending on time spent in the UK	Taxed on their worldwide income, taxes are levied at both federal and state level
Years to qualify for citizenship	5 years residence, during which max. 450 days out of the country including max 90 days out of the country in the 12 months preceding the application	5 years 'continuous' residence; 30 months physical residence
Language for citizenship	Yes	Yes
Permanent residence	Can be achieved within 2 years with 50% residence time (GBP 10 million option)	Green Card
Other requirements	Life in the UK test	Civics test
Dual citizenship	Yes	Yes

10.1   The Global Residence Program Index

The *Global Residence Program Index* (GRPI) 2016 gauges and reflects the relative worth of residence programs around the world through a benchmarking process. It analyzes a broad range of factors such as immigration law, tax, and quality of living, as well as transparency, risk and compliance issues, from multiple sources to produce an overall global view and ranking of the different investment migration programs.

The programs are ranked according to 10 indicators: Reputation, Quality of Life, Tax, Visa Free Access, Processing Time and Quality of Processing, Compliance, Investment Requirements, Total Costs, Time to Citizenship, and Citizenship Requirements.

Out of the 19 residence programs reviewed, Portugal's Golden Residence Permit Program has again emerged as the world's best residence-by-investment program, with a score of 80 out of 100. It is followed by Belgium (78) and Austria (77) in 2nd and 3rd places respectively.

Portugal offers a high quality of life and education, rich culture, mild climate and a high level of security. It has an excellent real estate offering, whether for lifestyle or investment, with a large geographic, environment and price-point diversity, and individuals may combine the mandatory qualifying stay with longer visits to Portugal, as either a second or holiday home, or as a permanent, safe place to reside or retire.

The tax burden on residents of Portugal is one of the lowest in the GRPI, both on corporate and personal levels. A Portuguese residence permit offers visa-free access to the Schengen area. Portugal also has extremely strict procedures and all individuals are carefully screened before their applications are approved.

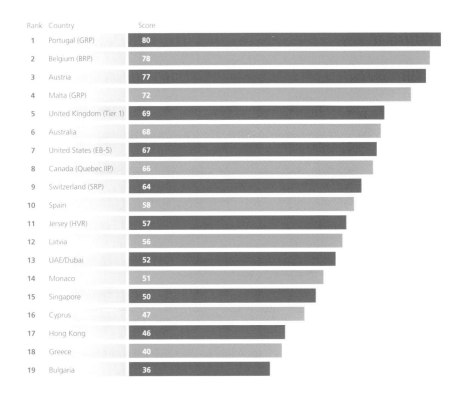

Rank	Country	Score
1	Portugal (GRP)	80
2	Belgium (BRP)	78
3	Austria	77
4	Malta (GRP)	72
5	United Kingdom (Tier 1)	69
6	Australia	68
7	United States (EB-5)	67
8	Canada (Quebec IIP)	66
9	Switzerland (SRP)	64
10	Spain	58
11	Jersey (HVR)	57
12	Latvia	56
13	UAE/Dubai	52
14	Monaco	51
15	Singapore	50
16	Cyprus	47
17	Hong Kong	46
18	Greece	40
19	Bulgaria	36

11
Australia

Australia is both a country and a continent, surrounded by the Indian and Pacific oceans. It comprises the mainland of the Australian continent, the island of Tasmania, and numerous smaller islands. It is the world's sixth largest country by total area. Its capital, Canberra, is inland, in contrast to all other major cities, such as Sydney, Brisbane, Melbourne, Perth and Adelaide which are all coastal.

Australia is highly developed and is one of the wealthiest countries in the world, with the world's 12th largest economy. It had the 5th highest per capita income in the world in 2014, and its military expenditure is 13th largest.

Australia ranks highly in many international studies and reports, for example in quality of life, health, education, economic freedom, and the protection of civil liberties and political rights. It is a member of the United Nations, G20, Commonwealth of Nations, ANZUS, Organisation for Economic Cooperation and Development (OECD), World Trade Organization, Asia-Pacific Economic Cooperation, and the Pacific Islands Forum.

Australia's immigration system is governed primarily by the Migration Act 1958 and Migration Regulations 1994. The immigration legislation is one of the most extensive and complex frameworks in Australian law.

All foreign nationals must hold a visa prior to travelling to Australia. Only New Zealand citizens can automatically obtain a visa on entry.

There are two types of migration for non-Australian citizens; temporary and permanent. Temporary resident visas allow non-Australian citizens to remain in Australia for a specified duration for purposes that may include tourism, visiting family, study, work and medical treatment. Many temporary visas provide a pathway to permanent residence eligibility.

Within the temporary and permanent residence programs, there are roughly 120 visas known as "subclasses".

11.1   Residence in Australia

There are four main permanent residence programs:

- *Family permanent residence* – available to partners, dependent children and aged parents of Australian citizens or permanent residents
- *Skilled permanent residence* – available to people with certain qualifications, employment history, investor and / or entrepreneurial expertise
- *Special eligibility residence* – is available to former citizens and permanent residents, absorbed persons and people of distinguished talent
- *Humanitarian residence* – for refugees

11.2   Requirements

Visa applicants must meet certain criteria prescribed to the appropriate visa subclass. The criteria prescribed to a visa application will include either "at time of lodgment" requirements, "at time of decision" requirements or a combination of both. Visa applications may be refused if an applicant does not demonstrate that they meet the criteria at the correct time. All visa subclasses include the requirement to satisfy health, character and certain public interest criteria.

Permanent residents are required to spend at least two years in five, or demonstrate significant ties to Australia, in order to maintain their residence status.

Skilled – Independent

Independent skilled residence requires a visa application to identify a particular occupation they have qualifications and/or work experience in from Immigration's occupation list, and then obtain a formal independent skill assessment in that occupation. They must then satisfy a points test, which is based on age, English proficiency, level of qualifications and work experience. The individual then submits an Expression of Interest to Immigration. They may then be invited to apply for the visa, at which time, they would provide their supporting documentation to Immigration for assessment.

Skilled – Company sponsored

There are three levels to securing company-sponsored visas (temporary or permanent). The temporary work visa is known as a 457. The permanent residence company sponsored visa is a commonly known as ENS.

The company must be an Australian trading entity who has committed a certain percentage of expenditure towards training Australians. They then must nominate a skilled position from Immigration's occupation list that they wish the foreign national to fill. This position must meet certain salary, market salary rate and, in some cases, labor market testing. The individual must then demonstrate that they meet certain skill, English language, health and character requirements.

Skilled – Investment / Entrepreneurial

There are five main streams under this program:

- *Business Innovation Stream* – individuals must be less than 55 years of age, pass a points test, have a successful business career with a business turnover of at least AUD 500,000 and net assets of AUD 800,000. They must obtain and maintain substantial ownership and management of an Australian business

- *Investor Stream* – individuals must be less than 55 years of age, pass a points test, have three years' investment experience, make a designated investment of AUD 1.5 million into an Australian state or territory bond for four years and have net assets of AUD 2.25 million

- *Significant Investor Stream* – individuals must invest at least AUD 5 million into complying Australian investments for at least four years

The above temporary visas offer a direct pathway to permanent residence after four years, subject to meeting certain residence and investment/business turnover requirements.

- *Business Talent (Significant Business History Stream)* – this visa is for successful business people, under the age of 55 years old, who own or part-own a business with a turnover of at least AUD 3 million for at least two of the last four fiscal years. Individuals must pass a points test, have a successful business career and have net assets of AUD 1.5 million. They must make a substantial investment into a new or established business in Australia and take an active role in managing the business

- *Business Talent (Venture Capital Entrepreneur Stream)* – individuals must have sourced AUD 1 million in venture capital funding to fund the start-up or product commercialization of a high value business idea in Australia and must establish (or participate in) that business

The above two streams offer direct permanent residence and applicants must quickly become involved in the relevant business.

11.3   Procedures and time frame

The Australian visa application process is very structured and based on laws, regulations, policy and legislative instruments. In addition to visa application legislation, the Department of Immigration also has the power to cancel visas, conduct compliance/monitoring exercises, regulate the professional migration agent industry and allow for legal review of visa decisions.

Certain visa applications for people outside Australia must be assessed by an Immigration attaché at the closest Australian Embassy. Other visa applications will be assessed by an Immigration office in Australia. The Department of Immigration is moving towards electronic online lodgment for all temporary and permanent residence visa applications.

Application processing time frames differ significantly depending on the visa being applied for. The immigration department uses a priority processing tier; whereby visa applications which yield the greatest economic benefit to the country (skilled visas) will be assessed quicker than those with little economic benefit (family visas).

Immigration advertises their Service Standards online for application time frames which are regularly updated.

Australian visas are attached electronically to passports and physical visa labels are no longer placed into them. Australia has an online portal which allows individuals and employers to check the visa status (and any applicable work conditions) of a visa holder.

11.4   Taxation

The Australian financial/tax year runs from 1 July to 30 June for individuals and businesses.

Income tax

Individuals must apply for a Tax File Number (TFN) to be registered with the Australian Taxation Office (ATO) and lodge annual tax returns. In most cases, tax from wages/salaries is withheld throughout the year and is known as "pay as you go" (PAYG). Tax is charged on the income you receive, including from salary, wages, investments, and shares etc.

The amount of income tax payable is based on how much you earn and your residence status. Australian residents are taxed on income sourced from Australia and overseas, and are entitled to a tax-free threshold of AUD 18,200. Residents are taxed at a progressive rate, the highest margin being 45% for salaries over the top taxable income currently set at AUD 180,001. In most cases, residents are also required to pay a health care levy (Medicare Levy) which is currently 2% of taxable income.

Non-residents are subject to tax only on Australian-sourced taxable income, though the tax rates are higher. There are a series of tests to determine "Residence for tax purposes" status, the primary being the "183-day test".

Between 1 July 2014 – 30 June 2017, a Temporary Budget Repair Levy of 2% is payable on resident and non-resident incomes over AUD 180,000.[129]

---

[129]   *exfin.com/australian-tax-rates*

Capital Gains Tax (CGT)

CGT applies to any capital gain made on the disposal of any asset, with the exception of the family home. Net gains are treated as taxable income and subject to CGT. Net capital losses in a tax year may be carried forward and offset against future capital gains.

Inheritance Tax

This death duty was abolished in 1979, and CGT is not payable on the capital gain (or loss) of assets in an estate if they are simply passed on to beneficiaries. If however the asset is sold by the executor and then the proceeds are distributed on, the sale of the asset is subject to CGT.

Goods and Services Tax (GST)

Australia has a GST of 10% which is charged on most goods and services consumed in Australia with the exception of basic foodstuff, education, medical services and government charges.

Corporate taxes

Businesses are liable for paying a number of taxes; including Payroll Tax, Fringe Benefits Tax and Corporate Tax (which is charged at a flat 30% rate).

Australia has an extensive network of double tax agreements.

11.5   Family law and inheritance aspects

Australian family law is governed by the Family Court of Australia (FCA) which has jurisdiction over all states and territories except for Western Australia. The FCA presides over matters regarding divorce/separation of married and *de facto* partnerships, child custody arrangements, adoption and property and financial divisions.[130] Australia does

---

[130] *familylawcourts.gov.au*

not allow same-sex marriage, though does recognize *de facto* relation-ships (including same sex relationships) in matters involving the FCA.

Inheritance and succession laws vary in each Australian state or territory, though a study has been undertaken and recommendations made to make these laws uniform throughout the country, which is slowly taking effect. Australian laws recognize valid wills and the executor of that will is responsible for complying with the applicable inheritance laws in that state or territory; including notifying beneficiaries, finalizing the estate, completing tax returns and paying all outstanding debts. Australia does not have a death duty/inheritance tax, though capital gains tax may be incurred on some financial transactions which are a result of the person's death.[131] Where there is no will, or any eligibility relatives, estates pass onto the State (Crown) to administer.

11.6   Citizenship

Citizenship is conferred in accordance with the Citizenship Act 2007.

A child born in Australia to an Australian permanent resident or citizen parent will automatically be entitled to Australian citizenship. A child born outside of Australia to an Australian citizen parent will also auto-matically be entitled to Australian citizenship.

After four years of lawful residence in Australia, with at least the past 12 months as an Australian permanent resident, it is possible to apply for Australian citizenship. There is a citizenship appointment and test that must be attended and passed, as well as a pledge that must be made, before citizenship will be granted.

It is compulsory for adult Australian citizens to vote in Federal, State and Local Government elections, and failure to do so may result in financial penalties. It is also a requirement for Australian citizens to exit and enter Australia using the Australian passport.

---

[131]   *legalanswers.sl.nsw.gov.au* and *ato.gov.au*

11.7 Dual citizenship

Australia allows dual citizenship.

11.8 Key advantages and disadvantages

Advantages

- High standards of living, multicultural
- Political, social and economic stability
- Objective, merits-based immigration system with predictable outcomes
- Compulsory 9.25% superannuation/pension payable by employers

Disadvantages

- Compulsory voting for Australian citizens over 18 years old
- Physical residence requirements for maintaining residence and obtaining citizenship
- Relatively high cost of living

11.9   General information

Official name	Commonwealth of Australia
Capital city	Canberra
Region	Oceania, Continent between the Indian Ocean and the South Pacific
Surface area	7,741,220 km²
Government	Federal Parliamentary Democracy
Language	English 25.9%, Mandarin 1.6%, Italian 1.4%, Arabic 1.3%, Greek 1.2%, Cantonese 1.2%, Vietnamese 1.1%, other 10.4%, unspecified 5%
Currency	Australian Dollar (AUD)
Population	22,751,014 (July 2015 est.)
Religion	Protestant 30.1%, Catholic 25.3%, other Christians 2.9%, Orthodox 2.8%, Buddhist 2.5%, Muslim 2.2%, Hindu 1.3%, other 1.3%, unspecified 9.3%
Ethnic groups	English 25.9%, Australian 25.4%, Irish 7.5%, Scottish 6.4%, Italian 3.3%, German 3.2%, Chinese 3.1%, Indian 1.4%, Greek 1.4%, Dutch 1.2%, other 15.8%, unspecified 5.4%
GDP	USD 1.489 trillion (2015 est.)
GDP per capita, PPP	USD 65,400 (2015 est.)
Major industries	Mining, agriculture, industrial and transportation equipment, steel, food processing
Main exports	Coal, iron ore, gold, meat, wool, alumina, wheat, machinery and transport equipment
Climate	Generally arid to semi-arid, temperate in south and east, tropical in north
UN Human Development Index (HDI)	2nd (2015)
World's healthiest countries (Bloomberg Rankings)	3rd (2015)
Henley & Partners Visa Restrictions Index	8th (2016), 6th (2015)
Legatum Prosperity Index	7th (2015)

Sources: CIA "The World Factbook" (2015), World Bank (2015),
UN Human Development Report (2015), Henley & Partners, The Legatum Institute

11.10 Climate

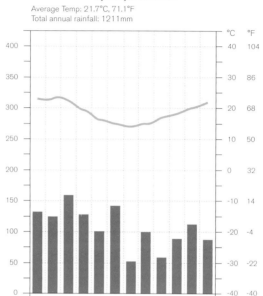

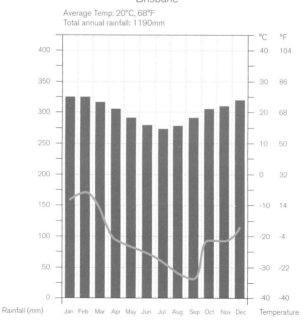

12

Austria

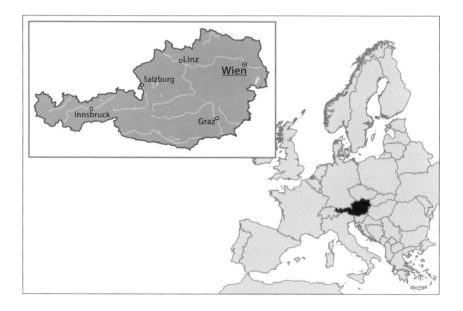

Austria is an attractive country with Vienna, its capital, regularly ranked as having a very high quality of life.[132] The combination of economic stability, a clean and safe environment and an excellent infrastructure make it an outstanding place of residence. The country has a vibrant culture and is home to many first-class museums, musical festivals and impressive architecture. Austria also lays claim to beautiful natural attractions, from snow-capped mountains to lush green countryside and lakes.

Austria ranks among the European community's richest countries. It has a well-developed economy with the service sector contributing approximately two-thirds of its GDP. The economy benefits from strong commercial relations with central, eastern and south-eastern Europe. Austria's economy relies on its export market with main exports including machinery and equipment, motor vehicles and parts, paper and paperboard, metal goods, chemicals, iron and steel, textiles and foodstuffs.

Despite the ongoing immigration debate and the strict quotas limiting residents' applications for persons of independent means, Austria offers the opportunity to become resident in a Schengen area member state with minimal bureaucratic requirements. However, the preparation of private residence applications requires significant experience and knowledge of the immigration system and procedures.

An Austrian residence permit allows visa-free travel to all Schengen states. A residence permit is initially issued for one year and can be renewed annually without problems or interruptions. After six to 10 years of uninterrupted residence in Austria, an application for Austrian citizenship can be lodged. If significant investments or other extraordinary engagements in Austria can be proven, citizenship may also be obtained in a much shorter period of time.

---

[132] The Mercer Quality of Living Survey 2015 rated Vienna the best city to live in for the fifth consecutive year. See *www.mercer.com/qualityofliving*

12.1   Residence in Austria

The main provisions regarding residence for foreign individuals are set out in the Domiciliation and Residence Act (*Niederlassungs – und Aufenthaltsgesetz, NAG*). This act distinguishes between 10 different types of residence permits. These permits differ firstly depending on whether the applicant is allowed to work in Austria, and secondly, if the person is allowed to work as an employee or as a self-employed person. Other permits exist for students and family members of persons who are already resident in Austria. For some of these permits, including those for persons of independent means, annual quotas apply that are implemented each year by decree. For all other residence permits, strict conditions have to be fulfilled.

The residence permit is issued by the Austrian authorities; however, usually the application has to be filed personally at the Austrian consulate or embassy in the applicant's current country of residence. Entrance is not permitted into the country until the residence permit has been approved. However, foreign nationals under the visa-waiver program[133] may file their application in Austria.

Residence permits (*Aufenthaltstitel*) are issued for a certain purpose and may not be extended after that purpose is fulfilled. Certain types of residence permits entitle the applicant to bring their spouse and children under 18 years into the country, and others do not.

Amongst others, Austria offers the following types of residence permits:

1. The *Highly Skilled Category* is a special category that allows foreigners to enter Austria if they are highly qualified[134] or qualify as a special executive[135] and contains the following permits:

---

[133] Visa waiver program extends to Australian, Brazilian, Canadian, Mexican and US citizens

[134] The applicant must have a university degree or equivalent, their area of expertise must be of importance to the employer, they must eventually create jobs and bring investment capital to Austria

[135] The applicant must earn more than EUR 4,200 per month in an executive position

a. Red-White-Red Card (employed)[136] covers the right of settlement and the right of being employed with a specific employer in Austria

b. Red-White-Red Card (self-employed) covers the right of settlement and the right of being self-employed in Austria

c. Red-White-Red Card (student) covers the right for graduates of universities and colleges of higher education in Austria to a further settlement of six months in Austria for the purpose of searching for employment

d. Blue Card EU covers the right of settlement and the right of being employed with a specific employer on the entire Federal Territory; however a university degree is mandatory

e. Red-White-Red – Card Plus covers the right of settlement and unrestricted access to the labor market; where the Integration Agreement has already been fulfilled

2. *Residence permit – family member (Aufenthaltstitel Familienangehöriger)* is issued to spouses and minor children of EU and EEA citizens that have permanently resided in Austria. The Integration Agreement must already be fulfilled

3. *Permanent residence permit – EC (Aufenthaltstitel Daueraufenthalt – EG)* is issued to foreign nationals who have had the right to stay in Austria for at least the last five years. The Integration Agreement must already be fulfilled

4. *Permanent residence permit – family member (Aufenthaltstitel Daueraufenthalt – Familienangehöriger)* is issued to individuals who have held a residence permit – family member *(Aufenthaltstitel Familienangehöriger[137])* for at least the last five years. The Integration Agreement must already be fulfilled

---

[136] The Red-White-Red Card program regulates the immigration according to a criteria-based model. In order to receive a Red-White-Red Card, the applicant has to achieve the sufficient amount of points (e.g. for education, professional experience, age, language skills); see *http://www.migration.gv.at/en/*

[137] *Familienangehöriger* is a title for spouses and children up to 18 years of Austrian citizens. With this title they have free access to work and do not need an additional work permit

5. *Registration certificate* (*Anmeldebescheinigung*) is issued to EU and EEA citizens, spouses and minor children of EU & EEA citizens (except Swiss nationals) who both work and therefore take up residence in Austria

6. *Permanent residence card* (*Daueraufenthaltskarte*) for non EU and EEA spouses and minor children of EU and EFTA citizens (except Swiss) who have taken up residence in Austria

7. The *Private Residence Category* is designed for financially independent persons, the key requirements are that the applicant must show funds, permanent accommodation in Austria in either a rental or purchase contract for a property to accommodate the applicant and any dependents included in the application, and health insurance providing full cover in Austria. A spouse and any children under 18 years may be included in an application.

Under this category, the individual is not allowed to take up gainful employment. The applicant and family must undertake to learn German within a certain period of time in accordance with the terms of the integration agreement

12.2   Requirements

Each permit has specific requirements that must be fulfilled to meet the criteria of the category. However, all applications require basic documentation such as passport copy, birth certificate, certificate of good conduct/criminal record. All foreign language documents must be translated into German by a professional translation service. In addition, most of the different kinds of permits also require basic German language skills before filing the application and demand that the holders learn German up to a specific level within a fixed period of time in line with the conditions of the Integration Agreement. People with a university degree or equivalent and minors under 14 years are exempted from this obligation.

12.3　Procedures and time frame

In the course of the application process, applicants must personally submit mandatory documentation to the Austrian consular or diplomatic representation in their current country of residence. Due to the strict quota constraints for some residence permits, timing of the submission of the application is of prime importance. Once the permit is granted, the applicant must pick up a special visa at the Austrian embassy which allows the applicant to travel to Austria to collect the residence permit at the relevant authority. There is a minimum processing period of one month but usually applications take three months to be approved.

The processing time for applications under the category of financially independent persons can take up to 14 months, depending on various factors.

Once the residence permit is issued, it must be collected in person from the issuing authority in Austria. In addition, all non-EU and non-EFTA citizens must sign an Integration Agreement if they will be residing in Austria for more than 24 months.

The residence and settlement permits are issued in the form of a card and can be renewed each year.

12.4　Taxation

Residents of Austria are subject to unlimited tax liability on their worldwide income. Non-resident individuals are only required to pay tax on Austrian-sourced income.

Austria does not levy any wealth or net worth taxes (except on Austrian real estate) and has abolished inheritance and gift tax.

Capital gains derived from financial assets acquired after 31 December 2010 are subject to income tax. For sales after 31 March 2012, a flat tax rate of 25% applies. Since 1 April 2012, capital gains from real estate held privately are also generally subject to income tax at the flat rate of 25%. Special provisions apply for real estate acquired before 1 April 2012; exceptions apply for real estate used as a main residence by the owner. Capital gains derived by private persons from other assets are not subject to income tax unless the disposal is seen as a speculative transaction completed within a specific period, in which case the capital gain would be subject to income tax.

A flat tax rate of 25% for individuals applies for most interest payments received from banks and dividends received from shares.

Other personal income is subject to a progressive rate of up to 50%. The tax burden is mitigated for employees by a flat tax rate of 6% on a 13th and 14th monthly salary. For self-employed people, tax mitigation is achieved through tax allowances.

The Austrian tax treatment of foreign trusts and the absence of controlled foreign corporation rules offer interesting pre-immigration planning opportunities for wealthy families.

Companies are subject to a flat-tax rate of 25%. For large corporations, Austria has introduced an attractive group taxation system with effect from 2005, which also provides for setting off losses incurred by foreign subsidiaries.

Austria has an extensive network of double tax agreements.

Most exchange controls have been abolished in recent years. There are no restrictions on the transfer of capital and currency transactions in place.

12.5   Family law and inheritance aspects

In Austria, a succession as a result of death will be determined according to the deceased's personal status at the time of their death, which is usually determined by nationality. However, if succession is settled in Austria, the acquisition of the estate and liability for the estate's debts will be governed by Austrian law. The transfer will be subject to Austrian estate law and settled before an Austrian court.

Austria recognizes wills and testaments that have been validly executed according to Austrian succession laws. If a person dies intestate, the estate is divided firstly amongst the spouse and children; then parents, siblings and their descendants are second in line, and finally grandparents, grandparents' siblings and their descendants will inherit.

In Austria, the law regulates two forms of matrimonial property regime, namely Separation of Property (*Gütertrennung*) and the Community of Property (*Gütergemeinschaft*). The Act on International Private Law (*Internationales Privatrechtsgesetz*) regulates international conflict of matrimonial property law and provides that the regime chosen by the spouses is observed. If no regime has been chosen, then the matrimonial property issues will be regulated according to the statute applicable at the time of the wedding. As the separation of property regime is the preferred regime this is usually applied to the couple.

12.6   Citizenship

The granting of Austrian citizenship is regulated by the Federal Law on Austrian Nationality, known as the Citizenship Act of 1985 (*Staatsbürgerschaftsgesetz StBG*) which was last amended in 2013. Citizenship by birth is granted to a child on its birth if at least one parent is a citizen of Austria, whether they are born in or out of wedlock. Before an amendment in August 2013, children born out of wedlock acquired Austrian citizenship by birth only if the mother was an Austrian citizen. Now, children born out of wedlock have the same status as those who are born in wedlock. A foreign spouse of an Austrian citizen can apply for citizenship after six years of uninterrupted residence in Austria.

A minimum of 10 years' uninterrupted residence is normally required before one can apply for Austrian citizenship. This period can be reduced to six years of uninterrupted residence in some cases. Furthermore, a knowledge of the German language is required as well the relinquishment of all other citizenships, except for applications made under Section 10 (6) of the Citizenship Act (see below) or if an exemption is granted.

In Austria it is also possible to qualify for citizenship without prior residence. Under the provisions of Section 10 (6) of the Austrian Citizenship Act, an applicant must provide exceptional benefits to the Republic of Austria in fields such as science, art, culture or economics. The Austrian Government then approves citizenship by a decision of all Government Ministers.

In order to be eligible for citizenship based on extraordinary economic contributions, an applicant is required to actively invest in the Austrian economy. The investment can take the form of a joint venture or a direct investment in a business creating jobs or generating new export sales. One can also make an extraordinary contribution that is in the interest of the Austrian Republic for example by making an important donation to a public institution. Passive investments in government bonds and real estate do not qualify. The grant of Austrian citizenship under this provision is subject to the discretion of the Austrian federal government.

12.7 Dual citizenship

Dual citizenship is generally not allowed in Austria. There are, however, a few exceptions. One exception is that of minors of Austrian citizens who were born in a foreign country and acquired the country's citizenship according to the country's laws.

Austria also allows dual citizenship if Austrian citizenship is acquired under the provisions of Section 10 (6) of the Austrian Citizenship Act.

A citizen will lose citizenship if they voluntarily relinquish the citizenship or if they voluntarily acquire foreign citizenship.

12.8 Key advantages and disadvantages

Advantages

- Minimal application requirements

- Residence permit gives visa-free access to the Schengen areas

- High quality of life

- Excellent transport and communications

- Citizenship possible after six to 10 years of residence

Disadvantages

- Application process will take at least 24 months

- Restrictions on dual citizenship apply

- Pre-immigration tax planning required (although Austria is an attractive place of residence from a tax point of view)

12.9   General information

Official name	Republic of Austria
Capital city	Vienna (1.8 million)
Region	Southern Central Europe
Surface area	83,871 km^2
Government	Federal Republic, Parliamentary Democracy
Language	German (official nationwide) 88.6%, Turkish 2.3%, Serbian 2.2%, Croatian (official in Burgenland) 1.6%, other (includes Slovene, official in Carinthia; and Hungarian, official in Burgenland) 5.3%
Currency	Euro (EUR)
Population	8,699,730 (2016)
Religion	Roman Catholic 73.8%, Protestant 4.9%, Muslim 4.2%, Orthodox 2.2%, other 0.8%, unspecified 2%
Ethnic groups	Austrians 91.1%, former Yugoslavs 4% (includes Croatians, Slovenes, Serbs, and Bosnians), Turks 1.6%, German 0.9%, other or unspecified 2.4%
GDP	USD 404.3 billion (2015 est.)
GDP per capita, PPP	USD 47,300 (2015 est.)
Major industries	Construction, machinery, vehicles and parts, food, metals, chemicals, lumber and wood processing, paper and paperboard, communications equipment, tourism
Main exports	Machinery and equipment, motor vehicles and parts, paper and paperboard, metal goods, chemicals, iron and steel, textiles, foodstuffs
Climate	Generally moderate and mild - varies from the Alpine region to the eastern plain. Summer can be hot with average temperatures from 20°C to 30°C, average winter temperatures are around 0°
UN Human Development Index (HDI)	21st (2015)
World's healthiest countries (Bloomberg Rankings)	12th (2015)
Henley & Partners Visa Restrictions Index	5th (2016), 5th (2015)
Legatum Prosperity Index	16th (2015)

Sources: CIA "The World Factbook" (2015), World Bank (2015), UN Human Development Report (2015), Henley & Partners, The Legatum Institute

12.10 Climate

Vienna

Average Temp: 9.9°C, 49.8°F
Total annual rainfall: 613mm

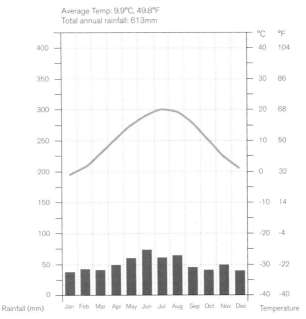

Rainfall (mm)   Jan Feb Mar Apr May Jun Jul Aug Sep Oct Nov Dec   Temperature

Salzburg

Average Temp: 8.9°C, 48°F
Total annual rainfall: 1169mm

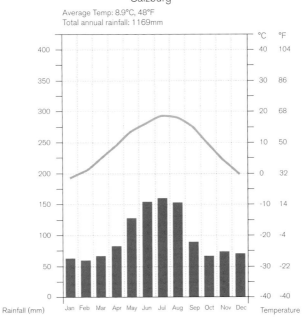

Rainfall (mm)   Jan Feb Mar Apr May Jun Jul Aug Sep Oct Nov Dec   Temperature

13

Belgium

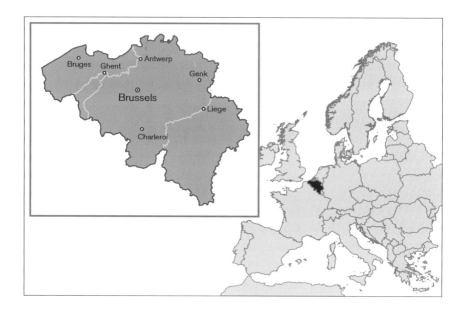

Although a small country, Belgium is often referred to as the capital of Europe, as it is the political nerve center of Western Europe. Officially known as the Kingdom of Belgium, the country is one of the founding members of the European Union (EU) and hosts the headquarters of the EU in Brussels, its capital city. Another important hub is the municipality of Antwerp, which is commonly referred to as the Diamond City, and is one of the biggest and fastest growing ports of the world as well as a main hub for diamond trade.

Belgium is both politically and economically stable. The King of Belgium, with limited prerogative, is head of state, and the country is based on a constitutional monarchy with bicameral federal parliament, comprising of a Senate and the Chamber of Representatives.

Despite its complex system of government, Belgium boasts efficient tax systems with numerous exemptions beneficial to both locals and foreigners. Belgium has interesting tax incentives and tax treaties for businesses, therefore residence in Belgium is a sensible solution for investors, financially independent persons and entrepreneurs.

Belgium has a highly developed economy and is one of the world's largest trading nations due to its central location and excellent transportation network.

Geographically, Belgium is divided into three organizational or administrative areas:

- The Brussels-Capital Region
- The Flemish Region (Flanders)
- The Walloon Region (Wallonia)

In addition to these three regions, Belgium is divided into 10 provinces and 589 municipalities.

Life in Belgium is comfortable as it provides a high standard of living and a healthy and safe environment. It also boasts an excellent healthcare system and a high level of school education. Culturally, Belgium is well known for its rich heritage, making it one of the most visited countries in the world.

The country, is a good base for business and residence. Moreover, a residence permit can be obtained within a reasonable time frame and application for citizenship is possible after five years of legal residence without fulfilling language or integration requirements. Belgium is a sensible and safe option for a family.

13.1 Residence in Belgium

The rights of foreign nationals to enter, reside and settle in Belgium are governed by the Law of 15 December 1980 and the Royal Decree of 8 October 1981.

Belgium adheres to its international commitments in respect to its obligations to the Benelux, the Schengen and the European Union arrangements with regards to entry and stay of foreign nationals.

Belgium can be visited by all nationals for up to 90 days (on the basis of a Schengen residence identity card or a passport). Specific visa requirements may apply for non-EEA/EFTA nationals depending on their nationality.

As with most EU member states, if a foreign (non-EU/EFTA) national wants to reside and settle in Belgium for longer than three months, they must apply for a residence permit.

Belgian law requires that a foreign national show a certain affiliation to the country, either personal or professional, in order to apply for residence. However, unless they have personal ties through a family connection, the foreign national will be most likely to apply for residence via the economic route.

More specifically, work permits are regulated by the Act of 30 April 1999 and the Royal Decree of 9 June 1999, and Professional cards for self-employed persons are regulated by the Act of 19 February 1965 and several Royal Decrees.

Due to its investor-friendly environment, there are interesting solutions to obtaining residence in Belgium under one of the economic categories. Various options are available including the set-up of an international holding structure in Belgium, or investment in an existing Belgian company, or investment in a foreign company through a Belgium holding company.

A person who is employed by a Belgian company or even any worldwide company, or a person who sets up or buys a Belgian company, can apply for residence in Belgium.

More specifically, there are two main economic routes under which a person could qualify for residence, either as (i) a manager or highly skilled employee; or (ii) an entrepreneur or self-employed individual.

In principle, foreign nationals may only apply for a work permit if there is a shortage in the Belgian and European labor market. However, some categories of employees are excluded from this rule, including persons executing a managerial function in Belgium.

In order to qualify as a highly-skilled employee or manager, the person must earn a yearly gross salary above a certain level as set by the Belgian authorities. Therefore, qualifying for this category of work permit would also entail a higher tax liability.

Interestingly, under this category, an applicant is not necessarily restricted to remain in Belgium and would have the freedom and flexibility to operate as, for example, a consultant abroad. The applicant can work as a consultant or employee of a third party Belgian company; or a Belgian company that requires the applicant to work in another jurisdiction for the purpose of the business; or alternatively, the applicant may work for a Belgian subsidiary or branch of an international company which may be headquartered in, for example, China. The most important factor would be that the applicant is employed on the Belgian pay roll and pays Belgian income tax. However, the Belgian authorities will expect that the local business set-up is genuine and has substance.

The alternative is to incorporate one's own company in Belgium. The individual operates the company and applies for a residence permit under the self-employment category. The advantage of this option is that there is no minimum salary level that the self-employed person must earn in order to qualify, but only need to earn sufficient money for a self-sustainable life. The individual's tax liability will be substantially less than that of the person who applies for a work permit. The disadvantage of this solution is that the professional card application and its execution will be reviewed by the authorities for a period of every two years and the procedure takes up about two to three months, whereas the work permit option usually takes approximately two to three weeks.

Residence permits can also be granted to family members of the main applicant through the family reunification procedure.

13.2   Requirements

Each category has its own set of criteria to qualify for the residence permit. However, all applications require a visa application form to be completed and submitted with qualifying documents such as a passport, as well as a birth certificate, medical certificate and criminal clearance record. The applicant must also secure appropriate accommodation in Belgium, which must be at the applicant's disposal at all times during the applicant's residence period in the country. However this does not prevent residents from travelling outside of Belgium during their residence period.

A spouse and children under 18 years can be included in most of the applications.

In the case of employment, the employer in Belgium must request an employer permit and work permit from the relevant sub-regional employment service. The employee will then submit his visa application at the Belgian consulate in his current place of residence. Initially the employee will receive only a temporary residence permit.

In order to apply for a residence permit as a manager, the applicant must provide a number of mandatory documents in addition to the work permit, including proof that the manager's yearly salary in question exceeds the annually adjusted lower limits (as specified in Article 65 of the law of 3 July 1978 governing labor agreements).

For highly skilled persons and managers, a work permit is usually granted for a maximum of four years which must be renewed annually. This period can be extended by another four years.

After three years of employment, a managerial employee can apply for a work permit that is valid for an unlimited duration along with a residence permit of unlimited duration. However, for highly skilled persons, after five years consecutively working for the same employer, a residence permit of unlimited duration will be granted.

The procedure for the application of a self-employed applicant is different in the sense that the applicant must first obtain authorization from the Federal Public Service Economy (FPS Economy). The FPS Economy grants the applicant the right to exercise a professional activity as a self-employed worker in writing. This approval must be submitted with other mandatory documentation to the Belgian consulate or embassy in order for the visa to be issued. A professional card (*carte professionnelle/ beroepskaart*) is also issued to the applicant.

13.3   Procedures and time frame

In the course of the visa application process, applicants must submit the usual documents, which include a criminal clearance certificate, medical records, as well as any additional documentary proof relevant to the particular permit category.

The Belgian consular and diplomatic authorities deal with the visa applications on a case-by-case basis. However, it is the Immigration Service at the Federal Public Service Home Affairs in Belgium that makes the final decision as to whether the visa will be granted. This decision will then be communicated to the embassy or consulate.

Once the visa is granted, the applicant must visit Belgium in person to apply for the residence permit at the municipality where they will reside.

Due to the case-by-case decision process, the whole visa and residence application process (from the time of lodging the application to the granting of the permit) can take between two to four months, depending on individual circumstances.

13.4   Taxation

Belgian taxation is favorable for executives, holding companies within international structures and individuals of independent means. Commonly known as a high-tax jurisdiction, Belgium is in fact a discreet tax haven for affluent individuals and families who do not live off employment income.

For individual residents in Belgium income tax is chargeable on their personal worldwide income. A person is considered tax resident if a domicile has been established in Belgium. A non-resident is liable only for Belgian-source income.

Special tax rules apply to foreign employees temporarily residing in Belgium. Foreign executives, specialists and researchers recruited or assigned to work in Belgium for a multi-national corporation with a Belgian operation, may apply for a tax concession. The employer and employee jointly apply for special expatriate status by sending written applications to the Belgian tax authorities. Under the special expatriate tax status, the employee is treated as a non-resident and therefore is only taxed on Belgian-source income. This can also be beneficial for the company, as the latter can decrease the gross remuneration as certain allowances (housing, tax equalization, moving expenses, education, etc.) can remain tax free.

Personal income is subject to a progressive rate of up to 50% (and increased with local surcharges).

There are no wealth or net worth taxes. In principle there is no capital gains tax on assets not used for a professional activity. However, certain exceptions do arise, for example, such as (short term) capital gains from property transactions or the transfer of a substantial shareholding to a non-EU/EEA resident company. There is a withholding tax of 25% on interests as well on dividends and liquidation tax of 10%, but certain exemptions apply.

Individual resident taxpayers have to annually report their existing accounts with financial institutions located in foreign countries.

With advanced tax planning it can be possible to pay only very limited inheritance or gift taxes, or even none at all. Belgian tax treatment of trusts offers interesting planning opportunities for wealthy families. For example, provided that the settlor of an irrevocable discretionary trust does not die as a Belgian resident – in which case further distributions would be subject to Belgian inheritance tax – Belgian resident benefi-ciaries may receive distributions from a foreign trust free of tax.

Companies are charged a general corporate tax rate of 33.99% (including a 3% surcharge). Under certain conditions reduced progres-sive corporate tax rates may apply. The Belgian tax regime provides for certain tax deductions. This includes the notional interest deduction regime, which can offset operational or financial income. The notional interest deduction allows a tax deduction calculated as a percentage of the "qualifying" equity of a Belgian company. This can be deducted on an annual basis.

Other special tax incentives also apply to particular categories such as intellectual property and shipping.

Belgium has even amended its legislation to the extent that withholding tax on interest payments and dividend distributions are in general no longer levied on a Belgian subsidiary, whose parent company is situated in a country with which Belgium has concluded a bilateral tax treaty that has a sufficient exchange of information provision.

Belgium has an extensive network of double tax treaties that provide for treaty relief for Belgian residents.

13.5   Family law and inheritance aspects

The Civil Code governs family relationships including marriage, divorce and inheritance.

In Belgium, the dissolution of an estate depends on whether the individual is resident in Belgium, in which case the entire estate is subject to Belgian inheritance laws. If the individual is not resident in Belgium, the inheritance laws will only apply to real estate held in Belgium.

If the deceased did not leave a will, or equivalent testamentary disposition, the estate will be dissolved by the strict inheritance laws which favor the immediate family members. A surviving spouse is entitled to the matrimonial property (all property acquired after the marriage) and a life interest in the property of the deceased.

Even if there is a will, Belgian law favors immediate family and therefore exclusion of certain heirs is disregarded – children and spouses are always entitled to a share of the estate.

Belgium recognizes the common property law regime, which involves an equal division of the marital assets (and losses), unless a legal prenuptial agreement is in place. Belgium recognizes the last location of a couple's common habitual residence. Thus, if divorce proceedings are held in another country, Belgium has no jurisdiction over the divorce proceedings. In order to obtain a divorce in Belgium, a petition must be filed on grounds of irretrievable breakdown, or by mutual consent.

13.6   Citizenship

Belgian citizenship is regulated by the Code of Belgian Nationality, dated 28 June 1984, which was last amended in 2013.

Birth within the territory of Belgium does not automatically confer citizenship. However, citizenship is automatically acquired by a child born in Belgium if at least one of the parents is a citizen of Belgium or if a child is born abroad and one of the parents is a native-born citizen of Belgium.

After five years of legal residence in Belgium, it is possible to apply for citizenship. The individual must show evidence of legal stay and be in possession of a Residence Permit of unlimited duration. There are further additional requirements.

13.7 Dual citizenship

Belgium allows dual citizenship.

13.8 Key advantages and disadvantages

Advantages

- Residence permit gives visa-free access to the Schengen area
- Excellent infrastructure in the heart of Europe
- Attractive corporate and private taxation system
- Citizenship possible after five years of legal residence

Disadvantages

- Establishment of a company in Belgium is required in most cases
- Pre-immigration tax planning required to take advantage of tax system
- Language requirements apply for citizenship applications (French, Dutch or German)

13.9   General information

Official name	Kingdom of Belgium
Capital city	Brussels
Region	Western Europe
Surface area	30,528 km²
Government	Federal State, Parliamentary Democracy
Languages	Dutch 60%, French 40%, German less than 1%, legally bilingual (Dutch and French)
Currency	Euro (EUR)
Population	11.239 million (2015)
Religion	Roman Catholic 75%, other (including Protestant) 25%
Ethnic groups	Flemish 58%, Walloon 31%, mixed or other 11%
GDP	USD 494.1 billion (2015 est.)
GDP per capita, PPP	USD 43,600 (2015 est.)
Major industries	Engineering and metal products, motor vehicle assembly, transportation equipment, scientific instruments, processed food and beverages, chemicals, base metals, textiles, glass, petroleum, diamond trade and cutting
Main exports	Machinery and electrical equipment, chemicals, vehicles, metals, diamonds
Climate	Temperate / moderate
UN Human Development Index (HDI)	21st (2015)
World's healthiest countries (Bloomberg Rankings)	20th (2015)
Henley & Partners Visa Restrictions Index	4th (2016), 4th (2015)
Legatum Prosperity Index	18th (2015)

Sources: CIA "The World Factbook" (2015), World Bank (2015), UN Human Development Report (2015), Henley & Partners, The Legatum Institute

13.10 Climate

Brussels

Average Temp: 9.9°C, 49.8°F
Total annual rainfall: 819mm

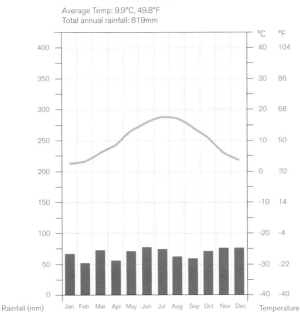

Rainfall (mm)   Jan Feb Mar Apr May Jun Jul Aug Sep Oct Nov Dec   Temperature

Bruges

Average Temp: 9.9°C, 49.8°F
Total annual rainfall: 757mm

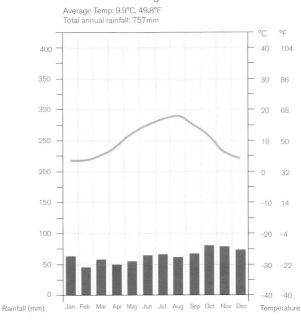

Rainfall (mm)   Jan Feb Mar Apr May Jun Jul Aug Sep Oct Nov Dec   Temperature

14
Canada

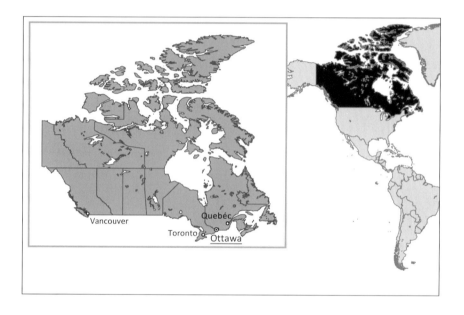

Canada is not only the second largest country in the world, but is also one of the wealthiest. Canada is regularly voted as one of the best countries to live in as it is known for its high standard of living, clean environment, low crime rate and excellent infrastructure. At the same time it is also a country where a good lifestyle is affordable. There is a high-quality education system, good working opportunities and a vast number of choices as to where to settle.

The entire country spans six time zones, with 10 provinces from which to choose. With such a large surface area, the longest coastline and highest mountains in North America, it is no surprise that Canada offers something for every individual. Each province has its own individual charm; Montreal, Toronto, and Vancouver are the largest cities in Canada, and are all popular destinations.

Historically, Canada was largely influenced by the English, French and the Aboriginals who originally lived in the area. The official languages in Canada are English and French. About nine million of the population are Francophone.

Canada offers the attractions and convenience of the US, and residents and citizens may benefit from the NAFTA agreement between the neighboring countries. Yet Canada manages to retain an identity of its own.

Although Canada is known as a high-tax country, this could in the past be circumvented in the first few years of residence with a five-year tax exemption on foreign income, designed to encourage migrants to invest in the country. This tax planning tool was however phased out following the 2014 Federal budget.

Canada is globally admired for its multicultural society and tolerant foreign policies – this multicultural ethos is in fact part of the Canadian legislation. It is the reason why Canada has the highest per-capita immigration rate in the world and continues to attract quality immigrants.

14.1 Residence in Canada

The right to enter and remain in Canada is regulated under the Immigration and Refugee Protection Act of 2002 (IRPA), and the relevant regulations that were provided under the Act.

The regulations deal with the specific requirements for immigration to Canada under the various categories. There are also operational bulletins and manuals available from the Immigration, Refugees and Citizenship Canada Department (IRCC), which are updated regularly and which provide clear instruction and guidance.[138]

The Province of Quebec[139] shares with the Canadian Federal Government the selection of immigrants who wish to establish themselves in Quebec under the Federal-Quebec Agreement of 1991. Quebec administers its own immigration programs under the Immigration Act of Quebec and its regulations. However, pursuant to the mobility rights in the Charter of Rights and Freedoms, persons selected under any of the Quebec Programs may reside in a Province of their choice.

There are several ways to become a permanent resident in Canada and, while each program has a different set of criteria that should be met, in general, it can be said that these requirements have become stricter and processing targets have decreased overall.

The programs are listed below:

1. *Federal Skilled Worker Program* for applicants who want to settle and work in Canada

2. The *Quebec Skilled Workers* Program for applicants who want to settle and work in Quebec

3. The *Federal Skilled Trades Program*, designed by federal government with provincial input for applicants whose trades are presently in demand on the Canadian labor market

---

[138] *www.cic.gc.ca*
[139] *www.immigration-quebec.gouv.qc.ca/en/index.html*

4. The *Canadian Experience Class* for applicants who have at least 12 months of full-time (or equivalent amount part-time) skilled work experience in Canada in the three years before application

5. The *Quebec Investor and Entrepreneur Category* for business applicants who are either passive investors or want to own and manage a business in Quebec that contributes to the economy

6. The *Federal Immigrant Investor Venture Capital Pilot Program* for experienced business immigrants who can actively invest a substantial amount in the Canadian economy

7. The *Federal Start-Up Visa Program* which links immigrant entrepreneurs with designated venture capital funds, designated angel investor groups and designated business incubators

8. The *Provincial Nominee Program* is a category specific to a province or territory, which can nominate a specific person who wishes to settle and work in that province or territory based on employment or business investment and job creation

9. *Family Class Sponsorship* is designed for family members sponsored by a Canadian permanent resident or Canadian citizen

The applicant must fulfil the specific criteria for the qualifying category, and they and any dependents are required to undergo a medical examination as well as security and criminal checks.

14.2   Requirements

As mentioned above, each category has a specific set of criteria that the applicant must fulfil in order to qualify for residence in Canada.

A brief overview of the specific requirements for the federal residence program is provided here.

Federal Skilled Worker Program

Persons applying under the Federal Skilled Worker Program must have the requisite professional work experience and are required to pass a minimum threshold language ability test for one of Canada's two official languages (English and French). The rules require that the applicant has at least one year of continuous full-time or equivalent paid work experience over the past 10 years in one of the National Occupation Classification (NOC) skill type (O, A or B). Further, the applicant must have a Canadian secondary (high school) or post-secondary certificate, diploma, or degree; or a completed foreign credential and an Educational Credential Assessment (ECA) report, by an agency approved by Citizenship and Immigration Canada (CIC), to show that their foreign education is equal to Canadian education standards.

The applicant must attain at least 67 points with regards to the following six selection factors: education, proficiency in one of the official languages, work experience, age, valid job offer in Canada and adaptability. Applicants must also show that they have the required settlement funds to support themselves and their dependents after arrival in Canada.

The Federal Skilled Worker Program is one of the programs under a new electronic system, "Express Entry", which manages applications for permanent residence in certain federal economic programs. Express Entry allows IRCC to actively recruit, assess, and select skilled immigrants for these programs.

Quebec Skilled Worker Program

To qualify for the Quebec Skilled Worker Program, applicants settle in Québec with the goal of being employed there and must:

- Hold at least one diploma that corresponds, in the Québec education system, to a Secondary School Diploma or a Diploma of Vocational Studies

- Have acquired training and occupational skills that will facilitate his or her integration into the job market

The following employability factors of the applicant will be taken into account:

- Schooling (applicant's level of education and area of training)
- Work experience
- Age
- Knowledge of French and English
- Stays in Quebec and family relationship with a Canadian citizen or a permanent Quebec resident
- Having a valid employment offer (this applies only if the applicant has received a job offer that meets certain conditions from a Quebec employer)
- Characteristics regarding the applicant's accompanying spouse or common-law spouse, if applicable

The Quebec Skilled Worker program is subject to an annual quota of 6,300 applicants.

Federal Skilled Trades Program

In order to qualify under the Federal Skilled Trades Program, applicants must have obtained 24 months of qualified work experience in the skilled trade in the last five years, and have an offer of full-time employment in Canada for at least one year's duration or a Certificate of Qualification issued from a provincial or territorial authority. In addition, applicants need to provide proof of minimum language level of Canadian Language Benchmark (CLB) 5 from a designated language testing organization, demonstrating that the applicant meets the minimum threshold set by IRCC. The Federal Skilled Trades Program is also one of the programs under Express Entry.

The Quebec Investor and Entrepreneur Category

To qualify for selection under the Quebec Investor and Entrepreneur Category, an applicant must:

1. Have management experience in a legal farming, commercial, or industrial business, or in a legal professional business where the staff, excluding the investor, occupies at least the equivalent of two full-time jobs, or in an international agency or a government or one of its departments or agencies

2. Have, alone or with his or her accompanying spouse, including a *de facto* spouse, net assets of at least CAD 1,600,000 obtained legally, excluding the amounts received by donation less than six months before the date on which the application was filed

3. Wish to settle in Quebec

4. Sign an agreement to invest CAD 800,000 with a financial intermediary authorized to participate in the Quebec Immigrant Investor Program

In addition, investor applicants will be selected on the basis of education, age, knowledge of French and English, and adaptability.

The *Ministère* will receive a maximum of 1,750 applications for a selection certificate under the investor program, including a maximum of 1,200 from applicants from China (including Hong Kong and Macao). These applications will be shared among financial intermediaries. The maximum number of applications for each financial intermediary has been determined based on the maximum number of applications received annually. The distribution of applications among the financial intermediaries is based on the relative historical importance of each one in relation to the whole group.

Investor applicants who demonstrate, by means of a test recognized by the *Ministère*, that they have an advanced intermediate knowledge of French are not subject to this maximum.

Federal Immigrant Investor Venture Capital Pilot Program

The Immigrant Investor Venture Capital Pilot Program was introduced by IRCC in January 2015 in order to attract experienced business immigrants who can actively invest in the Canadian economy, stimulating innovation, economic growth and job creation. This program was not well received by immigration practitioners nor prospective immigrants.

Federal Start-Up Visa Program

Under the Federal Start-Up Visa Program the applicant must:

- Have a Letter of Support from a designated angel investor group, venture capital fund or business incubator
- Meet the ownership requirements for a qualifying business
- Achieve scores of at least CLB 5 in all four categories for either English or French
- Have an adequate amount of money to settle and provide for the cost of living prior to earning an income

Provincial Nomination Programs

Most Canadian provinces have created provincial nomination programs (PNPs) as a means of attracting applicants who are more likely to make an immediate economic contribution to the province. These programs are tailored to respond to the economic needs of their province.

To apply for permanent residence under a PNP, applicants must be nominated by a province or territory. Each province and territory has established its own requirements and nomination procedures.

Family Class Sponsorship

To apply for residence on the basis of Family Class Sponsorship, a Canadian citizen or permanent resident must apply on behalf of the applicant as the applicant's sponsor, in order for the applicant to qualify for permanent residence.

CIC also requires that applicants pass the following:

- Medical examination
- Background check

Once the applicant becomes a permanent resident, he or she must comply with the residence obligation of being physically in Canada for at least two years in a five year period.

14.3   Procedures and time frame

The application process under the Canadian programs is very well regulated. In order to apply under the residence programs, an application must be submitted, usually to the applicant's local Canadian embassy or consulate or online. At the same time, a federal file number will be assigned to the case, allowing applicants to check the status of the immigration application at any time.

In some cases, a preliminary review is undertaken to determine whether the applicant must undergo a personal interview. The immigration authorities will make a final decision on the application based on the immigration requirements. Once the approval has been given, the passport is submitted to the applicant's local Canadian embassy or consulate, and the immigrant visa will be issued. Once the person arrives in Canada with the visa, the person is granted landed immigrant status.

It is important to note that during the application process – which can take up to three years or more in some cases – and until the applicant has been granted landed immigrant status, the applicant is generally not allowed to enter Canada, other than as a visitor or if the applicant makes a separate application for a work or study permit.

Application processing times differ, depending under which category and where the application was submitted. The IRCC website gives a breakdown of estimated processing times.

14.4 Taxation

Canada taxes residents on their worldwide income. Non-residents are only taxed on Canadian-sourced income. An individual will be deemed to be a resident in Canada if the person spends 183 or more days of a year in Canada, or if this person has significant personal links to Canada, such as familial, economic and social ties to the country, i.e. the common law test of residence to prove where a person has the closest ties is applied.

Provincial income tax rates are determined separately and are added to the federal rates to arrive at various combined marginal rates for individuals; these can currently reach up to approximately 54%. The maximum federal tax threshold is CAD 120,000 of taxable income.

A tax resident must file tax returns based on each calendar year (usually due by 30 April or 15 June for self-employed persons and spouses).

There are no inheritance or gift taxes, and Canada does not levy wealth taxes. However, there are capital gains taxes (taxed at a reduced rate for residents). These apply instead of gift or inheritance tax: a transmission of wealth as a result of a gift or death does not lead to any gift or estate tax; instead, there is a deemed disposition at fair market value resulting in capital gains tax payable by the person giving the gift, or by the estate of the deceased.

Canadian corporations are taxed on their worldwide active business income. There is a combined federal and provincial or territorial tax rate levied, which rate will be determined depending on where the business is located and the nature of its operations. Tax planning through corporations and income splitting is permitted under Canadian federal and provincial taxation laws and significantly reduces the higher taxation rates applicable to individuals.

Until July 2014, Canada's Income Tax Act allowed new immigrants to Canada to benefit from the creation of what is known as an 'immigration trust'. This was particularly beneficial to individuals who had a high net worth and retained liquid assets outside of Canada. If properly structured, any foreign earned income and capital gains earned from the assets held in an immigration trust were exempt from taxation for five years. This measure has now been removed.

Canada has an extensive network of double tax agreements.

It is also important to note that Canada imposes a 'departure tax' on persons who give up their residence in Canada. The rationale is that the person is deemed to dispose of all assets and is therefore taxed accordingly. However, there are special tax rules and exemptions that can mitigate this position. For example, an individual who has been resident in Canada for less than 60 months during a 120-month period preceding departure will be exempt from the departure tax.

14.5   Family law and inheritance aspects

Each province and territory follows its own matrimonial property law and succession law regimes as these laws are enacted by the provincial legislatures.[140] Generally the provinces follow the common-law system and a more equitable manner of sharing assets is now employed by the courts, whereas previously woman's rights to matrimonial property were rather restricted.

Inheritance tax was repealed in 1992. While there is no inheritance tax, provincial probate fees may apply. An estate is treated in the same way as if the assets were sold i.e. all sources on an accrual basis up to the date of the death of the person is deemed income, including accrued capital gains and losses. An exemption is applied for the surviving spouse.

14.6   Citizenship

The conditions of acquisition of Canadian citizenship were changed with the enactment of Bill C-24, the Strengthening Canadian Citizenship

---

[140]   Marriage and divorce matters are dealt with under federal jurisdiction; but most family law matters (including adoption, matrimonial property disputes, and custody unrelated to divorce) are governed by provincial laws

Act, which became law in June 2014 and included a number of important changes.

Applicants are now required to be physically present for four years (1,460 days) in a six-year period, and require applicants to be physically present in Canada for at least 183 days per year in four of the six years.

Under the old Citizenship Act, each day that applicants spent in Canada before they became permanent residents counted as a half day of residence toward fulfilling their residence requirement for citizenship. Under the new Act, time spent in Canada as a non-permanent resident will no longer count toward meeting citizenship residence requirements.

The Strengthening Canadian Citizenship Act requires citizenship applicants to declare their intention to reside in Canada before citizenship is granted. As well, the Act expands the age group from 18–54 to 14–64 of citizenship applicants, who are required to demonstrate official language proficiency and take the citizenship knowledge test. Language and/or knowledge requirements may be waived on compassionate grounds and on a case-by-case basis. In addition, new changes now require applicants to file Canadian income taxes, if required under the Income Tax Act, in order to be eligible to apply for citizenship.

The Act also amends the review process for decisions on citizenship applications. Until the passage of the legislation, an appeal of a citizenship judge's decision would go to the Federal Court but no higher. Now, decisions by citizenship officers, who have authority to decide certain cases under the Act, can be judicially reviewed and challenged in a higher court.

Under the Citizenship Act, judicial review of citizenship decisions will be subject to leave of the Federal Court. The Federal Court decision can then be appealed to the Federal Court of Appeal, where the Federal Court certifies a serious question of general importance. Further appeals are available to the Supreme Court of Canada with leave.

Once the applicant has acquired the citizenship certificate, an oath of citizenship must be taken at a ceremony. The oath is a personal commitment to accept the responsibilities and privileges of Canadian citizenship.

Any person born in Canada, regardless of the nationality of the parents, is a Canadian citizen.

14.7 Dual citizenship

Canada allows dual citizenship.

14.8 Key advantages and disadvantages

Advantages

- One of the highest standards of living in the world
- Multicultural and vibrant cities
- Excellent place to do business with access to the entire North American market (NAFTA)
- Citizenship available after four years of residence out of six years

Disadvantages

- Strict physical presence required to qualify for citizenship

14.9 General information

Official name	Canada
Capital city	Ottawa
Region	Northern North America
Surface area	9,984,670 km^2 km
Government	Parliamentary democracy, a federation, and a constitutional monarchy
Language	English (official) 58.8%, French (official) 21.6%, other 19.6%
Currency	Canadian Dollars (CAD)
Population	35.3 million (2014)
Religion	Roman Catholic 42.6%, Protestant 23.3%, other Christian 4.4%, Muslim 1.9%, other and unspecified 11.8%, none 16%
Ethnic Group	British Isles origin 28%, French origin 23%, other European 15%, Amerindian 2%, other, mostly Asian, African, Arab 6%, mixed background 26%
GDP	USD 1.632 trillion (2015 est.)
GDP per capita, PPP	USD 45,600 (2015 est.)
Major industries	Transportation equipment, chemicals, processed and unprocessed minerals, food products, wood and paper products, fish products, petroleum and natural gas
Main exports	Motor vehicles and parts, industrial machinery, aircraft, telecommunications equipment; chemicals, plastics, fertilizers; wood pulp, timber, crude petroleum, natural gas, electricity, aluminum
Climate	The climate varies from temperate in the south to sub-arctic and arctic in the North
UN Human Development Index (HDI)	9th (2015)
World's healthiest countries (Bloomberg Rankings)	14th (2015)
Henley & Partners Visa Restrictions Index	6th (2016), 4th (2015)
Legatum Prosperity Index	6th (2015)

Sources: CIA "The World Factbook" (2015), World Bank (2015), UN Human Development Report (2015), Henley & Partners, The Legatum Institute

14.10 Climate

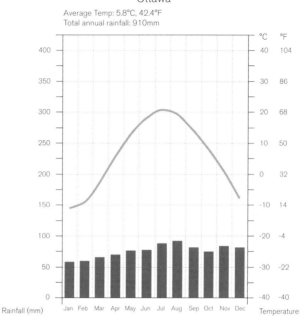

Ottawa
Average Temp: 5.8°C, 42.4°F
Total annual rainfall: 910mm

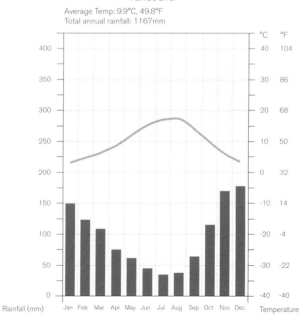

Vancouver
Average Temp: 9.9°C, 49.8°F
Total annual rainfall: 1167mm

15

Guernsey

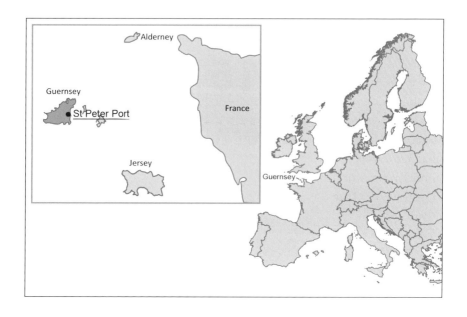

Guernsey is a beautiful island situated in the British Channel Islands in close proximity to the French and English coasts. Guernsey has an area of approximately 24 square miles, balancing the best of both worlds with its beautiful sandy beaches and a thriving town with a vibrant and forward-looking business environment.

Guernsey is a Crown Dependency which means that it is part of the British Isles, (but not the UK) and has its own constitutional government, the States of Guernsey, and independence in terms of changes in policy and legislation. It has its own taxation system characterized by low personal taxes and an absence of taxes applied elsewhere, such as general sales taxes, inheritance tax and a capital gains tax.

The economy of Guernsey is mostly underpinned by its internationally recognized finance services operating across the areas of banking, funds, fiduciary and insurance traditionally but also in newer innovative areas such as FinTech. Government, industry and the regulator, the Guernsey Financial Services Commission, work hard together to ensure that Guernsey has a robust level of regulation that is internationally commended while remaining flexible for exciting new business opportunities. The States of Guernsey takes an active role in supporting the existing sectors of the economy as well as creating an environment for new sectors to grow and thrive through its Economic Development Framework.

Tourism, hospitality and retail are other important areas to Guernsey's economy. Visitors and residents are never far from one of Guernsey's 27 sandy beaches which are some of the cleanest in the British Isles. The island also boasts miles of scenic cliff paths and a bustling town of St Peter Port with a number of independent shops selling a wide variety of unique and high quality items as well as a wide choice of cafes and restaurants to cater for all tastes.

Relocation to Guernsey can be achieved simply with help from the Locate Guernsey team.[141] Locate Guernsey is committed to marketing

---

[141] *locateguernsey.com* or email *enquiries@locateguernsey.com*

Guernsey as a destination for relocation of high net worth individuals and businesses. The team provides a welcoming experience for potential relocators ranging from liaison with other government departments to putting people in touch with estate agents and tax advisors.

The island is safe, politically stable and its residents enjoy an excellent quality of life.

15.1 Residence in Guernsey

There are controls on who can come to live and work in Guernsey, which are in addition to the immigration controls of the Guernsey Border Agency. There are two different Laws that are administered by the Housing Department of the States of Guernsey:

- The Housing Control Law divides Guernsey's housing stock into two tiers, known as the Open Market and the Local Market. The law controls who may live in all Local Market housing and it also controls who may live in certain types of Open Market housing

- The Right to Work Law requires any person in employment in Guernsey to hold a valid Right to Work document

The Open Market

There are approximately 1,600 Open Market Private Houses in Guernsey which are listed on "Part A" of the Open Market Housing Register.

An individual, couple or family living in an Open Market Private House, whether they own it or rent it from the owner, can live in the property indefinitely and will be able to do any job in the island if he/she is a British citizen, EEA national (that is EU nationals plus nationals of Iceland, Liechtenstein and Norway), Swiss national, a Commonwealth citizen who would be entitled to Right of Abode in the UK, or has a right of Abode in the UK through marriage or any other means. Open Market Part A occupants wishing to undertake employment in the island need to hold a "Right to Work" document (Declaration of Lawful Residence) which actually proves that they are lawfully housed. The issue of these documents are a mere formality as long as the occupant lives in this type of accommodation (and has immigration clearance to live in Guernsey).

If the individual, couple or family living in an Open Market Part A property do not intend to work, there is no need to liaise with the Housing Department regarding the occupation of that property.

As the controls on who can live in Open Market housing are more relaxed than for Local Market housing, Open Market housing tends to be more expensive. Further information regarding the Open Market can be obtained at the Locate Guernsey website.

The Local Market

An individual wishing to live in a Local Market property requires a housing licence to do so. There are two distinct types of housing licences:

1. An employment-related housing licence

2. A non-employment-related housing licence

If an individual does not have an existing right to occupy a Local Market property, it is highly unlikely that a non-employment-related housing licence would be granted. An individual who believes the post of employment which they might undertake in the island would be considered by the States of Guernsey to be "essential" to the island – as a result of the fiscal and other benefits that the island would receive as a direct consequence of it being undertaken - is strongly advised to contact Guernsey's Housing Department to receive further guidance on employment-related housing licences.

For individuals looking to become resident in Guernsey, the Locate Guernsey team is able to assist. Locate Guernsey is a dedicated Government unit which is committed to generating and responding to relocation queries.[142] The team imparts advice to all potential relocators

---

[142] *www.locateguernsey.com* or email *enquiries@locateguernsey.com*

but is primarily concerned with economically active high net worth individuals and businesses.

Guernsey has a positive reputation for its excellent business environment and its friendly and lively community. For these reasons, Locate Guernsey is committed to assisting relocators who will add value to the local economy through some mechanisms that may include (but not limited to) working with or commissioning work from local companies, inward investment or sponsorship of community activities, job creation on island, and up-skilling of employees.

Individuals who are interested in living in Guernsey, but who will not undertake or create employment are still able to relocate to a property in Guernsey's Open Market and are likely to find this route to residence, with a minimum of barriers, to be the most suitable for them.

Immigration

The Bailiwick of Guernsey has its own immigration legislation which, though operating separately from those in the UK, are integrated with and act parallel to UK immigration legislation.

In practice, UK Immigration Acts are extended to the Bailiwick by Order in Council. The primary Act is the United Kingdom Immigration Act 1971, as amended, and the day to day administration of the 1971 Act is set out in the Immigration (Bailiwick of Guernsey) Rules 2008.

Guernsey has not adopted the UK points based system; however the following immigration categories that allow for migration of non-EEA nationals to the island are catered for within the Immigration Rules:

- Investors
- Persons intending to establish themselves in business
- Writers, composers and artists

15.2   Requirements

As long as an individual/family has immigration clearance, there are no barriers to them being the tenant or owner of an Open Market Part A property. Estate agents and relocation agents in the island provide advice on the type and availability of Open Market properties and contact details can be found on the Locate Guernsey website.[143]

If an individual wishes to live in a Local Market property, an application for a housing licence must be submitted in advance of occupying such a property. Advice on making an application should be sought from the Housing Department prior to an application being submitted.

Investor immigration

An applicant seeking to enter as an investor must demonstrate that he has money of his own under his control and disposable in the Bailiwick of Guernsey amounting to no less than GBP 1 million, and intends to invest not less than GBP 750,000 of his capital in the Bailiwick of Guernsey or the UK in a manner that is of benefit to the Bailiwick. The applicant must intend to make the islands of Guernsey, Sark or Alderney his main home and must be able to maintain and accommodate himself and any dependents without taking employment (other than transacting business in connection with his investments).

Persons intending to establish themselves in business

An applicant seeking to establish himself in business can include taking over an existing business in the Bailiwick of Guernsey as a partner or director or establishing a new business in the Bailiwick. The main requirements are that he has a minimum of GBP 200,000 of his own money under his control and disposable in the Bailiwick of Guernsey which will be invested into the business and that there is a genuine need for his investment and services in the Bailiwick. Where a new business is being set up he must demonstrate that the business will create significant

---

[143]   *www.locateguernsey.com* or email *enquiries@locateguernsey.com*

new paid employment for persons already settled in the Bailiwick or the business will be in the general interests of the Bailiwick. An applicant seeking entry in this capacity must also demonstrate a suitable level of the English language at the time of application, unless he is a national of a majority English speaking country.

Writers, composers and artists

An applicant may seek to enter as a writer, composer or artist if he has established himself outside the Bailiwick and is primarily engaged in producing original work which has been published, performed or exhibited for its literary, musical or artistic merit. The applicant must be able to support himself and any dependents from his own resources without working except as a writer, composer or artist.

To qualify for settlement in the above mentioned immigration categories, the applicant must have spent a continuous period of five years in the Bailiwick in the capacity for which he sought entry and must have sufficient knowledge of the English language (unless already demonstrated at entry stage) and have passed a citizenship test. Once settlement has been granted all visa restrictions are removed. Permanent residence may be lost if absent from the UK and Islands for longer than two years.

15.3   Procedures and time frame

Housing

Applications for Right to Work documents to enable Open Market Part A occupants to work in Guernsey take approximately four weeks to process. Applications can be submitted in advance of the individual occupying the property. The document is not required to enable the individual to take up occupation of the property.

Immigration

Applicants seeking entry to the Bailiwick in any of the above categories must apply for a UK Entry Clearance whilst in their usual country of residence. It is not possible to apply from within the Bailiwick of Guernsey. Applications are initially submitted via the UK Visas and Immigration website[144] and applicants will then need to attend a visa application center to enroll their biometrics and submit all hard copy supporting documents. Applications are then referred to the Guernsey immigration authorities for a decision which can take approximately four weeks.

While individuals (or their representatives) are of course entitled and allowed to initiate and carry forward the relocation process, contact with Locate Guernsey on matters of process is available to assist in making relocation simpler.

15.4　Taxation

Guernsey has a fair and competitive tax regime which meets the OECD international standards of tax transparency and information exchange. There are no capital gains, inheritance or wealth taxes and no VAT in Guernsey. The tax year runs from 1 January to 31 December.

For companies the standard rate of tax is 0%, although some income from the provision of regulated financial services (such as fund administration and banking business) is taxed at 10%, and utilities and Guernsey property income streams are taxable at 20%. A company is resident in Guernsey if it is controlled by natural persons in Guernsey, or it is incorporated in Guernsey and has not been granted exempt status (collective investment vehicles are eligible to apply for exempt status upon payment of a fee).

For individuals the basic rate of income tax is 20%, which is applied after the deduction of personal and other allowable expenses.

An individual may be classed as "non-resident", "resident only" or "solely or principally resident" in Guernsey, for tax purposes. Full details of the criteria can be found in Section 3 of the Income Tax (Guernsey) Law 1975, as amended. However in essence an individual would become resident if they spend 91 days or more in Guernsey during a year of charge

---

[144]　*gov.uk/government/organisations/uk–visas–and–immigration*

and "principally resident" if they are in Guernsey for 182 days or more, or if they take up permanent residence. An individual, who is resident in Guernsey, would be classed as "solely resident", if they are not resident in any other place in the year of charge; to be resident in another place the individual would have to spend 91 days in that other jurisdiction in the year. An individual will be regarded as being in Guernsey, if they are resident in Guernsey at midnight, at the end of the day.

A "non-resident" individual has a liability to tax on certain Guernsey source income, such as employment, property or business income. That individual would be granted a proportion of the personal allowances for the time spent in the island. They would not be liable on Guernsey income such as bank interest or directors fees.

A "resident only" individual has the choice of paying tax on their worldwide income, against which they would receive a proportion of the personal allowances relating to the number of days spent in the island, or they may elect to pay the Standard Charge, which is GBP 30,000 for the calendar year 2016. If that individual chooses to pay the standard change, they will have no liability to tax on non-Guernsey income, but a liability will arise on their total Guernsey source income (other than bank deposit interest). The amount of the Standard Charge paid would be offset against the tax due on the Guernsey source income. An individual who elects to pay the standard charge has no entitlement to any allowances, reliefs or deductions. There are special provisions in the Law to cater for those who are resident only and who are in Guernsey solely for employment purposes.

Individuals who are "solely or principally resident" are taxable on their worldwide income and are granted the full personal allowances. There is however, a tax cap which is currently GBP 110,000 in respect of non-Guernsey source income (including Guernsey bank interest) with a higher GBP 220,000 cap on worldwide (including Guernsey) income, for 2016. Tax on income generated from Guernsey land and property is payable in addition to the tax cap.

Guernsey has entered into numerous Double Taxation Agreements (DTAs) with other countries to help alleviate the effects of double taxation; a full list of partial and comprehensive DTAs is available on the States of Guernsey website.[145] Guernsey has also signed over 50 Tax Information Exchange Agreements and also has intergovernmental agreements with the UK and US, which all enhance Guernsey's reputation as a responsible and transparent financial center.

15.5 Family law and inheritance aspects

Guernsey has its own legislation dealing with family and inheritance law matters although in many respects it is similar to English law. Local advice should be sought if required.

15.6 Citizenship

In Guernsey, the same regulations apply for citizenship as in the UK.

The British Government is responsible for administering the laws covering British citizenship through the British Nationality Act 1981, which also applies to Guernsey.

All naturalization and registration applications for Guernsey residents are dealt with by the Guernsey Customs and Immigration Service.

15.7 Dual citizenship

Dual citizenship is allowed.

15.8 Key advantages and disadvantages

Advantages

- Very high quality of life in a beautiful setting

- Good (40 minute) flight connections with London and other parts of the UK

---

[145] *www.gov.gg*

- Attractive tax system
- Very few barriers to entry, especially through Open Market housing

Disadvantages

- International airport in Guernsey has only limited international direct flight connections (except for to the UK)
- Prices of certain properties is relatively high

15.9   General information

Official name	Guernsey
Capital city	Saint Peter Port
Region	Western Europe, island in the English Channel, Northwest of France
Surface area	78 km^2
Government	Parliamentary Democracy
Language	English, French, Norman dialects spoken in country districts
Currency	Guernsey Pound
Population	66,080 (July 2015 est.)
Religion	Protestant, Roman Catholic
Ethnic groups	British, French, Norman descent with small percentages from other European countries
Gross Value Added	USD 3.451 billion (2014 est.)
GVA per capita	USD 52,300 (2014 est.)
Major industries	Agriculture, tourism, banking
Main exports	Flowers, vegetables
Climate	Temperate with mild winters and cool summers
UN Human Development Index (HDI)	n.a.
World's healthiest countries (Bloomberg Rankings)	n.a.
Henley & Partners Visa Restrictions Index	3rd (2016), 1st (2015) (as part of the UK)
Legatum Prosperity Index	n.a.

Sources: CIA "The World Factbook" (2015), World Bank (2015), Henley & Partners, The Legatum Institute, Policy & Research Unit Guernsey (2015)

15.10 Climate

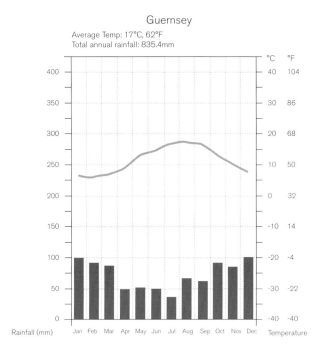

16
Hong Kong

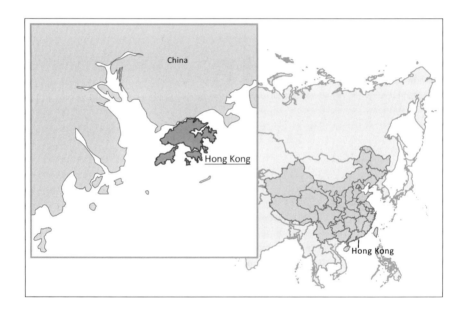

Hong Kong is a diverse metropolis offering a unique blend of Eastern and Western traditions. Hong Kong is one of two Special Administrative Regions (SAR) of the People's Republic of China (PRC), with the other being Macau. The Hong Kong region comprises of more than 260 islands with Hong Kong Island, the namesake of the SAR region, being the main activity hub.

From 1842 to 1997 Hong Kong was a colony of the UK. Consequently, Hong Kong adopted a hybrid legal system differing from that of the mainland, China. The law comprises of the legislated Basic Law and a tradition of Common Law inherited from British colonial rule.

Hong Kong is an open economy with a free market and low taxation, making it an important center for international finance and trade. It boasts a large presence of banks, insurance companies, venture capital companies and other financial intermediaries. According to the Global Financial Center Index 8,[146] Hong Kong is the 3rd largest financial center in the world after London and New York. Hong Kong is also the world's tenth largest trading economy, one of the world's largest gold markets, and Asia's third biggest stock market.

Since October 1983, the Hong Kong dollar has been pegged to the US dollar at a rate of HKD 7.80 to USD 1.00. Hong Kong acts as a regional business center in Asia, with well-established commercial links to most of the Asian countries. Hong Kong has a unique position with regard to business in China. This relationship is cemented by the bilateral free trade agreement known as the Closer Economic Partnership Agreement (CEPA)[147] that Hong Kong signed with Mainland China. China's entry into the World Trade Organization has strengthened Hong Kong's position to increase its role as China's major commercial and financial link with the outside world.

Hong Kong has adopted a liberal approach to its immigration policy. It welcomes professionals and businessmen to work and invest in the region.

---

[146] Published in March 2013
[147] The agreement was first signed in June 2003

The Hong Kong Special Administrative Region (HKSAR) Government has full autonomy on immigration control matters, even though Hong Kong is an inalienable part of the People's Republic of China.

16.1   Residence in Hong Kong

Article 154 of the Basic Law[148] provides that the Hong Kong Government may operate and apply its own immigration controls on foreign nationals' entry, stay and departure from the Region.

Nationals of about 170 countries and territories are allowed visa-free visits to Hong Kong for periods ranging from seven to 180 days.[149] Those who intend to stay for periods longer than the approved visa-free period are required to apply for permission to live, work or study in Hong Kong. The relevant entry visa must be obtained before arrival.

In particular Hong Kong has developed visa programs to attract professionals who possess special skills, knowledge and experience of value that may not be readily available in the Region. Moreover, individuals who make a substantial investment to the economy are also welcomed with open arms.

The rules and guidelines for immigration to Hong Kong are found in the Immigration Department's Regulation Booklets. These should be read in conjunction with chapter 115 of the Hong Kong Immigration Ordinance[150] to establish the basis for residence in Hong Kong.

There are various categories for individuals to obtain residence in order to work, live or study in the Region. The following provides a breakdown of these categories for foreign nationals to obtain residence in Hong Kong.[151]

---

[148]   *www.basiclaw.gov.hk/en/basiclawtext/images/Basic_Law.pdf*
[149]   *www.immd.gov.hk/eng/faq/top10_faq.html*
[150]   *www.legislation.gov.hk/eng/home.htm*
[151]   *www.immd.gov.hk/ehtml/hkvisas.htm*

1. The *Capital Investment Entrant Scheme* applied to applicants over the age of 18, with net assets of no less than HKD 10 million held for a period of two years prior to submission of the application. The applicant had to invest no less than HKD 10 million into permissible investments of financial assets. The Hong Kong Government has announced that the *Capital Investment Entrant Scheme* is suspended with effect from 15 January 2015 until further notice

2. *The Quality Migrant Admission Scheme* is a quota-based and points-based system that allows applicants over the age of 18, who can demonstrate that they are capable of supporting and accommodating themselves and their dependents. The applicant must be proficient in Chinese or English and have a good educational background to qualify for this category. Under the general points system, an applicant must score at least 80 points out of 195, as a combined mark from the subtotals under the five sections (age, academic/professional experience, work experience, language proficiency, and family background). Alternatively, an applicant who is exceptional in their field can qualify by scoring an overall mark of 195 points for their skill from an achievement–based point test

3. There are various categories under the employment/investment tier of applicants. The following employment permits exist:

    a. The *General Employment Policy (GEP) Permit* is an entry permit for an applicant employed as a professional or who provides a substantial investment. The person must have a good educational background and/or relevant experience, a confirmed employment offer in Hong Kong which is relevant to the person's professional abilities and a remuneration package that is commensurate with the prevailing market level in Hong Kong. Alternatively, the applicant must be in a position to make a substantial contribution to the economy of Hong Kong

    b. The *Employment under the Admission Scheme for Mainland Talents and Professionals Permit* is an entry permit for professional applicants from Mainland China in the commercial and financial sector, the arts, culture or sports sectors, or in the culinary profession. The applicant must provide a confirmed offer of employment relevant to their experience, which must not be readily available in the local Hong Kong work force. The remuneration package must correspond to the prevailing professional market

c. *Investment as Entrepreneurs* is the entry arrangement for persons who wish to enter/stay in the Hong Kong Special Administrative Region (HKSAR) for investment as entrepreneurs under the General Employment Policy (GEP), i.e. to establish or join a business in the HKSAR. An applicant with a good education background, good technical qualifications, proven professional abilities and/or relevant experience may also be accepted if they are in a position to make a substantial contribution to the economy of the HKSAR

d. The *Immigration Arrangements for Non-local Graduates Permit* is an entry permit for an applicant who has obtained a degree or higher qualification in a full-time and locally-accredited program in Hong Kong. The graduate is entitled to a 12-month visa to stay in Hong Kong, with the purpose of finding employment within this period. The applicant is not required to provide proof of secure employment for the initial application and can change employment during the 12-month period without affecting the validity of the visa. However, if the applicant submits the application to the Immigration Department six months after the graduation, the applicant will be required to provide proof of secure employment. Once the 12-month period is completed, the person cannot apply for an extension of this visa

e. The *Employment as Imported Workers Permit* allows employers to import laborers who provide labor at a technician level or below, of a category or type that cannot be sourced locally. Both the employer and employee must fulfill various conditions for this type of permit to be granted

f. The *Employment as Foreign Domestic Helpers Permit* allows employment of a foreign domestic worker

4. The *Permit for Residence as a Dependent* allows dependents including spouses, unmarried dependent children under the age of 18 and in some cases, parents aged 60 and above, who are sponsored by a permanent resident of Hong Kong, or a resident not subject to a limited stay to join the main applicant or permanent resident. Dependents in some of the visa categories are not permitted to work unless they have obtained special permission from the Immigration Department

5. A *Visa for Training* is provided to applicants for a limited period of less than 12 months to train the applicant to acquire special skills and knowledge not available in the applicant's country. The applicant must be sponsored by a well-established local company

6. In order to qualify for a *Study Permit* for Hong Kong, the applicant must apply to study in an educational institution that has been registered. The applicant must provide an acceptance letter from the institution as well as nominate a local sponsor in Hong Kong, which can be either the educational institution or an individual who is a permanent resident in Hong Kong

7. The *Working Holiday Scheme Permit* provides for a national of a participating country, aged between 18 and 30 years, to spend time in Hong Kong for a period of 12 months. The applicant should not work for the same employer for more than three months during their stay in Hong Kong. The participating countries include Australia, Canada, Germany, Ireland, Japan and New Zealand. There is no extension of the visa available once the applicant has completed the 12-month stay

16.2 Requirements

The authorities will approve an application based on the individual applicant's merits. The Hong Kong government does, however, require that the applicant also meets the standard immigration criteria. This includes a valid travel document with adequate returnability to their country of citizenship; a clean criminal record and, and like most countries, proof that the applicant will not be a burden on Hong Kong.

As the criteria of eligibility for each category will differ and are specific to the particular permit scheme, the applicant must fulfill the specific criteria for the grant of the entry permit. The eligibility criteria may be subject to change, so it is best to check with one's legal advisor or the Hong Kong Immigration Department[152] for the exact criteria requirements.

The Hong Kong Government has instituted restrictions on certain foreign nationals to preclude them from entering the resident permit program – each program with its own exclusion criteria. Certain programs are not available to foreign nationals of Afghanistan, Cambodia, Cuba, Laos, Korea (Democratic People's Republic of), Nepal and Vietnam, and Chinese residents of the mainland, Macau and Taiwan.

Under each program, the applicant must ensure that the criteria fulfilled to obtain the residence permit are maintained throughout the period of residence. For example, an applicant under the Capital Investment Entrant Scheme must maintain the investment continuously for a period of seven years. In the case of an employee, the visa is usually issued for the duration of the employment contract. Failing to meet the conditions of the permit will cause the resident to lose the initial status granted, unless the person changes to another resident scheme.

16.3 Procedures and time frame

The Immigration Department of the Hong Kong Special Administrative Region Government (HKSARG) administers the entry permit requirements for persons wishing to enter the Hong Kong Special Administrative Region (HKSAR) of the People's Republic of China (PRC).

The application process commences with submission of the application to the Immigration Department and if everything is in order, approval is granted. Once approval is obtained, the applicant must fulfill the conditions of entry as per the requirements for the specific immigration category. The timeframe for residence in the Hong Kong Region depends

---

[152] *www.immd.gov.hk*

on the different immigration schemes; in most cases the entry permit is issued for a period of two years.

Once the formal approval letter is received, the successful applicant and dependents can obtain their first residence visas and move to Hong Kong. The successful applicant will be required to activate their residence status with the Immigration Department within three months of entry into the region. All residents over the age of 11 must register for a Hong Kong identity card which must be carried at all times.

A further extension may be given to the applicant, provided all the requirements have been fulfilled by the applicant and the specific immigration category permits the extension. Under the Immigration Ordinance, six categories of people are eligible to enjoy the "right of abode" which entitles the resident to obtained permanent residence status in Hong Kong. A person who fulfils the transitional arrangement under the same Ordinance is also eligible to enjoy right of abode.

If a person belongs to one of the following categories, they are a permanent resident of the HKSAR and enjoy the right of abode:

Chinese Citizens

a. A Chinese citizen born in Hong Kong before or after the establishment of the HKSAR

b. A Chinese citizen who has ordinarily resided in Hong Kong for a continuous period of not less than seven years before or after the establishment of the HKSAR

c. A person of Chinese nationality born outside Hong Kong before or after the establishment of the HKSAR to a parent who, at the time of birth of that person, was a Chinese citizen falling within category (a) or (b)

Non-Chinese Citizens

d. A person not of Chinese nationality who has entered Hong Kong with a valid travel document, has ordinarily resided in Hong Kong for a continuous period of not less than seven years and has taken Hong Kong as his/her place of permanent residence before or after the establishment of the HKSAR

e. A person under 21 years of age born in Hong Kong to a parent who is a permanent resident of the HKSAR in category (d) before or after the establishment of the HKSAR if at the time of his/her birth or at any later time before they turn 21 years of age, one parent has the right of abode in Hong Kong

f. A person other than those in categories (a) to (e), who, before the establishment of the HKSAR, had the right of abode in Hong Kong only

16.4   Taxation

Taxation in Hong Kong is based on the territorial source principle and is therefore only levied on income sourced in Hong Kong. This is applicable to both individuals and companies and there is no distinction made between residents and non-residents.

Profit tax is charged on all income derived from business, trade or employment. Income derived from outside Hong Kong is exempt for individuals and companies. However, this exemption does not apply to financial institutions that conduct business in Hong Kong. In order to efficiently increase the operation of the territorial source concept, an advance ruling may also be obtained based on income or profits.

There are three separate income tax rates: profit tax at a standard rate of 16.5% on companies and 15% on unincorporated businesses; property tax at a standard rate of 15% (less a 20% deduction); and salaries tax at a standard rate of 15% on net income or at progressive rates on net chargeable income, whichever is lower.

Hong Kong has a very attractive taxation system because the income tax rates are low and there is no capital gains tax, no sales/value added tax, no wealth/net worth tax, no tax on inheritance or gifts, no tax on interest income and no withholding tax on dividends paid by Hong Kong companies.

Income derived from outside Hong Kong will be exempt from tax in Hong Kong, if the tax liability arises and is paid in the foreign jurisdiction. However, unless there is a double tax agreement in place, Hong Kong will not give a credit in lieu of the foreign tax paid.

Estate duty was abolished with effect from 11 February 2006 and therefore no estate duty is imposed on the value of an individuals' Hong Kong property at death.

16.5 Family law and inheritance aspects

The Wills Ordinance of Hong Kong Laws recognizes the testamentary intention of a deceased person if there is a valid will, executed in accordance with the law. If there is no will, the estate will be dissolved under the Intestate Succession Laws, which usually would entail movable assets to be distributed according to the laws of the deceased's country of domicile and immovable assets will be distributed according to the laws of the jurisdiction where the asset is located. Furthermore there are no forced heirship laws.

No community of property or other marital property regimes apply in Hong Kong.

The Matrimonial Reform Ordinance (Cap 178), and the Matrimonial Causes Ordinance (Cap 179) deal with matters pertaining to marriage as well as the dissolution of marriage in Hong Kong. The Matrimonial Proceedings and Property Ordinance (Cap 192) deals with the aspect of property dissolution in the event of divorce or death.[153]

16.6 Citizenship

The legal status of a permanent resident of Hong Kong may be acquired by any person, regardless of whether they are Chinese nationals or not.

---

[153] *www.hkfla.org.hk*

Article 24 of the Basic Law and Schedule 1 of the Immigration Ordinance (Cap 115), briefly sets out who is entitled to Hong Kong permanent resident status. In summary, they state that the following persons are permanent residents of Hong Kong:

a. A Chinese citizen born in Hong Kong before or after the establishment of the Hong Kong Special Administrative Region

b. A Chinese citizen who has ordinarily resided in Hong Kong for a continuous period of not less than seven years before or after the establishment of the Hong Kong Special Administrative Region

c. A person of Chinese nationality born outside Hong Kong before or after the establishment of the Hong Kong Special Administrative Region to a parent who, at the time of birth of that person, was a Chinese citizen falling within category (a) or (b)

d. A person not of Chinese nationality who has entered Hong Kong with a valid travel document, has ordinarily resided in Hong Kong for a continuous period of no less than seven years and has taken Hong Kong as his place of permanent residence before or after the establishment of the Hong Kong Special Administrative Region

e. A person under 21 years of age, born in Hong Kong to a parent who is a permanent resident of the Hong Kong Special Administrative Region in category (d) before or after the establishment of the Hong Kong Special Administrative Region, at the time of his birth or at any later time before he attains 21 years of age, enables one of his parents to claim the right of abode in Hong Kong

f. A person other than those residents in categories (a) to (e), who, before the establishment of the Hong Kong Special Administrative Region, had the right of abode in Hong Kong only

The Nationality Law of the People's Republic of China (the Nationality Law) determines the laws of citizenship. Article 7 of the Nationality Law provides that any foreign person who is willing to abide by China's constitution and laws and meets the criteria to qualify as a citizen, may be naturalized in Hong Kong upon approval of application for citizenship. The new Chinese citizen must provide proof that all previous citizenships have been relinquished.

16.7 Dual citizenship

China (and thus Hong Kong SAR) does not allow dual citizenship.

16.8 Key advantages and disadvantages

Advantages

- Straightforward, efficient residence program
- Well-established legal system based on common law and transparent regulations
- Strategic location and premier gateway for trade and investment to and from mainland China
- Freest economy in the world with limited corporate and personal taxes
- World-class international airport
- World-class medical facilities and education institutions

Disadvantages

- High property prices and scarcity of land
- Moderate air quality
- Population density very high
- Citizenship generally not available and of limited interest (Hong Kong is part of China, which does not allow dual citizenship)

16.9   General information

Official name	Hong Kong Special Administrative Region
Region	Eastern Asia, bordering the South China Sea and China
Surface area	1,108 km²
Government	Limited democracy
Language	Chinese (Cantonese) 89.5% (official), English (official) 3.5%, Putongua (Mandarin) 1.4%, other Chinese dialects 4%, other 1.6%
Currency	Hong Kong dollars (HKD)
Population	7,141,106 (July 2015 est.)
Religion	Eclectic mixture of local religions 90%, Christian 10%
Ethnic Group	Chinese 93.1%, Filipino 1.9%, Indonesian 1.9%, other 3%
GDP	USD 414.6 billion (2015 est.)
GDP per capita, PPP	USD 56,700 (2015 est.)
Major industries	Textiles, clothing, tourism, banking, shipping, electronics, plastics, toys, watches, clocks
Main exports	Electrical machinery and appliances, textiles, apparel, footwear, watches and clocks, toys, plastics, precious stones, printed material
Climate	Subtropical monsoon, cool and humid in winter, hot and rainy from spring through summer, warm and sunny in fall
UN Human Development Index (HDI)	12th (2015)
World's healthiest countries (Bloomberg Rankings)	17th (2015)
Henley & Partners Visa Restrictions Index	20th (2016), 16th (2015)
Legatum Prosperity Index	20th (2015)

Sources: CIA "The World Factbook" (2015), World Bank (2015), UN Human Development Report (2015), Henley & Partners, The Legatum Institute

16.10 Climate

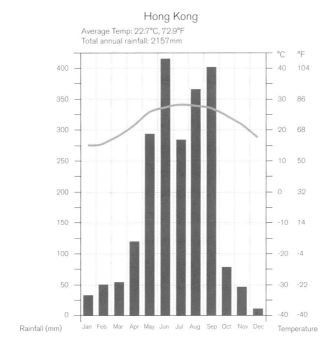

Hong Kong

Average Temp: 22.7°C, 72.9°F
Total annual rainfall: 2157mm

17

Jersey

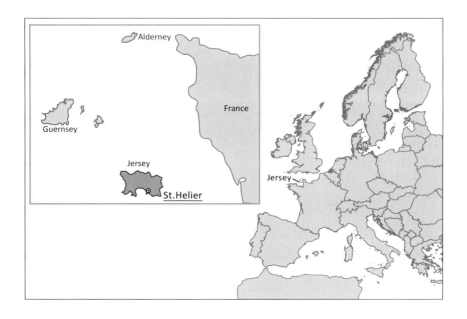

Jersey is a delightful island, with strong influences from both Britain and France, coupled with a rich history and culture that spans over 1,000 years. At just 118 square kilometers, Jersey is the largest of the Channel Islands, situated in the English Channel just a few miles from the French coast.

Jersey is a Crown Dependency. This means that it is part of the British Isles, but not part of the UK, which gives Jersey a unique constitutional link, as well as complete fiscal independence. Jersey is neither represented in the UK parliament at Westminster nor involved with, or subject to, the judicial systems of the UK. For immigration purposes, Jersey is part of the UK borders and the Common Travel Area, which comprises of the United Kingdom, Bailiwick of Jersey, Bailiwick of Guernsey, Isle of Man and the Republic of Ireland. Jersey is not a member of the European Union (EU), but has a special relationship with the member states, allowing free movement of goods and services. The government of Jersey is known as the States of Jersey or "the States", which comprises 49 elected members plus the Bailiff, who is President. Jersey has its own independent system of local administration, fiscal and legal systems, and courts of law. Jersey has a ministerial system of government, consisting of a Council of Ministers led by a Chief Minister.

Jersey's economy is based on international financial services, tourism and agriculture. In 2013 the finance sector accounted for about 40% of the island's Gross Value Added. However, the world-renowned Jersey breed of dairy cattle also represents an important export income. Tourism accounts for one-quarter of GDP. Jersey welcomes quality businesses from all over the world but maintains strict safeguards in order to protect its excellent reputation.

Jersey attracts many financial services companies which, depending upon their activity, will be regulated and/or registered by the Jersey Financial Services Commission which exerts close supervision over all the island's financial institutions and trust companies. The Jersey Financial Services Commission is also responsible for the Registrar of Companies. Jersey is well-renowned worldwide and recognized by both the International

Monetary Fund (IMF) and the Organization for Economic Cooperation and Development (OECD).

The island is a popular place to live due to low income tax, business opportunities and a high quality of life. The strong economy, coupled with the mild climate and the wealth of activities on offer, make Jersey an idyllic place to raise a family. It may appear small and quiet, but there is much to do ranging from exploring the countryside and coastline, to Michelin star dining as well as various cultural events and attractions.

17.1 Residence in Jersey

Where an immigration clearance is required, the Immigration and Asylum Act 1999 (Jersey) Order 2003 grants the Lieutenant-Governor of Jersey discretion to determine the right of entry and right of refusal into Jersey. The directions were duly adopted on 1 April 2005. The Directions of the Lieutenant-Governor determines the practice to be followed in the administration of immigration.[154]

Unless the applicant fulfils one of the permit free categories,[155] a work permit is required to take up employment in Jersey. The requirements for a work permit are governed by the Immigration (Work Permits) (Jersey) Rules 1995. The applicant can only take up employment if the employer has satisfied certain conditions, which include showing that the post cannot be filled by someone who is local, or the role qualifies under the permit free category. The applicant must also fulfil the criteria applicable to his particular sector.[156] The applicant will apply to the Jersey Customs and Immigration Service (Immigration Office), who will issue

---

[154] *www.gov.je*
[155] A British citizen or a British subject with the right of abode; national of a member state of the European Union (EU)/European Economic Area (EEA); non-EEA family member of an EEA national (may also work without a permit but must obtain an EEA family permit before entering Jersey); Swiss national; Commonwealth citizen admitted as a working holiday maker; Commonwealth citizen admitted on the grounds of UK ancestry; Commonwealth citizen with a certificate of entitlement to the right of abode; participant in the UK Youth Mobility Scheme; minister of religion; business visitor; and non EU/EEA passport holder who has no restrictions attached to the stay
[156] *www.gov.je*

the work permit if all criteria have been fulfilled by both the employer and employee. Presently, work permits are only issued to applicants employed in the following professions:

- Healthcare professionals
- Legal and finance professionals
- Chefs
- Entertainers

All other applications are reviewed on a case-by-case basis. A work permit does not automatically entitle the applicant to residence status.

There are also various alternative entry permits for special categories such as students, dependents, Ministers of Religion,[157] and Youth Mobility Scheme Applicants.[158]

Due to the limited accommodation available in Jersey, restrictions for property acquisition are placed on non-Jersey residents. Such residents may only purchase or lease "qualified" residential property once they have resided on the island for 10 years continuously, or if they meet other qualifying factors, including essential employment or on the grounds of economic benefit by way of High Value Residence or Inward Investor, collectively "Licensed".

Most people who come to work in Jersey can only live in "unqualified" accommodation, which includes private rental, lodging houses and lodging in private homes. This accommodation is comparatively expensive to the "qualified" options.

High Value Residency

A special residence category exists for high net worth individuals (HNWIs), which allows the individual to obtain residence by application for the

---

[157] Ministers of Religion must meet the requirements listed in the United Kingdom Statement of Immigration Rules (HC 1113/7701/349)
[158] Youth Mobility Scheme applicants must meet the requirements listed in the United Kingdom Statement of Immigration Rules (HC 1113/7701/349)

granting of a permit known as 2(1)(e), this being the relevant Article under the Control of Housing and Work (Jersey) Law 2012. The granting of such a permit is at the absolute discretion of the Chief Minister.

A successful High Value Residency applicant will be a person who is deemed to bring significant benefit to the island, usually on an economic, business or social level. Many qualifying factors will be taken into consideration along with the applicant's financial situation, such as high achievements or cultural benefits to the local community. Personal, financial, and business background information and references must be submitted for review.

There is no prescribed limit on the number of 2(1)(e) consents that the Chief Minister may grant each year although, in practice, the number is small. Each application is considered by the Chief Minister on its own merits, with regard to factors such as the individual's likely contribution to tax revenues, the business/social background of the applicant and their likely business activities (if any) in Jersey and other non-economic benefits which the island may obtain if consent is granted.[159]

17.2   Requirements

Successful 2(1)(e) applicants will retain their residential status as long as they remain resident in Jersey. They may only purchase property which has been classified or approved as suitable. In practice, such properties must be GBP 1.75 million or more.

The 2(1)(e) housing permits are generally issued on an unconditional basis, however conditions may be attached in individual cases.

The key requirement is that the applicant can show evidence of their ability to generate the requisite annual worldwide income of at least GBP 625,000 on a recurring basis from a robust source or sources to the Comptroller of Taxes, which would meet the minimum tax liability of GBP 125,000, being at a rate of 20%, with any worldwide income in excess of GBP 625,000 being taxed at 1%.

---

[159]   See *www.locatejersey.com*

A spouse and children under 18 years may be supplemented to the application once the main applicant is admitted.

Inward Investor

In addition to the High Value Residency option, which provides for a minimum annual tax collection to the States from the individual, Jersey also has a willingness to grant "Licensed" status to Inward Investors, either as employees or principals of new businesses, which meet the criteria for establishing a presence on the island, if the individual brings experience in a particular area of expertise.[160]

The "Licensed" consent is a special category for non-locals whose employment is deemed essential to a business. They must demonstrate that they fulfil the requirements of this role through ability, qualification or experience. The applicant would normally hold a position of some importance and the business must demonstrate that the post cannot be filled by someone already entitled to live and work in Jersey.

The grant of "Licensed" status gives the employee the right to purchase or rent property on the island.

Investor Category

The Investor visa requirements for Leave to Enter the Bailiwicks of Jersey or Guernsey requires an individual over the age of 18 years to have no less than GBP 1 million in capital under his/her control and disposal in the Bailiwick, and intends to invest not less than GBP 750,000 of that capital in a manner that is to the benefit of the Bailiwick.

What constitutes a GBP 750,000 investment "to the benefit of the Bailiwick" is a process that is determined on a case-by-case basis by the Bailiwick itself and is dependent on the applicant's own background, personal interest and medium to long-term objectives. A number of investment possibilities can be explored and will be considered.

---

[160] *www.locatejersey.com*

As for the portion above GBP 750,000, the investment can be by way of bank deposits or net equity in local real estate. The entire GBP 1 million investment must be maintained for at least five years. In addition to the investment, the principal applicant must make the Bailiwick their main home by spending more time in the Bailiwick than elsewhere in the world.

The applicant is not required to show any previous business experience or the ability to speak English at the time of application. The initial visa is valid for two years and, at its expiry, the applicant can apply for an extension of stay. The Bailiwick will grant a three-year extension if the applicant has maintained the required investment throughout the term.

To qualify for Indefinite Leave to Remain (ILR) in the Bailiwick, the applicant and dependents must prove that they have sufficient knowledge of life in the Bailiwick, and the principal applicant must have maintained the GBP 1 million investment for no less than five years and made the Bailiwick their main home by spending more time there than elsewhere in the world.

17.3   Procedures and time frame

For both the High Value Resident applicant and Inward Investor, there are no application forms as such. Each case is handled and assessed individually. A personal letter of application must be drafted, accompanied by a CV and background information, as well as a financial profile and references.

Before any case is submitted to the Jersey authorities, it is advisable to engage a suitably experienced Jersey tax practitioner to assist with all aspects of structure and tax planning.

In respect of High Value Residency, the application procedures in Jersey are extremely efficient and the entire application process can normally be completed within a time frame of as little as two weeks from the time of submission of a complete application package, unless additional information is required.

The Chief Minister considers each application on an individual basis before making a decision. The application is reviewed by the Comptroller of Taxes and thereafter approved by the Chief Minister. Even though the Chief Minister grants the right of residence, the Immigration Office issue the entry/residence permit.

Highly specialized senior employees will usually be granted an open-ended consent for residence. A "Licensed" employee will be granted residential status after a continuous 10-year period of essential employment on the island. This status will be lost if a total of five or more years is spent off-island.

Once the relevant authority has approved the application, an entry clearance (visa) will be issued and the applicant will be granted entry to Jersey for a specific period of time.

With regard to the Investor Category, the application and supporting documentation must be submitted to the UK visa post in the applicant's country of residence. The time frame from the submission of application to visa approval is dependent on the visa post receiving the application, but generally takes between two and six weeks. Once approved, the principal applicant, and all dependents associates with the application, are required to register at the Border Agency within seven days of their arrival in the Bailiwick.

Upon expiry of the initial two-year period, the main applicant must apply for an "extension of stay" from within the Bailiwick. The authorities will issue the principal applicant, and all dependents associated with the application, with a three-year extension, if all relevant criteria have been met.

On completion of five years of continuous lawful residence, the main principal applicant and dependents may apply for ILR, also known as Permanent Residence. To obtain ILR, the principal applicant must demonstrate that they have legally spent more time in the Bailiwick than elsewhere in the world, have maintained the conditions required by the Investor visa, and have maintained and accommodated themselves without taking employment (other than transacting business in connection with their investments) or without any recourse to public funds.

17.4   Taxation

The Jersey government is committed to maintaining the attractiveness of the Jersey tax regime as part of its overall economic strategy.

Jersey's income tax system is based on residence and income tax is charged on worldwide income and profits. There is no statutory definition of residence. There are two types of tax residence recognized, namely "resident and ordinarily resident" (ROR); or "resident but not ordinarily resident" (RNOR).

A person is considered a resident if they are physically present for at least six months of the tax year; or they are physically present in Jersey for an average of three months over any four-year period; or the person has accommodation available in Jersey and stays in this accommodation in the tax year.

A person is considered ordinarily resident if they are habitually resident. The Comptroller of Taxes in Jersey considers that a person is habitually resident if they have been resident for three concurrent tax years or if they move to Jersey with the intention of remaining permanently.

A person who is ROR is taxed on their worldwide income. A person who is RNOR is subject to tax on any Jersey source income and any foreign income that is emitted to.

Foreign tax paid is ordinarily allowed as a deduction from taxable income.

A non-resident is only levied tax on certain Jersey-source income excluding the following: bank interest, dividends from Jersey companies taxable at 0%, Jersey state pension, interest from a purchased life annuity, interest from a Jersey company, director's remuneration, royalty income and patent income.

The standard tax rate in Jersey is 20%. As described earlier, taxpayers with regulation 2(1)(e) status are subject to special tax rates. Income arising from Jersey property is subject to tax at the rate of 20%. This would be calculated on a pro-rata basis in the financial year (January to December) when the applicant moves to Jersey.

Capital gains are not subject to tax and there are no inheritance, gift or wealth taxes.

The island has no separate corporation tax code, although Jersey has now introduced a 'zero/ten' corporation tax regime. Under the zero/ten regime, companies will generally be taxed at 0% while a special 10% rate is applied to certain regulated financial businesses. Also public utility companies and property companies, including property developers, operating in Jersey are taxed at 20%.

Other attractions of the Jersey tax system include generous rules for the taxation of employee-share-ownership, social security payments capped at a low level, no stamp duty on equity transactions, and an excellent working relationship between the financial services industry and the tax authorities, which promotes openness and economic growth.

Jersey operates an indirect tax known as Goods and Services Tax (GST) which is applied at 5% on the value of goods and services supplied in Jersey by registered businesses. There is a turnover threshold below which traders are not required to register for GST. Currently, this threshold is GBP 300,000 per annum of taxable supplies.

Jersey has signed double tax arrangements with Estonia, Guernsey, Hong Kong, Isle of Man, Luxembourg, Malta, Qatar, Rwanda, Seychelles, Singapore and the UK; and has limited double tax arrangements with Australia, Denmark, Faroe Islands, Finland, France, Germany, Greenland, Iceland, New Zealand, Norway, Poland and Sweden.

17.5   Family law and inheritance aspects

Jersey has adopted the UK's legal system, therefore any family law issues would be dealt with in accordance with English law.

17.6   Citizenship

In Jersey, the same regulations apply for citizenship as in the UK. The British Government is responsible for administering the laws covering British citizenship through the British Nationality Act 1981, which also applies to Jersey.

All naturalization and registration applications for Jersey residents are dealt with by the Immigration Office.

17.7   Dual citizenship

Jersey allows dual citizenship.

17.8   Key advantages and disadvantages

Advantages

- Excellent location and lifestyle between Britain and France

- Strong and stable economy

- Convenient flight connections to London/the UK

- Attractive tax system

- Safe environment for children with a high standard of education

- High quality healthcare facilities

- Efficient immigration authorities and extremely fast procedures (one month)

Disadvantages

- Relatively high minimum tax requirements

- International airport in Jersey has only limited international direct flight connections (except to the UK)

- Property availability is limited and prices for certain properties are comparatively high

17.9 General information

Official name	Bailiwick of Jersey
Capital city	Saint Helier
Region	Western Europe, island in the English Channel, Northwest of France
Surface area	116 km²
Government	Parliamentary democracy
Languages	English 94.5% (official), Portuguese 4.6%, other 0.9%
Currency	Jersey Pounds (JEP)
Population	97,294 (July 2015)
Religion	Protestant (Anglican, Baptist, Congregational New Church, Methodist, Presbyterian), Roman Catholic
Ethnic groups	Jersey 46.4%, Britons 32.7%, Portuguese / Madeiran 8.2%, Irish, French, and other white 7.1%, other 2.4%
Gross Value Added	JEP 3.9 billion (2014)
GVA per capita	JEP 38,800 (2014)
Major industries	Tourism, banking and finance, dairy, agriculture, electronics
Main exports	Light industrial and electrical goods, dairy cattle, Jersey Royal potatoes, foodstuffs, textiles, flowers
Climate	The climate is temperate; mild winters and cool summers
UN Human Development Index (HDI)	n.a.
World's healthiest countries (Bloomberg Rankings)	n.a.
Henley & Partners Visa Restrictions Index	3rd (2016), 1st (2015) (as part of the UK)
Legatum Prosperity Index	n.a.

Sources: CIA "The World Factbook" (2015), World Bank (2015), Statistics Unit Jersey (2015), Henley & Partners

17.10 Climate

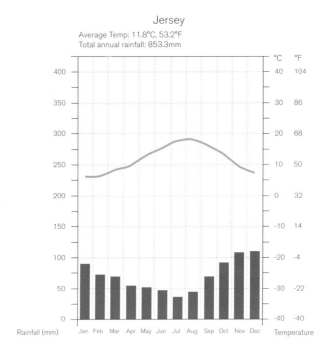

18

Malaysia

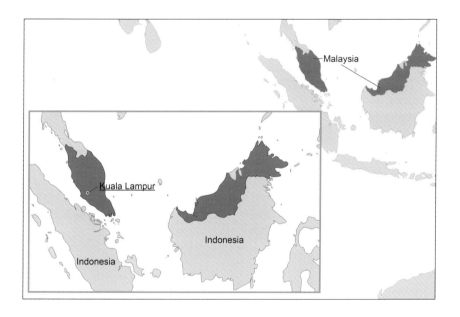

Malaysia is one of Southeast Asia's most vibrant economies, due to its continued industrial growth and political stability over the past few decades. It is a highly open upper-middle income economy and the third largest economy in the region.

The national language of Malaysia is Malay (Bahasa Melayu), with English is the second language. Similarly, the Malay culture is dominant in the country because the Malays are the dominant race in Malaysia and in the region, however, other cultures can be practiced very freely and there is a free intermingling of these different cultures.

After gaining independence from the UK, Malaysia joined the British Commonwealth. It is a member of the United Nations, Asia-Pacific Economic Cooperation (APEC), and a founding member of the Association of Southeast Asian Nations (ASEAN).

As one of the Southeast Asia's key tourist destinations, located near the equator, Malaysia offers excellent beaches, breath taking scenery and dense rainforests.

18.1   Residence in Malaysia

Any foreign national who is not a citizen of Malaysia and intends to enter and reside in Malaysia as a permanent resident may apply for an Entry Permit in accordance with Section 10 of the Immigration Act and Regulation 4 of the Immigration Regulations 1963.

There are four categories for Entry Permit applications for permanent residence:

1. Investors and Experts (A1)

   a. The Investor category (A1) is for individuals that invest a minimum USD 2 million fixed deposit at any bank in Malaysia for a minimum of five years. The investor's spouse and any children below the age of 18 years are eligible for Permanent Residence after five years of stay in Malaysia. This category requires one Malaysian sponsor

b. The Expert category (A1) is for individuals with expertise, talent and skills recognized as "World Class" by any international organization and requires recommendation by the relevant agency in Malaysia as well as a certificate of good conduct from the applicant's country of origin. This category also requires one Malaysian sponsor. Professionals (A2)

c. The Professional category (A2) is for professionals in any field with outstanding skills. This again requires recommendation by the relevant agency in Malaysia; a certificate of good conduct from the country of origin and one Malaysian sponsor. The applicant must work in a government agency or private company in Malaysia for a minimum period of three years and be certified by the relevant agency in Malaysia

2. Spouse and child/ren below the age of 6 of a Malaysian citizen

The applicant must be married to a Malaysian Citizen, who sponsors the applicant, and have been issued with a Long Term Visit Pass and have stayed continuously in Malaysia for a period of five years

3. The Points System

Applications are assessed through seven criteria: age, qualifications, duration of stay in Malaysia, familiarity with the Malaysia Institute, the values of investments, working experience in Malaysia, and proficiency in Bahasa Malaysia. Applicants need to achieve a minimum of 65 marks out of 120, have a Malaysian sponsor and a certificate of good conduct from their country of origin

Essentially, foreign nationals can apply for permanent residence once they have lived in Malaysia continuously for five years. For foreigners who are married to Malaysian citizens, the period required is 10 years. Every application for permanent residence must be sponsored by a Malaysian citizen.

Malaysia My Second Home Programme (MM2H)

The MM2H requires applicants to meet certain criteria and in exchange, applicants and their dependents are granted a 10 year multiple-entry visa. This is effectively a residence permit, enabling the successful applicant and their family to live in Malaysia.

The MM2H is open to citizens of all countries recognized by Malaysia regardless of race, religion, gender or age. Applicants are allowed to bring their spouses and unmarried children below the age of 21 as dependents.

Since the inception of the MM2H Programme in 2002, more than 29,000 applicants have been approved.

18.2   Requirements

Upon application, applicants are required to demonstrate the capability to support themselves financially in Malaysia without seeking employment or government assistance. The financial requirements for applicants below 50 years old are proof of bankable assets of at least MYR 500,000 and proof of offshore income of at least MYR 10,000 per month. For applicants 50 years old and above, the requirements are proof of bankable assets of at least MYR 350,000 and proof of offshore income of at least MYR 10,000 per month.

Upon approval and once an applicant receives a conditional approval letter, they must meet the requirements for applicants below 50 years old; a bank account must be opened with a deposit of at least MYR 300,000. After a period of one year, up to MYR 150,000 may be withdrawn for approved expenses relating to a house purchase, the education of children in Malaysia or medical purposes. A minimum balance of MYR 150,000 must be maintained from the second year onwards and throughout the stay in Malaysia under the program. For applicants 50 years old and above; a bank account must be opened with a deposit of at least MYR 150,000. After a period of one year, up to MYR 50,000 may be withdrawn for approved expenses relating to a house purchase, the education of children in Malaysia, or medical purposes.

A minimum balance of MYR 100,000 must be maintained from the second year onwards and throughout the stay in Malaysia under the program. With proof of receipt of a pension of at least MYR 10,000 per month, the applicant may be exempt from making a fixed deposit.

18.3 Procedures and time frame

The Ministry of Tourism and Culture is responsible for the processing of all applicants. The Immigration Unit will issue a conditional approval letter to each approved applicant. The applicant is then required to open a bank account in Malaysia and transfer the fixed deposit; purchase medical insurance from any insurance company in Malaysia; and obtain a medical report from any private hospital or registered clinic in Malaysia.

After submission of the fixed deposit certificate, the medical insurance policy and the medical report; the applicant may collect their MM2H visa. It is important to note that the visa does not allow the holder to work in Malaysia and it does not lead to permanent residence.

18.4 Taxation

Malaysia uses a territorial taxation system. Residents are only taxed on Malaysian sourced income and the progressive tax rate on chargeable income reaches a maximum of 25%. A 30% capital gains tax is levied on real estate belonging to non-citizens if the property is disposed of within four years of the purchase date. The standard rate of GST is 6%. Malaysia has an extensive network of double tax agreements with other countries, which means a resident of Malaysia may be able to claim a tax refund on foreign income taxed in overseas countries. There is no capital gains tax except when such gains comprise a portion of the income-earning activities of the business, in which case the corporate tax rate applies.

18.5 Family law and inheritance aspects

In Malaysia, family law relating to Muslims is governed separately from family law relating to non-Muslims. Secular high courts have jurisdiction over matters relating to non-Muslims, and religious courts, known as Syariah Courts, have jurisdiction over matters relating to Muslims. This applies to all personal matters including marriage, divorce, custody of children, division of assets in a divorce, and intestacy.

Section 76 of the Law Reform (Marriage and Divorce) Act 1976 allows the Malaysian court to order the division of any assets acquired during the marriage between the parties. The decision will distinguish between joint and sole assets. There is no assumption that matrimonial assets are equally shared.

There is no inheritance tax in Malaysia. The Distribution Act 1958 governs the distribution of an estate of a non-Muslim who dies intestate. The estate will be distributed among immediate family members.

18.6   Citizenship

The Ministry of Home Affairs is responsible for ascertaining and ensuring only qualified and deserving individuals are granted Malaysian citizenship status. All citizenship applications will be presented to the National Registration Department (NRD). Only those who meet the terms and conditions as stipulated by the Federal Constitution will be approved.

Foremost, applicants must hold an Entry Permit and Permanent Resident (PR) status to qualify to apply for citizenship. Those who have been stripped of or rejected Malaysian citizenship and have yet to hold PR status can submit their PR status application at the Malaysia Immigration Department through the entry permit application.

Applicants are then required to sit for a language test conducted by the NRD. The basic considerations for citizenship application include good behavior and no criminal record, residence in Malaysia for a long time, high commitment and deep-rooted interest in Malaysia, an understanding of the language, culture and national needs, having contributed to society and the Nation and being faithful and loyal to the Nation.

18.7   Dual citizenship

Malaysia does not allow dual citizenship.

18.8   Key advantages and disadvantages

Advantages

- Relatively low cost of living
- Attractive taxation system based on the territorial source principle
- Applicant may bring their spouse and unmarried children below 21 years old as dependents
- Applicant may purchase any number of residential properties at a minimum of MYR 1 million
- No physical presence requirements

Disadvantages

- Applicants are not allowed to work while staying in Malaysia
- MM2H is not a pathway to permanent residence or citizenship

18.9   General information

Official name	Malaysia
Capital city	Kuala Lumpur
Region	Southeast Asia
Surface area	330,803 km^2
Government	Federal government
Languages	Bahasa Malaysia (official), English, Cantonese, Mandarin, Hokkien, Hakka, Hainan, Foochow, Tamil, Telugu, Malayalam, Panjabi, Thai
Currency	Malaysian Ringgit (MYR)
Population	30,513,848 (July 2015 est.)
Religion	Muslim (official) 61.3%, Buddhist 19.8%, Christian 9.2%, Hindu 6.3%, Confucianism, Taoism, other traditional Chinese religions 1.3%, other 0.4%, none 0.8%, unspecified 1% (2010 est.)
Ethnic groups	Malay 50.1%, Chinese 22.6%, indigenous 11.8%, Indian 6.7%, other 0.7%, non-citizens 8.2% (2010 est.)
GDP	USD 815.6 billion (2015 est.)
GDP per capita	USD 26,300 (2015 est.)
Major industries	Rubber and oil palm processing and manufacturing, petroleum and natural gas, light manufacturing, pharmaceuticals, medical technology, electronics and semiconductors, timber processing, logging, agriculture processing
Main exports	Semiconductors and electronic equipment, palm oil, petroleum and liquefied natural gas, wood and wood products, palm oil, rubber, textiles, chemicals, solar panels
Climate	Tropical; annual southwest (April to October) and northeast (October to February) monsoons
World's healthiest countries (Bloomberg Rankings)	51st (2015)
UN Human Development Index (HDI)	62nd (2015)
Henley & Partners Visa Restrictions Index	12th (2016), 9th (2015)
Legatum Prosperity Index	44th (2015)

Sources: CIA "The World Factbook" (2015), World Bank (2015), UN Human Development Report (2015), Henley & Partners, The Legatum Institute

18.10 Climate

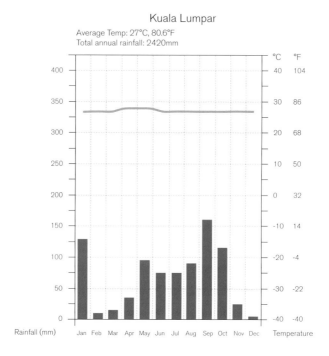

19

Malta

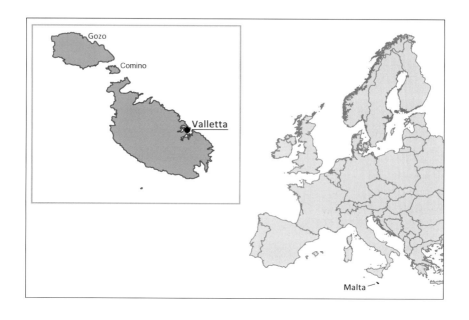

Malta lies in the middle of the Mediterranean Sea. The Maltese Archipelago consists of five islands: namely the main island, Malta; the second biggest island Gozo; Comino; Cominetto and Filfla, the latter two being uninhabited. These islands are located about 90 kilometers south of Sicily and 350 kilometers from the Libyan coast.

Valletta, the capital, has been declared a UNESCO World Heritage Site with beautiful building facades, each telling a different story about this small island steeped in history, dating as far back as 5000 BC. In fact, some of the earliest human settlements are found in Malta, dating back some 7,500 years.

The island has a population of just over 400,000 inhabitants. The national language is Maltese but the official languages of the country are Maltese and English with Italian also widely used among the natives.

In 1964, after more than 160 years of British rule, Malta gained its independence. In 1974 Malta became a republic with a parliamentary democracy system and a constitution in place. The President is Head of State and the Prime Minister and Cabinet hold the executive power. The legal system is based on Roman civil law but has a strong influence of English Common law, especially in respect of its commercial framework.

Malta has developed a good business infrastructure and over the last 15 years has actively positioned itself as an effective international business hub. The Government is proactive in its efforts to attract external investment. A variety of special regimes have been created for particular sectors including shipping and financial products.

Malta joined the EU in 2004 and has been using the euro since 2008.

In August 2015, the Government of Malta announced the Malta Residence and Visa Programme (MRVP), which offers international investors who are not EU, EEA or Swiss nationals indefinite residence.

19.1   Residence in Malta

The new program falls under the Immigration Act Legal Notice 288 of 2015 and is available for both the applicant and their dependants. The main applicant must be at least 18 years of age to qualify and must provide an affidavit declaring that from the date of the application they have an annual income of no less than EUR 100,000 or have in their possession capital of not less than EUR 500,000.

19.2   Requirements

In order to qualify for the MRVP the individual must:

1. Acquire property in Malta under one of the following criteria:

    a. Purchase a property for a minimum value of EUR 320,000 if the property is in Malta, or

    b. Purchase a property for a minimum value of EUR 270,000 if the property is in the South of Malta or in Gozo, or

    c. Rent a property for a minimum of EUR 12,000 annually, or

    d. Rent a property for a minimum of EUR 10,000 annually if the property is in the South of Malta or in Gozo

2. Commit to a qualifying investment of an initial value of EUR 250,000 which must be held for a minimum period of five years

3. Commit to pay a contribution of EUR 30,000 (of which EUR 5,500 is a non-refundable government administrative fee)

4. Have health insurance or health cover valid throughout the EU, worth at least EUR 30,000

5. Pass an international due diligence exercise

In order to retain the relevant permit under the program, the individual must ensure that a suitable address and a valid health insurance are maintained.

Although no physical presence is required for the MRVP, the individual must spend either six consecutive months or a total of ten months outside Malta in each four year period, and must sign a declaration to this effect.

19.3   Procedures and time frame

The MRVP application requirements and procedures are reasonable and straightforward. The application is submitted to the government agency responsible for the applications, Identity Malta, with a non-refundable deposit of the contribution of EUR 5,500. After stringent due diligence checks, successful applicants will be requested to complete the qualifying investments and will then be issued with a five-year residence permit. Identity Malta will also issue successful applicants with a Maltese Residence Certificate which will be deemed to be an indefinite permit. The certificate will be monitored annually for the first five years from its issue, and every five years thereafter.

19.4   Taxation

Individuals who are resident and domiciled in Malta pay income tax on their worldwide income. Personal income is taxed at progressive rates up to 35%. However, individuals who are resident but not domiciled in Malta pay tax on (a) income arising in Malta and (b) on income (excluding capital gains) remitted to Malta that arises outside the island (i.e. 'remittance basis'). The tax rate varies in accordance with the individual's tax status. Malta does not impose estate or gift tax but does levy a Capital Gains Tax (CGT) on various assets, mainly immovable property and shares. CGT is not levied on transfer of immovable property if the person transferring the property has owned it and occupied it as his main residence for a period of three consecutive years immediately preceding the date of transfer and if the property is transferred within 12 months from vacating the premises. Otherwise, tax may be levied at up to 35% on the gain if the property is sold within the first 12 years of ownership or 12% on the sales consideration if the transfer is made after 12 years of ownership. The 12% final tax, however, does not apply if the individual property owner is not resident in Malta. The standard VAT rate is 18%. The corporate tax rate is 35%; special tax concessions, however, apply for non-resident/non-domiciled owners. Malta has concluded double taxation treaties with around 60 countries. A number of other agreements are signed but not yet in force.

19.5   Family law and inheritance aspects

Matrimonial law is based on the community property regime, unless the couple specifically elect otherwise. This agreement would have to be notarized by public deed. If married outside of Malta, the couple will be subject to the community property regime in respect to property acquired in Malta, but only if they are deemed domiciled in Malta.

Until October 2011 it was not possible to get a divorce in Malta other than by having a foreign divorce recognized by the local authorities, provided that the decision was delivered by the competent court of the country in which either of the parties to the proceedings is domiciled or of which either of such parties is a citizen. Since October 2011, by Act XIV, 2011, a divorce law has been introduced in Malta, allowing both locals and foreigners to request a divorce decree from the Law Courts of Malta.

The domicile of the deceased at the time of death will determine the jurisdiction which will deal with dissolution of the deceased's estate. There is an exception with immovable property though, as immovable property situated in Malta will be subject to the law of Malta.

The deceased, having their domicile in Malta, is subject to the inheritance rules of Malta. If the deceased dies intestate (i.e. without a will) then their entire estate is divided equally between the spouse and the descendant's children. However if the deceased leaves a will, even though capable to dispose of his estate in the manner which pleases them most, the estate of the deceased is subject to the reserved portion, that is the right on the estate of the deceased reserved by law in favor of the descendants and surviving spouse of the deceased. The said right is a credit of the value of the reserved portion against the estate of the deceased.

There is no inheritance tax on the estate except for a stamp duty tax due on the transfer of immovable property and the transfer of certain securities. The maximum tax rate is 5%.

19.6 Citizenship

The Citizenship Act XXX of 1965, as amended, determines the citizenship rules in Malta.

Generally, Maltese citizenship is acquired by birth and descent or by naturalization. Most acquisitions of Maltese citizenship by naturalization are acquired by marriage or through a Maltese parent.

If a person is resident in Malta for an aggregate period of four out of six years, by law they can apply for citizenship, however, very few people obtain Maltese citizenship under this route as it is considered a very difficult process.

In Malta it is also possible to qualify for citizenship without prior residence. Under the provisions of Articles 10 (9) (b) and 24 (1) (i) of the Maltese Citizenship Act (Cap 188), and the Malta Individual Investor Programme Regulations, 2013, the grant of citizenship may be made to duly qualified, reputable foreign individuals and families who make a significant contribution to the economic development of Malta.

19.7 Dual citizenship

Malta allows dual citizenship.

19.8 Key advantages and disadvantages

Advantages

- Easy to integrate as mostly English speaking
- Good medical facilities
- High standard of living but affordable

- Safe environment for children
- Attractive tax regime
- Visa-free travel within the Schengen area

Disadvantages

- Physical presence requirements may apply
- Citizenship very difficult to obtain unless under the Malta Individual Investor Programme
- Not a main hub therefore accessibility can be limited

19.9 General information

Official name	Republic of Malta
Capital city	Valletta
Region	Southern Europe, islands in the Mediterranean Sea, south of Sicily (Italy)
Surface area	316 km^2
Government	Republic
Languages	Maltese (official) 90.2%, English (official) 6%, multilingual 3%, other 0.8%
Currency	Euro (EUR)
Population	413,965 (July 2015 est.)
Religion	Roman Catholic (official) 98%
Ethnic groups	Maltese (descendants of ancient Carthaginians and Phoenicians with strong elements of Italian and other Mediterranean stock)
GDP	USD 15.38 billion (2015 est5).)
GDP per capita, PPP	USD 35,900 (2015 est.)
Major industries	Tourism, electronics, ship building and repair, construction, food and beverages, pharmaceuticals, footwear, clothing, tobacco, aviation services, financial services, information technology services
Main exports	Electrical machinery, mechanical appliances, fish and crustaceans, pharmaceutical products, printed material
Climate	Mediterranean; mild, rainy winters; hot, dry summers
UN Human Development Index (HDI)	39th (2015)
World's healthiest countries (Bloomberg Rankings)	n.a.
Henley & Partners Visa Restrictions Index	9th (2016), 7th (2015)
Legatum Prosperity Index	23rd (2015)

Sources: CIA "The World Factbook" (2015), World Bank (2015), UN Human Development Report (2015), Henley & Partners, The Legatum Institute

19.10 Climate

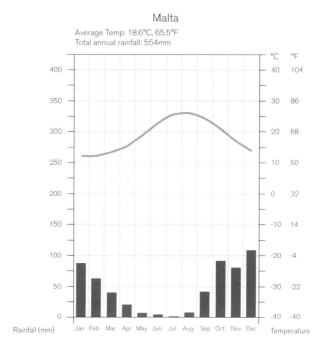

20

Monaco

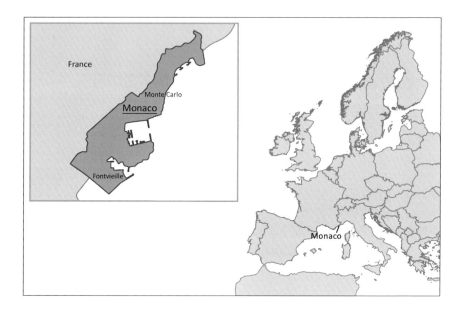

Monaco, with its location on the Cote d'Azur, enjoys a reputation as playground for the rich and famous. It is often described as the perfect place of residence with its French flair, temperate weather and absence of income/capital gains tax regime.

The Principality was founded in 1215. Until 1911, the country was ruled by the House of the Grimaldi Family. Following the Monégasque Revolution in 1910, the Prince of Monaco was forced to proclaim a constitution. The country still recognizes the Royal Family, with Prince Albert II as the head of the Family. In 2005, an historic treaty was signed with France which ended the French domination over the political landscape of Monaco and further confirmed the Principality as an independent sovereign state.

Monaco is the second smallest country in the world after Vatican City. It is approximately the size of Central Park in New York. Out of a population of around 37,000 residents, only 22% of the population is Monégasque. The other 78% of the population is a cosmopolitan mix of residents from the Americas, Europe, Middle East, Australia, and South Africa. Even though French is the official language, English is widely spoken.

It is located on the Mediterranean Sea, with France as its only neighbor. To travel by air, one has to arrive at Nice International Airport in France, 34 km from the Principality, which is a six-minute trip to Monaco by helicopter or 20-45 minutes by car depending on traffic.

Monaco has its own legal system but its law is, to a large extent, based on the French Civil Code. Monaco's political, military and economic interests are aligned with France – i.e. there is a customs and monetary union with France and French VAT applies.

Monaco is not a member of the European Union (EU) and therefore it is not subject to the EU regulations and directives. The country is a full member of the United Nations and the Council of Europe. Monaco is also home to famous sporting events such as the Monaco F1 Grand Prix, the Monte Carlo Tennis Open and the Monaco Yacht Show.

Monaco has traditionally been a residence of choice for wealthy and famous individuals, not least due to its non-taxation of individuals but also due to the level of personal security.

The requirements to become resident in Monaco are not as onerous as one would imagine. To become resident, the applicant must show sufficient means to be able to afford the lifestyle and proof of purchase or rental of property.

20.1 Residence in Monaco

As Monaco is not a member of the EU, EU/EEA citizens must apply for the right of residence in Monaco although the process for those applicants is simpler than for non-EU/EEA applicants.

The conditions for obtaining residence are governed by the Franco-Monégasque Neighbor Convention of 18 May 1963 (Convention Franco-Monégasque de Voisinage du 18 Mai 1963), and the subsequent Sovereign Ordinance No. 3153 of 19 March 1964 (*l'Ordonnance Souveraine No 3153 du 19 Mars 1964*).

Anyone over 16 years of age can apply for Monégasque residence. Once the Monégasque residence card is obtained, you will be required to physically reside in Monaco for at least three months each year although this condition is not always strictly enforced, provided you are not claiming Monaco as a primary residence for tax purposes. If this is the case and a residence certificate is needed, the residence requirement is six months.

By virtue of the relationship with France, and the absence of border controls, a Monégasque resident can travel freely within the EU.

20.2 Requirements

The procedure to become a Monégasque resident differs somewhat depending on whether the person is an EU/EEA national or not. However, regardless of the person's nationality, everyone must obtain a

Monégasque residence permit (*Carte de Résident*), from the Monégasque authorities.

A non-EU/EEA national who resides outside of France must apply for a long stay visa for Monaco before making an application to the Monégasque authorities for residence in Monaco. Under the *Franco Monégasque Convention of 1963* France administers visas on behalf of Monaco, which means that all visa applications must be submitted to a French embassy in the country where the applicant has resided for the six months prior to applying for the Monégasque residence permit (*Carte de Résident*).

For EU/EEA nationals, the long stay visa from France is not required and the applicant may apply directly for a *Carte de Résident* via the Residents section of Public Security in Monaco.

The applicant must submit various documents to the authorities in order to obtain the residence card. Included in this list is proof of accommodation by way of lease or purchase agreement and proof of sufficient funds to live in Monaco (being either a letter from a bank in Monaco, proof of employment in Monaco or the setup of a business there). The applicant is also required to provide standard documents such as birth certificate and proof of a clean criminal record.

Sometimes the applicant may also apply for a business license as Monaco has become a popular place to set up family offices, hedge fund management businesses or branches of overseas companies. Even though Monaco has a keen interest in attracting business to the Principality, the authorities will closely vet the business applications and in the past these could take quite a long time to process. However, a new Business Office has recently been established to provide multilingual assistance, furthermore the authorities have undertaken to confirm (or refuse) a new business license within two months of the complete dossier being presented[161]. Any business activity in Monaco without authorization from the authorities is prohibited. However, a separate work permit is

---

[161]   See *http://www.monaco-iq.com/entrepreneurs*

not required if a business license has been obtained. The exact process to obtain the business license differs depending on entity type and industry sector.

It is possible as a foreign national to obtain a work permit (*Permis de travail*) in Monaco. Law No. 629 of 17 July 1957 outlines the regulations applicable to employment of a foreigner. The work permit is specific to the employment obtained therefore if the employee changes jobs, a new application by the employer will be required. It is the employer's responsibility to show that there are no appropriate and qualified priority local candidates for the position. An employee does not need to be a resident to obtain a work permit and can live in the surrounding areas instead.

20.3   Procedures and time frame

Once the application for a visa has been submitted to the relevant French Consulate, it can take up to three months to be approved. The applicant can apply to the Monégasque authorities (Residents Section of the Directorate of Public Security) for a *Carte de Résident* once the initial visa process is completed and the applicant has received the visa. The applicant must apply for the *Carte de Résident* in Monaco within eight days of arrival in the Principality.

During the first three years, the *Carte de Résident* must be renewed annually; the 4th, 5th and 6th *Carte de Résident* are valid for three years and the seventh and beyond are valid for 10 years.

To renew the *Carte de Résident*, the applicant must demonstrate a certain presence in Monaco, for example by presentation of utility bills.

20.4   Taxation

In Monaco, all residents except most French citizens (who are subject to French taxation)[162], are not subject to income, capital gains tax, or wealth

---

[162]   If they arrived in Monaco before 1957 they are not taxed

tax. Inheritance taxes are due by both residents and non-residents but only on assets located in Monaco. There is no gift or inheritance tax between spouses, parents and children and the highest tax rates for gift and inheritance taxes between non-related persons or distant family members is 16%.

Monaco does not levy real estate tax or general property tax except for registration taxes on leases, the transfer of real estate and the transfer of ownership of legal entities owning real estate in Monaco.[163]

Local businesses may be taxed on net profit or on a percentage of their local operating costs. The net profit tax on commercial and industrial businesses is levied at 33.33%. However, businesses are exempt from this tax if under 25% of their turnover originates from outside Monaco. Moreover, as the profit tax is levied on net profit, a certain amount of directors' remuneration (depending on turnover and type of activity) can be deducted from the net profit thereby further reducing the tax liability to as little as around 5% in some cases.

Monaco is part of the EU Savings Directive which provides that interest payments made in Monaco to an EU resident are subject to a withholding tax of 35%. Monaco transfers 75% of such revenues to the EU state where the EU member is resident. An individual can avoid paying the withholding tax by authorizing the paying agent to disclose details of the interest payments to the tax authorities of his residence state. Monaco residents are not subject to the withholding tax treaty.

Monaco has also agreed to exchange information with certain countries on request in certain cases of tax fraud and where the requesting state has documentary evidence. As per the standard OECD form, so-called "fishing expeditions" are not permissible under such treaties.

Monaco has signed 32 tax agreements (of which 25 are in force) with countries including the US, Australia, India and, in Europe, France, Germany, Italy, Austria, Sweden, Denmark, Belgium and the Netherlands, and is in discussions with a similar number of other countries.

---

[163] Under a new law introduced in 2011

Monaco also signed the multilateral convention concerning mutual administrative coordination in fiscal matters in October 2014.

Since September 2009, Monaco has been on the OECD White List.

20.5   Family law and inheritance aspects

The Civil Code rules of intestacy or by will govern succession law in Monaco therefore Monégasque internal law currently will determine the dissolution of an individual's estate, regardless of the individual's wish, although this situation might change in the future.[164] Forced heirship rules favoring the immediate family members are closely observed in Monaco.

In 1936, legislation[165] was enacted in favor of individuals from common law countries who are resident in Monaco. This allows them to transfer or set up foreign law trusts in Monaco to regulate the dissolution of their estates as they wish with minimal taxation. All Monégasque residents concerned should be aware of these complex laws. In most cases it is advisable to obtain the necessary tax and trust advice to ensure that one's estate is structured in the correct manner.

Succession duty applies only to assets located in Monaco, regardless of where the deceased was resident. Moreover, there is no succession tax on assets passed to the spouse of the deceased, a parent, grandparent, child or other relative in the direct blood line.

The matrimonial regime is also fairly complex. The type of regime the spouses entered into at time of their marriage or anytime during the marriage, will determine how the matrimonial property will be divided at time of divorce or death.

Monaco recognizes various forms of pre-nuptial agreements. If however spouses do not enter into a pre-nuptial or a marriage contract, the

---

[164]   See the proposed law at *http://www.conseil-national.mc/lois.php?idcat=2&idsscat=13*
[165]   Law 214

statutory regime of limited community of goods (*communauté de biens réduites aux acquêts*) applies. Any assets acquired by the spouse before marriage, or by inheritance or gift during marriage, will remain the private property of the spouse. Upon death or divorce, the assets acquired during the marriage are split equally between each spouse.

20.6   Citizenship

Monégasque Citizenship is regulated by Law No. 1155 of 18 December 1992, as amended by Law No. 1276 of 22 December 2003 on nationality.

Acquired by descent, citizenship is established if a child is born to a Monégasque mother or father, or if both parents are Monégasque citizens. A minor who has been adopted by Monégasque parents has the right to acquire citizenship.

A foreign woman who has been married to a Monégasque citizen for more than five years may acquire citizenship by declaration.

Even after many years of residence, it is not easy to become a Monégasque citizen. Monaco is not a viable option if one is planning to acquire citizenship at some point after establishing residence, as one must have resided continuously in the country for at least 10 years as an adult over the age of 21 years, before one would qualify. Furthermore, an official letter must be submitted to the Prince to renounce any foreign nationality and the applicant is not permitted to perform national service abroad.

20.7   Dual citizenship

Dual citizenship is not permissible.

A Monégasque automatically forfeits their citizenship when acquiring a foreign nationality or performing foreign military service without prior authorization of the government of Monaco.

20.8   Key advantages and disadvantages

Advantages

- Residence permit gives visa-free access to all Schengen area

- Multi-cultural society

- Mild climate

- No income, capital gains tax or direct line inheritance tax

- High level of security

- Excellent access by road, sea, rail and Nice International Airport

- Modern and efficient infrastructure

Disadvantages

- Very high property prices (although rents are more reasonable)

- Landed property is extremely rare

- Physical presence is required: Monaco must be the main home to maintain tax residence status

- Reputation as haven for wealthy people who want to avoid tax

- Acquisition of citizenship is extremely difficult, even after extended periods of residence

20.9 General information

Official name	Principality of Monaco
Capital city	Monaco
Region	Western Europe, on the southern coast of France
Surface area	2 km²
Government	Constitutional Monarchy
Languages	French (official), English, Italian, Monegasque
Currency	Euro (EUR)
Population	37,000 (July 2015 est.)
Religion	Roman Catholic 90%, other 10%
Ethnic groups	French 47%, Monegasque 16%, Italian 16%, other 21%
GDP	USD 6.79 billion (2013 est.)
GDP per capita, PPP	USD 78,700 (2013 est.)
Major industries	Tourism, construction, small-scale industrial and consumer products
Climate	Mediterranean climate with mild, wet winters and hot, dry summers
UN Human Development Index (HDI)	n.a.
World's healthiest countries (Bloomberg Rankings)	n.a.
Henley & Partners Visa Restrictions Index	16th (2016), 17th (2015)
Legatum Prosperity Index	n.a.

Sources: CIA "The World Factbook" (2015), World Bank (2015), Henley & Partners, The Legatum Institute

20.10 Climate

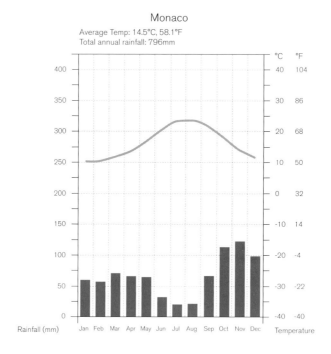

21

New Zealand

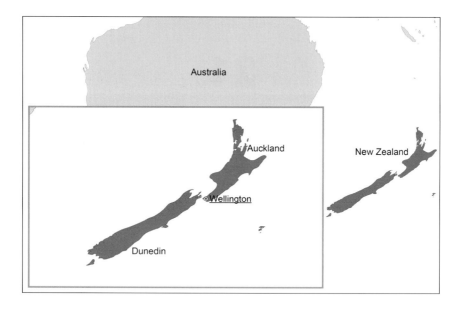

New Zealand is one of the world's most stable and well governed nations and offers an attractive destination for investment, business and raising a family. The country is consistently ranked in the top ten in terms of protecting investors, starting a business and for ease of doing business. New Zealand also recently ranked 4th by the Corruptions Perception Index for government transparency and lack of corruption.

With a population of approximately 4.5 million people, New Zealand is one of the least densely populated countries in the world. It has become an attractive jurisdiction for tax residence, offering no gift, estate, wealth or capital gains taxes, an extensive tax treaty network and a sound legal system based upon English law.

HSBC's 2016 Expat Explorer survey ranked New Zealand 2nd in the world for work-life balance and 3rd for "Quality of Life". The UN ranks New Zealand 9th out of 187 countries on its 2015 Human Development Index.

Compared to most countries in the world, New Zealand offers a great work-life balance with world-class education and healthcare systems.

21.1 Residence in New Zealand

To become a resident of New Zealand, applicants must meet the requirements of at least one of the residence categories available in the current residence program. There are specific requirements listed for each category, and beside those, each applicant, including partners and dependent children, must also meet health and character requirements. The categories available include those for skilled migrants, talent and entrepreneurs amongst others.

New Zealand has an immigration and investment policy that provides the opportunity for foreign nationals to obtain permanent residence through making a substantial investment into the country.

This can be achieved through investing between NZD 1.5 million (Investor 2 Resident Visa) and NZD 10 million (Investor 1 Resident Visa) in acceptable investments and maintaining these investments in

New Zealand for at least two years. Applicants must also meet the minimum annual residence requirements after the transfer of funds of between 44 days (Investor Plus) and 146 days (Investor).

21.2   Requirements

The Investor 2 Resident Visa is for experienced business people who have a minimum of NZD 2.5 million in available funds or assets. The applicant must invest NZD 1.5 million and keep the nominated funds invested in an acceptable investment in New Zealand for four years. Applicants must be 65 years old or under and there is an annual quota of up to 300 residence applications per year.

It allows applicants to live, work and study in New Zealand and applications can include the spouse and dependent children aged 24 and under. A points-based system is used to assess eligibility for Investor 2 Resident Visas. Successful applicants must spend at least 146 days in New Zealand in each of the last three years of the four-year investment period.

There is an English language requirement for all applicants who are required to either have an English speaking background, be a competent user of English, or have an International English Language Testing System certificate with an overall band score of three or more.

The Investor 1 Resident Visa requires the applicant to invest NZD 10 million in New Zealand over a three-year period in order to apply for New Zealand residence. It allows applicants to live, work and study in New Zealand and applications can include the spouse and dependent children aged 24 and under.

The Investor 1 Resident Visa has no maximum age limit, no language requirement and it does not require any business experience. Successful applicants must spend at least 44 days in each of the last two years of the three-year investment period in New Zealand.

Acceptable investments mean an investment that is capable of a commercial return, is not for the personal use of the applicant, is invested in New

Zealand in NZD, is invested in lawful enterprises or managed funds, and has the potential to contribute to the economy.

Acceptable investments include bonds issued by the New Zealand government or local authorities; firms traded on the New Zealand Debt Securities Market; firms with at least a BBB- or equivalent rating; registered banks or finance companies. Investments can also be made in equity in New Zealand firms (public or private including managed funds); registered banks, and residential property development(s). Applicants can nominate a mix of funds and/or assets to invest into.

21.3   Procedures and time frame

The process for the Investor 2 Resident Visa is initiated by first sending an Expression of Interest (EOI) to Immigration New Zealand outlining the applicant's business experience, investment and settlement funds. If the EOI is successful, the applicant and any spouse and dependents are invited to apply for New Zealand residence. Invites are generally issued within two weeks of lodgment of an EOI. Once invited to apply, the applicant will have four months to send the application.

An approval in principle is usually given within three months but is reliant on the quality of information provided as well as security and health checks. Immigration New Zealand will initially only approve in principle, and will not issue the visa until the funds have been transferred and invested and evidence of this is submitted to Immigration. The Resident Visa may then be issued within two to four weeks. Evidence that the invested funds have been maintained will be required at the end of the second and fourth years that the applicant resides in New Zealand.

In terms of the Investor 1 Resident Visa, applicants lodge a direct application. The application is generally allocated to case officers within two weeks of receipt for immediate assessment.

An approval in principle is usually given within three months, depending on the quality of information provided as well as security and health checks. Again, Immigration will only approve in principle and will not issue the Resident Visa until the funds have been transferred and invested and evidence of this is submitted to Immigration, after which, the Residence Visa will be issued within two to four weeks.

Successful applicants can travel in and out of New Zealand for the first two years of the investment period. If all of the conditions that apply to the first two years of the investment period are met, the applicant can apply for a variation of conditions to allow travel in and out of New Zealand for another two years. If all the conditions at the end of the three-year investment period are met, the applicant and family members can apply for a permanent resident visa.

21.4   Taxation

The Inland Revenue Department (IRD) is the government department that collects taxes in New Zealand. Individuals have to pay taxes and are considered a tax resident in New Zealand if physically residing there for more than 183 days within a 12-month period, or if they have an ongoing relationship with New Zealand.

New Zealand has negotiated double tax agreements with many other countries to prevent individuals from being taxed twice. Individuals may also qualify for a tax exemption on certain foreign income.

Taxes on New Zealand sourced income are deducted each pay period under a pay-as-you-earn system. The tax rate is a graduated up to a maximum of 33%.

The corporate tax rate is 30% and New Zealand has a goods and services tax of 15% that is levied on all goods and services other than financial services. Property tax is only levied on individuals that are in the business of developing properties. Homeowners are charged yearly rates as assessed by the local council and vary depending upon the area of residence.

New Zealand has no capital gains tax and there's also no estate duty.

21.5   Family law and inheritance aspects

The Family Court of New Zealand deals with all family issues, especially relating to children, and including births, deaths, marriage, and mental health.

Matrimonial property law is covered by the Property (Relationships) Act (PRA). In general, each party is considered to be entitled to half of all the relationship property, but this can be modified by many factors. New Zealand recognizes pre-nuptial agreements and also property agreements which effectively contract the parties out of the Act.

The PRA, which came into force in 2002, also governs rules of intestacy and wills, along with the Administration Act and the Family Protection Act. The PRA expanded the pool of people which must be provided for, and who are able to claim against an estate if not considered. This specifically now includes partners and children of *de facto* relationships (including step children) as eligible claimants. The courts have the ultimate power to ultimately decide and order what happens to an estate. It is therefore sensible to take professional legal advice. Family trusts and property agreements may be used to mitigate the effects of the PRA on inheritance.

21.6   Citizenship

Investors who have previously obtained residence under either of the above Investor programs are eligible to apply for New Zealand citizenship after they have held residence in New Zealand for five years, and have spent at least 1,350 days in total in New Zealand during the preceding five years, and at least 240 days in each of those five years.

21.7   Dual citizenship

New Zealand does allow dual citizenship.

21.8   Key advantages and disadvantages

Advantages

- High standards of living, multicultural society
- Political, social and economic stability
- Strong tax treaty network with a wide number of counter parties
- Solid legal system based upon English law

Disadvantages

- Physical residence requirements for maintaining residence and obtaining citizenship

21.9   General information

Official name	New Zealand
Capital city	Wellington
Region	Pacific Ocean
Surface area	268,000 km^2
Government	Constitutional monarchy with a parliamentary democracy
Languages	English (*de facto* official), Maori (*de jure* official)
Currency	New Zealand Dollar (NZD)
Population	4,438,393 (July 2015 est.)
Religion	Christian 44.3%, Hindu, Buddhist, Maori Christian among others
Ethnic groups	European 71.2%, Maori 14.1%, Asian 11.3%, Pacific peoples 7.6%, Middle Eastern, Latin American, African 1.1%, other 1.6%, not stated or unidentified 5.4%
GDP	USD 168.2 billion (2015 est.)
GDP per capita	USD 36,200 (2015 est.)
Major industries	Agriculture, forestry, fishing, logs and wood articles, manufacturing, mining, construction, financial services, real estate services, tourism
Main exports	Dairy products, meat and edible offal, logs and wood articles, fruit, crude oil, wine
Climate	Temperate with sharp regional contrasts
World's healthiest countries (Bloomberg Rankings)	15th (2015)
UN Human Development Index (HDI)	9th (2015)
Henley & Partners Visa Restrictions Index	7th (2016), 4th (2015)
Legatum Prosperity Index	4th (2015)

Sources: CIA "The World Factbook" (2015), World Bank (2015),
UN Human Development Report (2015), Henley & Partners, The Legatum Institute

21.10 Climate

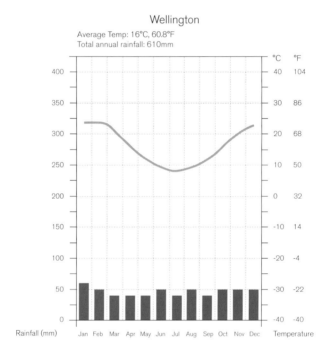

22

Portugal

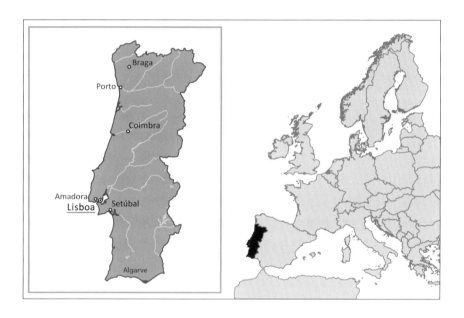

Portugal is the westernmost country of mainland Europe, situated on its Atlantic seaboard. With a long and impressive history and an important role in discovery, Portugal had colonies that, at one time, extended to western and eastern Africa, Brazil, Persia, Indochina and the Malayan peninsula. Its place in history starts from the discovery of the maritime trade route to India by Vasco da Gama in the late 15th century. It retains a strong association with its former colonies, now known as the Community of Portuguese-Speaking Countries, which includes Brazil, Mozambique and Angola. After centuries of being ruled by monarchy, which ended after the 1910 Revolution, the Portuguese First Republic was established, and was then superseded by the Estado Novo authoritarian regime. Democracy was restored after the Carnation Revolution in 1974. In 1986 the country joined the EU. Portugal is a developed country with a very high Human Development Index and it is also one of the world's most globalized and peaceful nations.

While Portugal is shifting towards business services, a third of its economy remains in manufacturing. It is also the world's largest supplier of cork and enjoys the benefits of a strong tourism industry. With little of its own hydrocarbon energy resources, Portugal is committed to creating renewable sources of energy such as hydro, wind and solar power. Over 40% of the energy created in Portugal is from such resources, including the most efficient wind tower in the world.

The capital, Lisbon and its surrounding urban area has a population of 2.8 million, and is the country's center of culture, tourism and business. Porto, located further north, is recognized as one of the cultural capitals of Europe and is the historic home of Port wine. It is a picturesque city at the mouth of the famous River Douro, and is also the center of the more industrialized North of the country.

Another scenic treasure is the Algarve in the south of the country, traditionally of farming importance but today is Portugal's most important tourism region. There is an international airport conveniently located in the center of the region, near its capital, Faro.

A relatively small country of approximately 11 million people, Portugal is considered very safe and boasts a low crime rate. Its healthcare is well developed, offering both public and private systems. Portuguese is the main language, but English is also widely spoken, particularly by younger people and especially in the tourist regions. The country is a member of the Schengen Agreement and has used the euro as its currency since 2002.

22.1   Residence in Portugal

The rights of foreign nationals to enter, reside and settle in Portugal are governed by the Law 23/2007 of 4ᵗʰ July 2007, which was further amended by the Law 29/2012 of 9ᵗʰ August 2012.

Portugal adheres to its international commitments and also its obligations as part of the Schengen area and the EU with regard to arrangements concerning the entry and stay of foreign nationals.

All holders of a Schengen residence identity card or passport may enter Portugal for up to 90 days without needing a visa. Specific visa requirements may apply for to non-EU nationals, depending on their nationality.

As with most EU member states, if a foreign (non-EU) national wants to reside and settle in Portugal, they must apply for a residence permit.

Residence permits for non-EU nationals are regulated by Law 29/2012 which introduced legislation allowing residence permits to be granted in the case of:

• Investments, via the Golden Residence Permit Program, or

• Highly qualified employment, via the EU Blue Card

Both residence options provide the opportunity for long-term residence and eligibility for citizenship, in accordance with the current legal provisions.

The Golden Residence Permit

The Golden Residence Permit program came into force in October 2012 and provides an opportunity for foreign investors from outside the EU to pursue an investment activity in Portugal. The program also covers shareholders of companies already set up in Portugal or in another EU member state with a stable presence in Portugal. When the investment requirements are met through a company, the investor's equity share is used to assess compliance with the investment criteria.

The current qualifying investment options for obtaining a Golden Residence Permit are:

Capital Investment Options

- Capital transfer of a minimum of EUR 1 million into a Portuguese bank account or specific approved investment options

- EUR 500,000 in investment or venture capital funds for capitalization of small and medium size companies

- EUR 350,000 in research activities which are part of the national scientific and technological system*

- EUR 250,000 in support of artistic production for the recovery or maintenance of national cultural heritage*

Property Acquisition

- A real estate investment of a minimum value of EUR 500,000*

- A real estate investment of a minimum value of EUR 350,000 for the refurbishment of properties older than 30 years or in an area of urban regeneration, including the costs of renovations*

Business

- Creation of a minimum of 10 new jobs*

---

*   If one of these options is chosen, the investment amount will be reduced by 20% if the investment takes places in a low population density area, defined as less than 100 inhabitants per square km or with a GDP per capita below 75% of the national average

The EU Blue Card Program

An alternative means of obtaining a residence permit in Portugal is the EU Blue Card Program, which was also introduced in October 2012 and provides an opportunity for highly qualified individuals from non-EU countries to reside and work in Portugal subject to meeting the criteria outlined below.

In both of these categories, residence permits can also be granted to family members of an eligible main applicant through the family reunification procedure. Civil union partners may also benefit from the family reunification procedure, subject to adequate proof.

22.2   Requirements

The Golden Residence Permit program is based on investment in Portugal and each category of investment has its own set of criteria to qualify for the residence permit. An application must be initiated online and concluded with submission of a full set of qualifying documents, including:

- A passport or other valid travel document
- Proof of legal entry and permanence in national territory, i.e. Schengen visa
- Proof of health insurance valid in Portugal
- A signed application enabling consultation of the Portuguese Criminal Record by SEF (Portuguese Immigration Border Services)
- A Criminal Record Certificate from the relevant authority of the applicant's home country or from any other country where the applicant has been residing for over a year
- Proof of the qualifying investment
- A declaration proving the absence of debts issued by the Inland Revenue and Customs Authority and by the Social Security

*   If one of these options is chosen, the investment amount will be reduced by 20% if the investment takes places in a low population density area, defined as less than 100 inhabitants per square km or with a GDP per capita below 75% of the national average

- An affidavit signed by the investor, on their word of honor that they will comply with the minimum quantitative requirements

- A receipt for the payment of the application fee

In addition to some of the requirements above, applicants for the EU Blue Card will be asked to provide the following:

- A contract or binding job offer with a salary of at least 1.5 times the average gross annual salary (or 1.2 times in certain professions). The OECD recorded annual gross salary for 2011 was EUR 17,000

- Proof of health insurance or evidence that the applicant is covered by the National Health Regime

- Registration with Social Security

- For regulated professions, documents establishing the applicant's specific qualifications and, for unregulated professions, the documents establishing the relevant higher professional qualification

The Golden Residence Permit (GRP) requires an applicant to undertake and maintain a qualifying investment for the minimum period of five years, attested by a *bona fide* declaration signed by the applicant.

Other requirements under general law state that applicants shall not have been imprisoned for more than one year, shall not have been the subject of an entry ban in national territory following a removal order from the country and shall not have been the subject of alerts in the Schengen Information System nor in SEF's own integrated information system.

There are minimum residence requirements in order to qualify for the renewal of the GRP. However, these are very modest; being seven days during the first year of residence in order to be entitled to the first renewal, and an average of 14 days for the two subsequent two-year renewal periods.

22.3   Procedures and time frame

All applications for the GRP and the EU Blue Card are reviewed by SEF. The application process starts online and is completed with submission of all of the required compliance documentation and a personal appearance for the purposes of identification and collection of biometric data.

The temporary residence permit will be granted initially for a period of one year and can then be extended for further periods of two years, subject to an application for extension of the permit being made at least 30 days prior to its expiry. At the end of a five-year period the applicant may continue to renew the Golden Residence Permit or may opt to make an application for permanent residence which, if granted, will last for a five-year period before requiring renewal. After completing six years as a resident, the applicant may also be eligible to apply for Portuguese citizenship; this is subject to prevailing legal criteria explained below.

Applications for residence permits and renewals usually take between three to eight months.

22.4   Taxation

In general, clients investing in Portugal under the GRP will be non-resident for tax purposes unless they stay in Portugal for more than 183 days during any period of 12 months or, if they do not meet this condition, have a property that they use as their habitual residence. The person will be considered resident from the day of arrival to the day of permanent departure.

Non-residents will be subject to tax on income or gains arising in Portugal. Most sources of income are taxed at fixed rates and withheld at source.

For new residents who wish to stay for longer periods of time and possibly reside in Portugal, there is a 'Non-Habitual Residents Regime' (NHR) which may be beneficial.

Once granted, this regime applies for 10 years, the main advantages being:

- For Portuguese-sourced employment and self-employment income deriving from a 'high-value-added' activity (as defined by Ministerial Order), a low 20% flat tax rate would apply

- For foreign source income, a tax exemption may be available for employment income, investment income, capital gains, pension income and rental income, other than income arising in a designated tax haven

Portugal does not apply a wealth tax, for either residents or non-residents. There is no tax on gifts or inheritances between parents, children and grandchildren. Other transfers of Portuguese assets by gift or inheritance may be subject to a 10% Stamp Tax.

Currently, the standard rate of corporate income tax is 21% and the standard rate of VAT is 23%.

22.5   Family law and inheritance aspects

The Civil Code governs family relationships including marriage, divorce and inheritance.

The law applicable to a foreign resident in Portugal who is an heir is, in general, the law of the country of the deceased's nationality. However, it is necessary to verify the law of that country in this respect, as it may defer to the law of the deceased's country of residence.

If the deceased did not leave a will, or equivalent testamentary disposition, the estate will be dissolved by the strict inheritance laws which favor the immediate family members. A surviving spouse is entitled to the matrimonial property (all property acquired after the marriage) and a life interest in the property of the deceased.

Even if there is a will, Portuguese law favors immediate family and, therefore, exclusion of certain heirs is possible – children and spouses are always entitled to a minimum of 50% share in the estate.

Portugal recognizes the common property law regime, which involves an equal division of the marital assets (and losses), unless a legal prenuptial agreement is in place. Portugal recognizes the last location of a couple's common habitual residence therefore, if divorce proceedings are held in another country, Portugal has no jurisdiction over the divorce proceedings. In order to obtain a divorce in Portugal, a petition must be filed on grounds of irretrievable breakdown or by mutual consent.

22.6   Citizenship

Portuguese citizenship is acquired mainly through descent from a Portuguese parent, marriage to a Portuguese citizen or naturalization in Portugal.

Descent from a Portuguese parent can follow one of these routes:

- The children of a Portuguese mother or father born abroad that register their birth in the Portuguese Civil registry or declare their wish to be Portuguese citizens

- Children of foreign citizens born in Portuguese territory to parents legally resident for at least five years at the time of their birth, and not in the service of their countries – if they declare their wish to be Portuguese citizens

- Those born in Portuguese territory that prove they do not possess any other nationality

With respect to naturalization, a foreign citizen can apply for Portuguese citizenship if all of the following conditions are met:

- The applicant is legally considered to be an adult, i.e. 18 years old

- The applicant has been resident in Portugal for more than six years

- The applicant has sufficient knowledge (International A2 level) of the Portuguese language

- The applicant has not been convicted of a crime punishable under Portuguese law with imprisonment of three years or more

A foreign minor or dependent whose mother or father has acquired Portuguese nationality since his birth, may also apply for nationality through his legal representatives.

Minors born in Portuguese territory, children of foreigners, providing they have a sufficient knowledge of the Portuguese language and no criminal convictions, or the minor has completed his primary education in Portugal, may also apply for citizenship.

Portuguese citizenship can also be acquired through marriage or *de facto* union. If a foreigner has been married to a Portuguese national for more than three years this is achieved by means of a declaration made during the marriage; or, if at the time of the declaration, they have been living in a *de facto* union with a Portuguese national for more than three years, following judicial recognition of the status by a civil court.

Citizenship can be conferred on second and third generation immigrants (born in Portugal) if the parent has resided in Portugal for at least five years, and/or the minor has concluded the first cycle of compulsory education in Portugal.

22.7   Dual citizenship

Portugal allows dual citizenship.

22.8   Key advantages and disadvantages

Advantages

- Residence permit gives visa-free access to the Schengen area
- Family reunification is available
- Low physical presence requirements
- Five years' residence which can count towards citizenship
- Excellent international and Portuguese schools and universities
- Attractive corporate and private taxation system

- International quality healthcare clinics and hospitals
- Excellent infrastructures at the heart of Europe with first class travel links
- Portugal's lifestyle: nature, gastronomy and traditions

Disadvantages

- Language requirements for eligibility to apply for citizenship applications (proficiency in Portuguese, A2 level)

22.9   General information

Official name	Portuguese Republic
Capital city	Lisbon
Region	Western Europe
Surface area	92,212 km²
Government	Republic
Languages	Portuguese
Currency	Euro (EUR)
Population	10,825,309 (July 2015 est.)
Religion	Roman Catholic 81%, other 19%
Ethnic groups	Homogeneous Mediterranean stock, <1% former African colonies
GDP	USD 289.8 billion (2015 est.)
GDP per capita, PPP	USD 27,800 (2015 est.)
Major industries	Agriculture, automobile assembly, chemicals, fishing, food processing, electronics, footwear, machinery, metal working, mining, textiles, tourism, wine and food products
Main exports	Chemicals, cork, leather goods, machinery, petroleum products, sardines, textiles and wine, agricultural and food goods
Climate	Mediterranean
UN Human Development Index (HDI)	43rd (2015)
World's healthiest countries (Bloomberg Rankings)	23rd (2015)
Henley & Partners Visa Restrictions Index	6th (2016), 4th (2015)
Legatum Prosperity Index	27th (2015)

Sources: CIA "The World Factbook" (2015), World Bank (2015),
UN Human Development Report (2015), Henley & Partners, The Legatum Institute

22.10 Climate

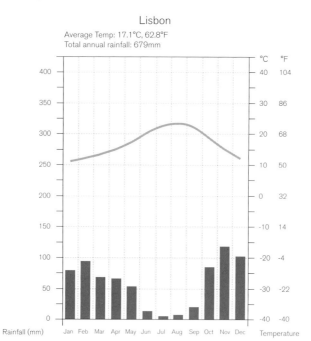

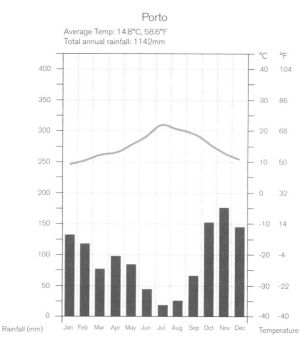

23
Singapore

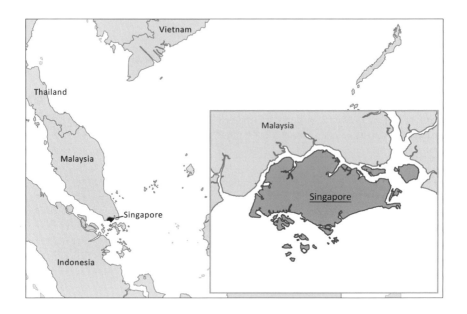

Singapore is considered one of the world's best places to live, and is frequently voted best Asian city to live in, due to its excellent infrastructure and public services. Singapore is one of the wealthiest countries in the world measured by GDP per capita.

The Republic of Singapore consists of the Singapore Island and 57 small neighboring islands, located close to the equator resulting in its tropical climate. Singapore was originally founded as a British trading colony in the early 19th century and gained independence in 1965. Today it has emerged as a world-class destination with its multiracial and multicultural society. Singapore is a city state, with a rich mixture of cultures that exist in harmony in an organized community.

Singapore has an excellent infrastructure and state of the art telecommunications, business and financial facilities. Singapore has grown into an international financial center, as is evident in the presence of many international banks and the volume of financial transactions which take place in this thriving city. Singapore is an exception to other large cities by virtue of the fact that it has one of the lowest crime rates in the world, and even littering is punishable.

Singapore is politically stable, as well as economically prosperous, and offers an extensive and reputable education system and highly reliable healthcare system.

Over the last 20 years, the Singaporean government has made great efforts to attract talent and good human capital to facilitate the continued growth of its economy. The government provides incentives and benefits to citizens, such as tax incentives to encourage first-time home owners, or encouraging citizens to have children, as well as education schemes for Singaporean students who perform well. However, in the past few years the government has increased the requirements for incoming talent and has slowed the number of Employment Passes and Permanent Residence approvals. Additionally, the rules of the Global Investor Programme (GIP) have been tightened, making it more challenging for entrepreneurs to move to Singapore.

English is the predominant language in Singapore and used specifically in administration, business and technology. The country comprises of large Asian communities, especially from China and India as well as Malaysia and the Philippines, which is evidenced by the blend of cultures on the street, and the other official languages which are Malay, Mandarin, Tamil, and English.

A stroll down the famous Orchard Road provides the evidence that Singapore attracts affluence. This factor, combined with the high quality of service and quality of life, makes it an ideal environment for residence and business.

23.1   Residence in Singapore

It is one of the Singaporean government's objectives to attract talent to live and work in the country. The government's intention is for foreigners to make Singapore their home by becoming permanent residents.

The Immigration Act, 1985 as amended (Cap 133) and the Immigration Regulations determine the immigration law in Singapore. The Immigration & Checkpoints Authority (ICA) deals with the immigration process.

There are defined categories of foreigners who are eligible to apply for permanent residence. These include spouses and unmarried children (below 21 years old) of a Singapore Citizen or a Singapore Permanent Resident (SPR); Aged Parents of a Singapore citizen; Employment Pass Holders under the Professional/Technical Personnel and Skilled Workers Scheme (PTS), and Investors/Entrepreneurs under the Global Investor Program (GIP). The Financial Investor Scheme (FIS) was officially closed for submission on 15 April 2012.

Foreigners interested in working and living in Singapore may apply for in-principle approval for a residence permit, by submitting an application before they enter Singapore, provided they satisfy the specific criteria. The advantage of obtaining permanent residence status is that the person is entitled to live and work in Singapore for at least five years.

However, the approval of permanent residence is at the sole discretion of the authorities and no reasons will be given in the event of a rejection.

A person holding a P, Q, or S work pass in Singapore may submit an application for permanent residence to the ICA after one year of employment and residence within Singapore. This is a very popular route for professional and highly skilled individuals, as no substantial investment is required to obtain these work passes.

The ICA will consider each application, giving specific attention to the applicant's academic and professional qualifications. Once permanent residence is obtained, the applicant no longer requires an employment pass, thereby giving the applicant more flexibility in his employment options.

Under the PTS, an applicant may include their spouse and unmarried children under 21 years of age in the permanent residence application.

The GIP is specifically for entrepreneurs or investors interested in making substantial financial investments in Singapore and is designed to attract wealthy foreign entrepreneurs and investors who wish to make Singapore their home.

23.2 Requirements

Each permanent resident category has a specific application form and particular set of documentary requirements that must be fulfilled. All permanent residence permits are issued by the ICA upon assessment of the applications.

An applicant holding a P, Q, or S pass must complete a Form 4A and provide full details of their work pass, academic and professional transcripts and certificates, pay slips, Income Tax Notices, Valid Business Registration Certificate (in case of applicants who are self-employed), and other standard documentation such as birth certificates.[166] The

---

[166] Explanatory Notes to Form 4A and Annex A for applying under the Professionals/ Technical Personnel and Skilled Workers Scheme

employer must complete the Annex A, stating the company's business and activities.

The GIP is jointly administered by the Singapore Economic Development Board (EDB), and the ICA.

The GIP is geared towards applicants with at least three years of entrepreneurial experience and a track record of successful business practice. The investors must own at least 30% equity of a company (or collection of companies) which has a turnover of at least SGD 50 million per annum in the most recent year, and at least SGD 50 million per annum on average for the past three years prior to the application. A one-time non-refundable application fee of SGD 7,000 is now chargeable before submitting the application forms.

The GIP offers two main investment options:

- Option "A" requires an investment of at least SGD 2.5 million in a new business entity, or expansion of an existing business operation
- Option "B" requires an investment of SGD 2.5 million in one of the GIP-approved venture capital natured funds

A GIP Family Office (FO) option also exists that requires an investment of at least SGD 2.5 million in a Singapore-based single family office with assets-under-management (AUM) of at least SGD 200 million. The AUM would include all financial assets, such as bank deposits, capital market products, collective investment schemes, premiums paid in respect of onshore life insurance policies and other investment products but excludes real estate. In order to be eligible to apply for permanent residence under the FO option, the applicants must have at least five years of investment, entrepreneurial or management track record and an individual, or direct family net worth of at least SGD 400 million.

Several sectors are approved for investment, including bio-medical sciences, clean energy, educational and professional services, electronics, energy, chemicals and engineering services, environment technology, info-communications and media, international organizations, non-government organizations and philanthropy, lifestyle and sports, logistics, new technologies, precision engineering and transport engineering.

A GIP applicant may include his spouse and children (below the age of 21 years), parents and parents-in-law in the application for permanent residence. However, as of 1 January 2011, parents and parents-in-law are no longer eligible to be included in the main applicant's GIP application for permanent residence status. Instead, they can apply for a five-year Long Term Visit Pass (LTVP), which is renewable and tied to the validity of the main applicant's re-entry permit.

Upon the formalization of the permanent resident status, the investor will be issued a Re-Entry Permit (REP). A valid REP is necessary whenever the permanent resident wishes to travel in and out of Singapore. It allows the client to retain permanent resident status while away from Singapore.

Subsequent to the first five years, the REP would be renewed if the client fulfills the following conditions:

1. For a three-year renewal: fulfil the investment conditions under either Option "A" or Option "B" of the GIP; and either

   a. Have set up a business in Singapore with five or more Singaporean employees and have incurred at least SGD 1 million in total business spending a year; or

   b. The applicant or at least one dependent who is also a PR under the GIP, resides in Singapore for more than half of the time

2. For a five-year renewal: fulfil the investment conditions under either Option "A" or Option "B" of the GIP; and

   a. Set up a business in Singapore with five or more Singaporean employees and have incurred at least SGD 1 million in total business spending a year; and

   b. The applicant and dependents who are also PR under the GIP must reside in Singapore for more than half of the time

To maintain permanent resident status, all permanent residents who intend to travel must first obtain re-entry permits and must return to Singapore within the validity period of the permit. Singapore permanent residents will lose their status if they remain outside of Singapore without a valid re-entry permit.

A re-entry permit may not be issued or renewed if the permanent resident does not comply with the terms and conditions applicable to each scheme, or does not maintain sufficient connections with Singapore.

23.3 Procedures and time frame

The GIP application procedure for permanent resident entry permit involves more processing than a work permit application. In order to obtain the resident permit, the applicant must submit a personal profile and a proposed investment plan via an e-application form.[167] Supporting documentation in hard copy must be compiled and sent to Contact Singapore[168]. The applicant is also required to attend an interview, usually within three to four months of submission of the application.

If the applicant meets all the criteria, the ICA will issue an Approval-in-Principle (AIP), valid for a six-month period. The applicant has six months from the date of the AIP to make the requisite investment under the specific investment option and submit the documentary proof, such as share certificates, which the Singaporean authorities will hold for five years. The ICA will then issue the final approval letter and the applicant is required to formalize his or her permanent residence status within 12 months from the date of the final approval letter.

The GIP applicants must undergo and pass a medical examination before Permanent Residence status will be granted.

Upon arrival in Singapore, the applicant should complete all the Permanent Residence formalities, including applying for an IC card.

---

[167] Refer to *www.contactsingapore.sg/GIP*
[168] Contact Singapore is an alliance of the Singapore Economic Development Board (EDB) and the Ministry of Manpower

All male citizens and permanent residents, aged 16 – 40 years are subject to the Enlistment Act[169] and must report for enlistment into the National Military Service for a defined period of time. In the case of first-generation permanent residents, they are automatically exempted from national service. However, male principal applicants or spouses of such will be required to register with the Central Manpower Base, if they are below 40 years of age, to receive an exemption notice. Subsequent male descendants are liable for national service.

23.4   Taxation

Singapore has a mild tax regime and over recent years has continued to introduce tax regulations favoring foreign investors. The country has introduced various incentive schemes to attract investment, enabling the growth of businesses.

Singapore's taxation system operates on a territorial basis. On an individual level, only local income derived from within the jurisdiction is taxable. Regardless of residence status, all foreign incomes are exempted, even if remitted to Singapore (unless remitted through a partnership in Singapore).

A Singaporean citizen is considered a tax resident if the individual normally resides in Singapore. A foreign resident is considered a tax resident if the individual is physically present or is employed for 183 days or more per tax year.

A scheme to attract global skills was introduced. Titled the "Not Ordinarily Resident" scheme (NOR), it provides various tax concessions for a five-year period. All applications, including the resident employee, must qualify under NOR conditions. These include the resident employee having been non-resident for three consecutive years prior to his first year of residence and correspondingly the first year of tax assessment.

Singapore has a very narrow tax base of taxable income. Personal income tax rates are low and levies are at progressive rates of up to 20%.

---

[169]   National Service is dealt with under the Enlistment Act, 1985

Capital gains taxes are only levied in very limited circumstances. There are no gift taxes and estate duty was abolished in 2008.

The standard corporate tax rate for the tax years 2010-2014 was 17%. Companies, both resident and non-resident, are taxed on income remitted to Singapore. Certain exemptions apply to resident companies regarding foreign remittances.

In 2008, a one-tier system of taxation was introduced that provided for the exemption of income tax on dividends, regardless of the method of paying out.

It is mandatory for Singaporean citizens and permanent residents employed in Singapore to contribute to the Central Provident Fund (CPF), a statutory savings scheme.

Singapore currently has double tax treaties with 60 countries. Notable among these are treaties with Australia, Belgium, Canada, China, France, the Russian Federation, South Africa and the UK. Limited treaties have also been signed with Chile, Hong Kong, Saudi Arabia, and the US[170].

23.5   Family law and inheritance aspects

The Family Court of Singapore adjudicates over family law matters, and has the jurisdiction to determine the division of marital property of spouses. The Court will not automatically divide the estate by half, but will rule according to what the court deems fair and equitable in each case. Property, including property acquired prior to the marriage, will be considered part of the martial property estate if the property in question was used by the spouse and children during the marriage, or if such property was substantially improved during the marriage.

There are no forced inheritance rules or estate duties in Singapore.

---

[170]   Agreements with the US cover only international air-transport or shipping operations

23.6   Citizenship

Citizenship is conferred in accordance with Part X of the Constitution of Singapore, dated 9 August 1965.

A child born in Singapore does not automatically obtain Singaporean citizenship, unless the child is born to a Singaporean citizen. If the child has a right to another citizenship from a foreign parent, the child must, by the age of 21, choose which citizenship they will retain.

After two years of permanent residence in Singapore, it is possible to apply for Singaporean citizenship.

The Singapore passport is one of the most widely accepted in the world. It provides the holder with visa-free access to over 160 countries, including all the EU countries, Canada, China, the US and others.

One must bear in mind that Singapore is a strictly single citizenship country and an applicant must relinquish all pre-acquired citizenships before naturalization is possible. As mentioned earlier, all male Singapore citizens are obliged to participate in the country's compulsory two-year National Service. This is not applicable in the case of a first generation permanent resident applicant.

23.7   Dual citizenship

Singapore does not permit dual citizenship, and this is strictly enforced. For this reason Singapore is not attractive if you are interested in holding more than one citizenship and passport.

23.8   Key advantages and disadvantages

Advantages

- Favorable tax laws

- International financial center

- Safe and orderly

- Excellent education and healthcare systems
- Warm tropical climate all year round

Disadvantages

- Property prices are relatively high
- Landed property is very scarce and extremely expensive
- Population density is very high
- National Service requirement for male citizens
- Second generation permanent male residents will need to serve National Service
- Dual citizenship is not allowed and this is strictly enforced
- Physical residence required for permanent residence status maintenance

23.9   General information

Official name	Republic of Singapore
Capital city	Singapore
Region	South-eastern Asia, islands between Malaysia and Indonesia
Surface area	697 km²
Government	Parliamentary Republic
Languages	Mandarin (official) 36.5%, English (official) 29.8%, Malay (official) 11.9%, Hokkien 8.1%, Tamil (official) 4.4%, Cantonese 4.1%, Teochew 3.2%, other Indian Languages 1.2%, other Chinese dialects 1.1%
Currency	Singapore dollars (SGD)
Population:	5,674,472 (July 2015 est.)
Religion	Buddhist 33.9%, Muslim 14.3%, Taoist 11.3%, Catholic 7.1%, Hindu 5.2%, other Christian 11% other 0.7%, none 16.4%
Ethnic groups	Chinese 74.2%, Malay 13.3%, Indian 9.2% other 3.3%
GDP	USD 292,74 billion (2015)
GDP per capita, PPP	USD 85,21 (2015)
Major industries	Electronics, chemicals, financial services, oil drilling equipment, petroleum refining, rubber processing and rubber products, processed food and beverages, ship repair, offshore platform construction, life sciences, entrepôt trade
Main exports	Machinery and equipment (including electronics), consumer goods, pharmaceuticals and other chemicals, mineral fuels
Climate	The weather is predominantly tropical - hot, humid, rainy. There are two distinct monsoon seasons (December to March and June to September); during the winter monsoon there are frequent afternoon and early evening thunderstorms
UN Human Development Index (HDI)	9th (2015)
World's healthiest countries (Bloomberg Rankings)	1st (2015)
Henley & Partners Visa Restrictions Index	5th (2016), 5th (2015)
Legatum Prosperity Index	18th (2015)

Sources: CIA "The World Factbook" (2015), World Bank (2015),
UN Human Development Report (2015), Henley & Partners, The Legatum Institute

23.10 Climate

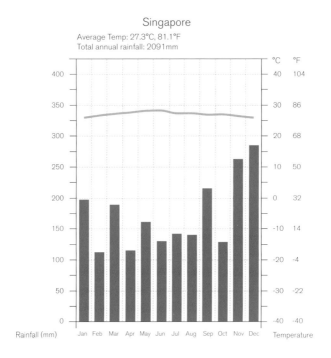

24

Switzerland

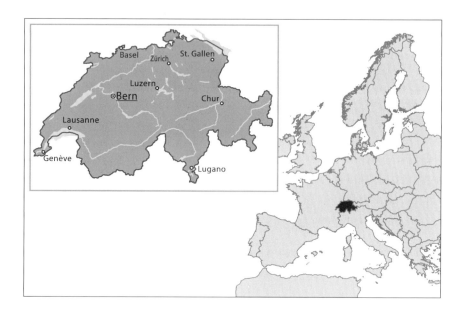

Switzerland, famous for banking, watch-makers and its popular tourism regions, ranks among the top countries to live in due to the overall high quality of life, with Zurich and Geneva frequently nominated as among the best cities in the world to live in.[171]

Historically, Switzerland has always maintained a neutral political stance internationally, a policy that has fostered a politically and economically stable environment. The combination of the country's rich culture and heritage and its liberal attitude has given rise to one of the richest, most independent and organized societies. Switzerland boasts a multicultural and multilingual society, with four official languages and a growing trend to teach English at elementary school level. An ideal combination of political and economic stability, a clean and safe environment, excellent communications and transport links, efficient public services and relatively low tax rates, makes it the ultimate choice for business and residence.

Switzerland is home to a large number of international organizations, such as the International Red Cross, the World Trade Organization, the Universal Postal Union, the World Intellectual Property Organization, the Office of the United Nations High Commissioner for Refugees, the International Labour Organization and the World Health Organization.

Many leading international corporations are relocating their headquarters to Switzerland, as the country is business-friendly by tradition and offers a solution to every need and expectation. Its 26 cantons offer companies a wide range of opportunities. The advantages associated with Switzerland as a whole are also complemented by the individual advantages that are specific to each of the 26 cantons.

The Swiss taxation system is consistent with the country's reputation as a center of international trade and finance. Many tax privileges have been introduced in order to encourage foreign investment in Switzerland, while there are very few restrictions on Swiss investment abroad. Investors and

---

[171] The Economist's "Where-to-be-born Index" 2013 puts Switzerland in 1st place. Mercer's Quality of Living Survey 2016 sees Zurich in 2nd place for the 5th year running

entrepreneurs as well as persons of independent means would normally have no problem obtaining a residence permit.

24.1 Residence in Switzerland

Switzerland has a dual system for granting foreign nationals access to Swiss residence and to the Swiss labor market. Due to the Agreement on the free movement of persons, it has become easy for citizens of EU and EFTA member states to become residents in Switzerland. Since 1 June 2016, and 1 May 2011, respectively, for citizens of all member states that have been part of the EU at least since 1 January 2007, the free movement of persons agreement has come into force without any restrictions, i.e. since then citizens of all EU/EFTA member states, except for Croatia, actually have a legal right to be granted a residence and work permit in Switzerland.

Specific transitional periods with regard to the granting of work permits still apply to Croatia which joined the EU on 1 July 2013. However, financially independent citizens of any EU Member State who are not gainfully occupied in Switzerland and have sufficient funds to live in Switzerland without working here may acquire a residence permit without further restrictions.

The criteria for admittance of non-EU/EFTA citizens are contained in the Federal Act on Foreign Nationals (*Ausländergesetz, AuG*), and in the Ordinance on Admittance, Residence and Employment *(Verordnung über Zulassung, Aufenthalt und Erwerbstätigkeit, VZAE)*. These criteria are further illuminated in the directives on the implementation of the Foreign Nationals Act.

Apart from special situations or permits for students, trainees and patients on health treatments, non-EU/EFTA citizens may obtain a residence permit only as gainfully employed persons, as pensioners with close ties to Switzerland, or as financially independent persons who are not gainfully occupied in Switzerland and who pay considerable annual taxes.

24.2 Requirements

In Switzerland, there are different categories of residence permits available, with a distinction between permits for EU/EFTA and non-EU/EFTA nationals. Applications for residence permits are generally administered on a cantonal level, however, in case of applications for non-EU/EFTA nationals, final approval must be sought at the federal immigration department.

EU/EFTA nationals can obtain a residence permit easily provided they show either a work agreement with a Swiss employer, or become self-employed persons in Switzerland, or – in case no gainful occupation in Switzerland is intended – they prove that they are financially independent persons with sufficient income or wealth to cover their living costs. In addition, the EU/EFTA national is not subject to geographical restrictions within Switzerland and can acquire real estate without prior authorization.

The following resident permits exist for EU/EFTA nationals:

1. *"B" Permit* is a residence/work permit for resident foreign nationals who reside in Switzerland for a certain purpose, with or without gainful employment – the "B" Permit is valid for five years if the person is in possession of a valid employment contract with at least a 12-month duration

2. *"C" Permit* is a settlement permit for foreign nationals who have resided in Switzerland for an uninterrupted period of five years. This permit grants the applicant the right to settle in Switzerland without any restrictions or conditions on his residence (certain restrictions apply for citizens of Bulgaria, Croatia, Cyprus, Malta, Romania and the EU-8 member states)

3. *"G" Permit* is applicable to EU/EFTA nationals who are resident in a foreign border zone and are gainfully employed within the neighboring border zone of Switzerland. The permit allows the national to work anywhere in Switzerland, on condition that they return to their place of residence in the EU/EFTA region once a week. The permit is

valid for five years, provided there is an employment agreement of unlimited duration, or of more than one year's duration

4. *"L" Permit* is a short-term permit for EU/EFTA foreign nationals resident in Switzerland for period of usually less than a year

The process to obtain residence for non-EU/EFTA nationals is significantly more challenging.

Like most countries, Switzerland gives its nationals priority in the domestic labor market. A foreign national may acquire a residence and work permit to become gainfully employed in Switzerland if the Swiss employer can prove that they are indispensable for a specific function in the company, that they possess the relevant qualifications for this function and that no suitable candidate can be found on the Swiss and European labor markets. Precedence is given to Swiss and EU/EFTA citizens. A fixed annual quota system to regulate the number of first time residence permits available to non-EU/EFTA citizens is in place. As a result it is generally extremely difficult to obtain a permit under this category. Only a limited number of management level employees, specialists and other qualified employees are admitted from non-EU/EFTA countries.[172]

If a foreign national establishes a company in Switzerland and is employed by it in a senior position, generally a residence and work permit will be issued within the scope of the economic promotion program. The rules vary between cantons but the compliance with the economic promotion program may be justified by economic reasons of sustained relevance to Switzerland. The criteria include the creation of new jobs for which domestic employees may be recruited, as well as the opening up of new markets, the securing of export sales and economically significant links abroad, and the creation of new tax revenue. The requirements fluctuate, depending on the canton in which the company is established.

To obtain a permit as a pensioner, the foreign national must be at least 55 years old, show close ties to Switzerland and have sufficient funds.

---

[172] Federal Office of Migration website – *www.sem.admin.ch*

The key condition here is the minimum age of 55 years. In many cases, it may also be difficult to fulfill the condition of close ties to Switzerland. However, despite these restrictive regulations, foreign nationals who do not meet the requirements under the "retired persons" category may still obtain a residence permit if they are financially independent.

Financially independent persons who are not gainfully occupied in Switzerland, but who agree to pay a certain minimum in net annual taxes, can usually acquire a residence permit regardless of their age, provided granting of residence to a potential taxpayer is considered as being in the "fiscal interest" of the canton of residence. The minimum annual taxes that must be paid in order to qualify for this specific immigration category vary considerably from canton to canton. In order to avoid being taxed on the basis of worldwide income and wealth, the minimum tax payable is, in most cases, fixed in a lump-sum tax arrangement. This special taxation arrangement is negotiated on an individual basis and is decided upon by the cantonal authorities. This makes Switzerland an even more attractive place of residence for financially independent persons who wish to relocate to a milder tax climate.

The following permits are issued to non-EU/EFTA nationals:

1. *Permit "B"* is a residence permit granted to a non-EU/EFTA national for a period of one year and can be renewed on an annual basis if the applicant has maintained the conditions upon which the permit was initially granted

2. *Permit "C"*, the settlement permit, is granted to foreign nationals who have resided in Switzerland for a continuous and uninterrupted period of 10 years. US and Canadian nationals are subject to special regulations

3. A non-EU/EFTA national may also apply under the *Cross-border commuter permit (Permit "G")*, if they are resident in a foreign border zone and are gainfully employed within the neighboring border zone of Switzerland

4. Subject to the quota system, a *Permit "L"*, the short-stay permit, is granted to foreign nationals resident in Switzerland for a period of

less than 12 months. Usually the terms and length of the permit will mirror the terms of the employment contract. However, if the employment period is less than four months, the application is not subject to the quota regulation

24.3   Procedures and time frame

Applications of EU/EFTA nationals to which the Agreement on the Free Movement of Persons fully applies are usually handled within just two to four weeks.

The procedures for non-EU/EFTA citizens to apply for Swiss residence are challenging. In the course of the application process, applicants must provide the usual documents. Once the application is approved in principle, the applicant is issued a visa to enter Switzerland, and consequently will be able to register upon their arrival in Switzerland. Thereafter, the applicant receives the residence permit by the canton in which they reside.

To obtain an employment permit, the employer must file the application with the specific cantonal labor authority. Upon approval, a resident permit will be issued by the police.

Due to the case-by-case decision process, applicants have to consider an estimated time frame of between two to six months after lodging their application depending on the canton and on individual circumstances.

24.4   Taxation

The legal basis of income, wealth, and lump-sum taxation in Switzerland is formed by the Federal Direct Tax Act *(Gesetz über die Direkte Bundessteuer, DBG)*, the Federal Tax Harmonization Act *(Steuerharmonisierungsgesetz, STHG)*, and – corresponding with the latter – the individual tax laws of the 26 cantons. Switzerland has a multi-layered tax system. Taxes are levied on federal, cantonal and community (municipal) levels whereas each canton determines its own tax rates. The cumulative cantonal and communal tax rates may vary considerably – currently ranging between less than 10% and more than 30% – whereas on federal level a maximum tax rate of 11.5% applies. In addition, net wealth taxes are levied at cantonal and municipal level.

A person resident or domiciled in Switzerland is liable for tax on federal, cantonal and municipal levels on worldwide income and net wealth, except on real estate situated abroad and income derived from a permanent business establishment. From the first day of residence an individual is liable for tax. A person is considered a resident if they hold a legal residence permit or intend to work in Switzerland for a period exceeding 30 days. Non-residents, however, are only liable for Swiss tax on certain income and assets, including from real estate or business interests in a permanent establishment in Switzerland.

As mentioned above, foreign nationals who fulfill certain requirements can avail themselves of a special tax arrangement whereby Swiss taxes are levied on the basis of expenditure and standard of living in Switzerland rather than on the usual worldwide income and assets. This fiscal arrangement is called lump-sum taxation (*forfait fiscal* in French) and is available throughout the country except in the cantons of Zurich, Basel-Stadt, Basel-Landschaft, Schaffhausen, and Appenzell Ausserrhoden. The Federal tax law and the relevant cantonal tax laws require that a foreign person wishing to benefit from this special tax regime must not have been resident in Switzerland during the last 10 years and may not carry out a gainful occupation in Switzerland. Under the lump-sum taxation regime, the Swiss tax authorities generally require the assessment of a minimum taxable income which must in general be equal to at least the tax resident's living expenditure. According to currently applicable federal and cantonal tax regulations the taxpayer's living costs are assessed to be at least seven times the annual rental value of the apartment or house in which the foreign national resides in Switzerland. In addition, the cantons must define in their tax laws a minimum taxable income and a minimum taxable net wealth in figures, whereas on federal level a minimum taxable income of CHF 400,000 applies.

If spouses move to Switzerland and wish to benefit from the lump-sum tax option, both spouses must fulfill the requirements – unless one spouse continues to live abroad and does not obtain residence in Switzerland.

Besides offering a unique lump-sum tax system of taxation, which effectively caps income and net wealth tax for qualifying foreign citizens, Switzerland is also an attractive place of residence with regard to inheritance and gift taxes. The country has no federal inheritance or gift taxes. Instead, the cantons levy inheritance and gift taxes in their own competence, which means that there are 25 different inheritance and gift tax regimes, while the canton of Schwyz has neither inheritance nor gift taxes. Switzerland has entered into several inheritance tax treaties including treaties with Austria, France, Germany, the UK and the US.

Companies are taxed according to the canton in which they are established and the maximum cantonal income tax rate can be as low as about 5%. For Swiss federal corporate income taxes, a flat rate of 8.5% applies. As tax planning through companies is permitted under Swiss taxation laws, dividends enjoy privileged taxation, which can significantly reduce the higher taxation rates applicable to individuals who are fully taxable (as opposed to individuals who opt for flat-rate taxation). Since January 2009, Swiss residents are only taxed on 60% of the dividend if the recipient owns at least 10% of the share capital of a Swiss company.

Individuals are exempt from capital gains tax from the sale of movable assets, but capital gains on immovable property will be levied on cantonal level. Furthermore, the Swiss tax treatment of trusts and the absence of controlled foreign corporation rules offer interesting pre-immigration planning opportunities for wealthy families.

Switzerland has close to 100 double tax agreements. However, some of these agreements (e.g. with Germany, France and other European countries) are not applicable to individuals who reside in Switzerland on a flat-rate tax basis.

24.5   Family law and inheritance aspects

The Swiss Civil Code deals with matrimonial property law in its Articles 182 to 251. Under Swiss law there are three basic matrimonial property regimes: an ordinary matrimonial property regime of participation in acquisitions (the Ordinary Regime), community of property, and the regime of separation of estates. In cases where no specific choice is made, the Ordinary Regime applies.

Under the Ordinary Regime, property brought into the marriage by means of a gift or inheritance, remains the property of the individual. Upon termination of the marriage, both parties retain their own property but the profit of the shared property is split equally between the parties.

Foreigners who move to Switzerland will continue their pre-existing matrimonial property regime, unless they choose to change to a regime as provided by Swiss law, or elect to participate in a marital property regime of one of their national laws – if this is more advantageous to them. If no marital property agreement or regime is in place, the Swiss law is applicable and will apply retroactively.

The Swiss Civil Code deals with inheritance law[173] in Switzerland and governs the dissolution of the deceased's estate if the deceased died intestate. The statutory heirs are divided into degrees, which determine the order of inheritance. In order for testamentary dispositions to be valid, the document must meet the formal requirements as specified in the law.

The estate of a foreign national whose last residence was in Switzerland will be subject to Swiss law, unless the deceased's will provides for the estate to be dealt with under the law of the deceased's nationality. The possibility to elect foreign law is popular amongst foreigners whose national law does not provide for close relatives to have a right to a compulsory portion of the estate. If a Swiss national dies and the last place of residence is Switzerland, the estate will be governed by Swiss law.

---

[173]   Articles 457 to 640I

In most cantons, resident foreigners are subject to inheritance tax and gift tax on worldwide assets, whereas non-residents are only subject to inheritance and gift tax on real estate located in Switzerland.

24.6 Citizenship

Swiss citizenship is governed at federal level by the Citizenship Act *(Bürgerrechtsgesetz, BüG)*. However, cantonal citizenship laws and even communal regulations also apply.

Citizenship can be acquired by descent, if at least one of the parents is a Swiss national. However, if the child is born abroad, the child must be registered as Swiss national before the age of 22.

One can apply for Swiss citizenship if one has resided in Switzerland for a minimum of 12 years. In addition to satisfying this federal law requirement, the person is subject to cantonal and communal requirements which will vary according to each canton and commune. Even after this long period of residence it can still take several years until citizenship is granted. In some communes the procedure is very arbitrary and further requirements must be met, such as language tests and an assessment of the person's integration into Swiss society.

If the particular residence requirements of the canton and commune are met and requirements provided by federal law are satisfied, the applicant is entitled to obtain a federal naturalization permit from the Federal Office for Migration. Citizenship is only acquired once the applicant has also been naturalized by the respective canton and commune.

To qualify for citizenship, the necessary time of residence time is reduced by half for children between the age of 10 and 20 years who live in Switzerland – i.e. only six years is required before an application for citizenship can be made. This may be the case, for example, if a child has studied in Switzerland during these years of their life, and would subsequently – after six years – also know the language and culture well enough to pass the citizenship tests.

24.7　Dual citizenship

Switzerland allows dual citizenship.

24.8　Key advantages and disadvantages

Advantages

- Residence permit gives visa-free access to all Schengen states
- Political, social and economic stability
- Multilingual society, English widely spoken
- First-class infrastructure and excellent banking facilities
- Attractive lifestyle and healthy environment
- World renowned schools and excellent education system
- Favorable taxation system

Disadvantages

- It is very difficult to acquire a citizenship (minimum residence time is 12 years and other requirements apply)
- In top locations, property to buy is difficult to find
- No "big city" life available in Switzerland

24.9   General information

Official name	Swiss Confederation
Capital city	Bern
Region	Central Europe, east of France, north of Italy
Surface area	41,277 km²
Government	Swiss Confederation
Language	German (official) 64.9%, French (official) 22.6%, Italian (official) 8.3%, Serbo-Croatian 2.5%, Albanian 2.6%, Portuguese 3.4%, Spanish 2.2%, English 4.6%, Rumantsch (official) 0.5%, others 5.1%
Currency	Swiss franc (CHF)
Population	8,121,830 (2015 est.)
Religion	Roman Catholic 38.2%, Protestant 26.9%, Muslim 4.9%, other Christian 5.7%, other 1.6%, unspecified 1.3%, none 21.4%
Ethnic groups	German 65%, French 18%, Italian 10%, Rumantsch 1%, other 6%
GDP	USD 482.3 billion (2015 est.)
GDP per capita, PPP	USD 58,600 (2015 est.)
Major industries	Machinery, chemicals, watches, textiles, precision instruments, tourism, banking, and insurance
Main exports	Machinery, chemicals, metals, watches, agricultural products
Climate	The weather in Switzerland is temperate, but varies with altitude. It is usually cold and cloudy with rain and snow in winter. Summers are humid with occasional showers
UN Human Development Index (HDI)	3rd (2015)
World's healthiest countries (Bloomberg Rankings)	4th (2015)
Henley & Partners Visa Restrictions Index	6th (2016), 5th (2015)
Legatum Prosperity Index	2nd (2015)

Sources: CIA "The World Factbook" (2015), World Bank (2015),
UN Human Development Report (2015), www.bfs.admin.ch (2012), Henley & Partners,
The Legatum Institute

24.10 Climate

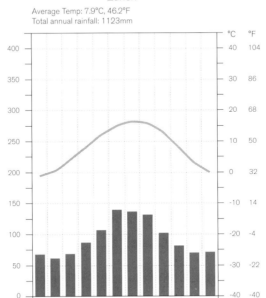

Zurich
Average Temp: 7.9°C, 46.2°F
Total annual rainfall: 1123mm

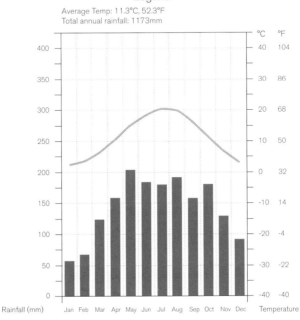

Lugano
Average Temp: 11.3°C, 52.3°F
Total annual rainfall: 1173mm

25

Thailand

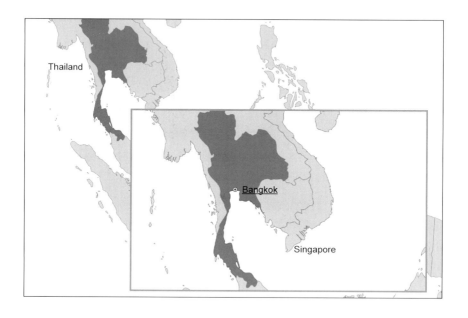

The Kingdom of Thailand is one of the most sought-after destinations in Southeast Asia, offering a low yet convenient standard of living. Over the last four decades, Thailand has made remarkable progress in social and economic development, moving from a low-income country to an upper-income country in less than a generation. Thailand has been one of the widely cited development success stories, with sustained strong growth and impressive poverty reduction, particularly in the 1980s.

Thailand is filled with spectacular natural, cultural, and historical attractions. Thailand's popularity as a tourist destination owes a great deal to its climate that predominantly has a tropical wet and dry or savannah climate while the south and the eastern tip of the east have a tropical monsoon climate.

Thai people are well known for their friendly nature and are extremely proud of their rich cultural heritage. The culture and lifestyle is influenced by their Buddhist or Hindu religions and their ethnic and cultural diversity is heavily celebrated and revered.

Thailand's attractions include scuba diving sites, golden beaches, tropical islands, exciting nightlife, flora and bird life, palaces, Buddhist temples and several World Heritage sites.

Thailand is a member of the World Trade Organization, the Association of Southeast Asian Nations and the Asia-Pacific Economic Cooperation.

25.1   Residence in Thailand

There are various residence visas available for Thailand including a retirement visa, a one-year visa, a business visa, a marriage visa, and a 90-day visa.

The Thai Retirement Visa is issued to applicants who wish to visit and retire in the Kingdom of Thailand. Applicants must first obtain a 90-day visa or a one-year non-immigrant visa from their home country or country of residence prior to applying for the Thai Retirement Visa.

The Thai Permanent Resident (PR) Visa is also available and has many advantages. It allows you to live permanently in Thailand, with no requirement to apply for an extension of stay. Successful applicants can also have their name on a house registration document, and will be able to buy a condominium without making a bank transfer from abroad. Getting a work permit is also made easier once you have PR status.

In addition to this, PRs can be eligible to become a director of a Thai public company, as well as eventually apply to become a naturalized Thai citizen. You will also be able apply for an extension of stay and PR status for your non-Thai family members.

25.2   Requirements

To be eligible for a Thai Retirement Visa, applicants must be 50 years of age or over and have a clean criminal record. Each applicant must make a security deposit of THB 800,000 in a Thai bank account for two months prior to the visa application, or provide proof of a monthly income or pension of at least THB 65,000, or provide a combination of the Thai bank account and yearly income for a total of THB 800,000.

The benefits of the Thai Retirement Visa include multiple-entry travel to Thailand for a period of one calendar year. The visa is renewable every year and can be renewed inside Thailand. Successful applicants also have the ability to open a bank account in Thailand and the option to apply for PR.

In order to apply to become a Thai PR, applicants must have had a Thai non-immigrant visa for at least three years prior to the submission of the application and must have three consecutive yearly extensions in order to qualify. The applicant must also be a holder of a non-immigrant visa at the time of submitting the PR application.

Applicants must qualify under one of the following categories to apply for PR status in Thailand:

- Investment
- Working/Business

- Family Support/Humanity Reasons

- Expert/Academic

- Other categories as determined by Thai Immigration

The regulations for obtaining an Investment Visa are outlined in Thailand's Immigration Act, under the Order of the Immigration Bureau No. 327/2557, the Criteria and Conditions for Consideration of an Alien's Application for a Temporary Stay in the Kingdom of Thailand.

To become eligible, an alien must have been granted a non-immigrant visa and demonstrate that they have transferred funds of at least THB 10 million into Thailand. They must also provide evidence of one of the following:

- A legally defined condominium unit (either freehold or a three-year minimum leasehold) at a purchase price or a rent of at least THB 10 million

- At least THB 10 million in a fixed deposit account in a Thai bank whose share capital is majority Thai owned

- Thai government or state enterprise bonds worth at least THB 10 million

These different investment options can be combined.

Once all the eligibility criteria for the Investment Visa are satisfied, it can be renewed annually as long as the qualifying investment is maintained.

Another significant benefit of the Investment Visa is that it also provides for long-term stay for the investor's family members including parents, spouse, children, adopted children and the spouse's children. Each family member must be granted a Non-Immigrant visa and have proof of the family relationship. A spouse must be both legally married and cohabiting. Children, adopted children and the spouse's children must not be married, must live with the Investment Visa holder as family, and must not be older than 20 years of age, unless they are ill or disabled and cannot live without the support of a father or mother.

An Investment Visa does not relieve its holder nor their family members of the 90-day reporting rule applicable for other long-term Thai visa holders. Also, it does not entitle the holder or their family members to work in Thailand, although a work permit can be obtained in addition to the visa.

25.3   Procedures and time frame

All applications for Thai PR are processed by the Royal Thai Immigration Commission. The annual quota for granting PR's in Thailand is a maximum of 100 persons per country. The opening date for applications in each year varies and is announced by the Minister of Interior. Once the announcement has been issued, applications may be submitted up to and including the last working day of the year. The committee initially evaluates applications for about five months, and then calls successful applicants for an interview. In general, the whole process can take up to a year.

Once an application for Thai PR is approved, a residence Blue Book is issued to the successful applicant who must then register the place of residence in Thailand and obtain a house card. A week after the receipt of the residence certificate, an application is then made for an alien book (Red Book) at the local police station, which is the equivalent of the Thai national ID card. Re-registration is required every year.

25.4   Taxation

Taxpayers are classified into "resident" and "non-resident". Resident means any person residing in Thailand for a period or periods aggregating more than 180 days in any tax (calendar) year. A resident of Thailand is liable to pay tax on income from sources in Thailand as well as on the portion of income from foreign sources that is brought into Thailand.

A non-resident is, however, subject only to tax on income from sources in Thailand. Personal income tax rates are progressive up to a maximum of 35%.

While a preliminary draft inheritance and gift tax law has been approved by the Thai Cabinet, it remains uncertain as to when the draft law will be officially announced. Thailand does not levy a net wealth tax.

The corporate income tax rate in Thailand is 20%.

25.5   Family law and inheritance aspects

Thailand's system of family law is contained in Book 5 of the Thailand civil code and includes divorce and division of property. Book 6 of the civil code deals with succession and inheritance.

Family law in Thailand is codified, however courts and independent judges have leeway in the exact interpretation of parts of the civil code, unless the supreme court has specified otherwise. The supreme court has total authority in certain elements of the law.

Thailand recognizes pre-nuptial agreements, although these cannot be used in contradiction of the the statutory legal system of property between husband and wife. This specifies that all property acquired during the marriage becomes jointly owned. Property that belonged to either spouse before the marriage remains their personal property after the marriage.

Inheritance law also provides that half of any common property must be left to the surviving spouse. There are no other requirements for distribution of the estate. If the deceased did not leave a will, section 1629 of the Civil and Commercial Code of Thailand specifies six classes of statutory heirs which are entitled to inherit in the following order: descendants, parents, brothers and sisters of full-blood, brothers and sisters of half-blood, grandparents, and uncles and aunts. In the case of intestacy, the spouse is still entitled to half of the common property.

25.6   Citizenship

An application for citizenship can be filed to become a Thai natural-ized citizen after holding Permanent Resident status in Thailand for 10 consecutive years.

25.7   Dual citizenship

Thailand does not allow dual citizenship.

25.8   Key advantages and disadvantages

Advantages

- Low cost of living
- Eligible to become a director of a public company
- Eligible to apply for an extension of stay for non-Thai family members
- Obtain a work permit quickly and easily

Disadvantages

- Complicated procedure that is not entirely transparent
- 90-day reporting rule for long-term Thai visas

25.9   General information

Official name	Kingdom of Thailand
Capital city	Bangkok
Region	Mainland Southeast Asia
Surface area	513,000 km²
Government	Constitutional monarchy
Languages	Thai (official) 90.7%, Burmese 1.3%, other 8% (2010 est.) English is a secondary language of the elite
Currency	Thai Baht (THB)
Population	67,976,405
Religion	Buddhist (official) 93.6%, Muslim 4.9%, Christian 1.2%, other 0.2%, none 0.1% (2010 est.)
Ethnic groups	Thai 95.9%, Burmese 2%, other 1.3%, unspecified 0.9% (2010 est.)
GDP	USD 1.108 trillion (2015 est.)
GDP per capita	USD 16,100 (2015 est.)
Major industries	Tourism, textiles and garments, agricultural processing, beverages, tobacco, cement, light manufacturing, computers and parts, integrated circuits, furniture, plastics, automobiles and automotive parts
Main exports	Automobiles and parts, computer and parts, jewelry and precious stones, polymers of ethylene in primary forms, refine fuels, electronic integrated circuits, chemical products
Climate	Tropical; rainy, warm, cloudy southwest monsoon (mid-May to September); dry, cool northeast monsoon (November to mid-March); southern isthmus always hot and humid
World's healthiest countries (Bloomberg Rankings)	77th (2015)
UN Human Development Index (HDI)	93rd (2015)
Henley & Partners Visa Restrictions Index	67th (2016), 69th (2015)
Legatum Prosperity Index	48th (2015)

Sources: CIA "The World Factbook" (2015), World Bank (2015),
UN Human Development Report (2015), Henley & Partners, The Legatum Institute

25.10 Climate

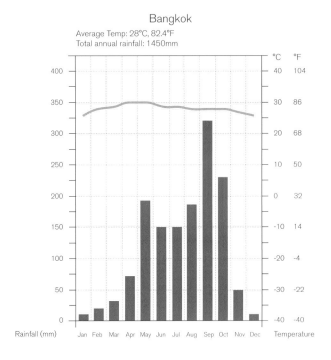

26

United Arab Emirates / Dubai

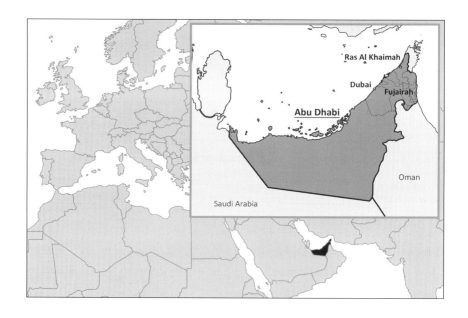

The United Arab Emirates (UAE) is an independent federal state comprised of seven member states: Abu Dhabi (where the federal capital, also called Abu Dhabi, is located), Dubai, Ras Al Khaimah, Fujairah, Umm Al Qaiwain, Sharjah and Ajman. The country covers a total area of approximately 83,600 square kilometers and is located on the eastern coast of the Arabian Peninsula between Oman and the Kingdom of Saudi Arabia.

The Supreme Council of the UAE, comprised of the rulers of the seven Emirates, is the highest federal authority. It is responsible for general policy matters involving education, defense, communications, foreign affairs and development and for ratifying federal laws. The UAE became a member of the United Nations and the Arab league in 1971. The UAE is also a member of the International Monetary Fund, the Organization of Petroleum Exporting Countries, and the World Trade Organization.

The UAE has concluded tax treaties with more than forty countries including China, Egypt, Finland, France, Germany, India, Indonesia, Ireland, Italy, Malaysia, Pakistan, Singapore, and the UK. It should also be noted that the UAE offers an investment-friendly environment so companies incorporated in this jurisdiction, if carefully structured with professional advice, may be useful vehicles to conduct international business, free of tax.

Dubai is the second largest Emirate and is situated between the Emirate Abu Dhabi and the Emirate Sharjah. The Emirate of Dubai is physically divided into nine sectors which are then further divided into over 130 communities or administrative regions. The city ranks as the UAE's most important port and commercial center and it has a long trading tradition that has earned Dubai the reputation within the Middle East as the 'City of Merchants'.

Arabic and English are the official business languages. Urdu and Hindi are widely spoken as well.

The non-oil sector of the UAE economy currently contributes over two thirds of the total produced domestic products and continues to see tremendous growth. The national economy has moved gradually from an oil-based economy to a diversified one and continues to attract foreign companies that seek opportunities in the region today.

In addition, the leaders of the Emirates have now embarked on a new race for excellence and creativity through the development of the Mohammed Bin Rashid City within Dubai. This new region will focus on expanding Dubai's strength in innovation and entrepreneurship while creating an area dedicated to progress in the fields of art, culture and education. This unique and integrated environment will aim to scale up the capacity of the city and further its goal of becoming a center of entrepreneurship, arts, culture, and large scale family tourism.

Particularly in Dubai, many different Free Trade Zones have been established, which allow foreign persons and entities to conduct their business, establish companies and buy property, subject to licensing requirements, which are different in each of the Free Zones. These have special authorities that issue licenses to operate businesses, and which manage the Free Zone. No business can be operated without a license, and depending on the activity and office area a certain number of work permits are available for foreign persons. A different license fee is payable every year. Furthermore, office space must be rented (or bought) in the relevant Free Zone.

26.1   Residence in Dubai

The main provisions regarding residence for foreign individuals in the Emirate of Dubai are set out by the General Directorate of Residency and Foreigners' Affairs. This government authority, working under the umbrella of the UAE, distinguishes between a range of residence permits. In general, these permits differ in their restrictions and length of validity, but are based on a legal sponsorship (e.g. company acts as a sponsor). In most cases the permits are valid for between one to three years but are all subject to renewal; some of the most common types of residence permits are:

1. *Employee Residence Permit* – As an owner, partner, investor or employee of a UAE company, the local UAE partner or Free Zone Authority can act a sponsor for the purpose of receiving a UAE Residence

Permit. Such permits are usually valid for a period of between one and three years and become invalid if the respected individual remains outside the UAE for a period exceeding six consecutive months

2. *Real Estate Investor Residence Visa* – A "Master Developer" can sponsor a foreign individual for the purpose of receiving a three year UAE Residence Visa. This applies only in the case where the aforementioned foreigner can prove that his income is AED 10,000 per month or greater, has purchased a property that is fully constructed and fit for habitation, and where the property is valued at AED 1 million or greater. It is important to note that only one such visa can be issued per property and that any such visa becomes invalid if the property is transferred to a third party

3. *Family Residence Permit* – A UAE Residence Permit Holder can sponsor their spouse and children to become dependent residents, as long as the sponsor has a minimum salary accepted by the authorities to allow them to be a sponsor

4. *Relative Residence Permit* – Through special application, a UAE Residence Permit Holder can sponsor their parents, parents-in-law, brother or sister. Note that the success of such an application is not automatic, and that it is dealt with on a case-by-case basis by the appropriate government authority

5. *Student Residence Permit* – Full-time tertiary level students at UAE colleges and universities can get annually renewable UAE residence permits through the sponsorship of the respective educational organization. Secondary and primary level students will normally be under the sponsorship of one of their parents that is a UAE Residence Permit holder

6. *Domestic Help Residence Permit* – The option of sponsoring a maid or nanny is open to families living in Dubai (bachelors are not eligible). The criteria for sponsorship of a house maid may vary slightly from one Emirate to another in the UAE

Dubai is the Middle East's trading hub and the meeting point for the Far Eastern and Western commercial worlds. The tax-free environment, sophisticated business and technological infrastructure and international strategic position are some of its key advantages. Dubai business licenses are available for both the mainland and Free Zones, but the licensing criteria varies according to the type of company being set up and the range of activities undertaken by that company. Therefore, depending upon the function to be carried out and the unique requirements of the company to be set up, there are a number of different ways of creating an establishment in Dubai, and the Companies Law (Federal Law No. 8 of 1984 concerning commercial companies) sets out the forms of companies, namely but not limited to:

1. *A Limited Liability Company (LLC)* – If the purpose of the entity is to sell within the UAE, the most common way of registering in Dubai is to acquire a commercial trading license from the Department of Economic Development. It is important to note that 100% foreign ownership of such an entity is not permitted, and that a local sponsor (a UAE national) must act as the majority (51%) shareholder of the entity. Despite the required split in shareholdings, the Companies Law permits shareholders of an LLC to agree on an economic benefit that deviates from this shareholding ratio when taking into consideration the efforts of the non-national partners in management, provision of technology or expertise. An amendment to the Companies Law in 2009 abolished the previous minimum share capital requirement of LLC's

2. *A Professional License* – For a professional license, a local service agent is required but a local shareholder is not. The agent has no involvement in the company's operations, management or profit sharing but serves as the company representative when drafting legal agreements, facilitating visa application and other administrative issues. A professional license from the Department of Economic Development will enable the provision of many services, as long as an office address can be verified by the Dubai Municipality and the licensee holds the relevant professional qualification

3. *A Branch or Representative Office* – Where the purpose of the entity is only to provide information and negotiate sales, a foreign company

may establish a branch or representative office. This entity can carry out promotional activities and facilitate contracts, but is subject to obtaining the necessary licenses as well as appointing a local (UAE national) service agent. Notably, the parent company must be well established and conducting sales or manufacturing within the UAE is not permitted

4. *A Free Trade Zone Company or Establishment* – Several Free Zones have been established in the UAE to ease foreign investment. Companies or establishments incorporated in the Free Zones are not subject to the many restrictions imposed on mainland companies, and most importantly, Free Zone Companies benefit from the option of 100% foreign ownership and corporate and income tax exemptions for a specified, guaranteed and renewable period of time. It is relatively straightforward to set up a company in a Free Zone, although the process differs from one Free Zone to another. It is also important to note that Free Zone Companies are restricted with regards to selling goods or providing services into the UAE; if they wish to do so, a local (UAE national) agent must be appointed and a 5% stamp duty will apply

There are more than twenty Free Zones operating in Dubai and each Free Zone is designed around one or more business industry sectors, offering licences to companies within those sectors, although sometimes boundaries are blurred. For most of the existing Free Zones, there are three options through which business can be carried out; a Free Zone Establishment, a Free Zone Company, and a branch office of a foreign or local company.

Once a company has been accepted into a Free Zone it will typically operate under one or more of the following four different licences: a commercial licence, a general trading licence, an industrial licence and/ or a service licence. The Free Zones have been set up with the specific purpose of facilitating investment and the procedures for investing in the zones are relatively simple. The companies operating in the Free Zones are treated as being outside the UAE for legal purposes and are suitable for companies intending to use the UAE as a regional manufacturing or distribution base, with the bulk of their sales business outside the UAE.

In all cases the following benefits apply:

- 100% foreign ownership
- 100% repatriation of capital and profits
- 100% corporate and personal income tax exemption (for a determined period of time)
- Goods may be imported into the Free Zones free of duty
- No currency restrictions
- Abundant and inexpensive energy
- Modern and efficient communications
- Excellent support services from local authorities

Each Free Zone is governed by an independent Free Zone Authority, which, amongst other things, is responsible for drafting and implementing the zone's regulations, policies, and strategies and for issuing the necessary operating licenses for operating within the zone, as well as the residence visas/permits for the employees of the relevant companies. The commercial activity that will be carried out normally dictates which Free Zone should be used. Free Zone Establishments and Free Zone Companies have differing minimum share capital requirements dependent upon the Free Zone of incorporation and must also pay annual license fees.

The following are examples of three different Free Zones in Dubai:

1. *The Jebel Ali Free Zone (JAFZ)* – The JAFZ is the largest and the oldest Free Zone in Dubai; it was established in 1985, now spreads over an area of 48 square kilometers, and is the home to over 6,400 companies (including 120 of the Fortune Global 500 companies). The world-class infrastructure, amenities, and logistics infrastructure (including an international port, office units, warehouses, and light industrial units) make it ideal for industrial, services, and trading companies to thrive in.

2. *Dubai International Financial Centre (DIFC)* – The DIFC is an international financial center strategically located between the east and west. It provides a secure and efficient platform for business and

financial institutions to reach the emerging markets of the region, while filling the time-zone gap for a global financial center between the leading financial centers of London and New York in the west and Singapore, Hong Kong and Tokyo in the east. The DIFC is now home to 21 of the world's top 30 banks, eight of the world's top 20 asset managers, six of the world's 10 largest insurance companies and six of the top 10 global law firms. The quality and range of the DIFC's independent regulation, common law framework and its supportive infrastructure make it the perfect base to take advantage of the region's rapidly growing demand for financial and business services.

3. *Jumeirah Lakes Towers (Dubai Multi Commodities Centre (DMCC) –* The DMCC Free Zone is the fastest growing mixed-use Free Zone in Dubai with several thousand licensed member companies from around the world. The Dubai Multi Commodities Centre Authority administers the DMCC Free Zone, which is recognized as the Free Zone of choice for all business activities, ranging from trading in oil, gold, diamonds and financial products, to providing logistical services, marketing, information technology and advertising. The DMCC Free Zone has been successful in attracting many leading global names and its strategic location on the Sheikh Zayed Road (the main artery connecting Dubai and Abu Dhabi) and its close proximity to the major ports and industry corridors continue to attract global businesses. It is also close to preferred residential and leisure areas.

As a Free Zone Company owner, partner, investor or employee, the relevant Free Zone acts as your sponsor for the purpose of acquiring a residence permit. This permit allows you to stay in the UAE as a resident and is usually valid for one to three years, but expires when the residence permit holder spends more than six consecutive months outside the UAE.

26.2   Requirements

Each residence permit has specific requirements that must be fulfilled to meet the criteria of the category. However, in general, applicants require basic documentation such as a passport, legalized/certified qualification certificates, marriage certificates (if applicable), and tenancy agreement if required. All foreign language documents must be translated into either English or Arabic by a professional translating service. There is no official language requirement other than the requirements of the employer or local partner.

26.3   Procedures and time frame

In the case of employment or company ownership, once the company has been fully set up and is in possession of the trade license the application process for a residence visa/permit involves the following steps:

1. The sponsor (local UAE partner) or Free Zone Company applies for a UAE entry visa (residence visa) for the applicant prior to their arrival in the UAE and requests all the associated application documents. At this stage, the applicant can travel to the UAE and use the entry visa to pass UAE immigrations and enter into the country

2. After entry, the applicant needs to apply for an Emirates ID card and arrange for an appointment for a medical check at an authorized government hospital or medical clinic. The medical check, comprised of a blood test and a chest X-ray, tests each applicant for HIV (AIDS), hepatitis B, hepatitis C, tuberculosis (TB), leprosy, and syphilis. If the results are positive for any of those conditions, the applicant is usually quarantined and deported immediately

3. Once the health check has been successfully completed and the applicant has received their medical results, the applicant or the company public relations officer (PRO) must now return to the relevant residence department and submit the application documents for processing. The documents required vary by residence department but generally include the applicant's passport, medical test results, copy of the company trade license, copy of the company establishment card, salary certificate (if applicable), tenancy agreement (if applicable), and any sponsor relationship verification documents (e.g. marriage certificate for a spouse); certificates should be notarized, attested and translated into English or Arabic.

4. If approved, the applicant will receive a "Residence Permit" stamp in their passport, validating the residence period and identifying the permit type. Thereafter, the applicant or PRO may collect the passport from the residence department/Free Zone office. Once approved, residence permit holders may settle in any of the seven emirates but must ensure that no more than six consecutive months are spent outside the UAE.

The time frame for the entire process is usually one to two months but can be shorter depending on the time and place of submission.

26.4   Taxation

There is no federal income taxation in the UAE. Citizens and residents of the UAE are not subject to personal income tax, property and capital gains taxes, or net worth taxes. However, UAE citizens do contribute a small percentage of their income to social security.

There are no corporate income taxes for most businesses located in the UAE; however, Dubai does tax the income from foreign banks and oil companies (from 20% to 80%). The Free Zones and companies established in them are exempted from any tax obligations for a guaranteed period of 15 years, at the end of which they may request an exemption for another 15 years. In addition, there are no import or export taxes in the Free Zones.

There is no sales tax, but there are high taxes on alcohol and other products that are considered *haram* (substances prohibited by Islamic law).

26.5   Family law and inheritance aspects

The general rule in the UAE is that inheritance issues related to the citizens of the UAE shall be dealt with in accordance with *Shari'ah* principles.

Residence permit holders are advised to seek the advice of a lawyer who will be able to accurately assess the family and inheritance aspects of their individual situation. A will is usually recommended.

26.6   Citizenship

UAE citizens are defined by law to be only those persons born to parents who are both UAE citizens or born to a father who is a UAE citizen. Henceforth, generally no foreigner is eligible for UAE citizenship. Naturalizations are extremely rare and granted only in absolutely exceptional circumstances.

26.7   Dual citizenship

The UAE does not recognize dual citizenship. Any UAE citizen holding dual citizenship will have their other passports confiscated by the UAE authorities upon discovery.

26.8   Key advantages and disadvantages

Advantages

- Residents can settle anywhere in the UAE

- Excellent modern infrastructure, transport and communications

- Favorable corporate and individual tax systems

- Multicultural and vibrant cities

- Excellent place to do business with easy access to the Middle East region

- Minimal application requirements for residence permits

- Minimal physical stay requirements for residents

Disadvantages

- Citizenship is not available

- Climate is unfavorable during the summer months

- Establishment of a company in the UAE is required in most cases to obtain a residence permit

26.9   General information

Official name	United Arab Emirates
Capital city	Abu Dhabi
Region	Eastern Coast of Arabian Peninsula, Middle East
Surface area	83,600 km^2
Government	Federation with specified powers delegated to the UAE federal government and other powers reserved for member emirates
Languages	Arabic (official), English, Persian, Hindi, Urdu
Currency	Emirati Dirham (AED)
Population	5,779,760 (July 2015 est.)
Religion	Muslim 76%, Christian 9%, other 15%
Ethnic groups	Emirati (19%), other Arab and Iranian (23%), South Asian (50%), other expatriates (8%)
GDP	USD 647.8 billion (2015 est.)
GDP per capita, PPP	USD 67,600 (2015 est.)
Major industries	Petroleum and petrochemicals, fishing, aluminum, cement, fertilizers, construction materials, textiles
Main exports	Crude oil (45%), natural gas, re-exports, dried fish, dates
Climate	Desert, cooler in eastern mountains
UN Human Development Index (HDI)	40th (2015)
World's Healthiest Countries (Bloomberg Rankings)	30th (2015)
Henley & Partners Visa Restriction Index	38th (2016), 40th (2015)
Legatum Prosperity Index	30th (2015)

Sources: CIA "The World Factbook" (2015), World Bank (2015),
UN Human Development Report (2015), Henley & Partners, The Legatum Institute

26.10 Climate

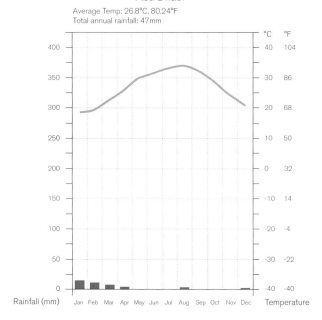

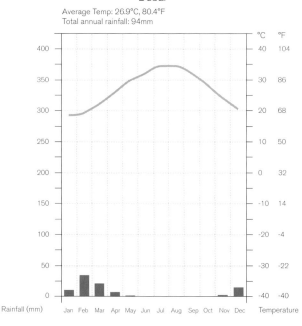

27

United Kingdom

The UK is one of the most attractive places in the world both as a business location and as a place for private residence. Over the past several centuries, the UK has emerged as a great economic and political power by conquering, colonizing and revolutionizing the world.

The UK is internationally known for having a stable democratic government and a respected system of law which has been adopted by countries across the globe including those as diverse as Australia, Canada, the Caribbean, India, Kenya, Malaysia, New Zealand, South Africa and the US.

The UK is well-located between America and Europe and is one of the best places to use as a base for travel to any part of the world. London has high-speed rail links to Paris, Brussels and onwards to the rest of Europe as well as mainline links to the rest of the UK. London is the busiest airport city in the world, boasting five international airports: Heathrow, Gatwick, London City, Luton and Stansted.

The UK constitutes the greater part of the British Isles. The largest island is Great Britain that comprises of England, Wales and Scotland. Northern Ireland also forms part of the UK. There is a constellation of smaller islands dotted around Great Britain that are tied administratively to the UK.[174]

The UK has a partially regulated free market economy. It is the sixth biggest economy in the world and the third largest in Europe. Despite giving rise to the Industrial Revolution, over the years the UK's economic edge declined in the manufacturing field. It is now the service sector that dominates the GDP, led by financial services.

This has resulted in the UK becoming one of the most attractive places in the world to do business. From a tax perspective, it can also be an attractive base for wealthy individuals and families taking advantage of the special tax treatment available to those who are not domiciled in the UK.

The UK is still currently one of the states of the EU but it remains to be seen how and when the "Leave" vote in its EU Referendum in June

---

[174] Isle of Anglesey, the Inner and Outer Hebrides, Orkney, the Isles of Scilly, the Shetland Islands and the Isle of Wight

2016 will affect its status in the future. It opted out of the European Monetary Union and continues with the pound as its currency. The UK is also a permanent member of the United Nations Security Council, a member of the Commonwealth of Nations and NATO.

The UK has a rich and colorful history, including a long history of immigration. The UK continues to attract immigrants and this has contributed to the cultural diversity of the country.

The UK boasts some of the best educational institutions in the world, from pre-school to university. These institutions of academic excellence attract students from across the globe. Many international students desire to obtain a British education.

The UK is also well known for its National Health Service (NHS) which provides free healthcare.

London is a leading global city and the world's most influential financial center, alongside New York. It is a cosmopolitan city and caters for every taste and culture. London has the highest GDP of any city in Europe and houses corporate headquarters of numerous multinational corporations, financial institutions, professional firms and major organizations. London ranks as the number one city in the world in a study based on economic activity, political power, influence and quality of life,[175] and has its own elected Mayor and Assembly.

Despite the recent reforms in the immigration policy, there are various options that an individual can explore to become a resident in the UK. The special tax treatment available to those who are not domiciled in the UK is also important.

27.1   Residence in the United Kingdom

The Immigration Act, 1971 forms the foundation of immigration law in the UK; Section 3(2) of the Act defines the Immigration Rules.

---

[175]   Knight Frank, Wealth Report 2016

In 2008, the UK Immigration authorities amended the application system for non-EU nationals who wish to gain entry and residence in the UK. Further changes are introduced on a regular basis but typically in April and November of each year. This current system is points-based and divided into five tiers. Each tier has a set of entry requirements, entitlements and conditions, and an applicant must score sufficient points to qualify under the relevant tier.

The five tiers are categorized as follows:

- *Tier 1* – High valued migrants including investors, entrepreneurs and exceptionally talented people
- *Tier 2* – Skilled workers, which includes general workers, intra-company transfers, sports people and ministers of religion
- *Tier 3* (currently suspended)
- *Tier 4* – Students
- *Tier 5* – Youth Mobility Scheme and temporary workers

Under Tier 1 and 2 an individual can potentially settle in the UK if they have met all the conditions of stay. Tier 5 is a temporary migration scheme and will not qualify the person for permanent residence. It is also important to note that one cannot change from a Tier 5 visa to a different scheme, whereas under Tier 1 and Tier 2, one is eligible to switch to another Tier, provided one meets all the requirements under the new Tier.

The Tier 1 category is aimed at attracting investors and entrepreneurs to contribute to the economy.

Until recently, highly skilled individuals including doctors, scientists, engineers, lawyers etc., could apply under the Tier 1 General category but this category is now closed to new applicants.

The law that governs Tier 1 applications has been incorporated into Part 6A, paragraphs 245B-245FC and Appendix A of the UK Immigration Rules of the UK Immigration and Nationality Directorate.

There are now three categories open under Tier 1, since two have been closed, namely:

1. *The Investor* category is aimed at attracting high net worth individuals to make a substantial investment in the UK. The investor must invest a minimum of GBP 2 million in the UK. The investor is free to work or study in the UK (with some minor exceptions)

2. *The Entrepreneur* category provides for individuals who intend to invest in the UK by establishing or taking over and becoming actively involved in the running of one or more businesses in the UK. The applicant must invest at least GBP 200,000 of disposable income, held in a regulated financial institution, in the business

3. *The Exceptional Talent* category is a unique category for people who are internationally recognized as world leaders or potential world-leading talent in the fields of science and the arts, and who specifically wish to work in the UK. This category is limited to only a small number of applicants[176] and the initial application must be endorsed by a "designated competent body"

4. *The Post-study Worker* category is now closed

5. *The Highly Skilled Migrant* category is now closed

In March 2011, the government announced new rules which provide the ability to achieve permanent residence[177] more quickly in the UK through an accelerated route. If an investor under Tier 1 invests GBP 10 million or more it would provide for permanent residence after two years, while an investment of GBP 5 million would lead to permanent residence after three years, instead of the standard five-year period. The two and three year periods are calculated from the day the initial investment has been increased to GBP 10 or 5 million. In December 2012, new guidelines were introduced to require evidence of the source of the additionally invested funds or evidence that the additional funds had been held for three months before the top-up was made.

---

[176] There was a limit of 1,000 endorsements between 9 August 2011 and 5 April 2012
[177] "Indefinite Leave to Remain" (ILR), which is equivalent to a permanent residence permit

The current system also provides that:

- A Tier 1 (Investor) migrant's leave will be curtailed if they fail to maintain the required level of investment for the duration of their leave

- Tier 1 (Investor) migrants may not work as professional sportspeople

- The investment may not be held in offshore custody

- The investment may not be financed as a loan

- The investment may not be a collective investment

- The investment does not need to be topped up if the value of the investment portfolio falls (unless the investor sells part of the investment)

The rule relating to financial institutions which do not satisfactorily verify financial statements is being expanded to cover the funds Tier 1 (Investor) applicants are required to invest.

There are four categories under Tier 2:

1. *Skilled workers* with a job offer, who can fill a gap in the work-force that cannot be filled by a settled worker

2. The *Intra-Company Transfers* category accommodates employees of multinational companies who are transferred by the overseas branch, either on a long-term basis, or for frequent short visits. Within this category, three sub-divisions distinguish established skilled staff to fill a post in the UK; graduate trainee for training in the UK; and skills transfer for new recruits

3. The *Minister of Religion* category accommodates ministers of religion who will fill a post in their faith community

4. The *Sportsperson* category is aimed at attracting elite sportsmen and coaches, whose employment will contribute significantly to the development of their sport at the highest level

Tier 3 is a temporary migration scheme. The scheme has replaced the various categories previously in place to accommodate unskilled labor for the purpose of filling gaps in the labor market, particularly on a seasonal basis. Currently this scheme has been suspended indefinitely in an attempt to adequately fill these positions by employees from the EU.

A foreign student can apply for a visa to study in the UK under the Tier 4 scheme. The applicant must be sponsored by an approved educational institution. Initially the visa will only be issued for the duration of the course. If a person has legally stayed in the UK as a student for an uninterrupted period of 10 years, this person is eligible for permanent residence.

The fifth category is a temporary scheme that only applies to a select group of countries[178] and gives young people an opportunity to experience life in the UK. This category will not lead to permanent residence, nor can a person change from a Tier 5 visa to another visa.

EEA and Swiss nationals have a right of residence if the person fulfils certain employment conditions and can prove that they are in a position to support themselves and their families without recourse to the social benefits system.

Under Tier 1 and Tier 2,[179] after the initial three-year residence period, the applicant can apply for an extension of stay for a further two years, as long as the applicant has met all the category's requirements. After five years, the person can apply for ILR.

27.2   Requirements – Tier 1 Investor Category

Each category has specific requirements that the applicant must fulfil in order to be granted a residence permit. This section will deal specifically with the requirements under the Tier 1 Investor category.

In order to qualify, the applicant must have held no less than GBP 2 million under his/her control in a regulated financial institution for three months in advance of the initial application or must be able to demonstrate

---

[178] Australia, Canada, Japan, Monaco, New Zealand
[179] This is not applicable to persons with a post-graduate work visa or an intra-company transfer visa

the source of funds (such as a deed of gift). The funds must be freely transferrable to the UK.

The applicant is then required to open up a UK investment account and must provide a criminal record certificate from any country where they have lived in for 12 months or more in the last 10 years. The application must include valid travel identification, a passport photo and tuberculosis test results if they come from a country where this is required. The applicant is not required to show business experience, the ability to speak English, or to undergo any interviews (in most cases). A mandatory tuberculosis test was introduced in 2013 for certain countries.

Within three months of entry to the UK the applicant is required to make an investment of at least GBP 2 million, which must be maintained throughout the period until permanent residence is granted.

The investor must invest in the UK by way of UK government bonds, share capital or loan capital in active and trading UK-registered companies, other than those principally engaged in property investment. Investment in offshore companies is not permitted. The investment must be maintained for five years.

The investor and their dependents are permitted to work and/or study in the UK. Once resident, the applicant's children will be entitled to the same public education benefits as British children, with certain restrictions applied only to college and university education (until settlement is granted).

Close to the expiry of the initial visa, the investor and their dependents must apply for an extension of stay. A two-year extension will be granted if the applicant has maintained the required investment throughout the term.

Investors are expected to make the UK their main home by spending more time in the UK than elsewhere. Up to a maximum of 180 days in any of the twelve calendar months preceding the date of application for settlement may be spent outside the UK. The UK Border Agency is very strict about physical presence and at the very least the main applicant must spend the requisite amount of time in the UK.

To qualify for settlement, the applicant must meet certain criteria, applicable to each category. All applicants must prove that they have sufficient knowledge of the language and life in the UK, and must pass a *Life in the UK* test as well as an English language exam at level B1 of CEFR.

Once settlement has been granted, all visa restrictions are removed. It is, however, important to maintain presence in the UK to avoid losing one's permanent resident status by entering the UK at least once every two years.

Partners (married or unmarried) and dependent children under 18 can apply to come to the UK with the investor. Furthermore, the UK recognizes civil partnerships that have been legally registered in the UK or in the home country.

27.3   Procedures and time frame

The application and supporting documentation must be submitted to the diplomatic post in the country of residence. If there is no diplomatic post in the country of residence, a diplomatic post in a country in close proximity will usually be in a position to accommodate the application. For example, a Russian citizen living in Moscow applying for a residence permit in the UK must do so at the British Embassy in Moscow, whereas a resident of St. Kitts must do so at the British High Commission in Barbados.

Applicants can only submit an application from inside the UK if changing their status from another qualifying category, e.g. a Student visa.

The processing time for the initial application is dependent on the embassy receiving the application. The approval can take between one and five weeks.

Once approved, the British government will grant entry clearance for three years and four months to the main applicant, his or her spouse and all dependents under the age of 18. Upon receiving entry clearance, a date is agreed whereby the applicant must travel to the UK within 30 days to obtain a stamp at the border post to start the residence period and to pick up the Tier 1 Investor biometric card from a post office. Applicants from certain countries are required to register with the police within seven days of arrival.

Upon expiry of the initial three year and four-months period, the main applicant must apply for an extension of stay from within the UK. The authorities will issue the applicant with a two-year extension.

On completion of five years of continuous lawful residence, the main applicant may apply for himself/herself and the respective family to be granted ILR. The main applicant would need to be able to demonstrate that they have legally spent a continuous period of five years in the UK, has maintained the conditions required by the permit, and that they and any dependents over 18 (but under 65), years of age have sufficient knowledge of the English language and sufficient knowledge about life in the UK.

Investors and their dependents must pass the *Life in the UK* test prior to gaining settlement. The *Life in the UK* test is very easy. It must also be demonstrated that they have sufficient knowledge of the English language. From October 2013, all applicants for settlement must present an English language speaking and listening qualification at B1 level or above of the Common European Framework of Reference for Languages (unless they are exempt). There is a criminality threshold to settlement applications that requires all applicants to be clear of convictions.

27.4   Taxation

The UK tax year runs from 6 April to 5 April.

Income Tax is chargeable at progressive rates with a maximum rate of 45% upon taxable income above GBP 150,000 annually from April 2013. Capital Gains Tax is charged at a maximum rate of 28%, but with an effective 10% rate upon the disposal of certain business assets, mainly related to unincorporated businesses and unquoted companies which are carrying on a trade or profession. The 10% rate is available on gains of up to GBP 10 million per individual upon the disposal of interests in such business and companies where the ownership period prior to disposal was at least one year. There is no wealth tax in the UK.

Inheritance Tax is charged upon death at a flat rate of 40% on the full value of the estate with an allowance on the first GBP 325,000 of the estate from this tax.

Furthermore, from April 2017, a Family Home Allowance will be added to the tax free allowance of GBP 100,000 for each individual. This Family Home Allowance will rise to GBP 175,000 by April 2020.

Married couples and civil partners can combine their allowance therefore, by 2020, a property worth up to GBP 1 million will be able to pass on to the beneficiaries completely free of inheritance tax.

Lifetime gifts made to trusts are taxed at 20% of the value transferred to the trust (with allowance given for the first GBP 325,000). Furthermore, the value of assets held in a trust is sometimes re-assessed at 10 yearly intervals and when assets leave a trust. In such circumstances a periodic Inheritance Tax charge can be imposed at a maximum effective rate of up to 6%.

The imposition of personal UK taxes is based on the two main concepts of residence and domicile.

Residence in the UK is determined by the Statutory Residence Test which was introduced in the Finance Bill 2013 whereby the individual will need to prove they are not a resident by satisfying four basic steps.

Step 1 considers whether the individual spent 183 days in the UK in that tax year. Those who did will be resident in the UK. If not:

Step 2 considers the three automatic overseas tests (these are mainly determined by days spent outside of the UK). If the individual meets one of these they are not UK resident. If they do not:

Step 3 considers if they are automatically UK resident (this is verified by the UK tests which are determined by the amount of time spent in the UK as well as within their home in UK. The UK tests also consider the amount of time spent working in the UK). If the individual meets one of these, they are UK resident. If they do not:

Step 4 considers the sufficient ties test (the sufficient ties test will consider the family ties, work ties, accommodation ties and the 90-day tie). If the individual meets this they are UK resident, if they do not meet this, they are not UK resident.

Domicile is determined by several factors. Essentially a person is presumed to be domiciled in the country which they regard as their permanent home. The purpose of determining domicile is to establish a legal "connection". Most notably, the person's domicile status will determine how their estate will be divided up. Various UK laws contain specific exceptions for non-domiciled people.

It is possible to be resident in the UK for tax purposes, but domiciled in a foreign country. If such a situation exists, this can offer considerable tax advantages.

An individual coming to the UK, who wishes to retain their foreign domicile of origin in order to retain tax advantages, may live in the UK until the age of 18 without forming the intention to settle permanently.

An individual who is UK resident but not UK domiciled can choose to be taxed on UK-source income and gains only, if they are willing to (and if necessary formally elect to) leave overseas-source income and gains outside the UK, and pay tax only on such overseas income and gains as they remit to the UK.

By contrast, if the individual is UK resident and domiciled, tax is imposed on worldwide income and gains, and Inheritance Tax is levied upon worldwide assets.

Many non-UK domiciled persons will make arrangements to separate overseas income and gains from UK source income and gains.

Furthermore it is possible for a non-UK domiciled individual to arrange for their overseas bank to separate their income and capital into different accounts. In this way, remittances from the original capital can continue to be made after UK tax residence has been acquired, whilst overseas income and gains continues to be tax free whilst unremitted.

The remittance basis of taxation has been complicated considerably by legislation introduced in 2008, 2012, and 2015.

The main effects of the changes are as follows:

1. Except for individuals with unremitted overseas income and gains of less than GBP 2,000 annually, the remittance basis must be claimed on a year-by-year basis, and the cost of such a claim is to sacrifice the basic personal allowances which exist for individuals to exempt the first slice of personal income and gains

2. For individuals who have been resident in the UK for at least seven out of the last nine preceding tax years, the remittance basis is conditional upon the individual both sacrificing his annual personal allowances, and upon making an additional payment of GBP 30,000 for each tax year for which the remittance basis is claimed

3. From 6 April 2015 a new level of charge for claiming remittance basis was introduced for individuals who have been UK tax resident for at least 12 out of 14 consecutive tax years. The charge was increased from GBP 50,000 to GBP 60,000. The charge of GBP 30,000 in clause 2 above remains the same. At the same time however the government has announced that it intends to offer a tax incentive to encourage non-UK domiciled (Non Dom) persons to remit income to the UK tax free if it is to be used for investment in UK business activity

4. From 6 April 2015, the Chancellor also announced a new charge. Non Dom individuals resident in the UK in more than 17 out of the last 20 tax years will now pay a charge of GBP 90,000 to claim the remittance basis

5. From April 2017, Non Doms will be deemed domiciled for tax purposes once the individual has been a resident in the UK for 15 out of the past 20 tax years

The UK has an extensive network of double tax agreements.

27.5   Family law and inheritance aspects

Unlike civil law jurisdictions, English law is based on a combination of statute and precedent. More specifically, it is important to further distinguish between the legal system of England and Wales and the Scottish legal system. Neither of them, however, recognizes a community of property regime.

In family matters, the UK generally does not take foreign law into account.

The UK made a policy decision to not apply private international law to matrimonial matters. Furthermore, irrespective of the spouses' domicile, English courts will apply English law. More specifically, the court is not obliged to give effect to the nuptial agreement in exercising its discretion under Section 25 of the Matrimonial Cause Act 1973 and will in most cases determine the financial arrangements between the parties. However, in the landmark Radmacher Case,[180] the courts enforced the pre-nuptial agreement.

For wealthy individuals who are married or living in a *de facto* relationship (which from a matrimonial property point of view may have the same consequences in the UK as if legally married), it is therefore important to obtain proper expert advice before establishing residence in the country.

The law of England and Wales does not impose forced heirship rules, but Scottish law does: by law the spouse and the deceased's children inherit a third of the estate.

---

[180] Radmacher (formerly Granatino) (Respondent) v Granatino (Apellant) 2009 [2010] UKSC 42

In England and Wales, the law recognizes a valid will. However, the Inheritance (Provision for Family and Dependents) Act 1975 empowers the court to make provisions for dependents who were financially dependent on the deceased. If there is no valid will, the law enforces the rules of intestacy.

27.6   Citizenship

The law covering British citizenship is in the British Nationality Act 1981 and in the British Overseas Territories Act 2002, and in the Nationality, Immigration and Asylum Act 2002 and the Immigration, Asylum and Nationality Act 2006.

In 1981, the UK ceased to recognize Commonwealth citizens as British subjects. However, people who are closely connected with the UK (including the Channel Islands and the Isle of Man) and the British Overseas Territories (excluding Akrotiri and Dhekelia in Cyprus), are British citizens.

UK citizenship is automatically acquired at birth by a child born in the United Kingdom to a parent who is a British citizen or a permanently settled UK resident at the time of birth.

If a child is born abroad, it can acquire UK citizenship by descent from a parent who is a British citizen other than by descent. Citizenship by descent is only transferable to one generation; therefore, if a parent was born outside of the UK and obtained citizenship by descent, this parent cannot transfer British citizenship to his or her child if it is born outside of the UK.

The Home Secretary may, if she thinks fit, naturalize a person who meets certain requirements which are set out in Section 6 of and Schedule 1 to the British Nationality Act 1981.

In order to qualify for citizenship, the family must satisfy the physical residence requirements, i.e. not to have spent more than 450 days outside the UK in the previous five years, and not to have spent more than 90 days outside of the UK in the year immediately preceding the application.

The person applying must be of good character, have sufficient knowledge of English, Welsh or Scottish Gaelic and demonstrate knowledge of life in the UK by passing the *Life in the UK* test.

Standard application forms must be completed and acceptance is at the discretion of the Home Office. The naturalized citizens must take a citizenship pledge at a formal ceremony.

Once citizenship has been granted, there is no restriction on the time that must be spent in the UK.

27.7   Dual citizenship

The UK allows dual citizenship.

27.8   Key advantages and disadvantages

Advantages

- International business environment – London is the financial capital of the world

- Attractive tax regime for high net worth individuals who are resident but not domiciled

- Direct international flight connections to almost all major cities in the world

- World-renowned schools and universities

- Fastest investor immigration application processing amongst the G8 countries

- No business or management experience required

- Very objective entry criteria, predictable outcome

Disadvantages

- Physical presence requirements apply both to maintaining the residence permit and qualifying for citizenship

- Citizenship is only available after a minimum of five years' residence

- Political uncertainty regarding future developments in immigration rules, citizenship requirements and taxation

27.9 General information

Official name	United Kingdom of Great Britain (England, Scotland, and Wales and Northern Ireland)
Capital city	London
Region	North Western Europe
Surface area	243,610km^2
Government	British Monarchy (constitutional monarchy and Commonwealth realm)
Languages	English
Currency	Pound Sterling (GBP)
Population	64,088,222 (July 2015 est.)
Religion	Christian (Anglican, Roman Catholic, Presbyterian, Methodist) 59.5%, Muslim 4.4%, Hindu 1.3%, other 2%, unspecified or none 30.9%
Ethnic groups	White (of which English 87.2%), Black African / Caribbean / Black British 3%, Asian / Asian British, Indian 2.3%, Asian / Asian British Pakistani 1.9%, Mixed 2%, other 3.7%
GDP	US$2.679 trillion (2015 est.)
GDP per capita	US$41,200 (2015 est.)
Major industries	Services, particularly banking, insurance, and business services
Main exports	Manufactured goods, chemicals, foodstuffs
Climate	The climate is temperate; moderated by prevailing southwest winds over the North Atlantic Current; more than one-half of the days are overcast
World's healthiest countries (Bloomberg Rankings)	14th (2015)
UN Human Development Index (HDI)	14th (2015)
Henley & Partners Visa Restrictions Index	3rd (2016), 1st (2015)
Legatum Prosperity Index	15th (2015)

Sources: CIA "The World Factbook" (2015), World Bank (2015),
UN Human Development Report (2015), Henley & Partners, The Legatum Institute

27.10 Climate

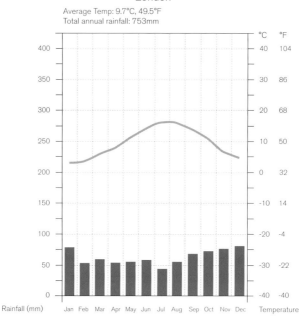

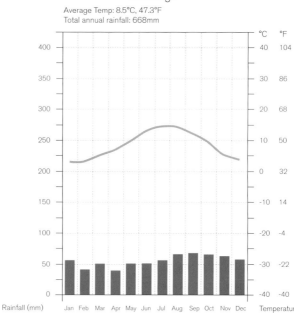

28

United States of America

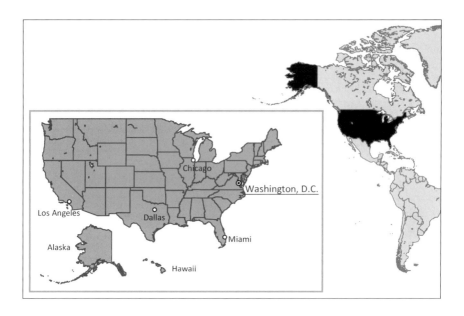

The US is the third largest country in the world by land and population and has been the economic and military powerhouse of the world for the last century. Its GDP accounts for nearly a quarter of the world's total GDP.

The US is a federal republic with 50 states. Each state enjoys quite extensive autonomy and has its own state government and legislature. The President of the United States is the Head of State as well as the Head of the Federal Government. The Congress is the legislative arm which is divided into the Senate and the House of Representatives.

The US is a diverse mix of cultures varying greatly across a great geographical expanse. Americans originate from various cultures and countries. The US was born from the original American Indians, the European settlers from Great Britain, Ireland, the Netherlands, Italy and other European nations, and the Africans who were brought to work in America on the plantations. More recently, there has been an influx of Asian and Hispanics who come to the US to live "the American dream". Despite the diversity in cultures, Americans have a strong sense of patriotism for their country.

Americans have a positive attitude toward and encourage entrepreneurship which is evident in the number of great companies and brands that originated in the US and are now household names all over the world. American culture has influenced the world for many decades.

Geographically, the country is enormous and has a vast range of landscapes, vegetation, complexity and diversity. The country is bounded by both the Atlantic and Pacific oceans and bordered by Canada and Mexico.

The US has a long history of welcoming immigrants from all parts of the world and still is a very attractive country to live, to work and for business.

The immigration laws and regulations of the US accordingly provide for many different types of visas and possibilities to enter, work and settle in the country. The permanent residence permit in the US is called the Green Card and may be obtained through different routes.

From a tax perspective, it may be desirable for a wealthy individual or family to have the right to spend time and reside in the US, yet not become a resident for tax purposes, or only during a limited period of time. In this regard, a Green Card would not be an optimal solution, because this establishes tax residence even if you do not actually spend much time in the US. Furthermore, giving up Green Card status later on may have other adverse tax consequences.[181] In such a situation it may be more advantageous to enter and remain in the US on another type of permit (e.g. treaty-investor visa or other, temporary permits which are renewable, in some cases without restrictions). Professional immigration and tax advice should be sought before entering the US with the intention to spend a longer period of time there.

This chapter only covers the EB-5 Program, which is a specific route to permanent residence (Green Card status) open to foreign persons who invest in the country.

28.1   Permanent residence through the EB-5 Program

The Immigrant Investor Program of the US, known as the EB-5 Program, was created by Congress in 1990 under Section 203(b)(5) of the Immigration and Nationality Act (INA) to stimulate the US economy through job creation and capital investments from foreign investors that wished to obtain permanent residence in the US. The Regional Center Pilot Program was established in 1992.

The US Congress authorized a three-year extension of the EB-5 Pilot Program when it passed bill S.3245 on 28 September 2012. There are two pathways to achieve permanent residence under the EB-5 Program, namely the Basic Program and the Regional Center Pilot Program. Both programs require the investor to make capital investment of either USD 1 million or USD 500,000 respectively in a new commercial enterprise located in the US. The new commercial enterprise must create at least 10 full-time jobs for qualified US workers within two years of

---

[181]   See chapter 3 for a discussion of these aspects

the grant of the conditional permanent residence. The USD 500,000 minimum investment is expected to increase at some point in the future.

There is an annual quota of 10,000 visas available under the EB-5 Program.

The Regional Center Pilot Program was created to promote economic growth in targeted employment and distressed areas. A Regional Center is defined as "any economic unit, public or private, engaged in the promotion of economic growth, improved regional productivity, job creation and increased domestic capital investment".[182] The United States Citizenship and Immigration Services (USCIS) has approved a number of regional center projects which qualify for the EB-5 Program.

Under the Regional Center Program, the investor is not required to be actively involved with the day to day management of the operations. As most Regional Center projects are structured as Limited Partnerships, the investor is able to easily meet the management requirements in a simplified way. This may include simply reviewing the reports and attending the annual Limited Partnership meeting. Furthermore, the Regional Centre is responsible for creating the minimum of 10 direct or indirect jobs that are required for each investor.

It is a legal requirement that the investment be "at risk", without any guarantees of return. The investor must invest the full minimum USD 500,000 or USD 1 million into the project. Most projects have a minimum investment hold period of five to seven years.

As these are active businesses, the investor must carefully assess the commercial viability and risk of the project. The investor should consider the experience of the management team, the project's track record under the EB-5 program, the financials of the company and the project, and in particular the commitment to create the required 10 full-time jobs.[183] The Investor should also understand the investment exit strategy that the Regional Centre has in place.

---

[182] *http://www.eb5globalventures.com/eb-5-regional-centers*
[183] This is a critical requirement which later on, if not met, may lead to the revocation of the permanent residence status

The investor may also invest in a business of their choice under the USD 1 million option. The investor must outline in a detailed business plan how the USD 1 million will be utilized and must show the creation of at least direct 10 jobs within two years. The investment may be in the form of cash, equipment, inventory, other tangible property, and cash equivalents. The assets will be valued at fair market value in US dollars. The investment capital cannot be borrowed.

28.2   Requirements

The EB-5 program has relatively few eligibility requirements. The applicant is not required to prove language skills or work or management experience.

The investor must be at least 21 years of age and meet the following requirements: a clean bill of health (no communicable diseases or serious mental disorders), proof of a clean criminal record (police record), no disqualifying US immigration background and evidence of legal source of funds (for at least five years), and the pathway of funds into the investment. The applicant must also demonstrate the ability to make the qualifying investment.

Under the Regional Center Pilot Program, the proposal must provide a framework within which the individual investor can satisfy the EB-5 eligibility requirements including creating the EB-5 jobs. The Regional Center Proposal must provide the necessary documentation of the transfer of the investors' capital into the enterprise that shall satisfy to USCIS that the investment complies with the eligibility requirements. When investing and applying through an EB-5 Regional Center, it is important that there are no issues in the agreements which could cause concern to the USCIS thereby jeopardizing the application.

The applicant must also demonstrate the ability to make the qualifying investment. One of the main benefits of the EB-5 Program is that an investor may use investment funds that have been gifted or inherited, as long as he is able to establish the legal source of the original funds. For example, it is possible for parents to gift the applicable funds to their child who is 21 years of age.

Under the Basic Program, the investor can only create jobs through direct employment, while the Regional Pilot Project allows the investor to satisfy the job creation requirements either through direct or indirect job creation.

An indirect job would include jobs held by employees of the producers of materials, equipment and services used by the commercial enterprise. There are economic models used to calculate the number of indirect jobs created.

Under the Regional Center Pilot Program, an individual or entity must file a Regional Center Proposal to request USCIS approval.

28.3   Procedures and time frame

Once the investor has decided on which route to proceed, the investor will enter into an arrangement to secure the investment. Usually the investment capital is placed in an escrow account with the Regional Center.

The investor must file an individual Form I-526 petition to establish eligibility for classification as an EB-5 investor under either program. This currently takes approximately 12 to 24 months to process. Given the popularity of the program and volume of applications, processing times have slowed down somewhat. Also, given the current volume of applications, applicants from certain countries, notably China, may face "visa retrogression" issues, further slowing down the process for them.

Upon approval of the Form I-526 petition, the investor can either apply under Form I-485 to register for permanent residence; or apply for an immigrant visa in the investor's home country to obtain the conditional permanent residence status (CPR). This will take an additional four to six months to process.

The EB-5 investor and their family are granted conditional permanent residence for a two-year period upon the approval of the I-485 application or upon entry into the US with an EB-5 immigrant visa.

As proof of that status, this person is granted a permanent resident card, commonly called a Green Card. A Green Card holder is someone who is granted authorization to live and work in the US on a permanent basis.

After the conditional two-year period, the conditions on the Green Card will be lifted as long as the applicable number of jobs has been created. Under some Regional Center Projects, the number of jobs created has not been sufficient in the eyes of the USCIS which means that conditions are not removed from the Green Card and the family does not achieve the permanent status. For this reason, it is important to choose a reputable and well-established project that has been proven to meet the job creation criteria.

Within 90 days prior to the two-year anniversary of the grant of the CPR, the investor must file the I-829 Form which should demonstrate that all terms and conditions of the EB-5 program have been met by the investor. If the USCIS approves this petition, the conditions are removed from the EB-5 applicant's status and the EB-5 investor and their family will be allowed to permanently live and work in the US.

Under the EB-5 Program, the applicant may work, study and live anywhere in the US. Unlike other US immigration categories, the EB-5 has no restrictions on what the investor can do and where the investor may reside in the US.

28.4   Taxation

US citizens and residents are subject to tax on their worldwide income. Certain exemptions and deductions are available. A Green Card holder will be considered resident for US tax purposes regardless of how much time they actually spend in the US.

Non-resident persons are subject to tax only on US sourced income. Taxes are levied at both federal and state level. State and municipal tax levels will vary from state to state. Some states do not levy an income tax.

Over and above the income tax, the US levies an employment tax, social security tax, Medicare tax, alternative minimum tax, gift tax, estate tax, capital gains tax and qualified retirement plan tax. Net worth tax is not levied on federal level but some states and municipalities may impose a net worth tax.

Everyone must file a tax return annually with the IRS and the state and local tax authorities. If you are a Green Card holder, you also need to file a Federal tax return and pay Federal tax even if you are not actually residing in the US.

The tax system in the US is onerous and complicated therefore it is critical to obtain appropriate tax advice prior to entering the US.

US citizens and residents can rely on double tax relief as the US has signed double tax treaties with a large number of countries.

28.5   Family law and inheritance aspects

Family law, including matters such as marriage and divorce, is almost exclusively a state matter which means in each state it is somewhat different. The various states recognize both pre-nuptial and ante-nuptial agreements.

The US recognizes the right of the deceased to dispose of their property as desired which is usually done by way of a will. If a person leaves behind a valid will, the courts will enforce it. If the person dies intestate, the person's estate will be disposed of according to the law of the state where the deceased was resident. Commonly, the state law provides that the intestate property will pass to the deceased's family.

Estate tax is levied on both a federal and state level and is levied on both residents and non-residents. The estate will be taxed in the state where the deceased was resident but should the deceased own property in another state, that property will be subject to the estate duty of the state in which the property is located. However, it is important to note that because each state has its own laws, the rules differ from state to state.

28.6   Citizenship

If an individual is born in the US, they will automatically acquire US citizenship at birth.

A person can also acquire citizenship by descent if at least one parent was a US citizen at the time of his or her birth.

A person is eligible for citizenship if they are over 18 years of age, has lived continuously in the US for five years without "abandoning" permanent resident status by leaving the US for extended trips (e.g. trips for continuous periods of six months or longer outside of the US may result in being deemed to have abandoned permanent residence), and is a person of good moral character. Applicants should also have accumulated 30 months of physical presence in the US within the five years, including the last three months in the state where the naturalization application is filed. Most naturalization applicants are required to take an English language and Civics test.

To become a US citizen, the applicant must take an Oath of Allegiance. The oath includes several promises the person makes to the government including to give up all prior allegiance to any other nation or sovereignty, to swear allegiance to the US and serve the country when required. The US however does not force people who become citizens to renounce their previous citizenship.

28.7   Dual citizenship

The US allows dual citizenship.

28.8   Advantages and disadvantages of EB-5

Advantages

- Can settle anywhere in the US
- Applicant may use funds that have been gifted, inherited or loaned

- The US offers a wide range of choice in lifestyle, culture, geography and climate

- Obtain same privileges as US citizens except being allowed to vote

- Excellent universities

- Great lifestyle, investment and business opportunities

Disadvantages

- Onerous taxation regime with comprehensive reporting requirements

- The Green Card under the EB-5 program is initially conditional

- Giving up Green Card status later on may have adverse tax consequences (exit taxes)

- Citizenship is only available after a minimum of five years' continuous residence

- Political uncertainty regarding future developments in tax regime

28.9   General information

Official name	United States of America
Capital city	Washington, D.C.
Region	North America, bordering both the North Atlantic Ocean and the North Pacific Ocean, between Canada and Mexico
Surface area	9,826,675 km²
Government	Constitution-based federal republic; strong democratic tradition
Languages	English 79.2%, Spanish 12.9%, other Indo-European 3.8%, Asian and Pacific island 3.3%, other 0.9%
Currency	US Dollars (USD)
Population	321,368,864 (July 2015 est.)
Religion	Protestant 51.3%, Roman Catholic 23.9%, Mormon 1.7%, other Christian 1.6%, Jewish 1.7%, Buddhist 0.7%, Muslim 0.6%, other or unspecified 2.5%, unaffiliated 12.1%, none 4%
Ethnic groups	White 79.96%, Black 12.85%, Asian 4.43%, Amerindian and Alaska native 0.97%, native Hawaiian and other Pacific islander 0.18%, two or more races 1.61%
GDP	USD 17.95 trillion (2015 est.)
GDP per capita, PPP	USD 55,800 (2015 est.)
Major industries	Highly diversified, world leading high-technology innovator, second largest industrial output in world; petroleum, steel, motor vehicles, aerospace, telecommunications, chemicals, electronics, food processing, consumer goods, lumber, mining
Main exports	Agricultural products 9.2%, industrial supplies (organic chemicals) 26.8%, capital goods (transistors, aircraft, motor vehicle parts, computers, telecommunications equipment) 49.0%, consumer goods (automobiles, medicines) 15.0%
Climate	Mostly temperate, but tropical in Hawaii and Florida, arctic in Alaska, semiarid in the great plains west of the Mississippi River, and arid in the Great Basin of the southwest; low winter temperatures in the northwest
UN Human Development Index (HDI)	8th (2015)
World's healthiest countries (Bloomberg Rankings)	33rd (2015)
Henley & Partners Visa Restrictions Index	4th (2016), 2nd (2015)
Legatum Prosperity Index	11th (2015)

Sources: CIA "The World Factbook" (2015), World Bank (2015),
UN Human Development Report (2015), Henley & Partners, The Legatum Institute

28.10 Climate

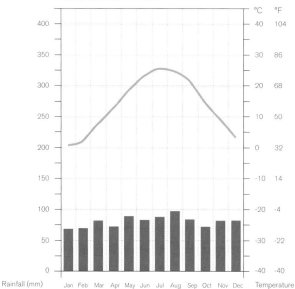

Washington D.C.
Average Temp: 13.7°C, 56.7°F
Total annual rainfall: 971mm

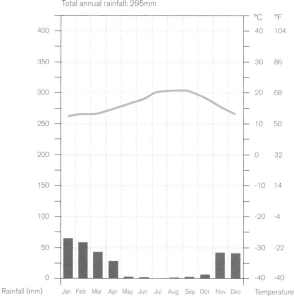

Los Angeles
Average Temp: 16.5°C, 61.7°F
Total annual rainfall: 295mm

PART IV

Citizenship-by-Investment

29

Overview of Citizenship-By-Investment Options

Residence permits are available to investors and wealthy individuals in most countries: Austria, Canada, Switzerland, and the UK are just a few examples of countries which offer residence to wealthy individuals and investors.

However, as explained in detail in earlier chapters, it is often desirable not only to hold an alternative residence permit, but also to obtain a second passport. The benefits are numerous but ultimately, possessing a second passport is equivalent to holding an insurance policy.

At different times, various countries have operated programs that officially allowed the acquisition of citizenship without residence requirements on the basis of an investment. These countries include Belize, Cape Verde, Grenada, Ireland and several others.

There are currently only eight countries which have clear provisions in their laws for granting citizenship-by-investment, i.e. for economic considerations and without lengthy residence requirements, and which also have a well-established practice to regularly grant citizenship for investments in the country. These are Antigua and Barbuda, Austria, Cyprus, Dominica, Grenada, Malta, St. Kitts and Nevis, and St. Lucia.

Countries which may have such provisions and may occasionally grant citizenship on these grounds, but which do not have a well-established practice, include Bulgaria, Slovakia and a few others, mainly in South America and Africa. In specific circumstances – particularly if one already intends to invest substantially in one of these countries – it may be worth exploring those possibilities. As a general rule, the expenses and complications (e.g. Slovakia) compared to other solutions, as well as lack of transparency and clear procedures (e.g. Bulgaria) make these options less interesting. In some countries, applicants could risk possible problems in the future, for example if there was to be a change of government (e.g. Bulgaria). Also, without clear rules, there is no certainty as to how long the process will take or whether one will in fact obtain the citizenship once the investment has been made.

It is therefore important to stress that there are currently no legal citizenship programs available anywhere else, including in Asia, Africa, Central or South America. Any information to the contrary and offers in this regard are fraudulent. The citizenship-by-investment programs described herein, however, offer you the opportunity to legally acquire a new citizenship quickly and in a straightforward manner, without any disruptions to your life.

Antigua and Barbuda

Antigua and Barbuda is one of the newer countries to offer a formal and legal citizenship-by-investment program, having introduced this as law in March 2013. The laws regarding the citizenship-by-investment program are contained in the Antigua and Barbuda Citizenship by Investment Act, 2013 and the Antigua and Barbuda Citizenship by Investment Regulations, 2013.

To qualify for citizenship, the individual must be over 18, meet the application requirements, and select one of the following options:

- An investment of at least USD 400,000 into one of the approved real estate projects
- A contribution to the National Development Fund (NDF) of a minimum non-refundable amount of USD 200,000 (for a single applicant)
- An investment of a minimum of USD 1.5 million directly into an eligible business as a sole investor or a joint investment involving at least two persons in an eligible business totaling at least USD 5 million, and each of those persons individually invests at least USD 400,000

Each route carries government processing fees of USD 50,000 each for the main applicant, spouse and any dependent over 18, and of USD 25,000 for dependents under 18.

Additionally, due diligence fees apply for all applications, of USD 7,500 each for the main applicant and spouse, USD 2,000 for dependents between ages 12 and 17, and USD 4,000 for dependents between ages 18 and 25 or over the age of 65.

The processing time is approximately three months. An Antigua and Barbuda passport offers a good level of visa-free travel, to over 130 countries, placing it 26th in the *Henley & Partners Visa Restriction Index 2016*. This is one of the newest citizenship-by-investment programs in the world, and one of the most efficient, having been designed and implemented with the professional assistance of Henley & Partners.

Austria

Since 1985, Austria has allowed the acquisition of citizenship on the basis of making an investment in the country. To qualify for citizenship without prior residence under the provisions of the Austrian Citizenship Act, Section 10 (6), an applicant must provide extraordinary scientific, cultural or economic benefits to Austria. Satisfaction of this condition must be confirmed by the Austrian Government. Following such confirmation, citizenship is granted to the successful applicant. Under the citizenship-by-investment provisions, an applicant is required to make a substantial investment in the Austrian economy, for example in the form of a joint venture or a direct investment in a business creating jobs or generating new export sales. Passive investments in government bonds, real estate, etc. normally do not qualify. Substantial professional fees apply, depending on the case and the number of persons in an application, as each case is handled on an individual basis. The processing time also varies from case to case, but the average time frame is at least 24 months. Knowledge of the German language is not required for the main applicant (but for spouse and children it is).

An Austrian passport is one of the best travel documents in the world. It allows extensive visa-free travel (including to the US) and gives you the right to live anywhere in the EU and also in Switzerland.

Cyprus

The citizenship-by-investment program of Cyprus was extensively revised again in March 2014. The regulations regarding citizenship-by-investment are contained in the Scheme for Naturalisation of Investors in Cyprus by Exception on the basis of subsection (2) of Section 111A of the Civil Registry Laws of 2002-2013. There are eight potential routes to citizenship based on extraordinary economic contributions, under which an applicant is required to actively invest in the Cyprus economy.

The first six of the eight options require an individual investment of at least EUR 5 million in one form or another. If any candidate had their deposits in Bank of Cyprus or Laiki Bank cut by at least EUR 3 million since March 15 2013 then they would also be eligible for naturalization. If the money was cut by less than EUR 3 million, candidates could potentially combine it with any of the other options. The main addition to the program was the introduction of the Collective Investment Scheme, which allows applicants to reduce the minimum investment amount from EUR 5 million to EUR 2.5 million by submission of applications to the government of Cyprus in a group, the total investment amount of which exceeds EUR 12.5 million. The investment within such groups does not necessarily need to be related and can be done though different investment options.

In all cases, the applicant must have a clean criminal record. Also, the name of the applicant must not be included in the list of persons on whose name there is a freezing or confiscation order of property within the boundaries of the EU.

In addition, every applicant must be the owner of a permanent residence in Cyprus, with a purchase price of at least EUR 500,000 plus VAT. It is understood that the members of the same family, who submit different applications as investors, can buy collectively a residence/house, provided that the total amount of the residence/house covers the amount of EUR 500,000 for each applicant.

Cypriot citizens are also citizens of the EU, with all the benefits that entails, and the right to live, work and buy property across all EU member countries.

Dominica

The Economic Citizenship Program of the Commonwealth of Dominica was established in 1991 and since then more than 3,000 families have received Dominica citizenship. The program is defined in the constitution and laws of Dominica: Section 101 of the Constitution and Section 8 of the Citizenship Act, chapter 1:10 of the Revised Laws and Section 20 (1) of the Citizenship Act.

Under the current regulations, there are five options for obtaining citizenship: the Single Applicant, and Family Applications One, Two and Three, as well as a Real Estate option.

- Under the Single Option, the applicant pays USD 100,000

- Under Family Application One (for applicant and spouse), USD 175,000

- Under Family Application Two (applicant, spouse, two children under 18), USD 200,000

- Under Family Application Three (applicant, spouse, and more than two children under 18), USD 200,000 and USD 50,000 for every additional person under 18 years

- Under the Real Estate option, a minimum investment in an approved real estate project of USD 200,000 is required for each main applicant. Two or more applicants may apply for citizenship-by-investment together by purchasing one piece of real estate, provided that each main applicant contributes the minimum investment of USD 200,000 towards the investment

From September 2016, these fees will increase as follows:

- Under the Single Option, the applicant will pay USD 175,000

- Under Family Application One (for applicant and spouse), USD 225,000

- Under Family Application Two (applicant, spouse, two children under 18), USD 250,000

- Under Family Application Three (applicant, spouse, and more than two children under 18), USD 250,000 and USD 50,000 for every additional person under 18 years

In addition to the above costs, the government charges a processing fee of USD 3,000 per application and certificate issuance and passport application fees of USD 1,950 per applicant. Furthermore, due diligence fees range from USD 7,500 to USD 2,000 per applicant, dependent upon age. The application process is relatively straightforward and currently takes three to six months from submission.

A Dominica passport enables travel to 119 countries without a visa, which is slightly lower than Antigua and Barbuda or St. Kitts and Nevis passport holders.

Grenada

Grenada is one of a number of the newest countries now offering a formal and legal citizenship-by-investment program. The legal basis for the Grenadian citizenship by investment is the Grenada Citizenship by Investment Act, No.15 of 2013 (as amended) which received Royal Assent on 2 August 2013 and regulations made thereunder. A Grenada passport offers a good level of visa-free travel and additionally and uniquely among the Caribbean countries offering citizenship-by-investment, carries with it visa-free travel to China and the right (subject to compliance) to a US E2 investor visa (see below). If a person has or wants to buy a material and *bona fide* business in the US, such a person may live for five years (renewable) on a non-immigrant basis in the US to run such a business.

Malta

The Malta Individual Investor Programme (MIIP) requires a person to make an economic contribution to the country. In return, and subject to a very thorough application procedure including detailed due diligence and background verification checks, the applicants and their families are granted full citizenship. To qualify for citizenship, the main applicant must be at least 18 years of age, meet all of the application conditions, make a non-refundable contribution to the National Development and Social Fund, and meet certain other requirements.

The contribution requirements are as follows:

- For main applicants, a contribution of EUR 650,000 is required

- An additional contribution of EUR 25,000 is required for a spouse and for each child under the age of 18

- The application may include children between the ages of 18 and 26 years if they are financially dependent on the main applicant and are not married; in such cases, the additional contribution is set at EUR 50,000 for each dependent

- Parents over the age of 55 may also be included in the application as dependents, if they are living with and are fully supported by the main applicant. In such cases, an additional contribution of EUR 50,000 is required per person

Due diligence fees are payable for all applicants: EUR 7,500 for the main applicant; EUR 5,000 for spouses, adult children and parents; and EUR 3,000 each for children between 13 and 17 years of age.

Additionally, the following investment requirements and other obligations must be met:

- *Property* – either the purchase of a residential property in Malta with a price of at least EUR 350,000 which must be held for five years, or the lease of a residential property with a rental of at least EUR 16,000 per annum, also held for five years

- *Investment* – EUR 150,000 in a prescribed investment, details of which are published from time to time by Identity Malta, which must be held for five years

- *Insurance* – the holding of a valid global health insurance policy with medical expense cover amounting to at least EUR 50,000 per family member

- *Residence* – the applicant must have been legally resident in Malta for one year prior to application for citizenship under the MIIP

- *Oath of Allegiance* – all applicants aged 18 years and over are obliged to visit Malta in person to undertake the Oath of Allegiance

The applicant must have a completely clean personal background and no criminal record.

The regulations further provide that a person who has been denied a visa to a country with which Malta has visa-free travel arrangements and has not subsequently obtained a visa to that country shall not be entitled to apply under the program.

A person who is deemed a potential national security risk, a reputational risk or is subject to criminal investigation will also be denied citizenship. Malta has developed a four-tier due diligence system which is considered the most thorough in the world for this kind of program.

The names of successful applicants will be published annually, along with all other naturalizations granted by the government.

There is a cap of 1,800 successful main applicants, after which the program will close, making this the most exclusive program available.

St. Kitts and Nevis

The citizenship-by-investment program of St. Christopher (St. Kitts) and Nevis was established in 1984, which makes it the longest established citizenship-by-investment program. Regulations regarding citizenship-by-investment are contained in Part II, Section 3 (5) of the Citizenship Act, 1984, and the Saint Christopher and Nevis Citizenship by Investment Regulations, 2011.

To qualify for citizenship, the government requires either an investment in designated real estate with a value of at least USD 400,000 plus the payment of government fees and other fees and taxes, or a contribution to the Sugar Industry Diversification Foundation (SIDF) of at least USD 250,000 (for a single applicant) inclusive of all government fees but exclusive of due diligence fees which are the same as for the real estate option. Furthermore, the real estate option may include purchase costs between zero and 12% of the purchase price; government fees of USD 50,047 for a single applicant plus USD 25,047 each for spouse and dependents under the age of 18 (and USD 50,047 each for dependents 18 years and older) and a USD 7,500 due diligence fee for the main applicant; plus USD 4,000 for dependents over the age of 16 years included in the same application. The application procedure under this option takes no longer than the SIDF option.

With the SIDF option, there are four different categories:

- Single applicant: USD 250,000 contribution required
- Applicant with up to three dependents (i.e. spouse and two children below the age of 18): USD 300,000 contribution required
- Applicant with up to five dependents (i.e. one spouse and four children): USD 350,000 contribution required
- Applicant with up to seven dependents: USD 450,000 contribution required

In each of these categories, the total amount includes all government fees but not the due diligence fees, which are USD 7,500 for the main applicant plus USD 4,000 per adult applicant included in the same application.

The documentation required for an application is reasonable and the application procedure is straightforward. The average processing time is usually four to nine months.

St. Lucia

St. Lucia is the latest Caribbean country to offer a formal and legal citizenship-by-investment program, having introduced this as law in 2015. The laws regarding the citizenship-by-investment program are contained in the St. Lucia Citizenship by Investment Act No. 14, 2015 and the St. Lucia Citizenship by Investment Regulations No. 89, 2015.

To qualify for citizenship, the individual must be over 18, meet the application requirements, and select one of the following options:

- An investment of at least USD 300,000 into one of the approved real estate development projects

- A contribution to the National Economic Fund (NEF) of a minimum non-refundable amount of USD 200,000 (for a single applicant)

- An investment in an approved enterprise project (as set out in the regulations) with a minimum investment of USD 3,500,000 plus the creation of no less than three permanent jobs

Investment made in the real estate and business enterprise options both have government administration fees. The main applicant is charged USD 50,000, a spouse USD 35,000, dependents aged 18 years and above USD 35,000 and dependents aged under 18 years of age USD 25,000.

Additionally, due diligence fees apply for all applications, of USD 7,500 for the main applicant and USD 5,000 for each qualifying dependent aged 16 years and above.

The government has established a Citizenship by Investment Board who are mandated to administer the citizenship program and a Citizenship by Investment Unit to process applications which they aim to complete within a three-month timescale. The program requires successful applicants to undertake an oath of allegiance either in person or at a St. Lucia Embassy, High Commission or Consulate office. A St. Lucia passport offers a good level of visa-free travel, to 125 countries, placing it 37th in the *Henley & Partners Visa Restriction Index 2016*. This is the newest citizenship-by-investment program in the world and in order to apply applicants must have a minimum net worth of USD 3 million.

Comparison tables

The following is an overview and comparison of the citizenship-by-investment provisions of Antigua and Barbuda (Antigua), Austria, Cyprus, Dominica, Grenada, Malta, St. Kitts and Nevis (St. Kitts) and St. Lucia.

Citizens of Antigua and Barbuda, Austria, Cyprus, Malta and St. Kitts enjoy extensive visa-free travel. The second table is an overview of the most important countries and territories to which citizens and passport holders of these countries, as well as Dominica, Grenada and St. Lucia, can travel without requiring a visa.

	Malta	Cyprus	Antigua Real Estate
Minimum investment in USD	899,000 (EUR 816,000)	2,875,000	400,000
Non-refundable contribution in USD	700,000 for single applicant	N/A	N/A
Standard Government Fees in USD	34,000 each for spouse and dependent children under 18 years. 68,000 per additional adult dependent	8,050 for adults, 92 for children under 18	50 000 per main applicant and dependent over 18 years and 25,000 per dependent child under 18 years of age
Due diligence fees in USD	8,000 for the main applicant; 5,300 for spouses, adult children and parents; and 3,200 each for children between 13 and 18 years of age	N/A	7,500 for main applicant and spouse, 2,000 per dependent child 12-17 years of age and 4,000 per dependent child 18-25 and dependent parent over 65 years
Other costs in USD	Real estate rental of 17,000 p/a for 5 years or real estate purchase for 375,000. Travel to Malta to swear an oath of allegiance	Travel to Cyprus for passport, stamp duty for real estate transaction, VAT 0-5%, escrow fees	0-6% taxes[1] and travel to Antigua or Embassy / High Commission for passport
Professional fees in USD	≥75,000	≥69,000	≥35,000
Average processing time	3 – 6 months	3 months	3 months
Interview required?	In some cases	No	In some cases
Visit required?	Yes	Yes	Yes
Oath of Allegiance required?	Yes	Yes	Yes
Residence required?	Yes	No	5 days within 5 years
Publication of applicant's details?	Yes	Yes	Yes
Visa-free travel[2]	•••••	•••••	••••
Rank in HVRI	9th	17th	30th
Reputation	•••••	•••••	••••

[1] Transfer Tax, stamp duty and indicative legal fees

[2] • = poor ••••• = excellent

	Antigua National Development Fund	Antigua Business Investments	Austria
Minimum investment in USD	N/A	400,000 or 1,500,000[3]	8,000,000
Non-refundable Contribution in USD	200,000 for a single applicant	N/A	N/A[4]
Standard Government Fees in USD	50 000 per main applicant and dependent over 18 years and 25,000 per dependent child under 18 years of age, or 100,000 for a family of four	50 000 per main applicant and dependent over 18 years and 25,000 per dependent child under 18 years of age[5]	2,000 per person
Due diligence fees in USD	7,500 for main applicant and spouse, 2,000 per dependent child 12-17 years of age and 4,000 per dependent child 18-25 and dependent parent over 65 years	7,500 for main applicant and spouse, 2,000 per dependent child 12-17 years of age and 4,000 per dependent child 18-25 and dependent parent over 65 years	5,000 to 10,000
Other costs in USD	Travel to Antigua or Embassy / High Commission for passport	Travel to Antigua or Embassy / High Commission for passport	Variable, travel to Austria
Professional fees in USD	≥35,000	≥35,000	> 500,000
Average processing time	3 months	3 months	12 - 18 months
Interview required?	In some cases	In some cases	Yes
Visit required?	Yes	Yes	Yes
Oath of Allegiance required?	Yes	Yes	Yes
Residence required?	5 days within 5 years	5 days within 5 years	No[6]
Publication of applicant's details?	Yes	Yes	No
Visa-free travel	••••	••••	•••••
Rank in HVRI	30th	30th	5th
Reputation	••••	••••	•••••

[3]   USD 1,500,000 is the minimum sole investment in an approved business. A collective scheme is available subject to a minimum total investment of USD 5 million and a minimum individual contribution of USD 400,000

[4]   Non-refundable philanthropic or public purpose contribution options are occasionally available depending on the applicant's profile, currently starting at USD 2.5 million

[5]   Referral to the Citizenship-by-Investment Unit may be required in certain cases where the investment is made through a body corporate

[6]   Formal residence required during application process; once citizenship is granted, there is no further residence requirement

	Grenada National Transformation Fund	Grenada Approved Project	St. Kitts Real Estate
Minimum investment in USD	200,000	350,000	400,000
Non-refundable Contribution in USD	200,000	N/A	N/A
Standard Government Fees in USD	Main applicant and spouse nil, children under 12-3,000	Main applicant and spouse nil, children under 12-3,000	50,000 for a single applicant, 25,000 for each dependent under 18 and 50,000 over 18
Due diligence fees in USD	5,000 per person	5,000 per person	7,500 for main applicant, 4,000 for dependents over the age of 16
Other costs in USD	None	None	0 - 12% taxes[7]
Professional fees in USD	≥35,000	≥35,000	≥35,000
Average processing time	60 business days	60 business days	4 - 9 months
Interview required?	No	No	In some cases
Visit required?	No	No	No
Oath of Allegiance required?	No	No	No
Residence required?	No	No	No
Publication of applicant's details?	No	No	No
Visa-free travel	▪▪▪▪	▪▪▪▪	▪▪▪▪
Rank in HVRI	39th	39th	32th
Reputation	▪▪▪▪	▪▪▪▪	▪▪▪▪

---

[7] Depending on the property development

	St. Kitts Sugar Industry Diversification Foundation	St. Lucia	Dominica
Minimum investment in USD	N/A	200,000	200,000
Non-refundable Contribution in USD	250,000 for a single applicant, 300,000 for a family of four	200,000	100,000 for a single applicant, 200,000 for a family of four
Standard Government Fees in USD	50,000 for a single applicant, 25,000 for each dependent under 18 and 50,000 over 18	2,000 for the main applicant and 1,000 per qualifying dependent	3,000 per application
Due diligence fees in USD	7,500 for main applicant, 4,000 for dependents over the age of 16	7,500 for the main applicant and 5,000 for each qualifying dependent aged 16 and above	7,500 for the main applicant and spouse, 4,000 for each dependent 16 and over and 2,000 for dependents aged 12 to 15 years
Other costs in USD	None	None	None
Professional fees in USD	≥35,000	>35,000	≥35,000[8]
Average processing time	4 - 9 months	4 months	3 months
Interview required?	In some cases	No	No
Visit required?	No	No	No[9]
Oath of Allegiance required?	No	Yes	Yes
Residence required?	No	No	No
Publication of applicant's details?	No	No	No
Visa-free travel	▪▪▪▪	▪▪▪▪	▪▪▪▪
Rank in HVRI	32nd	37st	41th
Reputation	▪▪▪▪	▪▪▪	▪▪▪

[8]   Variable fees; actual fee dependent on number of applicants and other factors

[9]   Interview must be attended in Dominica; however, for an additional fee and payment of expenses, a delegation from the Dominica government would travel to conduct the interview at a place of the applicant's choice outside Dominica, and in such cases a visit is not required

Countries and territories that allow visa-free access to holders of a passport from:

Malta	Cyprus	Antigua	Austria
Albania	Albania	Albania	Albania
Anguilla	Anguilla	Anguilla	Anguilla
Antigua and Barbuda	Antigua and Barbuda		Antigua and Barbuda
Argentina	Argentina		Argentina
Armenia	Armenia	Armenia	Armenia
Aruba	Aruba	Aruba	Aruba
Australia			Australia
Austria	Austria	Austria	
Bahamas	Bahamas	Bahamas	Bahamas
Bahrain	Bahrain		Bahrain
Bangladesh	Bangladesh	Bangladesh	Bangladesh
Barbados	Barbados	Barbados	Barbados
Belgium	Belgium	Belgium	Belgium
Belize	Belize	Belize	Belize
Bermuda	Bermuda	Bermuda	Bermuda
Bolivia	Bolivia	Bolivia	Bolivia
Bonaire, St Eustatius and Saba	Bonaire, St Eustatius and Saba	Bonaire, St Eustatius and Saba	Bonaire, St Eustatius and Saba
Bosnia and Herzegovina	Bosnia and Herzegovina		Bosnia and Herzegovina
Botswana	Botswana	Botswana	Botswana
Brazil	Brazil	Brazil	Brazil
	British Virgin Islands		
Brunei	Brunei		Brunei
Bulgaria	Bulgaria	Bulgaria	Bulgaria
Burkina Faso			Burkina Faso
Burundi	Burundi	Burundi	
Cambodia	Cambodia	Cambodia	Cambodia
Canada	Canada	Canada	Canada
Cape Verde Islands	Cape Verde Islands	Cape Verde Islands	Cape Verde Islands
Cayman Islands	Cayman Islands	Cayman Islands	Cayman Islands
	Central African Republic	Central African Republic	
Chile	Chile	Chile	Chile
Chinese Taipei	Chinese Taipei		Chinese Taipei
Colombia	Colombia	Colombia	Colombia
Comores Island	Comores Island	Comores Island	Comores Island

Grenada	St. Kitts	St. Lucia	Dominica
Anguilla	Anguilla	Anguilla	Anguilla
Antigua and Barbuda	Antigua and Barbuda	Antigua and Barbuda	Antigua and Barbuda
	Argentina	Argentina	
Armenia	Armenia	Armenia	Armenia
Aruba	Aruba	Aruba	Aruba
Austria	Austria	Austria	Austria
Bahamas	Bahamas	Bahamas	Bahamas
Bangladesh	Bangladesh	Bangladesh	Bangladesh
Barbados	Barbados	Barbados	Barbados
Belgium	Belgium	Belgium	Belgium
Belize	Belize	Belize	Belize
Bermuda	Bermuda	Bermuda	Bermuda
Bolivia	Bolivia	Bolivia	Bolivia
Bonaire, St Eustatius and Saba	Bonaire, St Eustatius and Saba	Bonaire, St Eustatius and Saba	Bonaire, St Eustatius and Saba
Botswana	Botswana	Botswana	Botswana
Brazil	Brazil		
	British Virgin Islands	British Virgin Islands	Croatia
Bulgaria	Bulgaria	Bulgaria	Bulgaria
Burundi		Burundi	Burundi
Cambodia	Cambodia	Cambodia	Cambodia
Cape Verde Islands	Cape Verde Islands	Cape Verde Islands	Cape Verde Islands
Cayman Islands	Cayman Islands	Cayman Islands	Cayman Islands
Central African Republic	Central African Republic		Central African Republic
Chad			
Chile	Chile	Chile	Chile
Colombia	Colombia	Colombia	Colombia
Comores Island	Comores Island	Comores Island	Comores Islands

Malta	Cyprus	Antigua	Austria
Cook Islands	Cook Islands	Cook Islands	Cook Islands
Costa Rica	Costa Rica	Costa Rica	Costa Rica
Croatia	Croatia	Croatia	Croatia
		Cuba	
Curacao	Curacao	Curacao	Curacao
Cyprus	Cyprus	Cyprus	Cyprus
Czech Republic	Czech Republic	Czech Republic	Czech Republic
Denmark	Denmark	Denmark	Denmark
Djibouti (Republic)	Djibouti (Republic)	Djibouti (Republic)	Djibouti (Republic)
Dominica	Dominica	Dominica	Dominica
Dominican Republic	Dominican Republic	Dominican Republic	Dominican Republic
	Dutch Caribbean		
Ecuador	Ecuador	Ecuador	Ecuador
Egypt (Arab Rep.)	Egypt (Arab Rep.)	Egypt (Arab Rep.)	Egypt (Arab Rep.)
El Salvador	El Salvador	El Salvador	El Salvador
Estonia	Estonia	Estonia	Estonia
			Ethiopia
Falkland Islands	Falkland Islands		Falkland Islands
Fiji	Fiji	Fiji	Fiji
Finland	Finland	Finland	Finland
France	France	France	France
French Guiana	French Guiana	French Guiana	French Guiana
French Polynesia	French Polynesia	French Polynesia	French Polynesia
French West Indies	French West Indies	French West Indies	French West Indies
Gambia		Gambia	
Georgia	Georgia	Georgia	Georgia
Germany	Germany	Germany	Germany
Gibraltar	Gibraltar	Gibraltar	Gibraltar
Greece	Greece	Greece	Greece
Grenada	Grenada	Grenada	Grenada
Guam			Guam
Guatemala	Guatemala	Guatemala	Guatemala
Guinea-Bissau	Guinea-Bissau	Guinea-Bissau	Guinea-Bissau
		Guyana	Guyana
Haiti	Haiti	Haiti	Haiti
Honduras	Honduras	Honduras	Honduras

Grenada	St. Kitts	St. Lucia	Dominica
Cook Islands	Cook Islands	Cook Islands	Cook Islands
Costa Rica	Costa Rica	Costa Rica	Costa Rica
	Croatia	Croatia	Croatia
Cuba	Cuba	Cuba	Cuba
Curacao	Curacao	Curacao	Curacao
	Cyprus	Cyprus	
Czech Republic	Czech Republic	Czech Republic	El Salvador
Denmark	Denmark	Denmark	Denmark
Djibouti (Republic)	Djibouti (Republic)	Djibouti	Djibouti (Republic)
Dominica	Dominica	Dominica	Dominica
Dominican Republic	Dominican Republic	Dominican Republic	Dominican Republic
Ecuador	Ecuador	Ecuador	Ecuador
Egypt (Arab Rep.)	Egypt (Arab Rep.)	Egypt (Arab Rep.)	Egypt (Arab Rep.)
	El Salvador	El Salvador	El Salvador
Estonia	Estonia	Estonia	Estonia
Falkland Islands			
Fiji	Fiji	Fiji	Fiji
Finland	Finland	Finland	Finland
France	France	France	France
	French Guiana	French Guiana	French Guiana
	French Polynesia	Greenland	
French West Indies	French West Indies	French West Indies	French West Indies
Gambia	Gambia	Gambia	Gambia
	Georgia	Georgia	Georgia
Germany	Germany	Germany	Germany
Gibraltar	Gibraltar	Gibraltar	Gibraltar
Greece	Greece	Greece	Greece
Grenada	Grenada	Grenada	Grenada
		Guam	
	Guatemala	Guatemala	
Guinea-Bissau		Guinea-Bissau	
Guyana	Guyana	Guyana	Guyana
Haiti	Haiti	Haiti	Haiti
	Honduras	Honduras	

Malta	Cyprus	Antigua	Austria
Hong Kong (SAR China)	Hong Kong (SAR China)	Hong Kong (SAR China)	Hong Kong (SAR China)
Hungary	Hungary	Hungary	Hungary
Iceland	Iceland	Iceland	Iceland
Indonesia	Indonesia		Indonesia
Iran			
Ireland (Republic of)	Ireland (Republic of)	Ireland (Republic of)	Ireland (Republic of)
Israel	Israel		Israel
Italy	Italy	Italy	Italy
Jamaica	Jamaica	Jamaica	Jamaica
Japan	Japan		Japan
Jordan	Jordan	Jordan	Jordan
Kenya	Kenya	Kenya	Kenya
Kiribati	Kiribati	Kiribati	Kiribati
Korea, Republic of	Korea, Republic of	Korea, Republic of	Korea, Republic of
Kosovo (Rep. of)	Kosovo (Rep. of)	Kosovo (Rep. of)	Kosovo (Rep. of)
Kuwait	Kuwait		Kuwait
Kyrgyzstan	Kyrgyzstan		Kyrgyzstan
Lao People's Dem. Rep.	Lao People's Dem. Rep.	Lao People's Dem. Rep.	Lao People's Dem. Rep.
Latvia	Latvia	Latvia	Latvia
Lebanon	Lebanon	Lebanon	Lebanon
Lesotho	Lesotho	Lesotho	Lesotho
	Liechtenstein		
Lithuania	Lithuania	Lithuania	Lithuania
Luxembourg	Luxembourg	Luxembourg	Luxembourg
Macao (SAR China)	Macao (SAR China)	Macao (SAR China)	Macao (SAR China)
Macedonia (FYROM)	Macedonia (FYROM)	Macedonia (FYROM)	Macedonia (FYROM)
Madagascar	Madagascar	Madagascar	Madagascar
Malawi	Malawi	Malawi	Malawi
Malaysia	Malaysia	Malaysia	Malaysia
Maldives	Maldives	Maldives	Maldives
Mali	Mali	Mali	
Malta	Malta	Malta	Malta
Marshall Islands	Marshall Islands		Marshall Islands
Mauritania			
Mauritius	Mauritius	Mauritius	Mauritius

Grenada	St. Kitts	St. Lucia	Dominica
Hong Kong (SAR China)	Hong Kong (SAR China)	Hong Kong (SAR China)	Hong Kong (SAR China)
Hungary	Hungary	Hungary	Hungary
Iceland	Iceland	Iceland	Iceland
		Indonesia	
	Iran	Iran	Iran
	Iraq	Iraq	
Ireland (Republic of)	Ireland (Republic of)	Ireland (Republic of)	Ireland (Republic of)
	Israel	Israel	Israel
Italy	Italy	Italy	Italy
Jamaica	Jamaica	Jamaica	Jamaica
Jordan	Jordan	Jordan	Jordan
Kenya	Kenya	Kenya	Kenya
Kiribati	Kiribati	Kiribati	
Korea, Republic of	Korea, Republic of	Korea, Republic of	Korea (Republic)
Kosovo (Rep. of)	Kosovo (Rep. of)	Kosovo (Rep. of)	Kosovo (Rep. of)
Lao People's Dem. Rep.	Lao People's Dem. Rep.	Lao People's Dem. Rep	Lao People's Dem. Rep.
Latvia	Latvia	Latvia	Latvia
	Lebanon	Liechtenstein	
Lesotho	Lesotho	Lesotho	Lesotho
Liechtenstein			
Lithuania	Lithuania	Lithuania	Lithuania
Luxembourg	Luxembourg	Luxembourg	Luxembourg
Macao (SAR China)	Macao (SAR China)	Macau	Macao (SAR China)
	Macedonia (FYROM)	Macedonia (FYROM)	
Madagascar	Madagascar	Madagascar	Madagascar
Malawi	Malawi	Malawi	Malawi
Malaysia	Malaysia	Malaysia	Malaysia
Maldives	Maldives	Maldives	Maldives
Mali	Mali	Martinique	Mali
Malta	Malta	Malta	Malta
			Mauritania
Mauritius	Mauritius	Mauritius	Mauritius

Malta	Cyprus	Antigua	Austria
Mayotte	Mayotte	Mayotte	Mayotte
Mexico	Mexico		Mexico
Micronesia (Federated States)	Micronesia (Federated States)	Micronesia (Federated States)	Micronesia (Federated States)
Moldova (Rep. of)	Moldova (Rep. of)		Moldova (Rep. of)
Montenegro	Montenegro		Montenegro
Montserrat	Montserrat	Montserrat	Montserrat
Morocco	Morocco		Morocco
Mozambique	Mozambique	Mozambique	Mozambique
			Namibia
Nauru	Nauru	Nauru	
Nepal	Nepal	Nepal	Nepal
Netherlands	Netherlands	Netherlands	Netherlands
New Caledonia	New Caledonia	New Caledonia	New Caledonia
New Zealand	New Zealand		New Zealand
Nicaragua	Nicaragua	Nicaragua	Nicaragua
Niue	Niue	Niue	
Norfolk Islands			
Northern Mariana Island			Northern Mariana Islands
Norway	Norway	Norway	Norway
Oman	Oman		Oman
Palau Islands	Palau Islands	Palau Islands	Palau Islands
Panama	Panama	Panama	Panama
Papua New Guinea			Papua New Guinea
Paraguay	Paraguay		Paraguay
Peru	Peru	Peru	Peru
Philippines	Philippines	Philippines	Philippines
Poland	Poland	Poland	Poland
Portugal	Portugal	Portugal	Portugal
Puerto Rico			Puerto Rico
			Qatar
Reunion	Reunion	Reunion	Reunion
Romania	Romania	Romania	Romania
Samoa	Samoa	Samoa	Samoa
			Samoa (American)

Grenada	St. Kitts	St. Lucia	Dominica
Micronesia (Federated States)	Micronesia (Federated States)	Micronesia (Federal States)	Micronesia (Federated States)
Mongolia			
Montenegro		Montenegro	
Montserrat	Montserrat	Monserrat	Montserrat
Mozambique	Mozambique	Mozambique	Mozambique
Nauru	Nauru		Nauru
Nepal	Nepal	Nepal	Nepal
Netherlands	Netherlands	Netherlands	Netherlands
	New Caledonia		
Nicaragua	Nicaragua	Nicaragua	Nicaragua
Niue	Niue	Niue	Niue
		Northern Mariana Islands	
Norway	Norway	Norway	Norway
Palau Islands	Palau Islands	Palau Islands	Palau Islands
Panama	Panama	Panama	Panama
Peru	Peru	Peru	Peru
Philippines	Philippines	Philippines	Philippines
Poland	Poland	Poland	Poland
Portugal	Portugal	Portugal	Portugal
	Reunion		
	Romania	Romania	Romania
Samoa	Samoa	Samoa	Samoa

Malta	Cyprus	Antigua	Austria
			Sao Tome and Principe
Senegal			Senegal
Serbia	Serbia		Serbia
Seychelles	Seychelles	Seychelles	Seychelles
Singapore	Singapore	Singapore	Singapore
Slovak Republic	Slovak Republic	Slovak Republic	Slovak Republic
Slovenia	Slovenia	Slovenia	Slovenia
Solomon Islands	Solomon Islands	Solomon Islands	Solomon Islands
	Somalia		
South Africa	South Africa	South Africa	South Africa
Spain	Spain	Spain	Spain
Sri Lanka	Sri Lanka	Sri Lanka	Sri Lanka
St. Kitts and Nevis	St. Kitts and Nevis	St. Kitts and Nevis	St. Kitts and Nevis
St Lucia	St Lucia	St Lucia	St Lucia
St. Maarten	St. Maarten	St Maarten	St. Maarten
St. Vincent and the Grenadines	St. Vincent and the Grenadines	St. Vincent and the Grenadines	St. Vincent and the Grenadines
Suriname		Suriname	Suriname
Swaziland	Swaziland	Swaziland	Swaziland
Sweden	Sweden	Sweden	Sweden
Switzerland	Switzerland	Switzerland	Switzerland
Tajikistan	Tajikistan		Tajikistan
Tanzania	Tanzania		Tanzania
Thailand	Thailand	Tanzania	Thailand
Timor Leste	Timor Leste	Timor Leste	Timor Leste
Togo	Togo	Togo	Togo
Tonga	Tonga		Tonga
Trinidad and Tobago	Trinidad and Tobago	Trinidad and Tobago	Trinidad and Tobago
Tunisia		Tunisia	Tunisia
Turkey	Turkey	Turkey	Turkey
Turks and Caicos Isl.	Turks and Caicos Isl.	Turks and Caicos Isl.	Turks and Caicos Isl.
Tuvalu	Tuvalu	Tuvalu	Tuvalu
Uganda	Uganda	Uganda	Uganda
Ukraine	Ukraine	Ukraine	Ukraine
	United Arab Emirates		United Arab Emirates

Grenada	St. Kitts	St. Lucia	Dominica
		Senegal	
Seychelles	Seychelles	Seychelles	Seychelles
Singapore	Singapore	Singapore	Singapore
Slovak Republic	Slovak Republic	Slovak Republic	Slovak Republic
Slovenia	Slovenia	Slovenia	Slovenia
Solomon Islands	Solomon Islands	Solomon Islands	Solomon Islands
		Somalia	Somalia
South Africa			
	South Sudan		South Sudan
Spain	Spain	Spain	Spain
Sri Lanka	Sri Lanka	Sri Lanka	Sri Lanka
St. Kitts and Nevis	St. Kitts and Nevis	St Kitts and Nevis	St. Kitts and Nevis
St. Lucia	St. Lucia		St. Lucia
St. Maarten	St. Maarten	St Maarten	St. Maarten
St. Vincent and the Grenadines	St. Vincent and the Grenadines	St Vincent and the Grenadines	St. Vincent and the Grenadines
Suriname	Suriname	Suriname	Suriname
Swaziland			
Sweden	Sweden	Sweden	Sweden
Switzerland	Switzerland	Switzerland	Switzerland
Tanzania	Tanzania	Tanzania	Tanzania
Timor Leste	Timor Leste	Timor Leste	Timor Leste
Togo			
	Tonga	Tonga	Tonga
Trinidad and Tobago	Trinidad and Tobago	Trinidad and Tobago	Trinidad and Tobago
	Tunisia	Tunisia	
Turkey	Turkey		Turkey
Turks and Caicos Isl.	Turks and Caicos Isl.	Turks and Caicos Isl.	Turks and Caicos Isl.
Tuvalu	Tuvalu	Tuvalu	Tuvalu
	Uganda	Uganda	Uganda

Malta	Cyprus	Antigua	Austria
United Kingdom	United Kingdom	United Kingdom	United Kingdom
United States		United States	United States
Uruguay	Uruguay		Uruguay
Vanuatu	Vanuatu	Vanuatu	Vanuatu
Venezuela	Venezuela	Venezuela	Venezuela
Virgin Islands (British)	Virgin Islands (British)	Virgin Islands (British)	Virgin Islands (British)
Virgin Islands (US)			Virgin Islands (US)
Zambia	Zambia	Zambia	Zambia
Zimbabwe	Zimbabwe	Zimbabwe	Zimbabwe

Grenada	St. Kitts	St. Lucia	Dominica
United Kingdom	United Kingdom	United Kingdom	United Kingdom
Uruguay			
Vanuatu	Vanuatu	Vanuatu	Vanuatu
Venezuela	Venezuela	Venezuela	Venezuela
Virgin Islands (British)	Virgin Islands (British)	Virgin Islands (British)	Virgin Islands (British)
Zambia	Zambia	Zambia	Zambia
Zimbabwe	Zimbabwe	Zimbabwe	Zimbabwe

29.1   The Global Citizenship Program Index

The GCPI gauges and reflects the relative worth of citizenship programs around the world through a benchmarking process. It analyzes a broad range of factors such as immigration law, tax, and quality of living, as well as transparency, risk and compliance issues, from multiple sources to produce an overall global view and ranking of the different investment migration programs.

For the second year in a row, Malta's Individual Investor Programme is the top ranking citizenship-by-investment program in the world, with a score of 73 out of 100. The Mediterranean island nation is followed by Cyprus (71), and Antigua and Barbuda (62) in 2nd and 3rd place respectively.

Malta boasts an excellent reputation with a splendid climate, very friendly people, and a low crime rate, offering a great quality of life. A Maltese citizen has the right of settlement in all 28 EU countries and enjoys visa-free travel to 168 countries worldwide including the EU, the US and Canada. For improved visa-free travel, permanent relocation, and financial security, Malta is the way to go.

The Malta Individual Investor Programme is a modern citizenship-by-investment program designed, implemented and globally promoted by Henley & Partners for the Government of Malta under a Public Services Concession. Moreover, it is considered the world's most advanced and most exclusive citizenship-by-investment program, being capped at 1800 applicants. Compliance and due diligence standards are recognized as the world's strictest, aiming to ensure that only the most respectable of applicants are admitted.

Rank	Country	Score
1	Malta	73
2	Cyprus	71
3	Antigua and Barbuda	62
4	Austria	60
5	Grenada	59
6	St. Kitts and Nevis	54
7	St. Lucia	51
8	Dominica	49

30
Antigua and Barbuda

Antigua and Barbuda is an independent Commonwealth state in the Eastern Caribbean. Antigua was first discovered by Christopher Columbus in 1493 and later became a British settlement. Under Lord Nelson, it became Britain's main naval base from which it patrolled the West Indies.

Antigua is 14 miles long and 11 miles wide and its flatland topography was well suited to produce its early crops of tobacco, cotton and ginger. The main industry, however, developed into sugar cane farming which lasted for over 200 years. Today, following its 34th year of independence from Britain, Antigua's key industry is tourism and related service industries. The next largest employers are the financial services industry, and the government.

Antigua and Barbuda is a constitutional monarchy with a British style parliamentary system of government. The Queen has a representative, an appointed Governor General, representing her as the Head of State. The Government is composed of two chambers: the elected 17-member House of Representatives, led by the Prime Minister; and the 17-member Senate. 11 of the Senate members are appointed by the Governor General under the guidance of the Prime Minister, four members are appointed under the direction of the Leader of the Opposition and two by the Governor General. General elections are mandated every five years and can be called earlier. The High Court and Court of Appeal are the Eastern Caribbean Supreme Court and the Privy Council in London.

With some 365 beaches of clean clear turquoise waters, the lush tropical island of Antigua is an inviting paradise and considered to be one of the most beautiful places in the world. As a result, tourism is the key driver of GDP and generates around 60% of the island's income, with key target markets being the US, Canada and Europe.

Antigua has experienced a challenging economic environment in recent years. However, the government has been credited with its implementation of the National Economic and Social Transformation Plan and a debt restructuring effort. One of the initiatives to support the island nation's economy is the introduction of a citizenship-by-investment program, in which Henley & Partners played a significant role in advising and assisting the government on the design, implementation and international placement.

Antigua's commitment to serving its tourism industry and increasing its GDP was demonstrated with the new airport expansion project completed in 2015. With a significant investment of over USD 90 million, it includes three passenger jet bridges and more than two dozen check-in counters, creating higher overall efficiency for passenger arrivals. This will also allow an increase in scheduled, charter and inter-island flights. There are already direct flights to Antigua from London, New York, Miami and Toronto in place.

Residents of Antigua and Barbuda benefit from no capital gains tax or estate taxes. Income taxes are progressive to 25% and for non-residents, they are at a flat rate of 25%. Recent amendments to Part 111 Section 5 of the Income Tax Act have changed taxation on worldwide income to taxation on income sourced solely within Antigua and Barbuda.

The currency is the Eastern Caribbean dollar (XCD), which is pegged to the USD at XCD 2.70 / USD 1. Antigua is a member of the United Nations (UN), the British Commonwealth, CARICOM and the Organization of American States (OAS), among many other international organizations. Holders of the Antigua and Barbuda passport enjoy visa-free travel to over 130 countries, including the UK, Canada and the countries of the Schengen area. Holders of this passport, like all Caribbean countries, do require a visa to enter the US as they are not a member of the Visa Waiver Program.

30.1   Legal basis

The citizenship-by-investment program, which the Government of Antigua and Barbuda launched at the annual Henley & Partners Global Residence and Citizenship Conference in November 2012, was passed by both Houses of Parliament in March 2013.

The laws regarding the Citizenship-by-Investment program are contained in the Antigua and Barbuda Citizenship by Investment Act, 2013 and the Antigua and Barbuda Citizenship by Investment Regulations, 2013.

30.2   Requirements

The citizenship-by-investment program requires a person to make a significant economic contribution to the country. In exchange, and subject to a stringent application procedure, including thorough background checks, the applicants and their families are granted citizenship.

To qualify for citizenship, the person must be over 18 years of age, meet the application requirements and select one of the following three options:

- An investment of at least USD 400,000 into one of the government approved real estate projects; such investments cannot be disposed of within a five-year period or before the proposed development in which the investment has been made has been substantially completed

- A contribution to the National Development Fund (NDF) of a minimum non-refundable amount of USD 200,000 (for a single applicant)

- An investment of a minimum of USD 1.5 million directly into an eligible business as a sole investor or a joint investment involving at least two persons in an eligible business totaling at least USD 5 million, with each of those persons individually investing at least USD 400,000

Under each of these options, there are government processing fees of USD 50,000 for the main applicant plus additional government processing fees of USD 50,000 for the spouse, any dependent child of 18 to 25 years of age and any dependent parent over the age of 65 years, as well as USD 25,000 for each dependent child under 18 years of age.

There are also due diligence fees of USD 7,500 for the main applicant and USD 7,500 for the spouse; USD 2,000 for any dependent child of 12 to 17 years; and USD 4,000 for any dependent child of 18 to 25 years of age or any dependent parent over the age of 65 years.

Government processing fees and due diligence fees apply to all three options.

The National Development Fund (NDF) is a special fund established under Section 42(2) of the Finance Act 2006 for the purpose of funding government sponsored projects, including private/public partnerships and approved charitable investments which deliver services in health-care, education, environmental management, youth development or the promotion of sports and culture.

The NDF is governed by the provisions of the Finance and Administration Act, which stipulates that there be established a special fund to be administered by a public officer. These funds will not be comingled with the Government's consolidated funds and will only be utilized for the specific aforesaid purposes. The citizenship-by-investment program will be subject to six-monthly reporting which will be published and presented to the House of Representatives no later than 30 days following completion of the report.

The program allows for a dependent between the ages of 18 to 25 years to be included in the application of the main applicant if the dependent is a full-time student at a recognized higher learning institution and is financially dependent on the main applicant. The program also allows for parents and grandparents over the age of 65 of the main applicant or their spouse to be included in the application as dependents, if the parent/s and grandparent/s are living with and are fully supported by the main applicant.

The main applicant and his or her dependents must have a clean back-ground, and (not having received a free pardon) have at no time been convicted in any country of an offence for which the maximum custo-dial penalty is in excess of six months' imprisonment. The regulations further provide that a person who has been denied a visa to a country with which Antigua and Barbuda has visa-free travel arrangements, and who has subsequently not obtained a visa to the country that issued the denial, shall not be entitled to apply under the program. A person who is deemed a potential national security risk, a reputational risk or is subject to criminal investigation will also be denied citizenship.

30.3 Procedures and time frame

The government authority responsible for administering the program, the Citizenship-by-Investment Unit (CIU), is responsible for the processing of all applications. The CIU examines the application thoroughly and, if deemed necessary, may request the applicant to attend an interview.

The CIU undertakes strict due diligence checks and will decline an application if the applicant makes a false statement or omits any relevant information in the application.

The applicant must apply on the prescribed government forms which can only be submitted through an agent who is the holder of a Citizenship-by-Investment Program License granted under the regulations.

The applicant is required to personally complete the form in English and submit the prescribed forms together with original or certified supporting documentation as specified by the government.

The documentary requirements of the Antigua and Barbuda Citizenship-by-Investment program are reasonable and the procedures are quite straightforward. It is recommended that investors visit the Islands before making a decision on the purchase of real estate. Once the application is approved, passports will be sent to the local license agent and thereafter sent to the client. It is estimated that the process will take between three and four months from submission of the application to issuance of the passport, assuming there are no areas of concern with the application. The regulations specify that, within three months of the submission of an application to the CIU, the CIU shall notify in writing to the licensed agent on behalf of the main applicant that the application has been approved, denied, or delayed for cause and is still being processed.

Under the real estate option, the time frame may vary depending upon the project. Therefore, it is important to select a real estate project that is able to provide the necessary paperwork required from the developer for the citizenship application.

If the real estate option is selected, it is important for an applicant to be aware of the investment potential, financial strength, track record and reputation of the developer before committing to the property. Once the applicant has chosen their preferred real estate, a sales and purchase contract is signed, which is usually conditional upon the person receiving citizenship. After approval by the government, the real estate purchase is completed and the ownership title transferred to the buyer. Applicants under the real estate option should also ascertain from the developer whether there are additional purchase and/or closing costs and the amount of those costs, prior to entering into any purchase contract.

Within 30 days of notification of approval, the applicant shall pay the balance of the processing fees and:

1. Deposit the required contribution into the National Development Fund; or

2. Complete and execute all necessary documents and pay the purchase price and all required disbursements to enable title to be registered in the applicant's name and allow for the implementation of the proposed real estate investment in accordance with the guidelines established by the CIU; or

3. Complete and execute all necessary documentation for the payment or investment of all sums due for the implementation of the proposed investment in business in accordance with the guidelines established by the CIU

30.4   Grant of citizenship

The citizen must visit an Embassy, Consular Office or High Commission of Antigua and Barbuda to swear the Oath of Allegiance or affirmation of allegiance. The passport will be valid for a period of five years and is renewable, provided that the requirements for renewal are met, including the residence requirements: the government may, by Order, deprive of their citizenship a citizen who has obtained citizenship under the citizenship-by-investment program if the citizen does not spend at least five days in Antigua and Barbuda during the period of five years after becoming a citizen. A standard 10-year passport will be issued at the five-year renewal stage and thereafter there is no residence requirement.

An Antigua and Barbuda citizen is entitled to take up residence in Antigua and Barbuda at any time.

30.5 Dual citizenship

There are no restrictions on dual citizenship in Antigua and Barbuda.

30.6 Taxation

There are no capital gains or inheritance taxes in Antigua and Barbuda. Personal income tax was re-introduced in 2005 and the current tax rates starts at 8% and increases to 25% on chargeable income in excess of XCD 15,500 per month or XCD 186,000 per annum. Each individual has a personal allowance of XCD 42,000 per annum. Individuals who have their permanent residence in the country or who are present for at least 183 days a year will qualify as residents of Antigua and Barbuda and will be subject to tax on their worldwide income. Individuals who are in the country temporarily will only be taxed on income arising in or derived from Antigua and Barbuda. However, recent amendments to Part 111, Section 5 of the Income Tax Act have changed taxation on worldwide income to taxation limited to locally sourced income alone.

The business and corporate tax rate is 25% of net profits, although attractive concessions are available to qualifying companies such as a tax holiday on profits up to a 20-year period and import/export customs duty waiver.

Antigua and Barbuda Sales Tax (ABST), which is similar to VAT, is applicable at a standard rate of 15% and levied on local consumption. Some exemptions exist and a reduced rate of 12.5% applies to the supply of hotel and holiday accommodation. ABST was introduced in 2007 and replaced a number of other taxes. The current threshold for business registration under ABST is an annual turnover of XCD 300,000 (although other variables also apply, so this is an approximate figure).

Property tax is levied on all properties in Antigua but not in Barbuda. The taxable value is based upon the property's current market value construction replacement cost with the applicable tax rate dependent upon the classification of the property (residential or commercial).

30.7   Advantages of Antigua and Barbuda citizenship

In 2009, the Antigua and Barbuda government signed a visa waiver agreement with the EU which allows an Antigua and Barbuda citizen to visit the Schengen area without a visa for a period of three months within any six-month period following the date of first entry into any EU country.

The Antigua and Barbuda passport is a good travel document for many international individuals. With an Antigua and Barbuda passport, a citizen can travel to over 130 countries in the world, including Canada, Hong Kong, Singapore, the UK and the EU with relative ease and without challenging visa requirements.

Full citizenship with passport is granted to the applicant and family, and there are no restrictions except a residence requirement during the first five years following the acquisition of citizenship. Antigua and Barbuda is a member of the Commonwealth, which entitles Antigua and Barbuda citizens to certain privileges in the UK and other Commonwealth countries.

A recent change in government means that several changes are expected to be made to this program. It remains to be seen to what extent these changes will positively or negatively affect the program.

30.8   General information

Official name	Antigua and Barbuda
Capital city	St. John's
Region	Central America, Caribbean
Surface area	Antigua 281 km²; Barbuda 161 km²
Government	Parliamentary democracy (independent sovereign state within the Commonwealth)
Language	English (Official), Antiguan Creole
Currency	Eastern Caribbean Dollar (XCD)
Population	92,436 (July 2015 est.)
Religion	Protestant 68.3%, Roman Catholic 8.2%, other 12.2%, unspecified 5.5%, none 5.9%
Ethnic groups	Black 87.3%, mixed 4.7%, Hispanic 2.7%, white 1.6%, other 2.7%, unspecified 0.9%
GDP	USD 2.097 billion (2015 est.)
GDP per capita, PPP	USD 23,600 (2015 est.)
Major industries	Tourism, financial services, construction, fish, cotton, livestock, vegetables
Main exports	Petroleum products, bedding, handicrafts, electronic components, transport equipment, food and live animals
Climate	Tropical maritime, cooled by trade winds, rain 1140mm, 45" annual fall
UN Human Development Index	61st (2015)
World's healthiest countries (Bloomberg Rankings)	n.a.
Henley & Partners Visa Restrictions Index	30th (2016), 26th (2015)
Legatum Prosperity Index	n.a.

Sources: CIA "The World Factbook" (2015), World Bank (2015), UN Human Development Report (2015), Henley & Partners

30.9 Climate

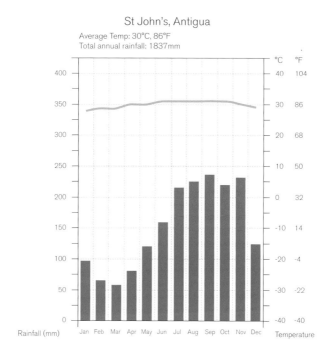

St John's, Antigua

Average Temp: 30°C, 86°F
Total annual rainfall: 1837mm

31
Austria

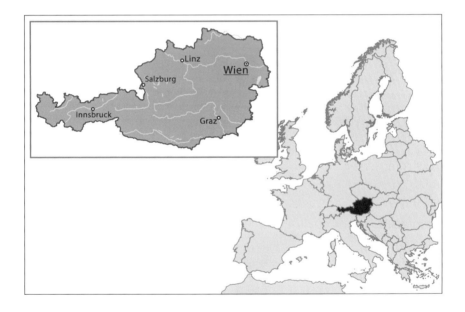

Austria is considered one of the most stable countries in the world and boasts a high standard of living. Although one of the smaller states of Europe, it has a world-class capital, Vienna, with a rich cultural and historic heritage. Austria also has beautiful countryside with Alpine peaks and spectacular scenery. An excellent place to establish residence within the European Union (EU), Austria is the only Western European country that offers the possibility to obtain citizenship and an EU passport without prior residence requirements, on the basis of a substantial investment in the country. Moreover, an Austrian passport is one of the best travel documents in the world.

31.1 Legal basis

Since 1985, Austria has allowed the acquisition of citizenship on the basis of substantial investment in the country. To qualify for citizenship without prior residence under the provisions of the Austrian Citizenship Act, Section 10 (6), an applicant must provide extraordinary scientific, artistic, cultural or economic benefits to the Republic of Austria. Various Austrian government authorities, as well as the Austrian government, must support the application and be satisfied that all the conditions have been met before the citizenship application is considered. Citizenship is then granted upon approval by all government ministers.

31.2 Requirements

Under the citizenship-by-investment provisions, an applicant is required to substantially invest in the Austrian economy, for example in the form of a joint venture or a direct investment in a business creating jobs or generating new export sales. Passive investments in government bonds, real estate, etc. generally do not qualify.

A completely clean personal record (certificate of no criminal record, etc.), a comprehensive Curriculum Vitae, background business information as well as impeccable references must be provided by all applicants.

Children up to 18 years of age can be included in the same application, but those over 18 cannot, and no exceptions are possible. However, a separate application may be prepared and lodged at the same time. That application may be included under the same investment, although the amount of the obligatory investment would then need to be higher than the minimum requirement.

Previously, basic knowledge of the German language was required, but this condition was abolished in early 2006. The language requirement no longer applies for the main applicant, but it remains in place for dependents, even though this rule is not applied very strictly in practice. There is no minimum stay requirement.

The grant of citizenship on the basis of an investment requires government approval at various levels, including, eventually, at the highest level (Cabinet). It is, therefore, essential that the applicant receives expert advice from the beginning, that the individual case is carefully prepared and that informal approvals from the key authorities are obtained before the formal application process is started.

31.3   Procedures and time frame

Substantial fees apply, depending on the case and the number of persons included in an application, as each person is handled on a separate basis. The processing time varies, but generally takes at least 24 months.

The successful applicant receives full citizenship of the Republic of Austria, and the application for an Austrian passport can be lodged immediately. The procedure results in citizenship status and a passport which is identical to those issued to other citizens. Austrian passports are valid for 10 years and are easily renewable at a nominal cost. Citizenship is irrevocable unless the application was fraudulent or involved a misrepresentation.

The grant of citizenship is not published or reported to any other country, as it falls within the strict Austrian official secrecy provisions (*Amtsgeheimnis*).

31.4 Grant of citizenship

The individual and the dependents become citizens of Austria upon attending a Citizenship Ceremony before a senior representative of the government. As soon as the individual receives citizenship they can apply for a passport.

31.5 Dual citizenship

The Austrian Citizenship Act generally does not permit dual citizenship therefore the country will require abandonment of the current citizenship as a prerequisite to grant Austrian citizenship. However, in case of a grant of citizenship under the provisions of Section 10 (6) of the Citizenship Act, the former citizenship can legally be maintained, i.e. the applicant is not required to give up his or her current citizenship. Although, once the person has obtained Austrian citizenship via this route, a further citizenship cannot be acquired without losing the Austrian citizenship. In extraordinary cases special permission may be obtained to remain an Austrian citizen.

31.6 Taxation

The acquisition of Austrian citizenship has no tax consequences *per se*. The individual becomes subject to Austrian taxation only when actually moving to Austria and taking up tax residence there, which is not mandatory. Although in some cases it is advisable to become resident in Austria during the application procedures, once citizenship is granted, residence is no longer required.

31.7 Advantages of Austrian citizenship

The Austrian passport is a well-recognized travel document and annually reaches the top ten of the *Henley Visa Restrictions Index*.[184]

---

[184] See chapter 9

As an Austrian citizen, the person is also an EU citizen. EU citizens have the freedom to settle anywhere within the EU without restrictions. Since 1 June 2002, the same also applies to EU citizens who wish to reside in Switzerland. Therefore, after obtaining Austrian citizenship, the individual has the right to live anywhere in the EU as well as in EEA/ EFTA states and in Switzerland.

31.8   General information

Official name	Republic of Austria
Capital city	Vienna (1.8 million)
Region	Southern Central Europe
Surface area	83,871 km²
Government	Federal Republic, Parliamentary Democracy
Language	German (official nationwide) 88.6%, Turkish 2.3%, Serbian 2.2%, Croatian (official in Burgenland) 1.6%, other (includes Slovene, official in Carinthia; and Hungarian, official in Burgenland) 5.3%
Currency	Euro (EUR)
Population	8,699,730 (2016)
Religion	Roman Catholic 73.8%, Protestant 4.9%, Muslim 4.2%, Orthodox 2.2%, other 0.8%, unspecified 2%
Ethnic groups	Austrians 91.1%, former Yugoslavs 4% (includes Croatians, Slovenes, Serbs, and Bosnians), Turks 1.6%, German 0.9%, other or unspecified 2.4%
GDP	USD 404.3 billion (2015 est.)
GDP per capita, PPP	USD 47,300 (2015 est.)
Major industries	Construction, machinery, vehicles and parts, food, metals, chemicals, lumber and wood processing, paper and paperboard, communications equipment, tourism
Main exports	Machinery and equipment, motor vehicles and parts, paper and paperboard, metal goods, chemicals, iron and steel, textiles, foodstuffs
Climate	Generally moderate and mild - varies from the Alpine region to the eastern plain. Summer can be hot with average temperatures from 20°C to 30°C, average winter temperatures are around 0°
UN Human Development Index (HDI)	21st (2015)
World's healthiest countries (Bloomberg Rankings)	12th (2015)
Henley & Partners Visa Restrictions Index	5th (2016), 5th (2015)
Legatum Prosperity Index	16th (2015)

Sources: CIA "The World Factbook" (2015), World Bank (2015),
UN Human Development Report (2015), Henley & Partners, The Legatum Institute

31.9 Climate

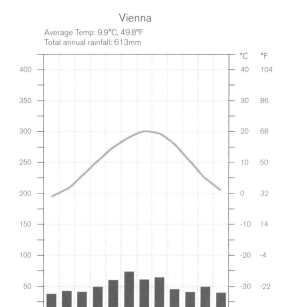

Vienna

Average Temp: 9.9°C, 49.8°F
Total annual rainfall: 613mm

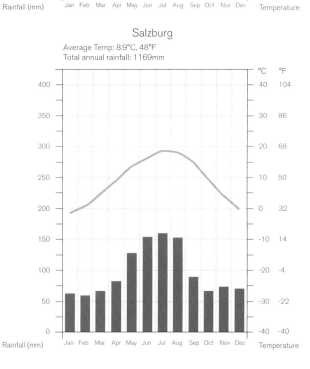

Salzburg

Average Temp: 8.9°C, 48°F
Total annual rainfall: 1169mm

32

Cyprus

Cyprus, with its warm and stable climate and convenient geographical position, is considered an attractive location for residence. Also, the investment landscape in Cyprus is desirable due to the island's well-qualified labor force and a reliable transport and telecommunications system.

Having some of the most beautiful beaches in the Mediterranean, 57 of which carry the eco-label Blue Flag[185], Cyprus is also the home of many historical monuments such as the Kourion Archaeological Site and the Neolithic Settlement of Choirokoitia, which are included in UNESCO's World Heritage List.[186]

Cyprus has a modern, free market, service-based economy, with an effective and transparent regulatory and legal framework, giving international investors and domestic businesses confidence to invest, grow and prosper. Cyprus was ranked 65th out of 144 countries in the World Economic Forum *Global Competitiveness Index 2015 – 2016*.[187] A number of new measures have been implemented to reboot the economy in the wake of the massive restructuring of the country's banking sector that aim, among other things, to help stimulate economic growth.

As well as being a perennially popular location for international consultants and independent contractors, the island also attracts active retirees attracted not just by the lifestyle, but by the large number of double taxation treaties meaning that retirement income from abroad will not usually be subject to withholding tax. Cyprus' strong commercial relations with eastern European and Middle Eastern countries enhance its economic and financial position.

32.1   Legal basis

The regulations regarding citizenship-by-investment are contained in the Scheme for Naturalisation of Investors in Cyprus by Exception on the basis of subsection (2) of Section 111A of the Civil Registry Laws of 2002-2013.

---

[185] *http://www.cyprusflag.net/cyprus-blue-flags.html*
[186] *http://whc.unesco.org/en/list/*
[187] *http://reports.weforum.org/global-competitiveness-report-2012-2013/#=*

32.2 Requirements

There are eight potential routes to citizenship based on extraordinary economic contributions, under which an applicant is required to actively invest in the Cyprus economy. The Council of Ministers revised the existing program in, 2014, enabling foreign nationals to gain citizenship if they meet certain criteria set out by the Ministry of Interior.

1. The first option requires an applicant to purchase state bonds of at least EUR 5 million

2. The second option requires an applicant to invest at least EUR 5 million in financial assets of Cypriot entities (e.g. bonds, securities or debentures registered and issued in the Republic of Cyprus)

3. The third option requires an applicant to invest at least EUR 5 million in real estate or other developments (residential, commercial or infrastructure projects)

4. The fourth option requires the applicant to acquire, incorporate or participate in companies residing and operating within Cyprus, investing into such companies an amount of at least EUR 5 million. Such companies must have a physical presence in Cyprus and employ at least five Cypriot nationals. It is noted that this criteria also provides for the compulsory conversion of deposits into shares

5. The fifth option would require the candidate or a company or trust of which they are the main beneficiary to have had deposits of up to EUR 5 million in a local bank for at least the last three years

6. The sixth option would involve making a combination of investments or donations under the above five options, again of at least EUR 5 million

7. If any candidate had their deposits in Bank of Cyprus or Laiki Bank cut by at least EUR 3 million since 15 March 2013 then they would also be eligible for naturalization. If the money was cut by less than EUR 3 million, candidates could potentially combine it with any of the other options

8. The latest additional option allows the council of Ministers to reduce the minimum investment amount required for an applicant to qualify for Cypriot citizenship from EUR 5 million to EUR 2.5 million if the investment is done through the Collective Investment Scheme. The Collective Investment Scheme involves a group of investors investing in the Cypriot economy under any of the options mentioned above provided that the total amount of funds invested by the group exceeds EUR 12.5 million. Note that under this category, investment for categories 1 to 4 can be performed through different sellers or providers

In all cases, the applicant must have a clean criminal record. Also, the name of the applicant must not be included in the list of persons on whose name there is a freezing or confiscation order of property within the boundaries of the EU.

In addition, every applicant must be the owner of a permanent residence in Cyprus, with a purchase price of at least EUR 500,000 plus VAT. It is understood that the members of the same family, who submit different applications as investors, can buy collectively a residence/house, provided that the total amount of the residence/house covers the amount of EUR 500,000 for each applicant.

32.3   Procedures and time frame

The government is keen to facilitate applicants and thus the processing of applications is treated with urgency, and time frames have been greatly reduced. There is no interview requirement and the applicant may submit the application personally or through an appointed representative or lawyer. Accordingly, the processing time for applications is around three months from the date of submission of the application with all the necessary supporting documentation.

32.4   Grant of citizenship

Once the Cabinet of Ministers approves the application and the applicant receives the official letter of approval, the Citizenship Certificate will be requested from the Migration Department. Once it is obtained, the applicant must visit Cyprus in order to appear before a Cypriot Court and sign the Citizenship Certificate before a Registrar. Afterwards, they must appear before the Civil Registry Department and file an application for a biometric passport which may be issued on the same day.

32.5 Dual citizenship

There are no restrictions on dual citizenship in Cyprus.

32.6 Taxation

In general, Cypriot tax residents are taxed at their worldwide income. Cyprus applies a personal income tax with a progressive rate structure. There are currently four brackets with rates set at 20%, 25% and 30% and, since 2011, an additional tax bracket with a top rate of 35% for income over EUR 60,000. Capital gains, and in particular dividends, interest income and income from the sale of securities are exempt from income taxation. Capital gains are, in general, not taxable. Gains on the disposal of immovable property located in Cyprus are taxed at 20%.

There are no net wealth taxes or inheritance or gift taxes. Immovable property is subject to a real estate tax levied on the estimated market value of the property in 1980. For natural persons, rates range from 0% to 0.8%, depending on the property value. A real estate transfer tax is levied in a progressive manner at 3%, 5% and 8% of the property value. The worldwide moveable property of a person domiciled in Cyprus is free of inheritance tax for those who die after 1 January 2000.

All residents (both physical persons and companies) are subject to the Defence Contribution, which has been a final levy on unearned income and not deductible for income tax purposes since 2003. It is applied with different rates to dividends, interest, rental payments and the taxable income of public corporate bodies. Dividends are currently subject to the Defence Contribution at a rate of 17%, with the contribution on domestic dividends withheld at source. Interest payments not accruing from ordinary business activities are taxed at a rate of 15%.

As of 16 July 2015, a new law came into force. It introduces a number of amendments to the Cyprus corporate and personal tax legislation.

These changes include:

- Introduction of the status of a non-domiciled (Non Dom) domicile tax resident, exempting such persons from certain tax obligations in Cyprus (for example, Non Dom residents will not pay Special Defence Contribution on dividends that is presently fixed at 17% and on passive interest income that is 30%)

- Reduction of transfer fees on real estate transactions by 50% until the end of 2016

- Exemption from capital gains tax on sales of land or land with buildings on it, provided that the acquisition takes place between 16 July 2015 and 31 December 2016

- Consolidation and modernization of immovable property tax and transfer fees

- Notional interest deduction on fresh capital injected into Cypriot companies

32.7   Advantages of Cypriot citizenship

There are minimal application and physical presence requirements, and the application process can take under three months. There is a tax-friendly regime which allows the applicant to enjoy the benefits of Cyprus citizenship without being exposed to severe financial obligations. The applicant automatically enjoys the right to work, reside and buy property in all 27 EU member countries, and seek for other business opportunities throughout the EU single market with over 450 million people.

32.8　General information

Official name	Republic of Cyprus
Capital city	Nicosia
Region	Mediterranean
Surface area	9,251 km² (of which 3,355 km² are in North Cyprus)
Government	Presidential representative democratic republic
Language	Greek (official) 80.9%, Turkish (official) 0.2%, English 4.1%, Romanian 2.9%, Russian 2.5%, Bulgarian 2.2%, Arabic 1.2%, Filipino 1.1%, other 4.3%, unspecified 0.6%
Currency	Euro (EUR)
Population	1,189,197 (July 2015 est.)
Religion	Orthodox Christian 89.1%, Roman Catholic 2.9%, Protestant / Anglian 2%, Muslim 1.8%, Buddhist 1%, other (includes Maronite, Armenian church, Hindu) 1.4%, unknown 1.1%, none/atheist 0.6%
Ethnic groups	Greek 98.8%, other 1% (includes Maronite, Armenian, Turkish-Cypriot), unspecified 0.2%
GDP	USD 28.06 billion (2015 est.)
GDP per capita, PPP	USD 32,800 (2015 est.)
Major industries	Tourism, food and beverage processing, cement and gypsum production, ship repair and refurbishment, textiles, light chemicals, metal products, wood, paper, stone and clay products
Main exports	Citrus, potatoes, pharmaceuticals, cement, clothing
Climate	Temperate; Mediterranean with hot, dry summers and cool winters
UN Human Development Index (HDI)	32nd (2015)
World's healthiest countries (Bloomberg Rankings)	11th (2013)
Henley & Partners Visa Restrictions Index	17th (2016), 14th (2015)
Legatum Prosperity Index	39th (2015)

Sources: CIA "The World Factbook" (2015), World Bank (2015), UN Human Development Report (2015), Henley & Partners, The Legatum Institute

32.9 Climate

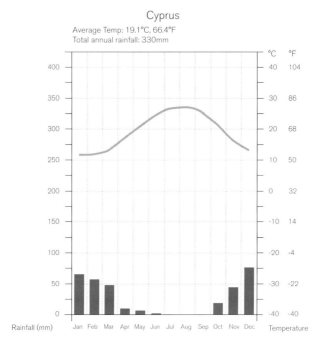

33

Commonwealth of Dominica

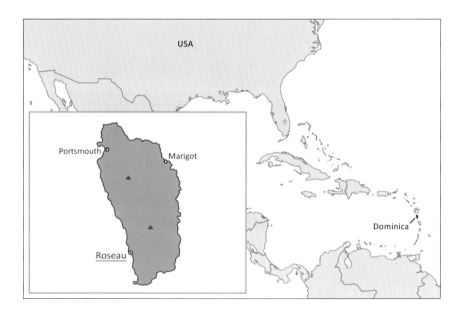

The Commonwealth of Dominica is an independent English-speaking island state[188] situated between the French islands of Martinique and Guadeloupe. It is a former British colony and a member of the Commonwealth of Nations (British Commonwealth) as well as the United Nations, the Organization of American States (OAS), Caribbean Community (CARICOM) and other international organizations. It should not be confused with the Spanish-speaking Dominican Republic to which it has no ties. Dominica has a pleasant climate, particularly during the cool months from December to March. It is one of the most beautiful countries in the Caribbean. Covering an area of almost 800 square kilometers, it has a population of more than 67,000 inhabitants, including about 3,000 of the last surviving native Carib people in the Caribbean. The Dominicans have been described by many travelers as the friendliest people in the Caribbean which is further supported by the almost non-existent crime rate. The currency is the Eastern Caribbean Dollar, which is pegged to the US dollar.

Also known as the Nature Island of the Caribbean, Dominica boasts a wide range of unique nature attractions, including fully preserved rain forests, an abundance of spectacular waterfalls, hundreds of rivers and streams, the second largest volcanic boiling lake in the world, and world-class hiking in the many nature reserves. The island is also a bird-watchers' paradise and offers fabulous diving opportunities around the coral reefs. Due to the mountainous terrain only about a quarter of the island is cultivated, but the very rich soil produces good domestic and export crops. Organic agriculture is being encouraged, and has great potential on this untouched island.

The economy is largely based on agricultural exports including bananas, citrus fruits, coffee, cocoa, coconut products including oil, tropical fruits, fruit juices and copra. Other exports are fish and various manufactured products including rum, soap, and timber. Tourism is an increasingly important sector of the economy.

---

[188] See Honychurch (1992); Evans and Honychurch (1989); Country Review Dominica 1999/2000; Commercial Data International, 1999

The Government of Dominica is adopting a structured approach to economic development through a number of programs, among them its citizenship-by-investment program.

33.1   Legal basis

The citizenship-by-investment program was established in 1991, and since then more than 3,000 families have received Dominica citizenship. Citizenship-by-investment is based on Section 101 of the Constitution and Sections 8 and 20 (1) of the Citizenship Act. It allows the government to operate a program under which citizenship is given to persons who qualify under criteria set by the government in its policy guidelines.

33.2   Requirements

Dominica's citizenship program requires making an economic contribution to the country. In exchange, applicants and their families are granted full citizenship. The economic contribution takes the form of a direct non-refundable payment made to the government.

Under the current regulations, there are five options for obtaining citizenship: the Single Applicant, and Family Applications One, Two and Three, as well as a Real Estate option.

- Under the Single option, the applicant pays USD 175,000

- Under Family Application One (for applicant and spouse), USD 225,000

- Under Family Application Two (applicant, spouse, two children under 18), USD 250,000

- Under Family Application Three (applicant, spouse, and more than two children under 18), USD 250,000 and USD 50,000 for every additional person under 18 years

- Under the Real Estate option, a minimum investment in an approved real estate project of USD 200,000 is required for each main applicant.

Two or more applicants may apply for citizenship-by-investment together by purchasing one piece of real estate, provided that each main applicant contributes the minimum investment of USD 200,000 towards the investment

In addition to the above costs, there are government processing fees of USD 3,000 per application and Certificate issuance and passport fees of USD 1,950 per person. Furthermore, due diligence fees of USD 7,500 for the main applicant and spouse, USD 4,000 for each qualifying dependent aged 16 years and above, and USD 2,000 for children aged 12 to 15 years of age apply.

The applicant must be at least 18 years of age and be of outstanding character. The applicant must provide a proof of clean personal record including certificate of no criminal record, etc., a comprehensive Curriculum Vitae, business background information as well as impeccable references.

33.3 Procedures and time frame

The documentary requirements of the program are reasonable and the procedures are quite straightforward with no requirement for an interview. The process takes four to six months from the submission of the application to issuance of the certificate of naturalization and passport, assuming there are no areas of concern with the application.

33.4 Grant of citizenship

Once the application has been pre-approved, the applicants are sent a document by which to take the Oath of Allegiance before a qualified lawyer or notary in a location of their choosing.

After pledging allegiance, the application for citizenship is processed further and certificates of citizenship are issued. Finally, the passport application can be lodged and the passports are usually issued within a couple of weeks.

There is no physical residence requirement. However, the government is of course keen to encourage new citizens to become involved further in the economy and substantial incentives are on offer to make this an attractive option. The applicant has the right to take up residence in Dominica at any time and for any length of time.

33.5   Dual citizenship

Dominica allows dual citizenship.

33.6   Taxation

Citizens are not liable for tax, unless they reside in Dominica.

33.7   Advantages of Dominica citizenship

Upon acquisition of citizenship under the Dominica citizenship program, the applicant enjoys full citizenship of the Commonwealth of Dominica. The passport allows the citizen visa-free travel to around 119 countries worldwide, including the UK and the Schengen area. Citizens of Dominica receive certain limited preferential treatment in the UK due to the country's membership of the Commonwealth.

33.8   General information

Official name	Commonwealth of Dominica
Capital city	Roseau
Region	Caribbean Island, between the Caribbean Sea and the North Atlantic Ocean, about half way between Puerto Rico and Trinidad and Tobago
Surface area	751 km²
Government	Parliamentary democracy
Language	English (official), French patois
Currency	East Caribbean dollars (XCD)
Population	73,607 (July 2015 est.)
Religion	Roman Catholic 61.4%, Protestant 20.6% (Seventh Day Adventist 6%, Pentecostal 5.6%, Baptist 4.1%, Methodist 3.7%, Church of God 1.2%), Jehovah's Witnesses 1.2%, other Christian 7.7%, Rastafarian 1.3%, other or unspecified 1.6%, none 6.1%
Ethnic groups	Black 86.8%, mixed 8.9%, Carib Amerindian 2.9%, white 0.8%, other 0.7%
GDP	USD 763 million (2015 est.)
GDP per capita, PPP	USD 10,700 (2015 est.)
Major industries	Soap, coconut oil, tourism, copra, furniture, cement blocks, shoes
Main exports	Bananas, soap, bay oil, vegetables, grapefruit, oranges
Climate	The climate is tropical; moderated by northeast trade winds; heavy rainfall
UN Human Development Index (HDI)	93rd (2015)
World's healthiest countries (Bloomberg Rankings)	n.a.
Henley & Partners Visa Restrictions Index	41st (2016), 41st (2015)
Legatum Prosperity Index	n.a.

Sources: CIA "The World Factbook" (2015), World Bank (2015), UN Human Development Report (2015), Henley & Partners

33.9 Climate

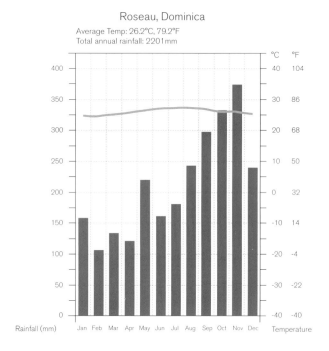

34

Grenada

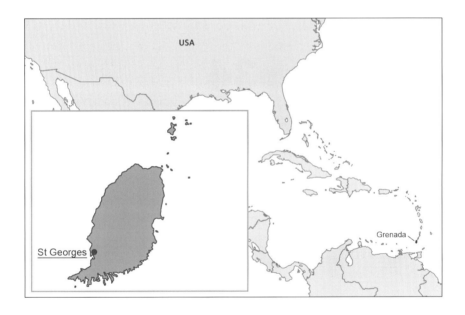

The State of Grenada lies in the Eastern Caribbean between Trinidad and Tobago to the south and St. Vincent and the Grenadines to the north. It is the southernmost island of the Windward Islands. Formerly colonized for many years, first by the French and then by the British, the islands of Grenada still retain traces of these European influences in their culture, architecture and place names. The capital, St. George's, is located on the south west coast of Grenada. It is the seat of government and the main commercial center.

Grenada is an independent nation within The Commonwealth of Nations (formerly called The British Commonwealth). Her Majesty, Queen Elizabeth II is Head of State and is represented locally by a Governor General, who is appointed on the advice of the Grenadian Prime Minister. Grenada has a Westminster-style parliamentary form of government. The Parliament which exercises legislative power consists of the House of Representatives and the Senate. Executive power lies with the Prime Minister and his Cabinet. General Elections are held every five years.

A Grenada passport offers a very good level of visa-free travel to 121 countries, placing it 39th in the *Henley & Partners Visa Restriction Index 2016*. Additionally, and uniquely among the Caribbean countries offering citizenship-by-investment, Grenadian citizenship carries with it visa-free travel to China and Brazil and the right (subject to compliance with all the rules) to a US E2 investor visa (see below). The basic principle is that if a person has or wants to invest in a material and *bona fide* business in the US, such person may live for five years (renewable) on a non-immigrant basis in the US to run such a business.

34.1   Legal basis

The legal basis and procedure is discussed in more detail below. In summary, Grenadian citizenship is acquired by investing in one of the following:

1. USD 200,000 in the National Transformation Fund (NTF)

2. USD 350,000 in a government approved project

After fees, commissions and expenses, the amounts paid by an applicant for either the NTF option or an approved project can be broadly similar depending upon the exact selection. The amounts may include the acquisition of citizenship for the spouse of the applicant. There are small additional fees for dependents (see below). The processing time should be no more than 60 business days. The applicant has to use a local agent. Only licensed marketing agents may promote Grenadian citizenship-by-investment. The applicant must pay all the money due for the investment and all other costs in advance.

There is no residence requirement in the acquisition of Grenadian citizenship-by-investment and (unlike some other countries) the applicant does not ever have to travel to Grenada.

34.2   Requirements

The program's purpose is to enable individuals to acquire citizenship of Grenada following investment.[189]

The regulations are Grenada Citizenship by Investment Regulations SRO. 17 of 2013, Grenada Citizenship by Investment (Amendment) No.2 Regulations SRO. 38 of 2014, Grenada Citizenship by Investment (Amendment) Regulations SRO. 23 of 2015.

To qualify for citizenship, applicants must:

• Be 18 years of age or over

• Meet the application requirements

• Apply on the prescribed forms and be accompanied by the processing fees, due diligence fees, and documentation including medical certificates and police certificates

---

[189]   Act No.15 of 2013, p 135

Investment must be made in one of the following:

- The National Transformation Fund (NTF), for a current minimum of USD 200,000 for a single applicant

- An approved project, for a current minimum of USD 350,000 for a single applicant

The Act defines an approved project as "a project that is approved by the Minister following the review and recommendation of the Citizenship by Investment Committee". Approval is evidenced by the Minister by Order identifying projects to be managed by identified bodies and organizations and approving such projects for the purpose of investment under the Act. Such approval is published in the *Gazette* and notified to the Citizenship by Investment Committee.

34.3   Procedures and time frame

If the approved project option is selected by the applicant, it is important for an applicant to be aware of the investment potential, financial strength, track record and reputation of the developer before committing to the project. Once the applicant has chosen an approved project option a contract should be executed, usually conditionally upon the grant of citizenship. Following the grant of citizenship the escrow funds will be disbursed and the contract completed with legal title of the interest in the approved project transferred to the applicant. Applicants should also ascertain from the approved project promoter whether there are additional purchase and/or closing costs and the amount of those costs, prior to entering into the contact.

The processing time should be no more than 60 business days as provided by the Act.

Following a grant of citizenship, citizenship certificates will be issued to the new citizens. The new citizens may then apply for Grenadian passports. This latter process is normally carried out by the Citizenship by Investment Committee and the Local Agent. A standard five-year passport will be issued.

A Grenada citizen is entitled to take up residence in Grenada at any time.

34.4   Grant of citizenship

The Citizenship Act 1976 as amended (and there are ten amending statutes) determines the citizenship rules in Grenada. Citizenship is (apart from by investment) acquired by descent not birth, *ius sanguinis* not *ius soli*.

34.5   Dual citizenship

There are no restrictions on dual citizenship in Grenada.

34.6   Taxation

Income tax depends on whether the individual is resident and domiciled for tax purposes in Grenada and being a citizen of Grenada does not produce tax liability unless the citizen is also resident and domiciled.

A person is resident for income tax purposes if they:

a. Have a permanent place of abode in Grenada and the person is physically present therein for some period of time in that year of assessment, or

b. Have physical presence in Grenada for period of not less than 183 days in that year of assessment, or

c. Are physically present in Grenada for some period of time in that year of assessment and such period is continuous with a period of physical presence in the immediately preceding or succeeding year of assessment of such duration as would qualify him for the resident status per (b)

An individual who is resident, ordinarily resident and domiciled in Grenada is subject to income tax on his or her income as it arises.

In ascertaining the chargeable income of an individual who is resident in Grenada, the amount of XCD 60,000 per annum is allowed as a deduction. A 30% tax rate is applied to the excess.

Non-residents are subject to tax on income accruing directly or indirectly from the carrying on of business in Grenada. Income of a non-resident arising in Grenada from any source other than from the carrying on of business is liable to withholding tax but does not form part of assessable income.

Tax residence should not be confused with tax domicile. Broadly, an individual is domiciled in the country or state which he regards as his permanent home. He acquires a domicile of origin at birth, normally that of his father, and retains it unless and until he acquires a new domicile of choice. To acquire a domicile of choice, a person must sever his ties with his domicile of origin and settle in another country with the clear intention of making it his permanent home. A new citizen of Grenada is not therefore necessarily tax domiciled in Grenada, and generally not even if resident in Grenada, and therefore not subject to tax other than local source income or income remitted to Grenada.

There are no capital gains or inheritance taxes in Grenada.

The business and corporate tax rate is 25% of net profits, although attractive concessions are available to qualifying companies such as a tax holiday on profits up to a 20-year period and import/export customs duty waiver.

Grenada applies VAT on outputs, currently at 15%. Business registration is not required where the annual turnover is XCD 300,000 or under (although other variables also apply, so this is an approximate figure).

Property tax is levied on all properties in Grenada. The tax is levied based upon the property's current market value construction replacement cost with the applicable tax rate dependent upon the classification of the property (residential or commercial).

34.7   Advantages of Grenadian citizenship

The Grenada passport gives visa-free travel to 121 countries, including the Schengen area, the UK, China and Brazil, and also the right to a US

E2 treaty investor visa. Therefore, other than the lack of visa-free access to Canada, Grenada offers the most interesting visa-free travel of all the Caribbean countries offering citizenship-by-investment programs. The Act requires that all applications are processed within 60 business days, making this a very fast process. There is no requirement to visit Grenada. It is an English speaking, Commonwealth country with a common law legal system and outstanding medical facilities. It is also one of the most beautiful, diverse and safe countries of the Caribbean.

34.8   General information

Official name	Grenada
Capital city	Saint George's
Region	Caribbean, island between the Caribbean Sea and Atlantic Ocean
Surface area	344.59 km²
Government	Parliamentary Democracy
Language	English (official), French Patois
Currency	East Caribbean dollar (XCD)
Population	110,694 (July 2015 est.)
Religion	Roman Catholic 44.6%, Protestant 43.5%, Jehovah's Witness 1.1%, Rastafarian 1.1%, other 6.2%, non 3.6%
Ethnic groups	African descent 89.4%, mixed 8.2%, East Indian 1.6%, other 0.9%
GDP	USD 1.401 billion (2015 est.)
GDP per capita, PPP	USD 13,100 (2015 est.)
Major industries	Food and beverages, textiles, tourism, construction, light assembly operations
Main exports	Nutmeg, bananas, cocoa, clothing and mace
Climate	Tropical, tempered by northeast trade winds
UN Human Development Index (HDI)	79th (2015)
World's healthiest countries (Bloomberg Rankings)	n.a.
Henley & Partners Visa Restrictions Index	39th (2016), 38th (2015)
Legatum Prosperity Index	n.a.

Sources: CIA "The World Factbook" (2015), World Bank (2015),
UN Human Development Report (2015), Henley & Partners, The Legatum Institute

34.9 Climate

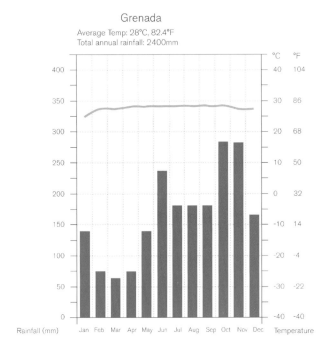

35
Malta

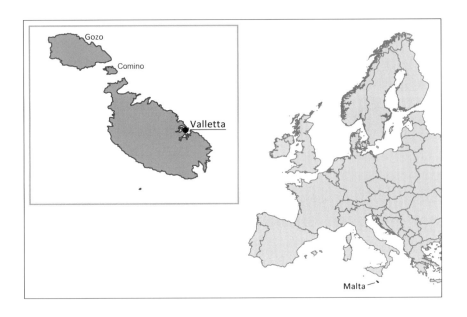

The Maltese archipelago lies virtually at the center of the Mediterranean and consists of three islands: Malta, Gozo and Comino, with a total population of over 400,000 inhabitants occupying an area of 316 square kilometers. Malta is the largest island and the cultural, commercial and administrative center. Gozo is the second largest island and is more rural, characterized by fishing, tourism, crafts and agriculture. Comino, the smallest of the trio, has one hotel but is otherwise is largely uninhabited. The official languages of the country are Maltese and English. Malta has an excellent climate, very friendly people, a low crime rate and is neutral, stable and safe.

In 1964, after more than 160 years of British rule, Malta gained independence. In 1974 Malta became a republic with a parliamentary democracy system and a constitution. Malta has been an EU member since 2004 and a member of the Schengen area since 2007.

Henley & Partners was awarded a Public Services Concession by competitive tender with regard to the design, implementation and international promotion of the Malta Individual Investor Programme (MIIP). The MIIP is a modern citizenship-by-investment program aimed at ultra high net worth individuals and families worldwide. It offers citizenship in an EU member state that is stable, neutral and highly respected, an efficient application process, and the world's strictest due diligence standards and vetting of applicants, thus ensuring only highly respectable clients will be admitted. Furthermore, the program is capped and only 1,800 applications will be admitted, making this the most exclusive such program in the world. It is also the most successful citizenship-by-investment program in the world ever, having not only established new standards of processing and due diligence, but also having secured already more than EUR 1 billion in new capital for Malta within the first 18 months of operation.

35.1 Legal basis

The MIIP allows for the grant of citizenship to duly qualified, reputable foreign individuals and families who make a significant contribution to the economic development of Malta. The legal basis regarding citizenship-by-investment is contained in Articles 10 (9) (b) and 24 (1) (i) of the Maltese Citizenship Act (Cap 188), and the Individual Investor Programme Regulations of the Republic of Malta, 2014. Furthermore, an agreement reached between the EU Commission and the Maltese Government on 29 January 2014 confers upon the MIIP a unique legal status with explicit EU treaty protection acknowledged and approved by the EU Commission.

35.2   Requirements

The MIIP requires a person to make an economic contribution to the country. In return, and subject to a very thorough application procedure including detailed due diligence and background verification checks, the applicants and their families are granted full citizenship. To qualify for citizenship, the main applicant must be at least 18 years of age, meet all of the application conditions, make a non-refundable contribution to the National Development and Social Fund, and meet certain other requirements.

The contribution requirements are as follows:

- For main applicants, a contribution of EUR 650,000

- An additional contribution of EUR 25,000 is required for a spouse and for each child under the age of 18

- The application may include children between the ages of 18 and 26 years if they are financially dependent on the main applicant and are not married; in such cases, the additional contribution is set at EUR 50,000 for each dependent

- Parents over the age of 55 may also be included in the application as dependents, if they are living with and are fully supported by the main applicant. In such cases, an additional contribution of EUR 50,000 is required per person

Due diligence fees are payable for all applicants: EUR 7,500 for the main applicant; EUR 5,000 for spouses, adult children and parents; EUR 3,000 each for children between 13 and 17 years of age.

Additionally, the following investment requirements and other obligations must be met:

- *Property* – either the purchase of a residential property in Malta with a price of at least EUR 350,000 which must be held for five years, or the lease of a residential property with a rental of at least EUR 16,000 per annum, also held for five years

- *Investment* – EUR 150,000 in a prescribed investment, details of which are published from time to time by Identity Malta, which must be held for five years

- *Insurance* – the holding of a valid global health insurance policy with medical expense cover amounting to at least EUR 50,000 per family member

- *Residence* – the applicant must have been legally resident in Malta for one year prior to application for citizenship under the MIIP

- *Oath of Allegiance* – all applicants aged 18 years and over are obliged to visit Malta in person to undertake the Oath of Allegiance

The applicant must have a completely clean personal background and no criminal record.

The regulations further provide that a person who has been denied a visa to a country with which Malta has visa-free travel arrangements and has not subsequently obtained a visa to that country shall not be entitled to apply under the program.

A person who is deemed a potential national security risk, a reputational risk or is subject to criminal investigation will also be denied citizenship. Malta has developed a four-tier due diligence system which is considered the most thorough in the world for this kind of program.

The names of successful applicants will be published annually, along with all other naturalizations granted by the government.

There is a cap of 1,800 successful main applicants, after which the program will close, making this the most exclusive program available.

35.3   Procedures and time frame

The MIIP was designed and is operated by Henley & Partners for the Government of Malta under a Public Services Concession. Each application is thoroughly checked and assessed, and, if deemed necessary, an interview may be requested.

Applications must be made on the prescribed forms and be accompanied by the appropriate fees and specific documents which, in addition to the usual personal documentation such as passport copies, birth certificates etc., include a medical report confirming that the main applicant and any dependents are not suffering from any contagious disease and that they are otherwise in good health; and a police certificate confirming that the applicants have no criminal record. Highly detailed due diligence checks are carried out and an application will be declined if it turns out that it contains false information or omissions.

The regulations stipulate that the process to achieve the issuance of a Certificate of Naturalisation under the MIIP shall be a minimum of six months and a maximum of two years from the date of submission of the application. This includes the time taken to fulfil the property and investment requirements, as well as the one-year residence requirement.

Before the submission of an application to government, all relevant information provided and the background of the applicant and any dependents are verified by one or several due diligence agents. All required due diligence fees, passport fees and bank charge fees as well as a non-refundable deposit of EUR 10,000 against the government contribution must have been received, the source of all funds must have been verified and a risk weighting procedure carried out.

35.4   Grant of citizenship

Once the application is approved in principle, the applicant is required to:

- Remit the contribution (less the deposit already paid)
- Demonstrate compliance with the property requirement

- Show proof of residence for one year

- Make the prescribed investment

- Be in possession of a valid health insurance policy for the entire family with the requisite level of cover

- Undertake the Oath of Allegiance in person in Malta, together with all dependents aged 18 years and above

Having satisfied all the above requirements, a certificate of naturalization will be issued, enabling the passport to be issued immediately thereafter.

35.5   Dual citizenship

There are no restrictions on dual citizenship in Malta. The Maltese Citizenship Act specifically provides that dual citizenship is allowed.

35.6   Taxation

Individuals who are resident and domiciled in Malta pay income tax on their worldwide income. Personal income is taxed at progressive rates up to 35%. However, individuals who are resident but not domiciled in Malta pay tax on (a) income arising in Malta and (b) on income (excluding capital gains) remitted to Malta that arises outside the island (i.e. remittance basis). The tax rate varies in accordance with the individual's tax status.

The acquisition of Maltese citizenship under the MIIP does not, in itself, trigger tax residence, but even if one decides to move and take up permanent residence in Malta, one would normally still retain the status of a non-domiciled person.

Malta does not impose estate or gift tax but does levy a capital gains tax (CGT) on various assets (mainly immovable property and shares). CGT is not levied on the transfer of immovable property if the person transferring the property has owned it and occupied it as his main residence for a period of three consecutive years immediately preceding the date of transfer and if the property is transferred within 12 months from vacating the premises. Otherwise, tax may be levied at up to 35% on the gain if the property is sold within the first 12 years of ownership or 12% on the sales consideration if the transfer is made after 12 years of ownership. The 12% final tax, however, does not apply if the individual property owner is not resident in Malta.

The standard VAT rate is 18%. The corporate tax rate is 35%; special tax concessions, however, apply for non-resident/non-domiciled owners.

Malta has concluded double taxation treaties with around 60 countries. A number of other agreements are signed but not yet in force.

All applicants are advised to seek appropriate tax advice from suitably qualified tax practitioners.

35.7   Advantages of Maltese citizenship

Malta is an attractive place to live or to own a second residence and is strategically located with excellent air links. Malta is a well-respected and stable EU country, and its citizens have the right of establishment in all 28 EU countries and visa-free travel to more than 150 countries worldwide. The country has an excellent reputation and offers the world's most advanced and most exclusive citizenship-by-investment program.

35.8   General information

Official name	Republic of Malta
Capital city	Valletta
Region	Southern Europe, islands in the Mediterranean Sea, south of Sicily (Italy)
Surface area	316 km^2
Government	Republic
Languages	Maltese (official) 90.2%, English (official) 6%, multilingual 3%, other 0.8%
Currency	Euro (EUR)
Population	413,965 (July 2015 est.)
Religion	Roman Catholic (official) 98%
Ethnic groups	Maltese (descendants of ancient Carthaginians and Phoenicians with strong elements of Italian and other Mediterranean stock)
GDP	USD 15.38 billion (2015 est.)
GDP per capita, PPP	USD 35,900 (2015 est.)
Major industries	Tourism, electronics, ship building and repair, construction, food and beverages, pharmaceuticals, footwear, clothing, tobacco, aviation services, financial services, information technology services
Main exports	Electrical machinery, mechanical appliances, fish and crustaceans, pharmaceutical products, printed material
Climate	Mediterranean; mild, rainy winters; hot, dry summers
UN Human Development Index (HDI)	39th (2015)
World's healthiest countries (Bloomberg Rankings)	n.a.
Henley & Partners Visa Restrictions Index	9th (2016), 7th (2015)
Legatum Prosperity Index	23rd (2015)

Sources: CIA "The World Factbook" (2015), World Bank (2015),
UN Human Development Report (2015), Henley & Partners, The Legatum Institute

35.9 Climate

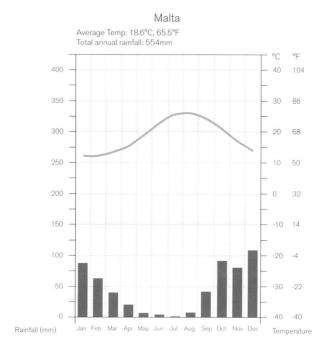

36

St. Kitts and Nevis

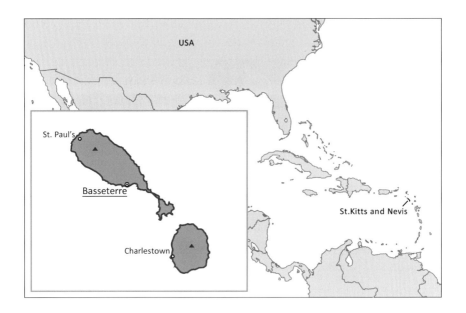

St. Kitts and Nevis, also known in the country's constitution as Saint Christopher and Nevis, was named by Christopher Columbus in 1493. The federation has a rich history with its varied influences from the British, French, Africans, and the native Carib people.

St. Kitts and Nevis gained its independence from Britain in 1983. The Federation comprises of two islands: the larger island, St. Kitts with an area of some 168.4 km² and Nevis with area of 93.2 square kilometers. The two islands are part of the group of islands known as the Lesser Antilles, located some 2,000 km southeast of Miami.

St. Kitts and Nevis is an exclusive Caribbean destination with impressive natural beauty. The islands offer twelve hours of sunshine almost year-round. With its tropical climate and cooling trade winds, it is an ideal place for relaxation. The two islands offer diverse vegetation from the many fine beaches to the attractive dense mountainous landscape. Differences in altitude and corresponding differences in soil types make it a paradise for tropical plants. The slogan of the local tourism authority, "Two islands – one paradise", is truly befitting.

The official language is English and the country is very proactive in promoting and attracting investment into the country. St. Kitts and Nevis has a well-regulated financial services sector and no restrictions on repatriation of profits or imported capital. The country has a modern infrastructure with an international airport. There are direct daily flights from Miami and bi-weekly direct flights from New York and London.

St. Kitts and Nevis has a democratically-elected government with the Prime Minister as Head of Government. The country has a National assembly which comprises of 15 members including 11 Elected Members representing the eight constituencies in St. Kitts and three constituencies in Nevis, and four Appointed Members. The Queen of England is Head of State. St. Kitts and Nevis is a well-functioning democracy based on the British parliamentary system and Her Majesty's Privy Council serves as the highest court of appeal.

The Federation is a member of the United Nations (UN), of the Organization of American States (OAS), the British Commonwealth, Caribbean Community (CARICOM) and many other international organizations. The Eastern Caribbean Central Bank has its headquarters on St. Kitts. It maintains the stability of the Eastern Caribbean dollar (XCD), the national currency of most Eastern Caribbean countries, which is pegged to the US dollar.

For over 400 years, St. Kitts and Nevis operated as mainly a sugar-producing country until 2005 when the government closed down the industry due to decreasing profitability. Today, the main economic drivers are tourism, real estate and financial services.

Since 1984, the St. Kitts and Nevis Citizenship Act has allowed foreign investors to acquire citizenship, making it the oldest existing citizen-ship-by-investment program. In 2007, Henley & Partners was mandated by the government to completely reform the program, and from 2007 until 2013 was mandated by the government as the global agent for promotion. It became the most successful program of its kind in the world for many years. More recently, however, the program has experi-enced several setbacks and irregularities, which lead to the withdrawal of visa-free access to Canada and an Advisory issued in May 2014 by the US Treasury Department's FinCEN[190]. The government has reacted to these issues finally and has taken various measures aimed at restoring the previous good reputation of the program.

36.1   Legal basis

The regulations regarding citizenship-by-investment in St. Kitts and Nevis are contained in Part II, Section 3 (5) of the Citizenship Act, 1984, and the Saint Christopher and Nevis Citizenship by Investment Regulations, 2011. These provisions allow the government to operate a program under which citizenship is granted to persons who qualify under the criteria set by the Government.

---

[190]   *https://www.fincen.gov/statutes_regs/guidance/pdf/FIN-2014-A004.pdf*

36.2 Requirements

The citizenship program of St. Kitts and Nevis requires a person to make an economic contribution to the country. In exchange, and subject to a stringent application procedure including thorough background checks, the applicants and their families are granted full citizenship.

To qualify for citizenship, the person must be over eighteen years of age, meet the application requirements and make an investment of at least USD 400,000 in one of the approved real estate developments or alternatively pay a contribution to the Sugar Industry Diversification Foundation (SIDF) of an amount starting from USD 250,000 (for a single applicant).

If the applicant chooses to invest in a government approved real estate development, this option may involve additional real estate purchase costs (depending on the developer), and government fees of USD 50,047 for the main applicant plus an additional USD 25,047 for each for spouse and dependents under the age of 18 (and USD 50,047 each for dependents 18 years and older). There is also a due diligence fee of USD 7,500 for the main applicant and USD 4,000 for dependents over the age of 16 years. Real estate that has been purchased and qualifies an applicant for citizenship under the citizenship-by-investment program must not be resold for a period of at least five years after the granting of citizenship. Where real estate has already been the subject of a citizenship-by-investment application, it cannot be used in a subsequent citizenship-by-investment application before January 2017. From January 2017, real estate that has been the subject of a grant of citizenship at least five years previously may be eligible for use in a subsequent citizenship-by-investment application.[191]

The SIDF is a non-profit foundation established for the purpose of, inter alia, supporting the former sugar workers, conducting research into the development of industries to replace the sugar industry, funding the development of these alternative industries and providing further support to secure the sustainability of the national economy.[192] The

---

[191] This provision was introduced by the Citizenship Regulations 2011, and takes effect as of 2017 (5 years from 1 January 2012)

[192] For more information see *www.sidf.org*

Foundation has been designated as a special approved project for the purposes of the Citizenship-by-Investment Program; its accounts are public and are annually audited by Grant Thornton LLP.

An applicant may make a contribution to the SIDF under the following four categories:

1. A single applicant is required to make a contribution of USD 250,000

2. An applicant with up to three dependents (i.e. one spouse and two children under the age of 18) is required to contribute USD 300,000

3. An applicant with up to five dependents (i.e. one spouse and four children under the age of 18) must make a contribution of USD 350,000

4. An applicant with up to seven dependents is required to make a USD 450,000 contribution

Under the SIDF, in each of these categories, the total amount includes all government fees, but excludes due diligence fees, which are the same for the real estate option (USD 7,500 for the main applicant and USD 4,000 for dependents over the age of 16 years).

The government allows for a dependent between the age of 18 and 25 years to be included in the application of the main applicant if the dependent is a full-time student at a recognized higher learning institution and is financially dependent on the main applicant.

The government also allows for parents and grandparents over the age of 65, of the main applicant or his or her spouse, to be included in the application as dependents, if the parent/s and grandparent/s are living with and are fully supported by the main applicant.

There is an additional government fee of USD 50,000 payable for each dependent over the age of 18.

The applicant must have no criminal record. The regulations further provide that a person who has been denied entry to a country with which St. Kitts and Nevis has visa-free travel arrangement and has subsequently not obtained a visa to the country after the first refusal shall not be entitled to apply under the program. A person that is deemed a potential national security risk, a reputational risk or is subject to criminal investigation will also be denied citizenship.

36.3   Procedures and time frame

The government authority responsible for administering the program, the Citizenship-by-Investment Unit (CIU),[193] is responsible for the processing of all applications. The CIU examines the application thoroughly and if deemed necessary, may request that the applicant attends an interview, although this is not generally a requirement. The CIU undertakes strict due diligence checks and will decline an application if the applicant makes a false statement or omits any relevant information on the application.

The applicant must apply on the prescribed government forms which are only available from the CIU or from an authorized service provider. The applicant is required to personally complete the forms in English and submit the prescribed forms together with original or certified supporting documentation as specified by the government.

The documentary requirements of the St. Kitts and Nevis citizenship-by-investment program are reasonable and the procedures straightforward.

Furthermore, most investors would normally visit the islands before making a decision on the purchase of real estate, which also needs to be taken into consideration. However, it is not a prerequisite for the application process.

The process usually takes between four to nine months from submission of the application to the CIU to approval. Under the real estate option, the time frame may vary depending on the development, therefore it is important to choose a real estate project that is efficient in acquiring and completing the paperwork needed for the citizenship application.

---

[193] *www.ciu.gov.kn*

If the real estate option is favored, it is important for an applicant to be aware of the investment potential, financial strength, track record and reputation of the developer before committing to the property.

Once the applicant has chosen their preferred real estate, a sales and purchase contract is signed which is usually conditional upon the person receiving citizenship. After approval by the government, the real estate purchase is completed and the ownership title transferred to the buyer.

Upon approval-in-principle of the application by the CIU, the funds for the real estate or SIDF contribution, government fees and other fees will be released to the various parties. Thereafter, the Prime Minister will sign the official Certificate of Registration which confirms that the applicant has been registered as a citizen of St. Kitts and Nevis. Once the Certificate of Registration is issued, the person is entitled to apply for a St. Kitts and Nevis passport.

36.4   Grant of citizenship

There is no formal ceremony that the citizen must attend and the grant of citizenship is not made public.

A St. Kitts and Nevis citizen is entitled to take up residence in St. Kitts and Nevis at any time and for any length of time. A St. Kitts and Nevis citizen may also reside in any other CARICOM country.

The citizen is issued with a biometric passport, which is valid for 10 years. In the event that the passport expires, is lost or destroyed, the citizen may apply for a new passport at the passport office in St. Kitts.

36.5   Dual citizenship

There are no restrictions on dual citizenship in St. Kitts and Nevis.

36.6   Taxation

There is no direct taxation in St. Kitts and Nevis. Even if a citizen resides on the islands, they will not be subject to personal income tax, estate duty, inheritance or succession taxes, gift taxes or net worth tax.

In St. Kitts and Nevis, there is a corporate income tax of 35% of net profits but the country offers qualified companies a tax holiday on corporate profits for up to 15 years. Nevis does not levy tax on companies and foundations as long as the business is not transacted on the island.

There is a 10% withholding tax payable by both individuals and companies remitting payments to persons outside of St. Kitts and Nevis, on the following: profits; administration, management or head office expenses; technical service fees; accounting and audit expenses; royalties; non-life insurance premiums; and rent.

There is also an annual property tax in St. Kitts and Nevis which is minimal and calculated on the market value of the property.

St. Kitts and Nevis has entered into Tax Information Exchange Agreements with Aruba, Australia, Belgium, Canada, Denmark, the Faroe Islands, Finland, France, Germany, Greenland, Iceland, Liechtenstein, Monaco, the Netherlands, the Netherlands Antilles, New Zealand, Norway, Portugal, San Marino, Sweden and the UK.

The current rate of VAT in St. Kitts and Nevis is 17%.

36.7   Advantages of St. Kitts and Nevis citizenship

In 2009, with the advice and assistance of Henley & Partners, the St. Kitts and Nevis government was among the first Eastern Caribbean states to sign a visa-waiver agreement with the Schengen area countries. This allows St. Kitts and Nevis citizens to visit the Schengen area without a visa for the period of three months within a six-month period following the date of first entry into any EU country. Generally, the St. Kitts and Nevis passport is a very good travel document to have, despite recent reputational issues due to irregularities with its citizenship-by-investment program and the US Treasury Department's FinCEN Advisory issued in May 2014. With a St. Kitts and Nevis passport, a citizen can travel to over 130 countries and territories in the world including Brazil, Europe, Hong Kong, Singapore and the UK.

Full citizenship with passport is granted to the applicant and family. St. Kitts and Nevis is a member of the Commonwealth, which entitles St. Kitts and Nevis citizens to certain limited privileges in the UK and other Commonwealth countries.

36.8   General information

Official name	Federation of Saint Kitts and Nevis
Capital city	Basseterre
Region	Central America, Caribbean
Surface area	261 km^2 (St. Kitts 168 km^2; Nevis 93 km^2)
Government	British Monarchy (parliamentary democracy and a Commonwealth realm)
Languages	English
Currency	East Caribbean Dollar (XCD)
Population	51,936 (July 2015 est.)
Religion	Anglican, other Protestant, Roman Catholic
Ethnic groups	Predominantly black; some British, Portuguese, and Lebanese
GDP	USD 1.379 billion (2015 est.)
GDP per capita, PPP	USD 24,600 (2015 est.)
Major industries	Tourism, real estate, salt, copra, light manufacturing
Main exports	Machinery, food, electronics, beverages, tobacco
Climate	Tropical, tempered by constant sea breezes; little seasonal temperature variation; rainy season (May to November)
UN Human Development Index (HDI)	73rd (2015)
World's healthiest countries (Bloomberg Rankings)	n.a.
Henley & Partners Visa Restrictions Index	32nd (2016), 27th (2015)
Legatum Prosperity Index	n.a.

Sources: CIA "The World Factbook" (2015), World Bank (2015), UN Human Development Report (2015), Henley & Partners

36.9   Climate

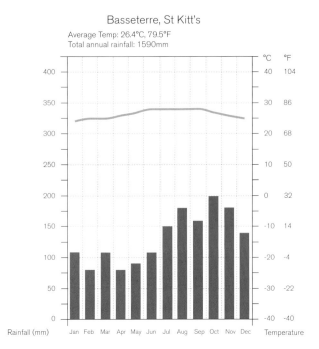

37

St. Lucia

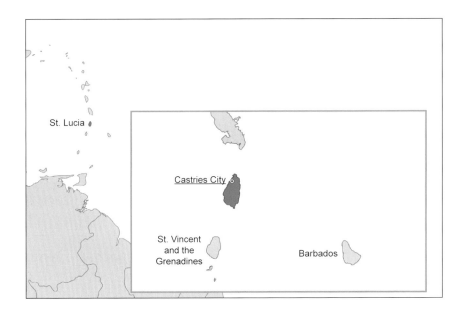

St. Lucia is an independent Commonwealth State, having gained independence from the UK on 22 February 1979, a day celebrated each year with a public holiday. The country's history has been influenced by the native Carib people, Africans, the British and the French who were the first European settlers and who gave the island its name after Saint Lucy of Syracuse in 1660, the only country to be named after a woman. Since the early days of the French settlers the island nation changed governance in excess of a dozen times until the British secured it in 1814, as part of the Treaty of Paris, ending the Napoleonic Wars. Thereafter St. Lucia was considered part of the British Windward Islands until independence.

St. Lucia is an island in the Lesser Antilles region of the Eastern Caribbean and covers 617 square kilometers. It is one of the Windward Islands and more mountainous than most Caribbean Islands, with the highest point being Mount Gimie, at 950 meters above sea level. Two other mountains, the Pitons, form the Island's most famous landmark. The natural beauty of the Island makes it a popular tourist destination for both European and North American travelers who are visit the rain forest, national parks, botanical gardens, a world heritage site, gorgeous Caribbean beaches and even a drive-in volcano. English is the official language of St. Lucia but most locals also speak French Creole.

The local climate is tropical, moderated by northeast trade winds, with a dry season between the months of December and May. Average daytime temperatures are around 29 degrees centigrade and average night time temperatures are 18 degrees centigrade with little seasonal variance as the Island is located close to the equator. The local population of 184,000 is evenly divided between urban and rural areas of which one third are located in the capital, Castries.

St. Lucia elected a new Prime Minister, Allan Chastanet, in June 2016, who is the head of the democratic government having secured 11 of the 17 seats within the House of Assembly. A further Chamber of Parliament, the Senate, has 11 appointed members. Queen Elizabeth II is the Head of State, represented on the island by her Governor General, Pearlette

Louisy. St. Lucia is a member of the United Nations, CARICOM, OECS and the Eastern Caribbean Currency Union (ECCU), a regional currency (East Caribbean Dollar, XCD) which is pegged to the US dollar at a rate of 2.70.

The island nation has been able to attract foreign business and investment, especially in its offshore banking and tourism industries. Tourism is St. Lucia's main source of jobs and income, accounting for 65% of GDP, and the island's main source of foreign exchange earnings. The manufacturing sector is the most diverse in the Eastern Caribbean area. Crops such as bananas, mangos, and avocados continue to be grown for export, but St. Lucia's once solid banana industry has been negatively impacted by strong competition. St. Lucia has experienced minimal growth since the onset of the global financial crisis in 2008, largely because of a slowdown in tourism and airlines cutting back on their routes to St. Lucia in 2012, a situation which is now slowly being reversed. VAT of 15% was introduced in 2012, becoming the last country in the Eastern Caribbean to do so. The government have identified three areas of future investment focus; tourism, smart manufacturing and infrastructure.

Travel connections to the Island are good with direct flights from the UK and the US cities of Miami, Atlanta, Philadelphia, Newark and Charlotte. There are two main airports on the island; Hewanorra International Airport at Vieux Fort is located 40 miles south of the capital of Castries, and George Inter Island Airport is located just outside the city.

37.1 Legal basis

St. Lucia's citizenship-by-investment program is regulated by the Citizenship by Investment Act No. 14 of 2015. Section 33 of this Act established the Saint Lucia National Economic Fund, which receives qualifying investments of donations from the program. These funds will be used by the government under the national development agenda.

37.2   Requirements

The citizenship-by-investment program requires a person to make a significant economic contribution to the country. In exchange, and subject to a stringent application process and due diligence checks, the applicants and their families are granted full citizenship. The main applicant must be at least 18 years of age to qualify, must sign a sworn affidavit declaring financial resources of at least USD 3 million, meet the application requirements and select one of the investment options below:

1. An investment in an approved real estate development with a minimum value of USD 300,000. Additional costs may also be incurred depending on the real estate developer. The property must be held for a minimum period of five years

2. An investment in an approved Enterprise Project (as set out in the regulations) with a minimum investment of USD 3.5 million plus the creation of no less than three permanent jobs

For the above two options, the following government administration fees will also apply:

- Main applicant USD 50,000

- Spouse USD 35,000

- Dependent under 18 years USD 25,000

- Dependent 18 years and older USD 35,000

3. A non-refundable contribution to the National Economic Fund of USD 200,000 (for a single applicant). An applicant may make the contribution under one of the four following categories:

   - Main applicant USD 200,000

   - Main applicant and spouse USD 235,000

   - Main applicant, spouse and up to two other qualifying dependents USD 250,000

   - Each additional qualifying dependent of any age USD 25,000

The following due diligence and government processing fees are charged in addition on all investment options:

Due diligence fees:

- Main applicant USD 7,500
- Each qualifying dependent aged 16 years and above USD 5,000

Government processing fees:

- Main applicant USD 2,000
- Each qualifying dependent USD 1,000

The main applicant and any dependents must have a clean personal background with no criminal record and not be under any criminal investigation (other than in respect of a minor offence). A person that is deemed a potential security risk or who is or has been involved in any activity that is likely to bring disrepute to St. Lucia shall not be approved for citizenship.

37.3   Procedures and time frame

The government authority responsible for administering the program, the Citizenship by Investment Board (CIB) provides oversight to a dedicated Citizenship by Investment Unit (CIU), which is responsible for the processing of all applications. The CIU examines the application thoroughly and undertakes strict due diligence checks. An application will be declined if the applicant makes a false statement or omits any relevant information in the application.

The documentary requirements of the St. Lucia citizenship-by-investment program are reasonable and the procedures are quite straightforward. We anticipate the application process will take no longer than four months from submission of the application to issuance of the passport, assuming there are no areas of concern with the application. Under the real estate option, the time frame may vary depending on the development.

The CIB will consider an application for citizenship and the outcome may either be to grant, to deny or to delay for cause. The average processing time from receipt of an application to notification of the outcome is three months. Where, in exceptional cases, it is expected that the processing time will be longer than three months, the authorized agent will be informed of the reason for the anticipated delay.

A citizenship-by-investment application must be submitted in electronic and printed form by an authorized agent on behalf of an applicant and all applications must be completed in English. All documents submitted with the application must be in English or an authenticated translation into English. An authenticated translation means a translation effected by either a professional translator who is officially accredited to a court of law, a government agency, an international organization or similar official institution, or if effected in a country where there are no official accredited translators, a translation effected by a company whose role or business is effecting professional translations.

All requisite supporting documents must be attached to applications before they can be processed by the CIU and all applications must be accompanied by the relevant non-refundable processing and due diligence fees for the principal applicant, his or her spouse and each qualifying dependent.

Any incomplete application forms will be returned to the authorized agent.

Where an application for citizenship by investment has been granted, the CIU will notify the authorized agent that the qualifying investment and requisite government administration fees must be paid before the Certificate of Citizenship can be granted. Where an application has been denied, the applicant may, in writing, request a review by the Minister.

The principal applicant must make the qualifying investment within 60 calendar days after notice by the CIU to the authorized agent of approval of their application. In the case of an investment in an approved real estate or enterprise project, the principal applicant must pay the government administrative fees due within 60 full days after notice by the CIU to the authorized agent of approval of their application. An applicant who is granted citizenship-by-investment must take the oath or affirmation of allegiance to St. Lucia in person in St. Lucia or at any St. Lucia Embassy, High Commission or Consulate, as prescribed by the Minister.

The Minister may, by order, revoke a grant of citizenship in exceptional circumstances as may be deemed necessary.

37.4 Grant of citizenship

Upon approval, the citizen can choose to visit St. Lucia or may elect to attend an Embassy, High Commission or Consular office in locations worldwide to enable the oath or affirmation of allegiance to St. Lucia in person, as prescribed by the Minister. The passport will be valid for a period of 10 years for all persons aged 16 and over and for a period of five years for all persons below the age of 16, which will be renewed at 16 to a 10-year passport, subject to the requirements for renewal being met. A citizen of St. Lucia is entitled to take up residence in St. Lucia at any time and may also benefit from membership of a CARICOM member country and a Commonwealth member country.

37.5 Dual citizenship

There are no restrictions on dual citizenship in St. Lucia.

37.6 Taxation

There are no capital gains or inheritance taxes in St. Lucia.

A personal income tax allowance of XCD is granted to the taxpayer, thereafter tax is progressive up to 30%: 10% on the first XCD 833.33, 15% on the second XCD 833.33, 20% on the third 833.33 and 30% thereafter.

Individuals who have their permanent residence in the country or who are present for at least 183 days a year will qualify as residents of

St. Lucia and will be subject to tax on their worldwide income. Individuals who are in the country temporarily will only be taxed on income arising in or derived from St. Lucia.

The business and corporate tax rate is 30% of net profits, although attractive concessions are available to qualifying companies such as a tax holiday on profits up to a 15-year period and import/export customs duty waiver. Company dividends paid to a resident or non-resident are not subject to tax and there is no holding company regime, but a special tax regime applies to International Business Companies (IBCs). IBCs have the option to elect to be liable to income tax on the profits and gains at a rate of 1% or to be exempt from income tax.

Under the Fiscal Incentives Act, approved enterprises engaged in the manufacture of an approved product are granted tax holidays and are exempt from import duties. The Tourism Incentive Act grants tax and import duty exemptions on approved tourism projects.

St. Lucia introduced a standard VAT rate of 15% in 2012, the last Caribbean country to do so, which is levied upon local consumption. A local company or person must register for VAT where the total value of supplies exceeds XCD in one year.

An annual property tax is levied on all properties in St. Lucia at a rate of 0.25%. The taxable value is based upon the property's current market value construction replacement cost with the applicable tax rate dependent upon the classification of the property (residential or commercial).

37.7 Advantages of St. Lucia citizenship

A St. Lucian passport provides visa-free travel to 125 countries, including the Schengen area, the UK, Hong Kong, Singapore and many others. There are no residence or visitation requirements and a range of investment options are available. The investment and processing costs are reasonable. St. Lucia recognizes dual citizenship, and citizenship gives a right of descent for future generations.

37.8   General information

Official name	St Lucia
Capital city	Castries
Region	Caribbean
Surface area	617 km^2
Government	Parliamentary Democracy (Independent sovereign state within the Commonwealth)
Languages	English (Official), French Creole
Currency	Eastern Caribbean Dollar (XCD)
Population	183,600 (2014 census)
Religion	70% Roman Catholic, 20% Christian Denominations
Ethnic groups	85% Afro Caribbean
GDP	USD 2.03 billion (2015 est.)
GDP per capita	USD 11,700 (2015 est.)
Major industries	Tourism, Financial Services, Agricultural Products and Petroleum Products
Main exports	Petroleum products, bananas and plantains, aerials and aerial reflectors and malted beer
Climate	Tropical, moderated by northeast trade winds
World's healthiest countries (Bloomberg Rankings)	N/A
UN Human Development Index (HDI)	89th (2015)
Henley & Partners Visa Restrictions Index	37th (2016), 35th (2015)
Legatum Prosperity Index	N/A

Sources: CIA "The World Factbook" (2015), World Bank (2015),
UN Human Development Report (2015), Henley & Partners, The Legatum Institute

37.9 Climate

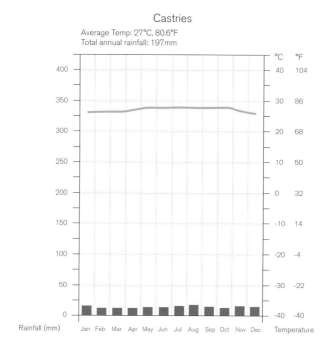

Castries

Average Temp: 27°C, 80.6°F
Total annual rainfall: 197mm

Useful Addresses and Websites

Henley & Partners Group Offices

For a complete and up-to-date list of all Henley & Partners group office locations worldwide, visit *henleyglobal.com*

Australia

Henley & Partners Australia Ltd
570 Bourke Street, Level 24
Melbourne, VIC 3000
Australia

Tel	+61 3 8658 5994
Fax	+61 3 8658 5800
Contact	Jennifer Lai
Email	*jennifer.lai@henleyglobal.com*

Austria

Henley & Partners Austria GmbH
Albertgasse 35
1080 Vienna

Tel	+43 1 361 6110
Fax	+43 1 361 6111
Contact	Dr. Jurg Steffen
Email	*juerg.steffen@henleyglobal.com*

Antigua and Barbuda

Henley & Partners Antigua Ltd
Suite 202, Village Walk Mall
Friars Hill Road, St. John's
Antigua

Tel	+1 268 562 2625
Fax	+1 268 562 2626
Contact	Gaye Hechme
Email	*gaye.hechme@henleyglobal.com*

Canada

Henley & Partners Canada Ltd
507 Place d' Armes, Suite 240
Montreal (Quebec) H2Y 2W8
Canada

Tel	+1 514 288 1997
Fax	+1 514 284 6258
Contact	Christopher Willis
Email	*christopher.willis@henleyglobal.com*

Henley & Partners Canada Ltd
885 West Georgia Street
Suite 1030
Vancouver, BC, V6C 3E8
Canada

Tel	+1 604 239 2170
Fax	+1 888 702 6945
Contact	Jon Green
Email	*jon.green@henleyglobal.com*

Croatia and Montenegro

Henley & Partners Croatia d.o.o.
Mihailova Sirina 3
HR-21000 Split
Croatia

Tel	+385 21 321 027
Fax	+385 21 321 028
Contact	Marko Jug-Dujakovic
Email	*marko.jug-dujakovic@henleyglobal.com*

Cyprus

Henley & Partners Cyprus Ltd
9, Spirou Kiprianou Avenue
Suite 301, 3070
Limassol
Cyprus

Tel	+357 2531 1844
Fax	+357 2531 1770
Contact	Yiannos Trisokkas
Email	*yiannos.trisokkas@henleyglobal.com*

Dubai/UAE

Henley & Partners Middle East DMCC
Reef Tower, JLT, Suite #1301
P.O. Box 213757
Dubai
UAE

Tel	+971 4 392 77 22
Fax	+971 4 392 77 33
Contact	Marco Gantenbein
Email	*marco.gantenbein@henleyglobal.com*

Grenada

Henley & Partners Grenada Ltd
Upper Floor
Netherlands Building
Grand Anse, St. Georges
Grenada, West Indies

Tel	+1 473 443 4000
Contact	Andrea St Bernard
Email	*andrea.stbernard@henleyglobal.com*

Hong Kong

Henley & Partners Hong Kong Ltd
1002A, Tower 1, Admiralty Center
18 Harcourt Road
Hong Kong

Tel	+852 3101 4100
Fax	+852 3101 4101
Contact	Jennifer Lai
Email	*jennifer.lai@henleyglobal.com*

Jersey

Henley & Partners International Ltd
Henley House
9 Hope Street
St Helier
Jersey, JE2 3NS
British Isles

Tel	+44 1534 514 888
Fax	+44 1534 514 999
Contact	Hugh Morshead
Email	*hugh.morshead@henleyglobal.com*

Latvia

Henley & Partners Latvia Ltd
Gertrudes Street 10
Riga LV-1010
Latvia

Tel	+371 66 05 1009
Contact	Dr. Peter Krummenacher
Email	*peter.krummenacher@henleyglobal.com*

Lebanon

Henley & Partners Lebanon Ltd
1st Floor, Foch Street
Marfa'a 230, Beirut
Lebanon

Tel	+961 76 834 632
Contact	Marc Menard
EmaiI	*marc.menard@henleyglobal.com*

Malaysia

Representative Office
Q Sentral, Level 35-2 (East Wing)
2A, Jalan Stesen Sentral 2
KL Sentral, 50470 Kuala Lumpur
Malaysia

Tel	+603 2731 9340
Fax	+603 2731 9399
Contact	Dominic Volek
Email	*dominic.volek@henleyglobal.com*

Malta

Henley & Partners Malta Ltd
Aragon House
Dragonara Road
St. Julian's, STJ 3140
Malta

Tel	+356 2138 7400
Fax	+356 2138 6401
Contact	Stuart MacFeeters
Email	*stuart.macfeeters@henleyglobal.com*

Philippines

Representative Office
Unit 10A, Net Lima Tower
5th Avenue, corner 26th Street
Bonifacio Global City, Manila
Philippines

Tel	+632 669 2771
Fax	+632 651 5902
Contact	Dominic Volek
Email	*dominic.volek@henleyglobal.com*

Portugal

Henley & Partners Portugal Lda
Palácio Alagoas
Rua da Escola Politécnica 183A
1250-101 Lisboa
Portugal

Tel	+351 213 970 977
Fax	+351 213 970 982
Contact	Emi Silva
Email	*emi.silva@henleyglobal.com*

Russia/CIS

Representative Office of
Henley Estates International Ltd.
Sechenovsky pereulok, 6
Moscow
Russia

Tel	+7 495 774 1501
Fax	+7 495 769 9253
Contact	Mechislav Polozov
Email	*mechislav.polozov@henleyglobal.com*

Singapore

Henley & Partners Singapore Pte. Ltd
36 Robinson Road
City House, Level 14-06
Singapore 068877

Tel	+65 6438 7117
Fax	+65 6438 7227
Contact	Dr. Juerg Steffen
Email	*juerg.steffen@henleyglobal.com*

South Africa

Henley & Partners South Africa Ltd
4 Niblick Way
Fairways Office Park
9 Somerset West
South Africa 7130

Tel	+27 21 850 0524
Fax	+27 21 850 0596
Contact	Karolina Laubscher
Email	*karolina.laubscher@henleyglobal.com*

St. Kitts and Nevis

Henley & Partners Caribbean Ltd
Sugar Bay Club
Zenway Boulevard
P.O. Box 2505
Frigate Bay
St. Kitts, West Indies

Tel	+1 869 465 6220
Fax	+1 869 465 6221
Contact	Chanée Isaac
Email	*chanee.isaac@henleyglobal.com*

South Korea

Representative Office
B-2405 Mokdong Twinville
Mok 5 dong, Yangcheon-gu
Seoul
07988

Tel	+82 10 5147 2300
Fax	+82 10 5147 2301
Contact	Peter Lee
Email	*peter.lee@henleyglobal.com*

Switzerland

Henley & Partners Switzerland AG
Henley Haus
Klosbachstrasse 110
8024 Zurich
Switzerland

Tel	+41 44 266 22 22
Fax	+41 44 266 22 23
Contact	Dr. Peter Krummenacher
Email	*peter.krummenacher@henleyglobal.com*

Turkey

Henley & Partners Danismanlik Ltd Sirketi
Louis Vuitton Building
Abdi Ipekci Caddesi
Bostan Sokak No. 15, 5th Floor
Nisantasi, 34367
Istanbul

Tel	+90 212 373 9588
Contact	Hakan Cortelek
Email	*hakan.cortelek@henleyglobal.com*

United Kingdom

Henley & Partners UK Ltd
20 Grosvenor Place
London SW1X7HN
United Kingdom

Tel	+44 207 823 1010
Fax	+44 207 235 4489
Contact	Mark Pihlens
Email	*mark.pihlens@henleyglobal.com*

Vietnam

Henley & Partners Vietnam Ltd
Representative Office
Harbour View Tower
35 Nguyen Hue Boulevard
Ben Nghe Ward, Dist 1
Ho Chi Minh City
Vietnam

Tel	+848 3911 1667
Fax	+848 3911 1669
Contact	Sylvie Ma
Email	*sylvie.ma@henleyglobal.com*

Useful Websites – General

International Professional Associations

Investment Migration Council	*investmentmigration.org*
Society of Trust and Estate Practitioners	*step.org*
International Bar Association	*ibanet.org*
International Tax Planning Association	*itpa.org*
International Fiscal Association	*ifa.nl*

Country Information

Economist Intelligence Unit	*eiu.com*
Country Watch	*countrywatch.com*
CIA World Fact Book	*cia.gov/library/publications/the-world-factbook/*
Mercer Quality of Living Reports	*mercer.com/qualityofliving*
US State Department Travel Information	*travel.state.gov*
IATA Travel Centre Visa Information	*iata-travelcentre.com*
European Citizenship Laws	*http://eudo-citizenship.eu/national-citizenship-laws*
European Succession Laws	*successions-europe.eu*

International Organizations

World Bank	*worldbank.org*
International Monetary Fund	*imf.org*
OECD	*oecd.org*
Financial Action Task Force	*fatf-gafi.org*
European Commission	*ec.europa.eu*
CARICOM	*caricom.org*
EFTA	*efta.int*

Useful Websites – Countries

Antigua and Barbuda

Government	*ab.gov.ag*
Citizenship-by-Investment Unit	*cip.gov.ag*
Antigua and Barbuda Investment Authority	*investantiguabarbuda.org*

Austria

Federal Government	*help.gv.at*
Vienna Government	*wien.gv.at*
Austrian Business Agency	*investinaustria.at*

Belgium

Federal Government	*belgium.be*
Investment Agency	*business.belgium.be*
Foreign Affairs and Foreign Trade	*diplomatie.be*

Canada

Federal Government	*canada.gc.ca*
Federal Immigration and Citizenship	*cic.gc.ca*
Border Agency	*cbsa.gc.ca*
Quebec Immigration	*immigration-quebec.gouv.qc.ca*

Cyprus

Web-portal of the Republic of Cyprus	*cyprus.gov.cy*
Ministry of Interior	*moi.gov.cy*
Cyprus Investment Promotion Agency	*investcyprus.org.cy*

Dominica

Government	*dominica.gov.dm*
Citizenship-by-Investment Unit	*cbiu.gov.dm*
Invest Dominica	*investdominica.dm*

Guernsey

Government	*gov.gg*
Locate Guernsey	*locateguernsey.com*
Guernsey Finance	*guernseyfinance.com*

Grenada

Government	*gov.gd*
Citizenship-by-Investment Unit	*citizenship.gd*

Hong Kong

Government	*gov.hk*
Immigration Department	*immd.gov.hk*
Tax Authorities	*ird.gov.hk*
Trade and Industry Department	*tid.gov.hk*

Jersey

Government	*gov.je*
Locate Jersey	*locatejersey.com*
Jersey Finance	*jerseyfinance.je*
Jersey Business	*jerseybusiness*.je
Chamber of Commerce	*jerseychamber.com*

Malta

Government	*gov.mt*
Ministry of Finance	*finance.gov.mt*
Tax Authorities	*ird.gov.mt*
Malta Financial Services Authority	*mfsa.com.mt*
Finance Malta	*financemalta.org*
Malta Enterprise	*maltaenterprise.com*
Identity Malta	*identitymalta.com*

Monaco

Government	*gouv.mc*
Laws of Monaco	*legimonaco.mc*

Portugal

Government	*portugal.gov.pt*
Portugal Global – Trade & Investment Agency	*portugalglobal.pt*
Immigration and Borders Service	*sef.pt*

Singapore

Government	*gov.sg*
Economic Development Bureau	*edb.gov.sg*
Entering Singapore for Business	*sedb.com*
Monetary Authority	*mas.gov.sg*

St. Kitts and Nevis

Government	*gov.kn*
Citizenship-by-Investment Unit	*ciu.gov.kn*
Sugar Industry Diversification Foundation	*sidf.org*

Switzerland

Federal Government	*admin.ch*
Federal Office for Migration	*auslaender.ch*
Federal Tax Authorities	*estv.admin.ch*
Business and Investment Portal	*swissnetwork.com*
Switzerland Global Enterprise	*s-ge.com*

United Arab Emirates / Dubai

Federal Government	*government.ae/en*
Ministry of Foreign Affairs	*mofa.gov.ae/mofa_english*
Abu Dhabi Government	*abudhabi.ae/en*
Dubai Government	*dubai.ae*
Jeleb Ali Free Zone	*jafza.ae*
Dubai International Financial Center	*difc.ae*
Jumeirah Lakes Tower Free Zone	*dmcc.ae*

United Kingdom

Government	*direct.gov.uk*
Immigration Authorities	*ukba.homeoffice.gov.uk*
Foreign and Commonwealth Office	*fco.gov.uk*
Tax Authorities	*hmrc.gov.uk*

United States of America

Federal Government	*usa.gov*
Tax Authorities	*irs.gov*
Department of Homeland Security	*dhs.gov*
Transportation Security Administration	*tsa.gov*
U.S. Citizenship and Immigration Services	*uscis.gov*
Association to Invest in the USA	*iiusa.org*

List of Abbreviations

APEC	Asia-Pacific Economic Cooperation
ABTC	APEC Business Travel Card
ANZCERTA	Australia-New Zealand Closer Economic Relations Trade Agreement
CAD	Canadian Dollar
CARICOM	Caribbean Community
CGT	Capital Gains Tax
CHF	Swiss Franc
CIC	Citizenship and Immigration Canada
CIP	Citizenship-by-Investment Program
CIS	Commonwealth of Independent States
CIU	Citizenship-by-Investment Unit
CLN	Certificate of Loss of Nationality
CPF	Central Provident Fund
ECCB	Eastern Caribbean Central Bank
ECOWAS	Economic Community of West African States
EEA	European Economic Area
EFTA	European Free Trade Association
EU	European Union
EUR	Euro
FATF	Financial Action Task Force
FBAR	Foreign Bank Account Reporting
FIRPTA	Foreign Investment in Real Property Tax Act
FIS	Financial Investor Scheme (Singapore)
GBP	British Pound
GCC	Gulf Cooperation Council
GDP	Gross Domestic Product

GIP	Global Investor Program (Singapore)
HDI	UN Human Development Index
HKD	Hong Kong Dollar
HKSAR	Hong Kong Special Administrative Region
HNWI	High Net Worth Individual
HVRI	Henley & Partners Visa Restrictions Index
IATA	International Air Transport Association
ICA	Immigration and Checkpoints Authority (Singapore)
ICAO	International Civil Aviation Organization
IHT	Inheritance Tax
ILO	International Labor Organization
ILR	Indefinite Leave to Remain (United Kingdom)
IMF	International Monetary Fund
IOM	International Organization for Migration
IRA	Individual Retirement Account
IRS	Internal Revenue Service (US)
MAS	Monetary Authority of Singapore
MFSA	Malta Financial Services Authority
N/A	Not Applicable
NAFTA	North American Free Trade Association
NATO	North Atlantic Treaty Organization
NHR	Non-Habitual Resident(s)
NOR	Not Ordinarily Resident
OAS	Organization of American States
OECD	Organization for Economic Cooperation and Development
OECS	Organization of Eastern Caribbean States
PPLI	Private Placement Life Insurance
PR	Permanent Residence / Permanent Resident
PRC	People's Republic of China

RNOR	Resident but Not Ordinarily Resident
ROC	Republic of China (Taiwan)
ROR	Resident and Ordinarily Resident
SADC	South African Development Community
SEF	Servico de Estrangeiros e Fronteiras
SGD	Singapore Dollar
SME	Small and Medium-sized Enterprises
TIEA	Tax Information Exchange Agreements
TTTA	Trans-Tasman Travel Arrangement
UHNWI	Ultra High Net Worth Individual
UK	United Kingdom
UKBA	United Kingdom Border Agency
UN	United Nations
USD	United States Dollar
US	United States
USCIS	United States Citizenship and Immigration Services
VAT	Value Added Tax
WHO	World Health Organization
WTO	World Trade Organization
XCD	East Caribbean Dollar

Bibliography

Aleinikoff, Thomas A. / Klusmeyer, Douglas (eds): Citizenship Today: Global Perspectives and Practices, Washington DC, 2001

– id. – / Martin, David A. / Motomura, Hiroshi / Fullerton, Maryellen: Immigration and Citizenship Process and Policy, New York, 1995

Alesina, Alberto / Spolaore, Enrico: The Size of Nations, Massachusetts, 2003

Anholt, Simon: Brand New Justice: How Branding Places and Products Can Help the Developing World, Oxford, 2005

– id. – : Competitive Identity, Wales, 2007

– id. – : Places: Identity, Images and Reputation, Eastbourne, 2010

Aust, Anthony: Modern Treaty Law and Practice, Cambridge, 2007

Baker & McKenzie International: Immigration Manual, Hong Kong, 2006

Barrington, Lowell W.: 'The Making of Citizenship Policy in the Baltic States'. 1999 revised version of a paper presented at a meeting of the Carnegie Comparative Citizenship Project, Virginia, USA, June, 1998

Barry, Kim: 'Home and Away: The Construction of Citizenship in an Emigration Context' (2006) 81 New York University Law Review 11-59

Bauböck, Rainer / Ersbøll, Eva / Groenendijk, Kees / Waldrauch, Harald (eds): Acquisition and Loss of Nationality Volume I: Comparative Analyses, Amsterdam, 2006

– id. – / – id. – / – id. – / – id. – / (eds): Acquisition and Loss of Nationality Volume 2: Country Analyses Policies and Trends in 15 European Countries, Amsterdam, 2006

– id. – / Perchinig, Bernhard / Sievers, Wiebke: Citizenship Policies in the New Europe, Amsterdam, 2007

Bauman, Robert E.: The Passport Book, Florida, 2009

Betten, Rijkele: Income Tax Aspects of Emigration and Immigration of Individuals, Amsterdam, 1998

Blitz, Brad K. / Lynch, Maureen: Statelessness and Citizenship, Massachusetts, 2011

Bredbenner, Candice Lewis: A Nationality of Her Own: Women, Marriage and the Law of Citizenship, Berkeley / Los Angeles, 1998

Brown, Jan H.: Dual Citizenship: Living on Both Sides of the Global Fence, New York, 2009

Brubaker, Rogers: Citizenship and Nationhood in France and Germany, New York, 1992

Brubaker, Rogers: Immigration and the Politics of Citizenship in Europe and North America, 1989

Brubaker, Rogers: Nationalism Reframed, London, 1996

Cairn, Alan C. / Courtney, John C. / MacKinnon, Peter / Michelmann, Hans J. / Smith, David E. (eds): Citizenship, Diversity, and Pluralism: Canadian and Comparative Perspectives, Montreal, 2010

Calder, Gideon / Cole, Phillip / Seglow, Jonathan (eds): Citizenship Acquisition and National Belonging: Migration, Membership and the Liberal Democratic State, Basingstoke, 2010

Caplan, Jane / Torpey, John (eds): Documenting Individual Identity, London, 2001

Denza, Eileen: Diplomatic Law, Oxford, 1998

Dzankic, Jelena: The Pros and Cons of Ius Pecuniae: Investor Citizenship in Comparative Perspective, San Domenico di Fiesole, 2012

Dufoix, Stéphane: 'Un pont par-dessus la porte, extraterritorialisation et transétatisation des identifications nationales', in Dufoix Stéphane, Guerassimoff Carine, de Tinguy Anne, Loin des yeux, près du cœur, Les États et leurs expatriés, Paris, 2010

Ernst & Young: The Global Executive, London, 2010

Evans, P.C.H. / Evans, S. / Honychurch, Lennox: Dominica: Nature Island of the Caribbean, Hertford, 1989

Fahrmeir, Andreas: Citizens and Aliens: Foreigners and the Law in Britain and the German States 1789-1870, London / New York, 2000

– id. – / Faron, Olivier / Weil, Patrick (eds): Migration Control in the North Atlantic World, London 2005

Feltham, Ralph G.: Diplomatic Handbook, Amsterdam, 2004

FitzGerald, David: 'Rethinking Emigrant Citizenship', (2006) 81 New York University Law Review, 90-116

Fransman, Laurie: Fransman's British Nationality Law, London, 2011

Frey, Linda S. / Frey, Marsha L.: The History of Diplomatic Immunity, New York, 1999

Grewal, David: Network Power: The Social Dynamics of Globalization, New Haven, 2009

Grundy, Milton: International Tax Planning Association: Retirement in Europe: The Tax Aspect, London, 2006

– id. – : International Tax Planning Association: Retirement in the Caribbean: The Tax Aspect, London, 2006

– id. – : International Tax Planning Association: Ten Retirement Destinations: The Tax Aspect, Jersey, 2007

Hailbronner, Kay / Renner, Günter / Maassen, Hans-Georg: Staatsangehörigkeitsrecht, München, 2010

Hansen, Randall: 'A European citizenship or a Europe of citizens? Third country nationals in the EU' (1998) 24(4) Journal of Ethnic and Migration Studies, 751-768

– id. – : Towards a European Nationality: Citizenship, Immigration and Nationality Law in the EU, New York, 2001

– id. – / Weil, Patrick (eds): Dual Nationality, Social Rights and Federal Citizenship in the USA and Europe, London, 2002

Hokema, Tido Oliver: Mehrfache Staatsangehörigkeit. Eine Betrachtung aus völkerrechtlicher und verfassungsrechtlicher Sicht, Frankfurt am Main, 2002

Honychurch, Lennox: Dominica: Isle of Adventure, London, 1992

Israel, Ron: Global Citizenship, Lexington, 2012

Jones-Correa, Michael: Dual Nationality in Latin America and its Consequences for Naturalization in the United States, in Hailbronner Kay / Martin David A. (eds), Rights and Duties of Dual Nationals, Amsterdam, 2003

Joppke, Christian: Citizenship and Immigration, Cambridge, 2010

Kälin, Christian H.: Internationales Immobilienhandbuch, 3rd Edition, Zurich, 2011

– id. – : Ius Doni, Zurich, 2016

– id. – : Switzerland Business & Investment Handbook, 3rd Edition, Zurich, 2011

– id. – / Taylor, Andrew J.: International Real Estate Handbook, 5th Edition, London, Zurich, Hong Kong, 2015

Kessler, James: Taxation of Non-Residents and Foreign Domiciliaries 2012-13, Oxford, 2012

Khoja, Sara: The European Union: An Area of Freedom, Justice and Security – But for Whom? An Examination of the Legal Status and Rights of Third Country Nationals within the European Union and their Possible Acquisition of European Union Citizenship, Berlin, 2005

Klaaren, Jonathan: 'Post-Apartheid Citizenship in South Africa', Aleinikoff Thomas A. / Klusmeyer D. (eds), From Migrants to Citizens: Membership in a Changing World, Washington DC, 2000, 221-252

Klusmeyer, Douglas B.: Between Consent and Descent: Conceptions of Democratic Citizenship, Washington DC, 1996

– id. – . / Aleinikoff, Thomas A.: Citizenship Policies for an Age of Migration, Washington DC, 2002

Knop, Karen: 'Relational Nationality: On Gender and Nationality in International Law', in Aleinikoff Thomas and Klusmeyer, Douglas (eds), Citizenship Today: Global Perspectives and Practices, Washington DC, 2001, 89-124

Langer, Marshall J: The Tax Exile Report, Cornwall, 1998

Lenz, Carl Otto / Borchardt, Klaus-Dieter: EU-Verträge – Kommentar nach dem Vertrag von Lissabon, Köln / Wien, 2010

Lloyd, Martin: The Passport: The History of Man's Most Travelled Document, Stroud, 2005

Lowe, Vaughan: International Law, Oxford, 2007

Lowe, Vaughan: Diplomatic Protection, Oxford, 2008

Magnette, Paul: Citizenship: The History of an Idea, Colchester, 2005

Mautino, Robert A. / Endelman, Gary: Nationality and Citizenship Handbook, Los Angeles, 1997

Meloni, Annalisa: Visa Policy within the European Union Structure, Heidelberg, 2006

Mercer: 2012 Quality of Living Worldwide City Rankings – Mercer Survey, New York, 2012

Miller, David: Citizenship and National Identity, Cambridge, 2009

Mussger-Fessler-Szymanski: Österreichisches Staatsbürgerschaftsrecht, Wien, 1999

Nascimbene, Bruno (ed): Nationality Laws in the European Union, Milan, 1996

Nevile, Ann: Human Rights and Social Policy: A Comparative Analysis of Values and Citizenship in OECD Countries, Cheltenham, 2010

OECD: International Migration Outlook 2013, Paris 2013

Ong, Ahiwa: Flexible Citizenship: The Cultural Logic of Transnationality, Durham, 1999

Orentlicher, Diane F.: 'Citizenship and National Identity', in David Wippman (ed), International Law and Ethnic Conflict, Ithaca and London, 1998, 296-325

Pastore, Ferrucio: 'A Community Out of Balance: Nationality Law and Migration Politics in the History of Post-Unification Italy', (2004) 9 Journal of Modern Italian Studies, 27-48

PKF: Worldwide Tax Guide, PKF Network, 2013

Salter, Mark B.: Rights of Passage: The Passport in International Relations, London, 2003

Saunders, Roy: The Peripatetic Resident – The ITPA Green Book 2010-2011, London, 2010

Schuck, Peter H. / Smith, Rogers M.: Citizenship without Consent: The Illegal Alien in American Polity, New Haven, 1985

Seddon, Duran: Immigration and Nationality Refugee Law, London, 2006

Soysal, Yasemin U.: Limits of Citizenship: Migrants and Postnational Membership in Europe, Chicago and London, 1994

Steiner, Niklaus: International Migration and Citizenship Today, Oxon, 2009

STEP Directory and Yearbook 2015: Jurisdictional Information and Step Branch Members, London, 2014

Stiller, Martin: Eine Völkerrechtsgeschichte der Staatenlosigkeit. Dargestellt anhand ausgewählter Beispiele aus Europa, Russland und den USA, Wien, 2011

Stool-Davey, Camille: Assessing the Playing Field, London, 2007

Thomas, Yan: Le droit d'origine à Rome: contributions à l'étude de la citoyenneté, (1995) 84(2) RCDIP, 253-90

– id. – : 'Origine et "Commune Patrie": étude de droit public romain' (89 av. J.-C.-212 ap. J.-C.). Collection de l'École française de Rome, vol. 221, Rome, 1996

Torpey, John: The Invention of the Passport, Cambridge, 2000

Trachtman, Joel P.: The International Law of Economic Migration: Toward the Fourth Freedom, Berkeley, 2009

United Nations Development Program: Overcoming Barriers: Human Mobility and Development, New York, 2008

Vertovec, Steven / Cohen Robin: Conceiving Cosmopolitanism: Theory, Context, and Practice, New York, 2008

Wallerstein, Immanuel: The Modern World System I, New York, 1974

Watson, Alan: Legal Transplants: An Approach to Comparative Law, Edinburgh, 1974

Weil, Patrick: 'Nationalities and Citizenships: The Lessons of the French Experience for Germany and Europe', in Ceserani David / Fulbrook Mary (eds), Citizenship, Nationality and Migration in Europe, London, 1996, 74-87

– id. – : The State Matters: Immigration Control in Developed Countries, New York, 1998

– id. – : Qu'est-ce qu'un francais?, Paris, 2002

– id. – / Hansen, Randall: Dual Nationality, Social Rights and Federal Citizenship in the USA and Europe, Oxford, 2005

– id. – : A la frontière de l'inégalité entre genres et des politiques d'immigration: la situation de la femme mariée à un homme d'une autre nationalité. Une comparaison internationale (19ᵉᵐᵉ–20ᵉᵐᵉ siècles), in Kastoryano Riva, les codes de la différence, religions races et origines (France, Etats-Unis, Allemagne), Paris, 2005

– id. – : How to be French? A Nationality in the Making since 1789, (translated by Porter, Catherine), Durham, 2008

– id. – : 'The New Strategic Link between the Citizen and the Nation-state in a Globalized World', I CON (2011)

Weiss, André: Traité Théorique et pratique de droit international privé, Tome premier: la nationalité, Paris, 1907

Wiessner, Siegfried: Die Funktion der Staatsangehörigkeit, Tübingen, 1989

Zolberg, Aristide R.: International Migration Policies in a Changing World System, in: McNeill, William H. / Adams Ruth J. (eds), Human Migration: Patterns and Policies, Bloomington, 1978, 241-286

Zureik, Elia / Salter, Mark B.: Global Surveillance and Policing, Devon and Portland, 2005

Index

accommodation/housing *see also* **real estate, acquisition of**
availability of accommodation 13
Belgium 222
domicile 12
double tax treaties 19
Germany 12
Guernsey 250–4
Jersey 281–3, 286
main family home, location of 12
Monaco 315, 317
Sweden 12
tax residence 16, 28, 30
advance passenger information and advance approval 151
advertising campaigns 81–2
Afghanistan 149, 166, 168
agents
Antigua and Barbuda 472
commission 45
Grenada 506, 507
Malta 518
real estate, acquisition of 39, 45
St Lucia 541
agricultural property 41
Albania 135, 148, 164
Allais, Maurice 80
American Revolution 103
ancestry/descent, citizenship by (*ius sanguinis***)** 48, 54–6, 100, 103–4
Croatia 56
dual citizenship 56
EU 56
flexibility 104
Grenada 508
Malta 307
Monaco 319
nationality 56, 104
Portugal 342
statelessness 104
Switzerland 372
United Kingdom 416
United States 56, 67, 430
Ancient Greece 103
Andean Community 108, 123

Anholt-GfK Roper City Brands Index 90–4
Anholt-GfK Roper Nation Brands Index (NBI) 76, 82–95
Antigua and Barbuda, citizenship-by-investment in 48, 438, 467–77
advantages 475
agents 472
airport expansion project 469
background 468
business and corporate tax 474
Business Investments 451
capital gains tax (CGT) 469
changes to programs 475
Citizen-by-Investment Unit (CIU) 472–3
climate 476
Commonwealth 468, 475
comparison table 450, 454, 456, 458, 460, 462, 464
criminal records 471
day counting and time spent in country 473–4
debt restructuring 468
dependents 439, 470–1
documentation 472–3, 475
dual citizenship 474
due diligence 439–40, 470, 472
economy 468–70
embassies, consular offices or High Commissions, attendance at 473
employment 468
estate tax 469
EU, visa waiver agreement with 475
families 439–49, 470–1
fees 439–40, 470–1, 473
financial services 468
general information 476
Global Citizenship Program Index (GCPI) 466
grant of citizenship 473–4
Henley & Partners 57, 149, 440, 469
income tax 469, 474
international organizations, membership of 469

interviews 472
legal basis 469–70
National Development Fund (NDF),
    contributions to 173–4, 439, 451,
    470–1, 473
National Economic and Social
    Transformation Plan 468
natural attractions 468
parents and grandparents 471
passports 440, 469, 473–4, 475
political system 468
procedures 472–3
property tax 475
real estate option 173–4, 450, 472–3,
    475
reporting 471
requirements/conditions 439–40,
    450–1, 470
sales tax (ABST) 474–5
Schengen area 475
security risks 471
spouses and families 439–40, 470–1
tax 469, 474–5
time frames 440, 472–3
tourism 468, 469
United Kingdom 468, 475
United States 469
visa-free travel 440, 448, 469
    comparison table 454, 458, 460,
        462, 464
    criminal records 471
Visa Restrictions Index (Henley &
    Partners) 149, 440
visa waiver agreement with EU 475
apartments 46
Arab League 164
Argentina 82, 163
ASEAN 164
Asia, quality of nationality in 164–5
**Asia-Pacific Economic Cooperation
(APEC)** 122–3
    APEC Business Travel Card (ABTC)
        scheme 123
    freedom of movement 108, 122–3
    member states, list of 123
asset protection 35, 43
Australia 191–202
    advantages and disadvantages 200

Australia embassies or consulates,
    applications at 196
background 193
birth, citizenship by (*ius soli*) 199
Business Innovation Stream 195
Business Talent (Significant Business
    History Stream) 196
Business Talent (Venture Capital
    Entrepreneur Stream) 196
Canberra 193
capital gains tax (CGT) 198, 199
cities 193
citizenship 199–200
civil liberties 193
climate 202
corporate taxes 198
Department of Immigration 196
documentation 195
double tax treaties 198
dual citizenship 200
economy 193
employment 194, 197
family law 198–9
family permanent residence 194
general information 201
goods and services tax (GST) 198
health 193, 194
Hong Kong, persons from 6
humanitarian residence 194
identity and brand of nations 82
immigration system 193
income tax 197
inheritance and succession 198–9
inheritance tax 198, 199
international organizations,
    membership of 193
intestacy 199
Investor Stream 195
Melbourne 193
Migration Act and Migration
    Regulations 193
nationality, quality of 163, 169
naturalization 56
New Zealand 136, 193
online portal 197
parents and grandparents 199
passports
    citizenship 199

electronic attachment of visas 197
permanent residence 193, 194–6
political rights 193
priority processing 196
procedures 196–7
public interest 194
quality of life/standard of living 193
requirements/conditions 194–6
residence 178–9
    citizenship 199
    family permanent 194
    humanitarian residence 194
    permanent 193, 194
    skilled permanent 194
    special eligibility 194
    temporary 193
same-sex relationships 199
Service Standards online 197
Significant Investor Stream 195
skilled - company sponsored 195
skilled - independent 194–5
skilled – investment/entrepreneurial
    195
skilled permanent residence 194
special eligibility residence 194
sub-classes of visas 194
Sydney 193
tax 197–8
temporary visas 193, 195
time frames 196–7
Trans-Tasman Travel Arrangement
    (TTTA)
visas 136, 193–6
    refusal 194
    requirements 194–6
    sub-classes 194
voting, compulsory 199
Austria 203–15 *see also* **Austria,**
    citizenship-by-investment in
advantages and disadvantages 212–13
Austrian consulates or embassies,
    applications at 206, 209
background 205
birth, citizenship by (*ius soli*) 211
capital gains tax 209–10
children 207, 211, 440, 482
citizenship 205, 211–12
climate 215, 486

controlled foreign corporation (CFC)
    rules 210
corporations, tax on 210
criminal records 208, 481
culture 205
dependents 208, 482–3
documentation 208–9
double tax treaties 210
dual citizenship 212
economy 205, 212
EEA 208
employment 206–8
EU 208
exceptional benefits 205, 212
exchange controls 210
families 206, 207–8, 210–11, 440, 482
    children 207, 211, 440, 482
    family law 210–11
    parents and grandparents 194, 211
    spouses and partners 207–8, 211,
      440
financially independent persons 209
general information 214
gift tax 209
Highly Skilled Category 206–7
illegitimate children 211
immigration laws 205
income tax 209–10
inheritance and succession 210–11
inheritance tax 209
Integration Agreement 207–9
intestacy 211
investments 205
language 208, 211
matrimonial property regime
    Community of Property 211
    Separation of Property 211
nationality, quality of 173
natural attractions 205
parents and grandparents 194, 211
permanent residence 207–8
private residence category 205, 208
procedure 209
quality of life/standard of living 205
quotas 205, 209
registration certificates 208
relinquishment of citizenship 212
residence 178, 179, 206–9, 437
    citizenship 211

duration 211
Global Residence Program Index
    (GRPI) 2016 188
permits 205–9
procedures 209
requirements/conditions 208
time frames 209
types of permits 206–9
Schengen area 117, 205
self-employed 206, 207, 210
settlement permits 209
spouses and partners 207–8, 211, 440
students 206, 207
tax 209–10
time frames 209
translations 208
trusts 210
Vienna 205
visas 205–6, 209
    visa-free travel 205
    visa-waiver program 206
wealth or net-worth tax 209
wills and testaments 211
Austria, citizenship-by-investment in
48, 57, 438, 479–86
advantages 483–4
ceremonies 483
climate 486
comparison table 451, 454, 456, 458,
    460, 462, 464
criminal records 481
culture 481
dual citizenship 483
economy 440, 481
EEA/EFTA 484
EU 440, 481, 484
expert advice 482
extraordinary scientific, cultural or
    economic benefits 440, 481
families 482
fees 440, 482
general information 485
grant of citizenship 482, 483
language 440, 482
legal basis 481
nationality, quality of 173
natural attractions 481
passports 440, 481, 482, 483
procedures 482

publicity 482
quality of life/standard of living 481
requirements/conditions 440, 451,
    481–2
reputation 481
residence 483
Switzerland 440, 484
tax 483
time frames 440, 482
Vienna 481
visa-free travel 440, 448, 454, 456,
    458, 460, 462, 464
Visa Restrictions Index (Henley &
    Partners) 483
Bahamas 34, 56
banking
accounts, transferring 12
citizenship planning 60
Cyprus 488–9
Germany, government access to
    accounts in 7
Malaysia 295–6
privacy 7
Thailand 380–1
Belgium 217–29
accommodation 222
accounts 225
advantages and disadvantages 227
Antwerp 219
background 219
Belgian embassies or consulates,
    applications at 222
birth, citizenship by (*ius soli*) 226–7
Brussels-Capital Region 219
capital gains tax 224–5
children 222
citizenship 116–17
climate 229
common property law regime 226
corporations 221–2, 225
criminal records 223
culture 219–20
diamond trade 219
divorce 226
documentation 223
double tax treaties 219, 225
dual citizenship 227
economy 219
education and schools 219

EFTA 220
employment 220–4
entrepreneurs 221
EU 219, 220
families
    children 222
    family law 226
    parents and grandparents 227
    reunification 222
    spouses and partners 222
Federal Public Service Economy (FPS
    Economy) 223
Flemish Region 219
forced heirship 226
general information 228
gift tax 225
habitual residence 226
headquarters, as EU 219
health 219, 222, 223
highly-skilled persons 221, 223
holding structures 221, 224
income tax 224
inheritance and succession 226
inheritance tax 225
integration 220
investments 221
language 220
managerial functions, persons with
    221, 222–3
matrimonial property regime 226
nuptial agreements 226
parents and grandparents 227
professional cards 223
province and municipalities 219
quality of life/standard of living 219–20
residence 178, 180, 220–4
    citizenship 227
    duration 220, 223, 227
    Global Residence Program Index
        (GRPI) 2016 188
    permits 220, 222–4, 227
    procedures 223–4
    requirements/conditions 222–3
    tax 28
    time frames 220, 222, 223–4
Schengen area 117, 220
self-employed 220, 221–2, 223
spouses and partners 222, 226
tax 219, 221–2, 224–5

expatriate status 224
    haven, as 224
    residence 28
time frames 222
Visa Restrictions Index (Henley &
    Partners) 148
visas 148, 220, 222, 223–4
Walloon Region 219
wealth or net worth tax 224
wills or testaments 226
withholding tax 225
work permits 220, 221–2, 223
Belize 437
biometric passports
    Cyprus 491
    EU 135
    privacy 134
    St Kitts and Nevis 530
    United Kingdom 411
    visa-free entry 135
birth, citizenship by (*ius soli*) 54–5, 100,
    103, 104–5
    Australia 199
    Austria 211
    Belgium 226–7
    birth tourism 55
    Canada 244
    diplomats or officials, children of 105
    Grenada 508
    Hong Kong 272
    Ireland 104–5
    Malta 307
    Monaco 319
    residence for certain periods of time
        55, 104
    Singapore 357
    United Kingdom 416
    United States 48, 55, 67, 104, 430
blackmail 59–60
Bolivia 148
Bosnia 135, 148
branding *see* **cities, identity and brand
    of; identity and brand of nations**
Brazil
    domicile of origin 10
    Grenada 505, 509
    identity and brand of nations 82
    nationality, quality of 171
    St Kitts and Nevis 532

United States 171
visas 171
bribery, passports obtained by 59–60
BRICs (Brazil, Russia, India, China)
164
Bulgaria 59, 115–18, 122, 170, 437
Canada 231–46
advantages and disadvantages 244
APEC Business Travel Card (ABTC)
scheme 123
background 233
birth, citizenship by (*ius soli*) 244
Canadian embassies or consulates,
applications at 240
Canadian Experience Class 235
capital gains tax 241–2
Charter of Rights and Freedoms 234
cities 233
citizenship 242–4
climate 246
corporations, tax on 241
criminal records 235
culture 233
departure tax 242
dependents 235
double tax treaties 242
dual citizenship 244
economy 239
education and schools 233
educational level 236
employment 235, 237, 241
families
Family Class Sponsorship 235,
239–40
family law 242
spouses and partners 237–8, 241
Federal Immigrant Investor Venture
Capital Pilot Program 235, 239
Federal Skilled Trades Program
(FSTP) 234, 237
Federal Skilled Worker Program
(FSWP) 234, 236
Federal Start-Up Visa Program 235,
239
general information 245
gift tax 241
health 235, 240
Hong Kong, persons from 6
identity and brand of nations 82

immigration trusts 241–2
income tax 233, 241–2, 243
inheritance and succession 242
inheritance tax 241, 242
integration 236
job creation 235, 239
languages 233, 236, 243
matrimonial property regime 242
multiculturalism 233–4
NAFTA 233
nationality, quality of 163, 169
naturalization 56
procedures 240
Provincial Nominee Programs 235,
239
quality of life/standard of living 233
Quebec 234–7
Quebec Investor and Entrepreneur
Category 235, 238
Quebec Skilled Workers Program
234, 236–7
quotas 237
real estate, acquisition of 20–1
residence 178, 180, 234–40, 437
duration of residence 243
permanent 234, 243
procedures 240
requirements/conditions 235–40
time frames 240
security risks 235
self-employed 241
Singapore 357
spouses and partners 237–8, 241–2
St Kitts and Nevis 526
Switzerland 367
tax 7, 233, 241–2, 243
time frames 240
time zones 233
United States 233
wealth tax 241
Cape Verde 437
capital gains, tax on
Australia 198, 199
Austria 209–10
Belgium 224–5
Canada 241–2
Cyprus 491, 492
Guernsey 249
Malaysia 296

Malta 305–6, 519–20
Portugal 340–1
real estate, acquisition of 43, 45–6
Singapore 356
St Lucia 542
Switzerland 370
United Kingdom 411–12
United States 70, 72
CARICOM (Caribbean Community)
108, 124
Caribbean Free Trade Association
(CARIFTA) 124
CARIPASS (Regional Travel Card
system) 124
freedom of movement 108, 124
members, list of 124
nationality, quality of 173
passports 124
cash planning 34
caveat emptor 44, 58–9
celebrities 77
change of residence
bank accounts, transferring 12
businesses, moving 12
cancellation of licences and
membership 12
difficulties 11
domicile 12, 15–16
electoral register, amending the 12
factors to take into consideration 12–13
habitual residence 11–12
hard factors 13
inheritance tax 11–12
intention 12
matrimonial property regime 11–12
soft factors 13
tax residence 11–13
Chastanet, Allan 537
children *see also* **education and schools**
Austria 207, 211, 440, 482
Belgium 222
citizenship planning 55
diplomats or officials 105
Dominica 442–3, 498–9
EU 113
Hong Kong 267
Jersey 283
Malaysia 293–4, 295, 297
Malta 306, 444, 516–17

Monaco 317
New Zealand 325–6, 329
passports 130, 134, 136
Portugal 341–3
real estate holding structures 43
residence planning 18, 27, 43
Singapore 349, 351, 353
St Kitts and Nevis 446, 528
Switzerland 372
Thailand 381
United Arab Emirates/Dubai 391
United Kingdom 409, 415
United States 67
Chile 163
China
Closer Economic Partnership
Agreement (CEPA) 263
France 50
Grenada 443, 505, 509
Hong Kong 6, 51, 138, 263–4,
268–70, 272–3
identity and brand of nations 82
nationality, quality of 164
Singapore 357
United Kingdom 50
United States 427
World Trade Organization 263
cities
Anholt-GfK Roper City Brands
Index 90–4
Australia 193
Austria 205, 481
Belgium 219
Canada 233
City Brands Hexagon 91–4
culture 90–1
government 90, 94–6
Grenada 505
Guernsey 249
identity and brand 90–4
language 91
Malta 303
measurement of images 90–4
place 76, 91, 93
people 76, 91, 93–4
Portugal 335
potential 76, 91–2, 93–4
presence 76, 91, 93
prerequisites 76, 91, 93

pulse 76, 91, 93–4
reputation 76–80
science 91
St Lucia 537
status and standing 91, 94
Switzerland 363
tourism 90
United Kingdom 403, 404
citizenship 14, 99–106 *see also* **ancestry/
descent, citizenship by (*ius
sanguinis*); birth, citizenship by (*ius
soli*); dual citizenship; citizenship-
by-investment; citizenship
planning; dual citizenship**
American Revolution 103
ancestry/descent, citizenship by (*ius
sanguinis*) 100, 103–4
Ancient Greece 103
Australia 199–200
Austria 205, 211–12
automatic acquisition 104
Belgium 116–17
birth, citizenship by (*ius soli*) 100, 103,
104–5
Canada 242–3
case law 101–2
checklist 25–6
civil status, change in 104
customary international law 102
definition 100–1
domicile 9
double tax treaties 32–3
exceptional means, acquisition by 105
extraordinary achievements, persons
with 102
France 17, 103
freedom of states 101–2
French Revolution 103
Global Residence Program Index
(GRPI) 2016 188
Guernsey 257
Hong Kong 271–3
Jersey 288
legal status 101
Malaysia 297–8
Malta 307
marriage, citizenship by (*ius
matrimonii*) 48, 54, 67, 100, 103,
105, 319, 342–3

military/national service 100–1, 106
Monaco 319
multiple citizenship 6
nationality 100–4, 106
definition 100–1
differences from citizenship 101
quality 161
state succession 103
Universal Declaration of Human
Rights 103
naturalization 100, 103, 105
collective 105
conditions 100
integration factors 105
language 105
marriage 105
residence, length of 105
Netherlands 16
New Zealand 329
parents and grandparents 55–6, 104
passports 130, 132–3, 135
Portugal 336, 342–3
renunciation 100, 105–6
Roman law 103
Singapore 357
sportspersons 102
St Lucia 447, 540–1, 543
state, relationship with 101, 102–3
statelessness 100, 102–3
statutory law 101–2
Switzerland 372
taxation
citizenship 16–17
residence 26
Thailand 380, 384
United Arab Emirates (UAE)/Dubai
398
United Kingdom 416–17
United States 16, 64, 65, 430
Universal Declaration of Human
Rights 100, 103
citizenship-by-investment 437–9 *see also*
**Antigua and Barbuda, citizenship-
by-investment in; Austria,
citizenship-by-investment in;
Cyprus, citizenship-by-investment
in; Dominica, citizenship-
by-investment in; Grenada,
citizenship-by-investment in;**

Malta, citizenship-by-investment in; St Kitts and Nevis, citizenship-by-investment in; St Lucia, citizenship-by-investment in
Belize 437
Bulgaria 59, 437
Cape Verde 437
CARICOM 173
caveat emptor 58–9
Comoros 174
comparison table 448–65
Cyprus 149
due diligence 57
Global Citizenship Program Index (GCPI) 466
honorary citizenship 58
Iceland 58
Ireland 437
Malta 149
Montenegro 174
nationality, quality of 158, 161, 168–9, 171–4
naturalization 171
passports for non-citizens 58
reputation of services companies 59
second passports, importance of 437
security 58
Seychelles 174
Slovakia 437
statelessness 54
United States 67
Visa Restrictions Index (Henley & Partners) 149
citizenship planning 47–62
ancestry/descent, citizenship by (*ius sanguinis*) 48, 54, 55–6
banking and business environment 60
benefits of alternative citizenship 48–54
birth, citizenship by (*ius soli*) 48, 54, 55
birth tourism 55
blackmail 59–60
bribery, passports obtained by 59–60
caveat emptor 58–9
children 55
citizenship-by-investment programs 48, 54, 57–9
corruption 59–60

criteria when acquiring citizenship 59–62
cyber-crime 53
data abuse 53
diversification 52
domicile 51, 54
dual citizenship 48, 56–7, 60–2
economy 49, 53, 60
EU 50–1, 112–13
families 52, 55
flexibility 48–9, 52
freedom of movement 49, 109
frequent travellers 48
grant, citizenship by 48
Henley & Partners, concept created by 48–9
identity and brand of nations 82, 84, 89, 95
identity theft 53
illegal means, passports obtained by 59–60
income tax on non-residents 50
investors 52
kidnappings 52–3
languages 60
legal advisors 58
location of country 60
marriage, citizenship by 48, 54
Middle East, political upheaval in the 53
military service 54
multiple nationalities 52–4, 56
nationality, threats arising from 49
naturalization 54–5, 56–8
non-citizens, passports for 58, 60
organized crime 53
passports 48–53, 59–60
political circumstances 49–50, 52–3, 60
privacy 48, 56
reasons for becoming citizen of more than one country 49–52
recognition of passports 58, 60
regulations in selected countries, overview of 60–2
reputation 48
residence 50–1, 54–5
Schengen area 50
second citizenship 48–62

obtaining 54–62
persons interested in 52–4
security 48, 53, 56–8
September 11, 2001, terrorist attacks
on US 49
statelessness 54
tax 48, 50–1, 54
domicile 50, 54
planning 48, 50–1
residence 50, 54
United States, taxation of
non-residents in 50
terrorism 49, 52–3
tie-breaker rules in double tax treaties
51
trade sanctions 49
violence 49, 52–3
visas
procedure 50
restrictions 49
Schengen area 50
visa-free travel 48, 50, 53, 60
clichés and stereotypes of nations 79–80
climate
Antigua and Barbuda 476
Australia 202
Austria 215, 486
Belgium 229
Canada 246
Cyprus 488, 494
Dominica 497, 502
Grenada 512
Guernsey 260
Hong Kong 275
identity and brand of nations 76–7,
91, 95
Jersey 280, 290
Malaysia 300
Malta 310, 466, 515, 522
Monaco 322
New Zealand 332
Portugal 188
Singapore 349, 360
St Kitts and Nevis 525, 534
St Lucia 537, 545
Switzerland 375
Thailand 379, 386
United Arab Emirates (UAE)/Dubai
400

United Kingdom 420
United States 433
Clinton, Bill 73
Colombia 148
Colombus, Christopher 467, 525
colonialism
Grenada 505
Hong Kong 263
Malta 315
Portugal 335
St Lucia 537
United Kingdom 403, 505
Commonwealth
Antigua and Barbuda 468, 475
domicile 10
Dominica 497, 500
Grenada 505
St Lucia 537, 543
United Kingdom 416
**Commonwealth of Independent States
(CIS)** 108, 124–5
freedom of movement 108, 124–5
members, list of 125
nationality, quality of 161, 164
communications, access to 42
Comoros 174
companies *see* **corporations;**
corporations, tax on
construction projects 39–40
consumer power 95
corporations *see also* **corporations, tax
on**
Austria 210
Belgium 221–2
Cyprus 489, 491–2
real estate holding structures 42–3
structures 19
Switzerland 363
United Arab Emirates (UAE)/Dubai
392–7
corporations, tax on
Antigua and Barbuda 474
Australia 198
Austria 210
Belgium 225
Cyprus 491–2
Grenada 509
Guernsey 255
Jersey 287

Malta 306, 520
New Zealand 328
Portugal 341
Singapore 356
St Kitts and Nevis 531
St Lucia 542
Switzerland 370
Thailand 383
corruption 59–60, 95
criminal records
    Antigua and Barbuda 471
    Austria 208, 481
    Belgium 223
    Canada 235
    Cyprus 441, 490
    Dominica 499
    EU 115
    Hong Kong 267
    Malaysia 297
    Malta 445, 517
    Monaco 315
    Portugal 338, 342–3
    St Kitts and Nevis 528–9
    St Lucia 540
    Thailand 380
    United Kingdom 409, 411
    United States 426
Croatia 28, 56, 115–18, 122, 168, 170, 364
culture
    Austria 205, 481
    Belgium 219–20
    Canada 233
    checklist 24
    cities, identity and brand of 90–1
    Grenada 505
    identity and brand of nations 76–7, 82, 83, 85–6, 89
    Jersey 282
    Malaysia 293, 297
    Malta 515
    Portugal 188, 335, 337
    quality of life/standard of living 83
    Singapore 349
    Switzerland 363, 372
    Thailand 379
    United Arab Emirates (UAE)/Dubai 390
    United Kingdom 404

United States 423
customary international law 102, 136
cyber-crime 53
Cyprus, citizenship-by-investment in 48, 57, 438, 487–94
    advantages 492
    background 488
    banks
        deposits 489
        restructuring of 488
    biometric passports 491
    capital gains, tax on 491, 492
    Citizenship Certificate 490–1
    climate 488, 494
    Collective Investment Scheme 441, 490
    comparison table 450, 454, 456, 458, 460, 462, 464
    corporations 489, 491–2
        notional interest deductions 492
        tax 491–2
    criminal records 441, 490
    Defence Contribution 491–2
    documentation 490
    double tax treaties 488
    dual citizenship 491
    Eastern Europe, connections with 488
    economy 441, 488–9
    employment 488, 492
    EU 441–2, 492
    extraordinary contributions 489
    families 441, 490
    freezing or confiscation orders 441, 490
    general information 493
    gift tax 491
    Global Citizenship Program Index (GCPI) 466
    grant of citizenship 490–1
    income tax 491
    inheritance tax 491
    interviews 490
    legal basis 488
    Middle East, connections with 488
    nationality, quality of 170, 173
    natural attractions 488
    naturalization 441, 489
    non-domiciled (Non Dom) status 492
    passports 491

procedures 490
real estate, acquisition of 173, 441–2,
    489, 490, 492
requirements/conditions 441–2, 450,
    489
retirees 488
revision 441, 489
Scheme for Naturalisation of
    Investors in Cyprus 441
Schengen area 117–18
tax 488, 491–2
time frames 490, 492
tourism 488
visa-free travel 448, 454, 456, 458,
    460, 462, 464
Visa Restrictions Index (Henley &
    Partners) 149
wealth tax 491
withholding tax 488
World Economic Forum. Global
    Competitiveness Index 2015-16
    488
Czech Republic 117–18, 148
dampness 41
data abuse 53
Data Protection Directive 121
day counting and time spent in country
    Antigua and Barbuda 473–4
    birth, citizenship by (*ius soli*) 55
    Canada 243
    domicile 12
    EU 113–14
    Grenada 508
    Malta 305
    naturalization 105
    New Zealand 326, 328, 329
    Portugal 339, 340
    tax residence 12, 16, 27–9
    Thailand 382
    United Kingdom 409–10, 412–13,
        416–17
    United States 64–5, 71
Democratic Republic of Congo (DRC)
    164
demographics 83, 90
Denmark
    domicile of origin 10
    Nordic Passport Union 118, 126
    Schengen area 117–18

dependents *see also* **children; families;**
    parents and grandparents; spouses
    and partners
    Antigua and Barbuda 439, 470–1
    Austria 208, 482–3
    Canada 235
    Dominica 443–4, 499
    EU 112
    Guernsey 253
    Hong Kong 265, 267
    Jersey 279, 281, 283–5
    Malaysia 295
    Malta 516, 518–19
    New Zealand 325, 327
    Portugal 343
    Singapore 353
    St Kitts and Nevis 446, 527–8
    St Lucia 447, 539, 541
    United Arab Emirates/Dubai 391
    United Kingdom 409, 411
descent, citizenship by (*ius sanguinis*) *see*
    ancestry/descent, citizenship by (*ius
    sanguinis*)
developing countries 36
diplomatic or consular passports and
    visas 130, 136, 139
diplomats or officials, children of 105
discrimination 6, 112–14
diversification 6, 38, 52
divorce
    Belgium 226
    domicile 10
    Hong Kong 271
    London 18
    Malaysia 297
    Malta 306
    Monaco 318–19
    New Zealand 329
    Portugal 341–2
    Thailand 383
    United Kingdom 18
    United States 429
documentation *see also* **identity cards;**
    passports; visas
    Antigua and Barbuda 472–3, 475
    Australia 195
    Austria 208–9
    Belgium 223
    bribery 59

Cyprus 490
Dominica 499
EU 113, 115
Grenada 506
Guernsey 251, 255
Hong Kong 267, 269
Jersey 285
Malta 518
Monaco 315, 317
Portugal 339
Singapore 351, 354
St Kitts and Nevis 446, 529, 531–2
St Lucia 540–1
United Arab Emirates/Dubai 396
domestic workers 266, 391
domicile
Anglo-Saxon common law 9, 15
business connections 12
change of residence 12, 15–16
choice, of 10, 16, 509
citizenship 9, 51, 54
Commonwealth 10
death 10
definition 9
determination 12
divorce 10
duration of stay 12
effects 9
family connections 12
Grenada 508–9
inheritance tax 10, 15–16
intention 15
main family home, location of 12
Malta 306, 519
nationality 9, 12
one domicile at a time, having 9
origin, of (parents/birth) 10, 509
residence
factors to consider 15–16
inheritance tax 18–19
planning 9–10
status, determination of 10
tax 12, 15–16, 50, 54, 508–9
United Kingdom 10, 65, 412–15
United States 65
Dominica, citizenship-by-investment in 48, 54, 438, 495–502
advantages 500
background 497
children 442–3, 498–9
climate 497, 502
Commonwealth 497, 500
comparison table 453, 455, 457, 461, 463, 465
Constitution 442, 498
criminal records 499
dependents 443–4, 499
documentation 499
dual citizenship 500
due diligence 443, 499
Economic Citizenship Program 442
economy 442, 497–8
families
children 442–3, 498–9
Family Applications 442–3, 498–9
spouses and partners 443, 499
fees 442–3, 498–9
general information 501
grant of citizenship 499–500
international organizations, membership of 497
interviews 499
language 497
legal basis 498
nationality, quality of 173
natural attractions 497
naturalization 499
Oath of Allegiance 499
passports 443, 499
people 497
procedures 499
Real Estate option 442, 498–9
requirements/conditions 442–3, 453, 498–9
Schengen area 500
Single Option 442, 498
spouses and partners 443, 499
tax 500
time frames 499
tourism 497
United Kingdom 497, 500
visa-free travel 443, 448, 455, 457, 459, 461, 463, 465, 500
double tax treaties
Australia 198
Austria 210
Belgium 219, 225
Canada 242

centre of vital interests 19–20
citizenship 32–3
close connection 19–20
Cyprus 488
definition 31
gift taxes 32
Guernsey 256–7
habitual residence 20, 32–3
Hong Kong 271
inheritance tax 32
Jersey 287
Malaysia 296
Malta 306, 520
Monaco 317
mutual agreements 20, 33
New Zealand 325, 328
OECD model treaty 10, 32, 317
real estate 32
Singapore 356
Switzerland 370
tax residence 32–3
tie-breaker rules 19–20, 32
United Arab Emirates (UAE)/Dubai 389
United States 65, 70, 429
drugs, fight against 118
dual citizenship
ancestry/descent, citizenship by (*ius sanguinis*) 56
Antigua and Barbuda 474
Australia 200
Austria 483
Belgium 227
Canada 244
citizenship planning 48, 56–7, 60–2
Cyprus 491
Dominica 500
Grenada 508
Guernsey 257
Hong Kong 273
Jersey 288
Malaysia 298
Malta 307, 519
Monaco 319
New Zealand 329
Portugal 343
Singapore 357
St Kitts and Nevis 530
St Lucia 543

Switzerland 373
Thailand 384
United Arab Emirates (UAE)/Dubai 398
United Kingdom 417
United States 66–7, 430
Dubai *see* **United Arab Emirates (UAE)/Dubai**
due diligence
Dominica 443, 499
Grenada 506
Malta 304, 305, 444, 466, 515–18
real estate, acquisition of 45
St Kitts and Nevis 446, 527–9
St Lucia 447, 539–40
Visa Restrictions Index (Henley & Partners) 149
Economic Community of West African States (ECOWAS) 108, 125
economic migrants 6
economy
Antigua and Barbuda 468–70
Australia 193
Austria 205, 212, 440, 481
Belgium 219
Canada 239
checklist 23–4
citizenship planning 49, 53, 60
Cyprus 441, 488–90
Dominica 442, 497–8
EU 108–9, 169–72
global economic crisis of 2008 17
Guernsey 249, 252
Hong Kong 263, 265
Jersey 279, 287
Malaysia 293
Malta 443
Portugal 335
quality of nationality index 161–5, 169–72, 174
residence planning 6, 9, 13–14, 17, 27, 39
Singapore 349
St Kitts and Nevis 527
St Lucia 538
Switzerland 363
Thailand 379
United Arab Emirates (UAE)/Dubai 389–90

United Kingdom 403
United States 423–5
education and schools 14–15 *see also*
    students
    Belgium 219
    boarding schools abroad, sending to
        15
    Canada 233
    curricula 15
    EU 114
    identity and brand of nations 83, 90
    integration 15
    international schools 15
    language 15
    private schools 14
    real estate, acquisition of 40
    residence 14–15
    Singapore 351
    United Arab Emirates (UAE)/Dubai
        390–1
    United Kingdom 404–5, 408–9
Egypt 82
electoral register, amending the 12
electronic communications
    Electronic System for Travel
        Authorization (ESTA) 140
    e-visas 155
    immigration checkpoints, processing
        at 110
    passports
        attachment of visas to 197
        monitoring 133–4
employment and job creation *see also*
    professionals; work permits
    Andean Community 123
    Antigua and Barbuda 468
    Australia 194, 197
    Austria 206–8
    Belgium 220–4
    Canada 234–7, 239, 241
    Cyprus 488–9, 492
    EU 108, 112–13, 115–16
    free movement 110, 112, 115–16, 122
    Guernsey 250–1, 253–4
    Hong Kong 265–7, 270
    Jersey 280–1, 283, 285–7
    Malaysia 295
    Malta 173
    migrant workers 123

Monaco 315–16
Portugal 336, 341
Singapore 349, 351–3, 355–6
South Africa, socio-political context
    in 110
Switzerland 364–8
Thailand 380, 382
United Arab Emirates (UAE)/Dubai
    390–1, 394–6
United Kingdom 405–8
United States 72, 423, 424–9
visas 139, 141
equal treatment 114
estate planning *see* **inheritance tax and**
    estate planning
estate tax
    Antigua and Barbuda 469
    Hong Kong 271
    United States 429–30
Estonia 117–18, 170
European Economic Area (EEA)
    Agreement
    Austria 208, 484
    EFTA 108, 116
    entry into force 116
    EU 116
    freedom of movement 108, 116
    Iceland 108, 116
    internal market 108
    Liechtenstein 108, 116
    nationality, quality of 163, 166–7
    Norway 108, 116
    Monaco 314, 315
    United Kingdom 408
European Free Trade Association
    (EFTA) 108, 116
    Austria 484
    EEA 108, 116
    EU 108, 116
    freedom of movement 108, 116
    Iceland 108, 116
    Liechtenstein 108, 116
    Norway 108, 116
    Switzerland 108, 116, 121–2, 364–6,
        368
European Union 108–10, 111–22 *see also*
    Schengen area
    3 month residence period 113–14
    5 year residence period 114

Amsterdam Treaty 112
ancestry/descent, citizenship by (*ius sanguinis*) 56
Antigua and Barbuda 475
Austria 208, 440, 481, 484
Belgium 219–20
biometric passports 135
borders 108
Brexit 111, 403–4
Bulgaria, transitional provisions for 115–16, 122
children 113
citizenship
    nationality, quality of 161, 163–5, 166–73
    planning 50–1, 112–13
criminal records 115
Croatia, transitional provisions for 115–16, 122, 364
Cyprus 441–2, 492
Data Protection Directive 121
database 108
dependents 112
documentation 113, 115
economic activities, engagement in 113
economy 108–9, 169–72
EEA 116
education, access to 114
EFTA 108, 116
employment 108, 112–13, 115
enter and stay, right to 113–14
equal treatment 114
expulsion 114–15
family members 113
freedom of movement 108, 110, 112, 115–21
identity cards 113
Lisbon Treaty 112
Malta 303, 466, 515–16, 520
member states
    list of 111
    transitional provisions for new states 115–16
Monaco 313, 314, 315, 317
Montenegro 174
move, right to 113–14
nationality
    discrimination 112

family members 113
    quality 174
Nice Treaty 112
parents and grandparents 113
passports 108, 134–5, 164–5
permanent residence 114
political rights 169
Portugal 335, 336–9, 340
public policy, public security or public health 114–15
residence
    conditions 113–14
    permits 113–14
    right of 113–14
    student grants or loans 114
restrictions on right of entry 114–15
resources 113
right to reside 113–14
Romania, transitional provisions for 115–16, 122
Savings Directive 317
self-employed 113, 115
Singapore 357
social security 114
social services 113
spouses and partners 113
students 113, 114, 115
supranationalism 109–10
Switzerland 116, 121–2, 364–6, 368
transitional provisions for new member states 115–16
Treaty on European Union 112, 169
Treaty on the Functioning of the EU (TFEU) 112
United Kingdom 65, 111, 403–4
visas 108, 113, 139, 475
vocational training 113
exceptional/extraordinary contributions and highly-skilled persons
Austria 205, 206–7, 212, 440, 481
Belgium 221, 223
citizenship 102, 105
Cyprus 489
Guernsey 250
Hong Kong 265
identity and brand of nations 77, 95
Jersey 281–2, 283, 284–5
Malta 515

Monaco 314
Portugal 336, 338
reasons for becoming resident in
    another country 7
United Kingdom 405–8, 411
exit, departure or emigration taxes
Canada 242
claw backs 31
definition 31
residence 17, 29, 30–1
sovereign debt problems, countries
    with 16
United States 64, 66, 68–74
experts *see* **professional and expert
    advice**
exports 76, 83, 85
**factors to consider when choosing a new
    residence** 13–26
business environment 13, 14
change of residence 15–16
checklist 22–6
    business and economy 23–4
    infrastructure 22–3
    people, culture and lifestyle 24
    physical environment 23
    residence permits 25
citizenship
    checklist 25–6
    requirements for obtaining 14
    tax 16–17
criteria, list of 14–26
death of spouses 18
domicile 15–16
education and schooling 14–15
exit taxes 17
family law 18
health insurance 21–2
inheritance tax 18
inheritance tax and estate planning
    18–19, 34–5
location 14
matrimonial property regime 14, 18
personal situation 14
political and economic stability 14
real estate, acquisition of 20–1
residence permits, obtaining and
    maintaining 14
tax 13, 16–20
    citizenship 16–17

exit taxes 17
inheritance tax and estate planning
    18–19
residence 16
treaties and tie-breaker rules
    19–20
temporary visits, dangers of 13
timing 21
visa-free travel 14
families *see also* **children;
    dependents; family law; parents
    and grandparents; same sex
    relationships; spouses and partners**
Antigua and Barbuda 439–49, 470–1
Austria 206, 207–8, 210–11, 482
Belgium 222, 226
Canada 235, 239–40, 242
citizenship planning 52, 55
Cyprus 441, 490
domicile 12
Dominica 442–3, 498–9
EU 113
Hong Kong 267, 271
Jersey 282, 287
Malaysia 294
Malta 444, 516
nationality 113
New Zealand 325–7, 329
passports 130, 136
personal situations 14
Portugal 338, 342–3
Singapore 350–3
St Kitts and Nevis 446, 527–8
St Lucia 447, 539
Switzerland 370
tax residence 30
Thailand 380–2
United Arab Emirates (UAE)/Dubai
    391, 397
United Kingdom 409–12
United States 428, 429–30
family law
Australia 198–9
Austria 210–11
Guernsey 257
Hong Kong 271
Jersey 287
Malaysia 296–7
Malta 306–7

Monaco 318–19
New Zealand 329
Portugal 341–2
residence 18
Singapore 350
Switzerland 371–2
Thailand 383
United Kingdom 415–16
United States 429–30
fees
Antigua and Barbuda 439–40, 470–1, 473
Austria 440, 482
Dominica 442–3, 498–9
Grenada 506
Malta 444, 516, 518
legal advisors 45
real estate, acquisition of 45
St Kitts and Nevis 446, 527–8, 530
St Lucia 447, 539–40, 541, 543
financial planning 33–5
asset protection 35
cash planning 34
currencies, in other 34
pensions 34
seizure of assets, risk of 35
tax advisers in original jurisdiction, using 34
financial services *see also* **banking**
Antigua and Barbuda 468
Guernsey 249, 255
Hong Kong 263
Jersey 279–80, 287
Singapore 349
St Kitts and Nevis 525, 526
St Lucia 538
United Arab Emirates (UAE)/Dubai 394–5
United Kingdom 403
Finland 117–18, 126, 148, 168, 170
forced heirship
Belgium 226
France 18
Malta 306
Monaco 318
Scotland 415
foundations 19, 44
France
Chinese travellers 50

citizenship, taxation based on 17
forced heirship 14
French Revolution 103
identity and brand of nations 82
inheritance tax 34
Jersey 279
Monaco 313, 314, 315
nationality, quality of 164
real estate holding structures 43
Schengen area 50, 117
SCLs 43
Visa Restrictions Index (Henley & Partners) 148
freedom of movement
Andean Community 108, 123
Asia-Pacific Economic Cooperation (APEC) 108, 122–3
CARICOM (Caribbean Community) 108, 124
citizenship planning 49, 109
Commonwealth of Independent States (CIS) 108, 124–5
Croatia 122
Economic Community of West African States (ECOWAS) 108, 125
European Economic Area Agreement (EEA) 108, 116
European Free Trade Association (EFTA) 108, 116
European Union 108–10, 111–22
Gulf Cooperation Council (GCC) 108, 125
immigration checkpoints, electronic processing at 110
integration 110
International Covenant on Civil and Political Rights 109
labour, free movement of 110, 122
Monaco 314
Nordic Passport Union 108, 110, 126
reasons for becoming resident in another country 5–6
regional arrangements 107–27
residence 109
Schengen area 117
Southern African Development Community (SADC) 110
statelessness 54

Switzerland 116, 121–2, 368
Trans-Tasman Travel Arrangement
(TTTA) 108, 126
travel, ease of 110
UK-Ireland Common Travel Area
108, 110, 126–7, 279
United Nations 109
Universal Declaration of Human
Rights 109
G20 nationalities 164
gender 83, 90
Georgia 161
Germany
accommodation available for use,
having 12
bank accounts, government access to 7
identity and brand of nations 82
nationality, quality of 163, 164, 170
privacy 7
Visa Restrictions Index (Henley &
Partners) 148
gift tax
Austria 209
Belgium 225
Canada 241
Cyprus 491
double tax treaties 32
inheritance tax 19
Portugal 341
reasons for becoming resident in
another country 9
Switzerland 370, 372
Thailand 383
United States 64–5, 66, 69, 71–2
**Global Citizenship Program Index
(GCPI)** 466
global economic crisis of 2008 17, 538
Global Peace Index (GPI) 161, 163, 170
**Global Residence Program Index
(GRPI) 2016** 188–9
Austria 188
Belgium 188
citizenship requirements 188
compliance 188
indicators 188
investment requirements 188
Portugal's Golden Residence Permit
Program 188
processing time 188

quality of life/standard of living 188
reputation 188
tax 188
time to citizenship 188
total costs 188
visa-free travel 188
globalization 5–6, 161, 335
goods, tax on *see* **sales and goods tax/
VAT**
governance 76, 83, 85, 96
governmental social responsibility 94–6
grandparents *see* **parents and
grandparents**
grant of citizenship
Antigua and Barbuda 473–4
Austria 482, 483
Cyprus 490–1
Dominica 499–500
Grenada 508
Malta 518–19
St Kitts and Nevis 530
Greece 20–1, 117–18
Grenada, citizenship-by-investment in
48, 57, 437–8, 503–12
advantages 509–10
agents 506, 507
ancestry/descent, citizenship by (*ius
sanguinis*) 508
Approved Project 452, 505, 507
birth, citizenship by (*ius soli*) 508
Brazil, travel to 505, 509
China, travel to 443, 505, 509
Citizenship by Investment Committee
507
Citizenship Certificates 507
climate 512
colonialism 505
Commonwealth 505
comparison table 452, 457, 459, 461,
463, 465
corporations and businesses, tax on
509
culture 505
day counting and time spent in
country 508
documentation 506
domicile 508–9
dual citizenship 508
due diligence 506

fees 506
general information 511
grant of citizenship 508
health 509
income tax 508–9
language 510
legal basis 505–6
National Transformation Fund
    (NTF), contribution to 452,
    505–6, 507
nationality, quality of 173
passports 505, 507
political system 505
procedures 507–8
property tax 509
requirements/conditions 443, 452,
    505–7
residence 508
Schengen area 509
single applicants, approved projects
    for 507
spouses 506
St George's 505
tax 508–9
time frames 506, 507–8, 510
United Kingdom 505, 509
United States visas, right to 443, 505,
    509–10
VAT 509
visa-free travel 443, 448, 505
    Brazil, travel to 505, 509
    China, travel to 443, 505, 509
    comparison table 455, 457, 459,
        461, 463, 465
    Schengen area 509
    United Kingdom, travel to 509
    Visa Restrictions Index (Henley &
        Partners) 505
withholding tax 509
guarantees 45
Guernsey 247–60
advantages and disadvantages 257–8
background 249
business, persons intending to
    establish themselves in 253–4
capital gains tax 249
citizenship 257
climate 260
corporations, tax on 255

Crown Dependency of UK, as 249
dependents 253
documentation 251, 255
double tax treaties 256–7
dual citizenship 257
economy 249
employment 250–1, 253–4
family law 257
financial services 249, 255
general information 259
high net worth individuals 250
hospitality 249
housing 250–2
    licensing 251–2
    Local Market property 251–2, 253
    Open Market Private Houses
        250–1, 252, 253, 254
    time frames 254
immigration 252, 254–5
income tax 255–6
inheritance and succession 257
inheritance tax 249
investor immigration 253
Locate Guernsey Team 249–50,
    251–3, 255
naturalization 257
non-residents, tax on 255–6
OECD standards of tax transparency
    255
procedures 254–5
quality of life/standard of living 250
registration 257
reputation 252
residence 178, 181, 250–4
    permanent 254, 256
    procedures 254–5
    requirements/conditions 253–4
    time frames 254–5
resident only tax 256
retail 249
Right to Work documents 250
St Peter Port 249
solely or principally resident, tax on
    individuals are 256
States of Guernsey 249
tax 249, 255–7
time frames 254–5
tourism 249
UK Entry Clearance 254–5

United Kingdom 249, 252, 254–5, 257

visas 255

writers, composers and artists 254

Guinea 148

Gulf Cooperation Council (GCC) 108, 125, 161, 164

habitual residence

Belgium 226

change of residence 11–12

civil rights 10–11

definition 8

double tax treaties 20, 32–3

income tax 10

inheritance tax 10

Jersey 286

OECD Model Treaty 10

Portugal 340

health and health checks *see also* **health insurance**

Australia 193, 194

Belgium 219, 222, 223

Canada 235, 240

Grenada 509

hospitals, access to 40

Malaysia 295, 296

Malta 518

New Zealand 325, 327

Portugal 336

real estate, acquisition of 40

Singapore 349, 354

Switzerland 364

United Arab Emirates (UAE)/Dubai 396

United Kingdom 404

United States 426

vaccinations 143

Visa Restrictions Index (Henley & Partners) 151

visas 130, 142–3, 151

health insurance

checklist 38

choice of doctor and hospital 36, 37

comprehensive cover 36–7

continuing cover 36

developing countries 36

emergencies 36

importance 21–2

local insurers 36–7

Malta 304, 445, 517, 519

Portugal 338, 339

private hospitals 36

residence 21–2, 35–6

state insurance 35

specialist advisers 34

temporary residence 36

worldwide cover 37

Henley & Partners *see also* **Henley & Partners - Kochenov Quality of Nationality Index (QNI); Henley & Partners Visa Restrictions Index (HVRI)**

Antigua and Barbuda 440, 469

citizenship planning 48–9

Malta 466, 515, 518

St Kitts and Nevis 526, 531

Henley & Partners - Kochenov Quality of Nationality Index (QNI) 157–74

2011-2015 160

Afghanistan 166, 168

Albania 164

Arab League 164

Argentina 163

ASEAN 164

Asia 165

Australia 163, 169

Austria 173

Brazil 171

BRICs 164

Bulgaria 170

Canada 163, 169

Chile 163

citizenship 161

citizenship-by-investment schemes 158, 161, 168–9, 171–4

Commonwealth of Independent States citizenship 161, 164

content and structure 160–1

Croatia 168, 170

Cyprus 170, 173

Democratic Republic of Congo 164

diversity of settlement freedom 161–2, 163, 166–7, 170

diversity of travel freedom 162, 163, 165, 167–8, 170

economic strength of country 161–2, 163–5, 169–72, 174

EEA countries 163, 166–7

Estonia 170
EU citizenship 161, 163–5, 166–73
expert commentaries 158, 161, 168–74
external factors 158, 160, 161–6
External Value of Nationality
    Ranking 162, 166
Finland 168, 170
France 164
full access countries 161–2
G20 nationalities 164
GDP 161
General Ranking 162–5, 166
Georgia citizenship 161
Germany 163, 164, 170
Global Peace Index (GPI) 161, 163, 170
globalization 161
Gulf Cooperation Council (GCC)
    161, 164
high quality 158, 163, 165
Human Development Index (HDI)
    (UN) 161–2, 163, 170
Hungary 167
Iceland 169
importance of Index 159–60
India 164
Indonesia 164
internal factors 158, 160, 161–3
international organizations 161–4
Iran 171
Israel 164
Japan 163, 168, 169
Latvia 161, 167
Liechtenstein 164, 167, 169
low quality 158, 163, 165
Malta 172, 173
medium quality 158, 163, 165
MERCOSUR 165
Mexico 164
Middle East 165
Mozambique 166
NATO members 164
New Zealand 163
North Africa 165
Norway 169
OECD members 164
Pacific Region states, citizenship of
    161, 165
Panama, non-citizens passports and
    173

peace and stability 161, 163, 170
Poland 170
ranking 161–8
regions 161
Romania 170
Schengen area 171
Settlement Freedom Ranking 161–2,
    163, 165–7, 173
    diversity of 161–2, 163, 166–7, 170
    weight of 162, 163, 166–7, 170
Singapore 163, 168
Slovakia 167
South America citizenships 161, 165
South Korea 163
Switzerland 163, 167, 169
Travel Freedom Ranking 167–8
    diversity of 162, 163, 165, 167–8, 170
    ranking 162
    weight of 162, 163, 166, 167–8,
        170
Turkey 164
United States citizenship 161, 163,
    165, 169, 171
very high quality 158, 163
visa-free travel 162, 171
weight of settlement freedom 162,
    163, 166–7, 170
weight of travel freedom 162, 163,
    166, 167–8, 170
**Henley & Partners Visa Restrictions
    Index (HVRI)** 145–56
2016 highlights 148–50
2016 rankings 152–4
advance passenger information and
    advance approval 151
Afghanistan 149
Albania 148
Antigua and Barbuda 149, 440
Austria 483
Belgium 148
Bolivia 148
Bosnia 148
citizenship-by-investment 149
Colombia 148
Cyprus 149
Czech Republic 148
definition of index 147
due diligence 149
enforcement 155–6

e-visas 155
Finland 148
France 148
Germany 148
Grenada 505
Guinea 148
health 151
Hungary 148–9
IATA 139, 147, 150
investment migration, importance of
    149–50
Iraq 149
Italy 148
Liberia 148
Liechtenstein 148
Luxembourg 148
Malaysia 149
Malta 148–9
methodology 150–6
Pakistan 149
Palau 148
passports 149–51, 155
Portugal 149
requirements/conditions 150, 155
residence 149
Serbia 148
Sierra Leone 148
Slovakia 148
Somalia 149
South Korea 148
Spain 148
St Lucia 447
Sweden 148
temporary visas 155
Timor Leste 148
Tonga 148
underlying assumptions 155–6
United Arab Emirates (UAE) 148
United Kingdom 148
website 150
**high-tension lines and mobile phone
    masts** 41
highly-skilled persons *see* **exceptional/
    extraordinary contributions and
    highly-skilled persons**
historical properties 41
Hong Kong 261–75
    advantages and disadvantages 273
    Australia 6

background 263
birth, citizenship by (*ius soli*) 272
Canada 6
Capital Investment Entrant Scheme
    265, 268
children 267
China 6, 51, 138, 263–4, 268–70,
    272–3
    Closer Economic Partnership
        Agreement (CEPA) 263
    passports 138
citizenship 271–3
climate 275
colonial rule 263
contributions to economy 265
criminal records 267
dependents 265, 267
divorce 271
documentation 267, 269
double tax treaties 271
dual citizenship 273
economy 263, 265
educational background 265, 266
employment 265–7, 270
    Employment as Foreign Domestic
        Helpers Permit 266
    Employment as Imported Workers
        Permit 266
    Employment under the Admission
        Scheme for Mainland Talents
        and Professionals Permit 265–6
estate duty 271
exceptional individuals 265
extension of stay 267, 269
families
    children 267
    family law 271
    parents and grandparents 267, 269,
        272
    Permit for Residence as a
        Dependant 267
    spouses and partners 267
financial services 263
General Employment Policy (GEP)
    Permit 265, 266
general information 274
identity cards 269
Immigration Arrangements for
    Non-local Graduate Permit 266

immigration policy 263–4, 267–9
income tax 270–1
inheritance and succession 271
intestacy 271
investment 265–6
Investment as Entrepreneurs 266
language 265
matrimonial property regime 271
nationality 272–3
naturalization 56, 272–3
parents and grandparents 267, 269,
    272
Permit for Residence as a Dependant
    267
political discrimination 6
procedure 268–70
professionals 264, 265–6
profit tax 270
Quality Migrant Admission Scheme
    265
quotas 265
residence 178, 181, 264–70
    Chinese citizens 269–70
    citizenship 271–2
    non-Chinese citizens 269–70
    permanent 269, 271–2
    permits 268
    procedures 268–70
    requirements/conditions 267–8
    tax 28
    time frames 268–70
second passports 51
spouses and partners 267, 271
St Kitts and Nevis 532
St Lucia 543
Study Permits 267
tax 28, 263, 270–1
time frames 268–70
United Kingdom 6, 263
United States 6
visas 266–7
    dependents 267
    Visa for Training 267
    visa-free travel 264
wills and testaments 271
Working Holiday Scheme Permit 267
World Trade Organization 263
housing see accommodation/housing;
    real estate, acquisition of

HSBC's 2015 Expat Explorer survey
    325
human capital 79
Human Development Index (HDI)
    (UN) 161–2, 163, 170, 325, 335
human rights
    Canadian Charter of Rights and
        Freedoms 234
    habitual residence 10–11
    International Covenant on Civil and
        Political Rights 109
    political rights 169
    Universal Declaration of Human
        Rights 100, 103, 109
humanitarian residence 194
Hungary 117–18, 148–9, 167
Iceland 58, 108, 116–18, 126, 169
identity and brand see cities, identity
    and brand of; identity and brand of
    nations
identity and brand of nations 75–96
    advertising campaigns 81–2
    age 83, 90
    Anholt-GfK Roper Nation Brands
        Index (NBI) 76, 82–95
    Argentina 82
    Australia 82
    Brazil 82
    Canada 82
    celebrities 77
    changing a nation's image 78, 81–2
    China 82
    citizenship planning 82, 84, 89, 95
    clichés and stereotypes 79–80
    climate 76–7, 91, 95
    co-branding 78
    consumer power 95
    corruption 95
    culture 76–7, 82, 83, 85–6, 89
    demographics 83, 90
    developing countries 78
    education 83, 90
    Egypt 82
    ethical standards 95
    exports 76, 83, 85
    France 82
    gender 83, 90
    Germany 82
    governance 76, 83, 85, 96

governmental social responsibility 94–6
high-net-worth-individuals 77, 95
human capital 79
immigration 76, 84–6
India 82
investment 76, 79, 82, 84–6, 96
Italy 82
Japan 82
marriage question 87, 89
mass-marketing 81–2
measurement of image of nations 80, 82–90
media 77
Mexico 83
Nation Brand Hexagon 83–4
Netherlands
passports, loss of 86, 89
people 76, 79, 83–5, 90, 96
Poland 83
pollution 95
quality of life/standard of living 83, 84, 87
regions, reputation of 76–80
reputation 76–82, 95–6
residence planning 95
Russia 83
sectoral promotion 81
social responsibility 95
soft factors 77, 89
South Africa 83
South Korea 83
spouses and partners 89
Sweden 83
Switzerland
tax 79, 95
tourism 76, 81–2, 84–6, 96
transparency 95
Turkey 83
United Kingdom 83
United States 83
identity cards
EU 113
Hong Kong 269
passports 130, 132–3, 136, 137
Portugal 336
United Arab Emirates (UAE)/Dubai 396
identity theft 53

Ideos Publications *see* **Henley & Partners - Kochenov Quality of Nationality Index (QNI)**
immigration checkpoints, electronic processing at 110
immigration
Australia 193
Austria 205
Guernsey 252, 254–5
Hong Kong 263–4, 267–9
identity and brand of nations 76, 84–6
Jersey 280–1, 288
New Zealand 325
United Kingdom 404–10
United States 71–2, 423
visas 130, 141
income tax
Antigua and Barbuda 469, 474
Australia 197
Austria 209–10
Belgium 224
Canada 233, 241–2, 243
citizenship planning 50
Cyprus 491
Grenada 508–9
Guernsey 255–6
habitual residence 10
Hong Kong 270–1
Jersey 280, 272, 286–7
Malaysia 296
Malta 305, 519
New Zealand 328
Portugal 340–1
reasons for becoming resident in another country 8
Singapore 355
St Lucia 542
Switzerland 368–70
tax residence 16, 26–7, 29, 30–1
Thailand 382
United Kingdom 65, 411–13
United States 65–9, 72–4, 428
independent means, persons of
Austria 209
Belgium 219
EU 113, 115
identity and brand of nations 77
Switzerland 364–5, 367
visas 141

India 82, 164
Indonesia 164
infrastructure 6, 22–3, 39–40
inheritance and succession *see also*
    forced heirship; inheritance tax and
    estate planning; intestacy
    Australia 198–9
    Austria 210–11
    Belgium 226, 242
    domicile 10, 15–16
    Guernsey 257
    Hong Kong 271
    Jersey 287
    Malaysia 296–7
    Malta 306–7
    matrimonial property regime 18
    Monaco 318–19
    Portugal 341–2
    real estate holding structures 42
    Singapore 356
    Switzerland 371–2
    Thailand 383
    United Arab Emirates (UAE)/Dubai
        397
    United Kingdom 415–16
    United States 426, 429–30
inheritance tax and estate planning
    18–19
    Australia 198, 199
    Austria 209
    Belgium 225, 241, 242
    change of residence 11–12
    company structures 19
    Cyprus 491
    double tax treaties 32
    foundations 19
    gift tax 19
    Guernsey 249
    habitual residence 10
    life insurance structures 19
    Malaysia 297
    Malta 307
    Monaco 317–18
    Netherlands 16–17
    Portugal 341
    reasons for becoming resident in
        another country 8–9
    residence 11–12, 30
        change of 11–12

    domicile, difference from 18–19
    factors to consider 18–19, 34–5
    gift tax 19
    habitual residence 10
    St Lucia 542
    Switzerland 370, 372
    Thailand 383
    trusts 19
    United Kingdom 412–13
    United States securities 19
insurance 19 *see also* **health insurance**
integration, citizenship tests and
    ceremonies *see also* **oaths of**
    allegiance
    Australia 199
    Austria 207, 208–9, 483
    Belgium 220
    Canada 236
    education and schools 15
    freedom of movement 110
    naturalization 105
    Switzerland 372
International Air Transport Association
    (IATA) 139, 143, 147, 150
International Civil Aviation
    Organization (ICAO) 130, 134–5
International Covenant on Civil and
    Political Rights (ICCPR) 109
International Monetary Fund (IMF)
    279–80
international organizations,
    membership of
    Antigua and Barbuda 469
    Australia 193
    Dominica 497
    Malaysia 297
    Monaco 313
    nationality, quality of 161–4
    St Kitts and Nevis 526
    St Lucia 538
    Switzerland 363
    Thailand 379
    United Arab Emirates (UAE)/Dubai
        389
    United Kingdom 403–4, 410, 411, 417
interviews
    Antigua and Barbuda 472
    Cyprus 490
    Dominica 499

Malta 518
St Kitts and Nevis 529
Thailand 383
intestacy
Australia 1993
Austria 211
Hong Kong 271
Malaysia 297
Malta 306
Monaco 318
New Zealand 329
Portugal 341
Switzerland 371
Thailand 383
United Kingdom 416
United States 429
investments *see also*
citizenship-by-investment
Austria 205
Belgium 221
citizenship planning 52
Global Residence Program Index
(GRPI) 2016 188
Guernsey 253
Hong Kong 265–6
identity and brand of nations 76, 79,
82, 84–6, 96
Jersey 281, 283–4, 285
Malaysia 293
Malta 303–4, 307
migration, importance of 149–50
New Zealand 325–8, 329
Portugal 336–8, 340
privacy 7
real estate, acquisition of 20
reasons for becoming resident in
another country 6, 7
Singapore 349, 350–5
Switzerland 363–4
Thailand 380–2
United Arab Emirates (UAE)/Dubai
389, 393
United Kingdom 405–10
United States 424–7
Iran 171
Iraq 149
Ireland
ancestry/descent, citizenship by (*ius
sanguinis*) 104–5

citizenship-by-investment 437
domicile of origin 10
inheritance tax 34
Schengen area 117–18r
UK-Ireland Common Travel Area
108, 110, 126–7, 279
Israel 133, 139, 164
Italy
identity and brand of nations 82
rules and regulations, complexity of 8
Schengen area 117–18
small businesses 8
Visa Restrictions Index (Henley &
Partners) 148
ius sanguinis see **ancestry/descent,
citizenship by (*ius sanguinis*)**
ius soli see **birth, citizenship by (*ius soli*)**
Japan 82, 163, 168, 169
Jersey 277–90
accommodation 281–2, 286
advantages and disadvantages 288
agriculture 279
background 279
children 283
citizenship 288
climate 280, 290
Common Travel Area with UK, Ireland,
Guernsey and Isle of Man 279
corporations, tax on 287
Crown Dependency of UK, as 279
culture 282
dependents 279, 281, 283–5
documentation 267, 269, 285
double tax treaties 287
dual citizenship 288
economy 279, 287
employment 80–1, 283, 285–7
extension of stay 284–5
families 282, 287
children 283
family law 287
financial services 279–80, 287
France 279
general information 289
Goods and Services Tax (GST) 287
habitual residence 286
high net worth individuals 281–2
High Value Residency 281–2, 283,
284

highly specialized senior employees 285
IMF 279–80
immigration 280–1, 288
income tax 280, 282, 286–7
Indefinite Leave to Remain (LTR) 284, 285
inheritance and succession 287
Investor Category 283–4, 285
Inward Investor 281, 283, 284
Leave to Enter 283–4
Licensed Status 283
naturalization 288
OECD 280
procedures 284–6
professionals 281
real property acquisition 281
registration 288
residence 178, 182, 280–6
    definition 286
    permanent 285–6
    permits 280, 285
    procedures 284–6
    requirements/conditions 282–4
    tax 286
    time frames 284–6
security risks 287
spouses and partners 283
States of Jersey 279
tax 280, 282, 284, 286–7
    resident and ordinarily resident (ROR) 286
    resident but not ordinarily resident (RNOR) 286
time frames 284–6
tourism 279
United Kingdom 279, 288
work permits 280–1
job creation *see* **employment and job creation**
Kälin, Christian 159–60
kidnappings 52–3
Kochenov, Dimitry 160 *see also* **Henley & Partners - Kochenov Quality of Nationality Index (QNI)**
language
Austria 208, 211, 440, 482
Belgium 220
Canada 233, 236, 243

cities, identity and brand of 91
citizenship planning 60
Dominica 497
education and schools 15
English, dominance of 5–6
Grenada 510
Hong Kong 265
Malaysia 293, 297
Malta 303, 515
Monaco 313, 315
naturalization 105
New Zealand 326
Portugal 336, 343
real estate, acquisition of 39
reasons for becoming resident in another country 5–6
Singapore 350
St Kitts and Nevis 525, 529
St Lucia 537, 541
Switzerland 363, 372
United Arab Emirates (UAE)/Dubai 389, 396
United Kingdom 409, 410, 411, 417
United States 426, 430
Latvia 117–18, 161, 167
Liberia 148
Liechtenstein 108, 116, 118, 148, 164, 167, 169
liens 46
life insurance 19
Lithuania 117–18
Louisy, Pearlette 537–8
Luxembourg 117, 148
Macedonia 135
Malaysia 291–300
    advantages and disadvantages 298
    background 293
    bank accounts, deposits in 295–6
    capital gains tax 296
    children 293, 295, 297
    citizenship 297–8
    climate 300
    criminal records 267
    cultures 293, 297
    dependents 295
    divorce 297
    double tax treaties 296
    dual citizenship 298
    economy 293

employment 295
Entry Permits 293–4, 297
Expert category 294
families
    children 293, 295, 297
    family law 296–7
    spouses and partners 293–5
    time frames 296
financial requirements 295
general information 299
goods and services tax (GST) 296
health 295, 296
income tax 296
inheritance and succession 296–7
inheritance tax 297
international organizations,
    membership of 293
intestacy 297
Investors and Experts 293
language 293, 297
Malaysia My Second Home
    Programme (MM2H) 295, 296
matrimonial property regime 297
National Registration Department
    (NRD) 297
passports 138
Peninsular Malaysia and Eastern
    Malaysia, travel between 138
Points System 294
procedures 296
Professional category 294
real property 295
residence 178, 182, 293–7
    duration of residence 294
    Entry Permits 293–4
    permanent 293–4, 296–7
    permits 295
    procedures 296
    requirements/conditions 295–6
    time frames 296
spouses and partners 293–5, 297
tax 296
time frames 296
tourism 293
United Kingdom 293
Visa Restrictions Index (Henley &
    Partners) 149
visas 149, 295

Malta 301–10 *see also* **Malta,
    citizenship-by-investment in**
    advantages and disadvantages 307–8
    ancestry/descent, citizenship by (*ius
        sanguinis*) 307
    background 303
    birth, citizenship by (*ius soli*) 307
    capital gains tax 305–6
    children 306, 444, 516
    citizenship 307
    climate 310, 466, 515
    corporate tax 306
    criminal records 445, 517
    day counting and time spent in
        country 305
    dependents 516, 518–19
    divorce 306
    domicile 306
    double tax treaties 306
    dual citizenship 307
    due diligence 304, 305
    economy 43
    employment 173
    EU 303
    families
        children 306, 444, 516
        family law 306–7
        parents and grandparents 307,
            444, 516
    forced heirship 306
    general information 309
    health insurance 304
    Identity Malta 305
    income tax 305
    inheritance and succession 306–7
    inheritance tax 307
    intestacy 306
    investments 303–4, 307
    islands 303
    language 303
    Malta Individual Investor Programme
        307
    Malta Residence and Visa Programme
        (MRVP) 303–5
    matrimonial property regime 306
    naturalization 307
    parents and grandparents 307, 444,
        516
    procedures 305

real estate
    acquisition of 304
    holding structures 43
    inheritance and succession 306
    stamp duty land tax 307
residence 178, 183, 303–5
    citizenship 307
    day counting and time spent in
        country 305
    duration 307
    indefinite 303–5
    permits 305
    procedures 305
    real estate, acquisition of 304
    requirements/conditions 303–4
    tax 28
    time frames 305
Schengen area 117–18
security risks 445, 517
stamp duty land tax 307
taxation 28, 305–6, 307
time frames 305
United Kingdom 303
Valletta 303
VAT 306
wills and testament 306
Malta, citizenship-by-investment in 48,
    57, 438, 513–22
advantages 520
agents 518
background 515
capital gains tax (CGT) 519–20
children 517
climate 515, 522
colonialism 515
Comino 515
comparison table 450, 454, 456, 458,
    460, 462, 464
corporate tax 520
criminal records 445, 517
culture 515
documentation 518
domicile 519
double tax treaties 520
dual citizenship 519
due diligence 444, 466, 515–18
EU 466, 515–16, 520
families 444, 516–17
fees 444, 516, 518

general information 521
Global Citizenship Program Index
    (GCPI) 466
government bonds, investment in 173
Gozo 515
grant of citizenship 518–19
health
    insurance 445, 517, 519
    reports 518
Henley & Partners Public Services
    Concession 466, 515, 518
high net worth individuals 515
income tax 519
inheritance tax 34
interviews 518
language 515
legal basis 515–16
Malta Individual Investor Programme
    (MIIP) 443–4, 466, 515–22
National Development and Social
    Fund, contributions to 173, 444, 516
nationality, quality of 172, 173
naturalization 445, 518–19
Oath of Allegiance 445, 517, 519
parents 517
passports 149, 518–19
procedures 518
publicity 445, 517
quality of life/standard of living 466
quotas 445, 517
real estate, acquisition of 173, 444–5,
    517–18
reputation 466, 520
requirements/conditions 444–5, 450,
    516–17
residence 445, 517, 519
Schengen area 515
security risks
spouses 516
tax 34, 519–20
    domicile 519
    residence 519
time frames 518
ultra high net worth individuals 515
United Kingdom 515
VAT 520
visa-free travel 445, 448, 517
    comparison table 454, 456, 458,
        460, 462, 464

Global Citizenship Program Index
(GCPI) 466
Visa Restrictions Index (Henley &
Partners) 148–9
marriage *see also* **divorce; matrimonial
property regimes; nuptial
agreements; spouses and partners**
citizenship by marriage (*ius
matrimonii*) 48, 54, 67, 100, 103,
105, 319, 342–3
identity and brand of nations 87, 89
naturalization 105
Thailand 379
mass-marketing 81–2
matrimonial property regimes
Austria 211
Belgium 226
Canada 242
change of residence 11–12
express choice 12
Hong Kong 271
Malaysia 297
Malta 306
Monaco 318
New Zealand 329
Portugal 341–2
residence 14, 18
Singapore 356
Switzerland 371
Thailand 383
United Kingdom 415
United States 65
media 77
MERCOSUR 165
Mexico 83, 164
Middle East
nationality, quality of 165
political upheaval 53
military/national service
citizenship 54, 100–1, 106
Monaco 319
Singapore 355, 357
Monaco 311–22
accommodation, proof 315
adoption 319
advantages and disadvantages 320
ancestry/descent, citizenship by (*ius
sanguinis*) 319
background 313

birth, citizenship by (*ius soli*) 319
businesses
licences 315
tax 317
children 317
citizenship 319
climate 322
criminal records 315
divorce 318–19
documentation 315, 317
double tax treaties 317
dual citizenship 319
EEA 314, 315
employment 315–16
EU 313, 314, 315, 317
families
children 317
family law 318–19
parents and grandparents 317, 319
spouses and partners 317–19
forced heirship 318
France 313, 314, 315
Franco-Monégasque Neighbor
Convention 314, 315
fraud, exchange of information on
tax 317
French embassies, applications at 315
freedom of movement within EU 314
general information 321
Grimaldi family 313
high net worth individuals 314
inheritance and succession 318–19
inheritance tax 317–18
intestacy 318
interest payments 317
international organizations 313
language 313, 315
leases, registration tax on 317
long-stay visas 315
marriage, citizenship by 319
matrimonial property regime 318
military/national service 319
naturalization 56
parents and grandparents 317, 319
people 313
pre-nuptial agreements 318–19
procedures 314–15, 316
profit tax 317
quality of life/standard of living 313

real estate
    acquisition of 314
    tax 317
renunciation of foreign nationality 319
residence 28, 178, 183, 314–16
    citizenship 319
    duration 319
    permits/cards 314–15, 316
    primary 314
    procedures 314–15, 316
    renewal of cards 316
    requirements/conditions 314–15
    tax 314
    time frames 316
Savings Directive 317
security 314
Sovereign Ordinance No 3153 of
    1964 314
sporting events 313
spouses and partners 317–19
succession tax 318
sufficient funds, proof of 315
tax 314, 316–18
    fraud 317
    mutual administrative
        coordination, convention on
        318
    OECD White List 318
    residence 28
    trusts 318
time frames 316
trusts 318
visas
    France, administration of 315, 316
    long-stay 315
withholding tax 317
work permits 315–16
Montenegro 174
Morgan, JP 77
Mozambique 166
multiculturalism
    Canada 233–4
    Singapore 349
    Switzerland 363
Nation Brand Hexagon 83–4
national development funds,
    contributions to
    Antigua and Barbuda 173–4, 439,
        451, 470–1, 473

Grenada 452, 505–6, 507
Malta 173, 444, 516
St Lucia 447, 539
national service *see* **military/national
    service**
nationality *see also* **Henley & Partners
    - Kochenov Quality of Nationality
    Index (QNI)**
    ancestry/descent, citizenship by (*ius
        sanguinis*) 56, 104
    citizenship 49, 52–4, 56, 100–4, 106
    definition 100–1
    differences from citizenship 101
    discrimination 112
    domicile 9, 12
    EU 112–13
    families 113
    Hong Kong 272–3
    multiple nationalities 52–4, 56
    state succession 103
    threats arising from nationality 49
    Universal Declaration of Human
        Rights 103
**NATO (North Atlantic Treaty
    Organization)** 164, 174
natural attractions
    Antigua and Barbuda 468
    Austria 205, 481
    Cyprus 488
    Dominica 497
    St Kitts and Nevis 525
    St Lucia 537
    Thailand 379
natural hazards 41
naturalization 100, 103, 105
    Australia 56
    Bahamas 56
    Canada 56
    caveat emptor 58
    citizenship planning 54–5, 56–8
    collective naturalization 105
    conditions 100
    Cyprus 441, 489
    Dominica 499
    Guernsey 257
    Hong Kong 56, 272–3
    Iceland 58
    integration factors 105
    Jersey 288

language 105
Malta 307, 445, 518–19
marriage 105
Monaco 56
nationality, quality of 171
Portugal 342
privacy 56
residence, length of 105
security 57
Singapore 56, 357
Switzerland 56, 372
tax 56
Thailand 380, 384
United Arab Emirates (UAE)/Dubai
    398
United Kingdom 56, 416
United States 430
Nelson, Horatio 467
Netherlands
aggressive fiscal and regulatory
    environment 7
inheritance tax 16–17
Schengen area 117
New Zealand 323–32
advantages and disadvantages 330
Australia 136, 193
background 325
children 325–6, 329
citizenship 329
climate 332
corporate tax 328
corruption 325
day counting and time spent in
    country 326, 328, 329
dependents 325, 327
divorce 329
double tax treaties 325, 328
dual citizenship 329
Expression of Interest (EOI) to
    Immigration NZ 327
families 325–7
    children 325–6, 329
    family law 329
    spouses and partners 327
    trusts 329
general information 331
health 325, 327
Human Development Index 325
immigration 325

income tax 328
inheritance and succession 329
intestacy 329
investments 325–8, 329
Investor 326
Investor 1 Resident Visa 325–7
Investor 2 Resident Visa 325–7
Investor Plus 326
language 326
matrimonial property regime 329
permanent residence 325, 328
points-based system 326
pre-nuptial agreements 329
procedures 327–8
property tax 328
quality of life/standard of living 325
residence 178, 184, 325–8
    citizenship 329
    day counting and time spent in
        country 326, 328, 329
    duration 329
    permanent 325, 328
    procedures 327–8
    Resident Visas 325–8
    tax 325, 328
    time frames 327–8
security risks 327
spouses and partners 327, 329
tax 325, 328
time frames 327–8
trusts 329
visas 325–8
noise 40, 42
Nordic Passport Union (NPU) 118, 126
North Africa, quality of nationality in
    165
North American Free Trade Agreement
    (NAFTA) 233
Northern Ireland 403
Norway
domicile of origin 10
EEA 108, 116
EFTA 108, 116
nationality, quality of 169
Nordic Passport Union 118, 126
Schengen area 117–18
nuptial agreements
Belgium 226
Monaco 318–19

New Zealand 329
Portugal 342
residence 14, 18
Thailand 382
United Kingdom 18, 415
oaths of allegiance
Dominica 499
Malta 445, 517, 519
United States 71, 430
OECD (Organisation for Economic Co-operation and Development) 164, 280
organized crime 53
Pacific Region states, citizenship of 161, 165
Pakistan 149
Palau 148
Panama
non-citizens passports 173
real estate holding structures 43
parents and grandparents *see also* **children; families**
Antigua and Barbuda 471
Austria 194, 211
Australia 199
Belgium 227
citizenship 55–6, 104
EU 113
Hong Kong 267, 269, 272
Malta 307, 444, 516–17
Monaco 317, 319
Portugal 341–3
Singapore 350, 353, 357
Thailand 381, 383
United Arab Emirates/Dubai 391, 393
United Kingdom 416
United States 67
partners *see* **same sex relationships; spouses and partners**
passports 129–38 *see also* **biometric passports**
alien (or non-citizen) passports 130, 133, 136
alien residence cards or permits 137
Antigua and Barbuda 440, 469, 473–4, 475
APEC 123
Australia 197, 199

Austria 440, 481, 482, 483
bribery, passports obtained by 59–60
camouflage passports 137
CARICOM (Caribbean Community) 124
children 130, 134, 136
citizenship 130, 132–3, 135, 199
citizenship-by-investment 58, 437
planning 48–53, 59–60
customary international law 136
Cyprus 491
definition 130, 132
diplomatic or consular passports 130, 136
Dominica 443, 499
ECOWAS 125
electronic attachment of visas 197
electronic monitoring 133–4
emergencies 130, 136–7
EU 134, 135, 164–5
families 130, 136
foreign relations 138
fraud 134–5
Grenada 505, 507
Hong Kong 51, 138
Hong Kong, Macau and mainland China, travel between 138
ICAO 130, 134–5
identity and brand of nations 86, 89
identity cards/permits 130, 132–3, 136, 137
illegal means, passports obtained by 59–60
internal travel, passports for 138
Israel, travel to 133
joint passports 130, 136
loss of passports 86, 89
machine-readable passports 130, 134
Malaysia 138
Malta 149, 518–19
medieval Europe 131
modern system 131
more than one passport, holding 130, 132–3
non-citizens 58, 60
Nordic Passport Union 118, 126
official passports 130, 136
one person, one passport policy 134
Panama, non-citizens passports and 173

Portugal 336, 338
privacy 134–5
recognition of passports 58, 60
Red Cross Laissez-Passer 130, 136
repatriation, place of 132
requirements/conditions 136
restrictions 138
retiree residence programs 60
Russia, travel within 138
Schengen area 118, 137
second passports, importance of 51,
   132, 140, 437
security printing 135
security risks 138
service passports 130, 136
Singapore 357
special passports 130, 136
St Kitts and Nevis 530, 531–2
St Lucia 447, 540, 543
standard format 130, 134–5
state, connection with a 131, 132
temporary passports 130, 136–8
terrorism 135
travel documents, legal effect of other
   137
types of passport 136–8
United Arab Emirates (UAE)/Dubai
   396, 398
United Kingdom 132, 409
visas 130, 131–3, 135–6, 139–40, 197
   developing countries 135
   electronic attachment of visas 197
   fees 135
   tourists 136
   US visa-waiver program 135
   visa-free travel 137
   Visa Restrictions Index (Henley &
     Partners) 149–51, 155
   visitors 135–6
peace and stability
Global Peace Index (GPI) 161, 163,
   170
nationality, quality of 161, 163, 170
reasons for becoming resident in
   another country 6, 7
pensions 34
permanent residence
Australia 193, 194–6
Austria 208

Canada 234, 243
citizenship planning 51
EU 114
Guernsey 254, 256
New Zealand 325, 328
Portugal 340
Schengen area 120
Singapore 349–53, 357
Thailand 380–2, 384
United Kingdom 405–6, 408–10, 416
personal situations 14
Poland 83, 117–18, 170
police and judicial cooperation 118–21
political circumstances 6, 7, 14, 49–50,
   52–3, 60
political rights 169
pollution 41, 95
Portugal 333–46
advantages and disadvantages 343–4
Algarve 335
ancestry/descent, citizenship by (*ius
   sanguinis*) 342
background 335
Blue Card (EU) 336, 338–9, 340
businesses, creation of 337
capital gains tax 340–1
children 341–3
citizenship 336, 342–3
climate 188
colonies 335
common property law regime 342
corporate income tax 341
criminal records 338, 342–3
culture 188, 335, 337
day counting and time spent in
   country 339, 340
dependents 343
divorce 341–2
documentation 339
dual citizenship 343
economy 335
educational level 343
employment 336, 341
EU 335, 336–9, 340
families
   children 341–3
   citizenship 342–3
   family law 341–2
   parents and grandparents 341–3

residence permits 338
reunification 338
spouses and partners 341
general information 345
gift tax 341
Global Residence Program Index
    (GRPI) 2016 188
Golden Residence Permit Program
    188, 336, 337, 338, 339
    businesses, creation of 337
    capital investment options 337
    real estate acquisition 337
    reviews 340
habitual residence 340
health 336, 338, 339
highly qualified employment 336, 338
Human Development Index 335
identity cards 336
income tax 340–1
inheritance and succession 341–2
inheritance tax 341
intestacy 341
investments 336–8, 340
language 336, 343
Lisbon 335
marriage, citizenship by 342, 343
matrimonial property regime 341–2
naturalization 342
Non-Habitual Residences Regime
    (NHR) 340
parents and grandparents 341–3
passports 336, 338
permanent residence 340
Porto 335
prenuptial agreements 342
procedures 340
professionals 339
quality of life/standard of living 188
real estate acquisition 337
renewable energy 335
residence 178, 184, 336–40
    citizenship 336, 343
    day counting and time spent in
        country 339, 340
    duration 340, 343
    long-term 336
    permanent 340
    permits 336, 338, 340
    procedures 340

requirements/conditions 338–9
tax 340
temporary permits 340
time frames 340
same sex relationships 338, 343
Schengen area 117–18, 188, 336, 339
Schengen Information System (SIS) 339
security 188
self-employed 341
spouses and partners 341–2
stamp tax 341
tax 188, 340–1
tourism 335
time frames 340
Visa Restrictions Index (Henley &
    Partners) 149
visas 149, 188, 336
wills and testament 341
withholding tax 340
poverty reduction 379
**pre-emption rights, duty to inform
    buyer of** 45
pre-nuptial agreements *see* **nuptial
    agreements**
privacy
    banking 7
    biometric passports 134
    Germany, bank accounts in 7
    citizenship planning 48, 56
    naturalization 56
    passports 134–5
    real estate holding structures 43
    reasons for becoming resident in
        another country 7–8
    United States 8
professional and expert advice *see also*
    agents
    Austria 482
    citizenship planning 58
    fees 45
    health insurance 34
    real estate, acquisition of 39, 44–5
    tax 34
    United Arab Emirates (UAE)/Dubai
        397
    United Kingdom 44
    United States 69, 71, 74, 424, 429
professionals *see also* **professional and
    expert advice**

Belgium 223
Hong Kong 264, 265–6
Jersey 281
Malaysia 294
Portugal 339
Singapore 351
United Arab Emirates (UAE)/Dubai
    392
property *see* **property tax; real estate,**
acquisition of
property tax
Antigua and Barbuda 475
Grenada 509
Monaco 317
New Zealand 328
St Lucia 543
quality of life/standard of living
Australia 193
Austria 205, 481
Belgium 219–20
Canada 233
Global Residence Program Index
    (GRPI) 2016 188
Guernsey 250
identity and brand of nations 83, 84, 87
Malta 466
Monaco 313
New Zealand 325
Portugal 188
real estate, acquisition of 20, 38, 46
reasons for becoming resident in
    another country 7
Singapore 350
Thailand 379
United Kingdom 403
quality of nationality index *see* **Henley**
& Partners - Kochenov Quality of
Nationality Index (QNI)
quotas
Austria 205, 209
Canada 237
Hong Kong 265
Malta 445, 517
Switzerland 366–8
Thailand 382
United States 425
real estate, acquisition of 20–1
access and access authorization 41
advisers, appointment of 39

agencies 39, 45
agricultural property 41
Antigua and Barbuda 173–4, 450,
    472–3, 475
apartments 46
asset diversification 38
authorizations 45
broker's commission 45
building, factors with regard to the
    actual 41–2
capital gains tax 45–6
capital growth 39
caveat emptor 44
communications, access to 42
construction projects 39–40
Cyprus 173, 441–2, 489, 490, 492
dampness 41
defects, duty to inform buyer of 44
disclosure 45
Dominica 442, 498–9
double tax treaties 32
due diligence 45
encumbrances/third party claims 42,
    45, 46
exclusion of liability 45
fees 45
finding the right property 39–42
guarantees 45
high-tension lines and mobile phone
    masts 41
historical properties 41
holding structures 42–4
hospitals and healthcare 40
improvements to location 40
infrastructure 39–40
investments 20
Jersey 281
language 39
legal advisors 45
legal issues 20, 39, 42
liens 46
location 39–40
Malaysia 295
Malta 173, 304, 306–7, 444–5, 517–18
Monaco 314
natural hazards 41
noise 40, 42
notaries' fees 45
owners' associations 46

pollution 41
Portugal 337
pre-emption rights, duty to inform
    buyer of 45
prestige 20
quality of life/standard of living 20,
    38, 46
quality of local municipality 40
registers of land 42, 43
rental properties, benefits of initial 38
representations and warranties 45
reserve or renovation funds 46
residence planning 38–46
restrictions 20–1, 39
re-zoning 39–40
risk 44
rural property 41
sales agreements 45
schools 40
security 41
shopping 40
size and shape of plot 40
smell 40
St Kitts and Nevis 451, 526, 527,
    529–30, 531
St Lucia 539, 540–2, 543
surveillance 41
Switzerland 122, 265, 269
tax 20, 39, 45–6
Thailand 380–1
title 42, 44
transactions 44–6
transport 39–40
United Arab Emirates (UAE)/Dubai
    391
United States 70
value maintenance 39, 42
VAT 45
water pressure 41
water, properties located near 41
wind exposure 40–1
reasons for becoming resident in
    another country 5–9
business opportunities 6
diversification 6
economic migrants 6
freedom of travel 6
globalization 5–6
high-net-worth-individuals 7

investment opportunities 6, 7
language 5–6
lifestyle 6
movement of people 5
personal and business planning,
    optimizing 6
political instability 6, 7
privacy 7–8
quality of life/standard of living 7
refugees 6
rules and regulations, complexity of 8
security 6, 7
tax planning 7–9
technological infrastructure 6
Red Cross Laissez-Passer 130, 136
refugees 6
regions
freedom of movement 107–27
reputation 76–80
registration
Austria 208
Guernsey 257
Jersey 288
land 42, 43
Malaysia 297
Switzerland 372
Thailand 382
United Kingdom 411
reputation
Austria 481
cities, identity and brand of 76–80
citizenship planning 54–5
Global Residence Program Index
    (GRPI) 2016 188
Guernsey 252
identity and brand of nations 76–82,
    95–6
Malta 466, 520
regions 76–80
services companies 59
St Kitts and Nevis 526, 532
Switzerland 363–4
residence *see also* **habitual residence;**
    permanent residence; residence
    planning; tax residence
alien residence cards or permits 137
Australia 178, 179, 193–4, 199
Austria 178, 179, 188, 205–9, 211,
    437, 483

Belgium 178, 180, 188, 220–4, 227
Canada 178, 180, 234–40, 243, 437
checklist 22–6
China 269–70
citizenship 14, 16–17, 188
    list 25–6
    taxation based on 16–17
change of residence 11–13, 15–16
definition 9
domicile 15–16, 18–19
economy 14
education and schools 14–15
effects 9
EU 113–14
factors to consider 13–26
gift tax 19
Global Residence Program Index
    (GRPI) 2016 188–9
Grenada 508
Guernsey 178, 181, 250–5
health insurance 21–2, 35–6
Hong Kong 178, 181, 264–70
humanitarian residence 194
inheritance tax 18–19, 34–5, 109
Jersey 178, 182, 280–6
location 14
Malaysia 178, 182, 293–7
Malta 178, 183, 303–5, 307, 445, 517,
    519
Monaco 178, 183, 314–16, 319
matrimonial property regime 14, 18
New Zealand 178, 184, 325–9
Nordic Passport Union 126
quality of life/standard of living 188
permits, obtaining and maintaining
    14
personal situations 14
political stability 14
Portugal 178, 184, 188, 336–40, 343
premier options, overview of 177–89
real estate, acquisition of 20–1
reputation 188
retiree residence programs 60
Schengen area 120
Singapore 178, 185, 349–55, 357
St Lucia 542
students 114
Switzerland 122, 178, 185, 364–9,
    372, 437

temporary residence 36
temporary visits, dangers of 13
Thailand 178, 186, 379–82
timing 21
total costs 188
United Arab Emirates (UAE)/Dubai
    178, 186, 390–7
United Kingdom 65, 178, 187,
    404–17, 437
United States 65, 178, 187, 423–31
visas 141
    visa-free travel 14, 188
    Visa Restrictions Index (Henley &
        Partners) 149
residence planning 3–46
    children 18, 27, 43
    domicile 9–10
    economy 6, 9, 13, 17, 27, 39
    factors to consider when choosing a
        new residence 13–26
    financial planning 33–5
    health insurance 35–8
    identity and brand of nations 95
    reasons for becoming resident in
        another country 5–9
    residential real estate 38–46
    security risks 7, 9, 13, 41
    spouses and partners 12, 18, 27
    tax residence
        change of 11–13
        considerations and implications
            26–33
    use of term 4
retirees
    Cyprus 488
    EU 115
    retiree residence programs 60
    security 51
    Switzerland 364, 366–7
    Thailand 379, 380
    visas 141
Roman law 103
Romania 115–18, 122, 170
rural property 41
Russia 83, 138
sales and goods tax/VAT
    Antigua and Barbuda 474–5
    Australia 198
    Grenada 509

Jersey 287
Malaysia 296
Malta 306, 520
real estate, acquisition of 45
St Kitts and Nevis 531
St Lucia 538, 543
United Arab Emirates (UAE)/Dubai 397
Salter, Mark 132
same-sex relationships
Australia 199
Portugal 338, 343
United Kingdom 410
Sarkozy, Nicholas 17
Savings Directive 314
Schengen area
Amsterdam Treaty 117
Antigua and Barbuda 475
Austria 117–18, 205
Belgium 117, 220
Bulgaria 117–18
citizenship planning 50
conditions of entry 119
courts and legal systems
Croatia 117–18
Cyprus 117–18
Czech Republic 117–18
Data Protection Directive 121
Denmark 117–18
Dominica 500
drugs, fight against 118
establishment
Estonia 117–18
Finland 117–18
framework 118–20
France 50, 117
free movement of persons 117
Greece 117–18
Grenada 509
Hungary 117–18
Iceland 117–18
Ireland 117–18
Italy 117–18
Latvia 117–18
Liechtenstein 118
list of member states 117
Lithuania 117–18
Luxembourg 117
Malta 117–18, 515

nationality, quality of 171
Netherlands 117
Nordic Passport Union 118, 126
Norway 117–18
opt-outs 118
passports 118, 137
permanent residence 120
Poland 117–18
police and judicial cooperation 118–21
Portugal 117–18, 188, 339
residence permits 120
Romania 117–18
Schengen *acquis*, establishment of 117–18
Schengen Information System (SIS) 118–21, 339
Schengen Information System II (SIS II) 120–1
Slovakia 117–18
Slovenia 117–18
Spain 117–18
St Kitts and Nevis 531
St Lucia 543
Sweden 117–18
Switzerland 117–18
terrorism 118
third country nationals 120
United Kingdom 118
visas 50, 118–20, 138
refusal 119–20
residence permits 120
schools *see* **education and schools**
Scotland 403, 415, 417
security risks
Antigua and Barbuda 471
Canada 235
citizenship planning 48, 53, 56–8
Jersey 287
Malta 445, 517
naturalization 57
New Zealand 327
passports 138
Portugal 188
real estate, acquisition of 41
reasons for becoming resident in another country 6, 7
residence planning 7, 9, 13, 41
Singapore 7
St Kitts and Nevis 529

Switzerland 7, 363
United Kingdom 7, 403
seizure of assets, risk of 35
self-employed
    Austria 206, 207, 210
    Belgium 220, 221–2, 223
    Canada 241
    EU 113, 115
    Portugal 341
    Switzerland 365
September 11, 2001, terrorist attacks on US 49
Serbia 135, 148
service passports 130, 136
Settlement Freedom Ranking 161–2, 163, 165–7, 173
    diversity of 161–2, 163, 166–7, 170
    weight of 162, 163, 166–7, 170
Seychelles 174
Sierra Leone 148
Singapore 7, 347–60
    advantages and disadvantages 357–8
    Approval-in-Principle (AIP) 354
    background 349
    birth, citizenship by (*ius soli*) 357
    Canada, visa-free travel to 357
    capital gains tax 356
    Central Manpower Base, registration with 355
    Central Provident Fund (CPF), contributions to 356
    children 349, 351, 353
    China, visa-free travel to 357
    citizenship 357
    climate 349, 360
    corporate tax 356
    culture 349
    dependents 353
    documentation 351, 354
    double tax treaties 356
    dual citizenship 357
    economy 349
    education and schools 349
    educational level 351
    employment 349, 351–3, 355–6
    Employment Pass Holders 349
    EU countries, visa-free travel to 357
    families 350–3
        children 349, 351, 353

    family law 350
    GIP Family Office (FO) option 352
        Long Term Visit Pass (LTVP) 352
    Financial Investor Scheme (FIS), closure of 350
    financial services 349
    general information 359
    Global Investor Program (GIP) 349, 350–3
    health 349, 354
    incentives 349
    income tax 355
    infrastructure 349
    inheritance and succession 356
    investments 349, 350–5
    language 350
    Long Term Visit Pass (LTVP) 353
    matrimonial property regime 356
    military/national service 355, 357
    multiculturalism 349
    nationality, quality of 163, 168
    naturalization 56, 357
    Not Ordinarily Resident (NOR) scheme 355
    parents and grandparents 350, 353, 357
    passports 357
    permanent residence 349–53, 357
    procedures 354–5
    professional qualifications 351
    quality of life/standard of living 350
    Re-Entry Permit (REP) 353–4
        conditions for renewal 353–4
        investments 353
    relinquishment of other citizenships 357
    residence 178, 185, 350–5
        categories of foreigner 350
        citizenship 357
        duration 350, 357
        permanent 349–53, 357
        permits 350–3
        procedures 354–5
        requirements/conditions 351–2
        tax 28, 355
        time frames 354–5
    spouses and partners 351, 353, 355–6
    St Kitts and Nevis 532
    tax 355–6
        incentives 349

residence 28, 355
telecommunications 349
time frames 354–5
United Kingdom 349
United States, visa-free travel to 357
visa-free access 357
work passes 351
Slovakia 117–18, 148, 167, 437
Slovenia 117–18
smell 40
social responsibility 95
social security 114
social services 113
Somalia 149
South Africa
  identity and brand of nations 83
  socio-political context 110
South American citizenships 161, 165
South Korea 83, 148, 163
Southern African Development
  Community (SADC) 110
sovereign debt problems, countries with 16
Spain
  inheritance tax 34
  Schengen area 117–18
  Visa Restrictions Index (Henley &
    Partners) 148
special passports 130, 136
sportspersons 102, 405, 407
spouses and partners *see also* **same-sex**
  relationships
  Antigua and Barbuda 439–40, 470–1
  Austria 207–8, 211, 440
  Belgium 222
  Canada 237–8, 241
  death 18
  Dominica 443, 499
  EU 113
  Grenada 506
  Hong Kong 267
  identity and brand of nations 89
  Jersey 283
  Malaysia 293–5
  Malta 516
  Monaco 317–19
  New Zealand 327
  Portugal 341
  residence planning 12, 18, 27
  Singapore 351, 353, 355–6

St Kitts and Nevis 527
St Lucia 447, 539, 541
Switzerland 370
Thailand 381, 383
United Arab Emirates/Dubai 391
United Kingdom 410–11, 412, 415
United States 65–6, 71
St Kitts and Nevis, citizenship-by-
  investment in 48, 57, 438, 445–6,
  523–34
  advantages 531
  biometric passports 530
  Brazil, travel to 532
  Canada 526
  categories 446
  Certificate of Registration 530
  children 446, 528
  Citizenship-by-Investment Unit
    (CIU) 529–30
  climate 525, 534
  comparison table 451–2, 455, 457, 459,
    461, 463, 465
  corporate income tax 531
  criminal records 528–9
  dependents 446, 527–8
  documentation 446, 529, 531–2
  dual citizenship 530
  due diligence 446, 527–9
  economy 527
  families 446, 527–8
  fees 446, 527–8, 530
  financial services 525, 526
  general information 533
  grant of citizenship 530
  Henley & Partners 526, 531
  Hong Kong, travel to 532
  inheritance tax 34
  international organizations,
    membership of 526
  interviews 529
  irregularities and setbacks 526, 532
  language 525, 529
  legal basis 526
  nationality, quality of 171, 172, 173
  natural attractions 525
  passports 530, 531–2
  political system 525
  procedures 529–30
  real estate 451, 526, 527, 529–30, 531

reputation 526, 532
requirements/conditions 446, 451–2, 527–9
Schengen area 531
security risks 529
service companies, reputation of 59
Singapore, travel to 532
spouses and partners 527
sugar industry
    shut down of 526
    Sugar Industry Diversification Foundation (SIDF) 446, 452, 527–8, 530
tax 28, 34, 531
Tax Information Exchange Agreements 531
time frames 446, 529–30
tourism 525
United Kingdom 525, 532
United States 525, 532
VAT 531
visa-free travel 448, 528–9
    Canada, withdrawal of access by 526
    comparison table 455, 457, 459, 461, 463, 465
    Schengen area 531–2
visa-waiver agreement with Schengen area countries 531
withholding tax 531
St Lucia, citizenship-by-investment in 57, 438, 535–45
advantages 543
agents 541
background 537
capital gains tax (CGT) 542
Castries 537
Certificates of Citizenship 541
citizenship 543
Citizenship by Investment Board 447, 540–1
Citizenship by Investment Unit (CIU) 540, 541–2
climate 537, 545
colonialism 537
Commonwealth 537, 543
comparison table 453, 455, 457, 459, 461, 463, 465
corporate and business tax 542

criminal records 540
dependents 447, 539, 541
documentation 540–1
dual citizenship 543
due diligence 447, 539–40
economy 538
embassies, consular offices or High Commissions, attendance at 542, 543
Enterprise Project 539
families 447, 539
fees 447, 539–40, 541, 543
financial services 538
general information 544
global economic crisis of 2008 538
Hong Kong, travel to 543
income tax 542
inheritance tax 542
International Business Companies (IBCs) 542
international organizations, membership of 538
language 537, 541
National Economic Fund (NEF), contributions to 447, 539
nationality, quality of 173
natural attractions 537
oath of allegiance 447, 542, 543
passports 447, 540, 543
political system 537–8
procedures 540–2
property tax 543
real estate, acquisition of 539, 540–2, 543
requirements/conditions 447–8, 453, 539–40
residence 542
Schengen area 543
Singapore, travel to 543
spouses and partners 447, 539, 541
tax 538, 542–3
    residence 542
    tourism 542
time frames 540–2
tourism 537, 538, 542
travel connections 538
United Kingdom 537, 538, 543
United States 538
VAT 538, 543

visa-free travel 447–8
  comparison table 455, 457, 459,
    461, 463, 465
  Schengen area 543
  Visa Restrictions Index (Henley &
    Partners) 447
standard of living *see* **quality of life/
standard of living**
state succession 103
statelessness
  ancestry/descent, citizenship by (*ius
sanguinis*) 104
  citizenship 54, 100, 102–3
  freedom of movement 54
stereotypes and clichés of nations 79–80
students
  Austria 206, 207
  EU 113, 114, 115
  grants or loans 114
  Hong Kong 267
  residence 114
  Switzerland 364
  United Arab Emirates (UAE)/Dubai
391
  United Kingdom 405, 408
succession *see* **inheritance and
succession; inheritance tax and
estate planning; intestacy**
surveillance 41
Sweden
  accommodation available for use,
having 12
  identity and brand of nations 83
  Nordic Passport Union 126
  Schengen area 117–18
  Visa Restrictions Index (Henley &
    Partners) 148
Switzerland 361–75
  advantages and disadvantages 373
  age 366–7
  ancestry/descent, citizenship by (*ius
sanguinis*) 372
  asset protection 35
  Austria 440, 484
  'B' residence permits for EU/EFTA
citizens 365
  background 363
  'C' residence permits for EU/EFTA
citizens 365

Canada 367
cantons 363, 365–72
capital gains tax (CGT) 370
children 372
citizenship 372
climate 375
close ties to Switzerland, requirement
  for 366–7
communes 368–9, 372
community of property 371
corporations
  relocation of 363
  tax 370
Croatia, transitional provisions
  relating to 364
cross-border commuter permit
  (Permit 'G') 367
culture 363, 372
day counting and time spent in
  country 12
double tax treaties 370
dual citizenship 373
economic promotion program 366
economy 363
education and schools 15
EFTA 108, 116, 121–2, 364–6, 368
employment 364–6, 368
EU 116, 121–2, 364–8
families 370–2
  children 372
  family law 371–2
  spouses and partners 370
free movement of persons 116, 121–2,
  368
'G' residence permits for EU/EFTA
  citizens 365–6
general information 374
Geneva 363
gift tax 370, 372
health treatments 364
income tax 368–70
independent means, persons of 364–5,
  367
inheritance and succession 371–2
inheritance tax 370, 372
integration 372
international organizations,
  membership of 363
intestacy 371

investments 363–4
'L' residence permits for EU/EFTA
   citizens 366
labor market, access to 364, 366
language 363, 372
lump-sum taxation 367, 368–70
matrimonial property regime
   community of property 371
   Ordinary Regime 371
   separation of estates 371
multiculturalism 363
nationality, quality of 163, 167, 169
naturalization 56, 372
non-EU/ETFA citizens 364–6,
   367–9, 372
pensioners 364, 366–7
permanent establishments 369
Permit 'B' for non-EU/EFTA citizens
   367
Permit 'C' for non-EU/EFTA citizens
   367
Permit 'G' for non-EU/EFTA citizens
   367
Permit 'L' for non-EU/EFTA citizens
   367–8
procedures 368
quotas 366–8
real estate
   acquisition of 20–1, 122, 365, 369
   capital gains tax (CGT) 370
   gift tax 372
   inheritance tax 372
registration of citizenship 372
reputation 363–4
residence 178, 185, 364–9, 437
   categories 365–8
   citizenship 372
   duration 372
   EU 122
   permits 122, 364–9
   procedures 368
   requirements/conditions 365–8
   tax 28
   time frames 368
Schengen area 117–18
Schwyz, no inheritance or gift tax in
   370
secure base, as 7, 363
self-employed 365

separation of estates 371
short-stays 367–8
spouses and partners 370–1
students 364
tax 28, 363–4, 366–7, 368–70, 372
time frames 368
tourism 363
trusts 370
United Kingdom 403–4, 412–15
United States 367
visas 138–9, 368
wealth tax 368–70
work permits 364, 366
Zurich 363
tax see also capital gains, tax on;
   corporations, tax on; double
   tax treaties; exit, departure or
   emigration taxes; gift tax; income
   tax; inheritance tax and estate
   planning; property tax; sales
   and goods tax/VAT; wealth tax;
   withholding tax
advisers 34
Antigua and Barbuda 469, 474–5
Australia 197–8
Austria 209–10, 483
Belgium 219, 221–2, 224–5
Canada 7, 241–2, 243
citizenship 16–17, 48, 50–1, 54
Cyprus 488, 491–2
Dominica 500
Guernsey 249, 255–7
Hong Kong 263, 270–1
identity and brand of nations 79, 85
Jersey 280, 282, 284, 286–7
Malaysia 296
Malta 305–6, 307, 519–20
Monaco 314, 316–18
naturalization 56
Netherlands 7
New Zealand 328
OECD standards of tax transparency
   255
real estate, acquisition of 20, 39, 42–6
reasons for becoming resident in
   another country 7–9
Singapore 355–6
St Kitts and Nevis 531
St Lucia 538, 542–3

Switzerland 363–4, 366–7, 368–70,
    372
Thailand 382–3
timing 21
United Arab Emirates (UAE)/Dubai
    389, 391–3, 397
United Kingdom 7, 28, 33, 403–4,
    412–15
United States 7, 27, 50, 64–72, 428–30
tax residence
accommodation available for use,
    having 16, 28, 30
ambiguity in laws and regulations
    27–8
Austria 483
business interests 30
change of residence 11–13
citizenship 16–17, 26, 48, 50–1
considerations and implications 13,
    16–19, 26–33
criteria 26–8
day counting and time spent in
    country 12, 16, 27–9
domicile 50, 54
double tax treaties 19–20, 32–3
exit taxes 17, 29, 30–1
    claw backs 31
    definition 31
extended income taxes 30–1
factors to consider 13, 16–19
family interests 30
Global Residence Program Index
    (GRPI) 2016 188
Grenada 508–9
income tax 16, 26–7, 29, 30–1
inheritance tax 18–19, 30
New Zealand 325, 328
Portugal 188, 340–1
residence criteria 26–7
source income 26–7, 29
St Lucia 542
termination 33
Thailand 382
United Kingdom 33
United States 27
wealth tax 16
technological infrastructure 6
terrorism 49, 52–3, 118, 135
Thailand 377–86

90-day visas 379
1-year visas 379
advantages and disadvantages 384
age 380–1
background 379
bank accounts, security deposits in
    380–1
Blue Book 382
business visas 379
children 381
citizenship 380, 384
climate 379, 386
corporate income tax 383
criminal records 380
culture 379
day counting and time spent in
    country 382
directors of public companies 380
divorce 383
dual citizenship 384
economy 379
employment 380, 382
families 380–2
    children 381
    family law 383
    parents and grandparents 381, 383
    spouses and partners 381, 383
general information 385
gift tax 383
house cards 382
income tax 382
inheritance and succession 383
inheritance tax 383
international organizations,
    membership of 379
interviews 382
intestacy 383
investment 380–2
marriage visas 379
matrimonial property regime 383
natural attractions 379
naturalization 380, 384
parents and grandparents 381, 383
permanent residence 380–2, 384
poverty reduction 379
pre-nuptial agreements 383
procedures 382
quality of life/standard of living 379
quotas 382

real estate, acquisition of 380–1
Red Book 382
registration 382
residence 178, 186, 379–82
    Blue Book 382
    certificates 382
    day counting and time spent in
        country 382
    permanent 380–2, 384
    procedures 382
    requirements/conditions 380–1
    time frames 382
retirement visas 379, 380
spouses and partners 381, 383
taxation 382–3
time frames 382
tourism 379
visas 379–82
work permits 380, 382
time frames
Antigua and Barbuda 440, 472–3
Australia 196–7
Austria 209, 440, 482
Canada 240
change of residence 21
Cyprus 490, 492
Dominica 500
Grenada 505, 509
Guernsey 254–5
Hong Kong 268–70
Jersey 284–6
Malaysia 296
Malta 305, 518
Monaco 316
New Zealand 327–8
Portugal 340
Singapore 354–5
St Kitts and Nevis 446, 529–30
St Lucia 540–2
Switzerland 368
synchronization 21
tax and estate planning 21
Thailand 382
United Arab Emirates (UAE)/Dubai
    396–7
United Kingdom 410–11
United States 427–8
time spent in country *see* **day counting**
    and time spent in country

Timor Leste 148
Tonga 148
tourism
Antigua and Barbuda 468, 369
cities, identity and brand of 90
Cyprus 488
Dominica 497
Guernsey 249
identity and brand of nations 76,
    81–2, 84–6, 96
Jersey 279
Malaysia 293
Portugal 335
St Kitts and Nevis 525
St Lucia 537, 538, 542
Switzerland 363
Thailand 379
UN World Tourism Organization
    (UNWTO) 142
United Arab Emirates (UAE)/Dubai
    390
visas 141, 142
trade sanctions 49
transport, access to 39–40
**Trans-Tasman Travel Arrangement
    (TTTA)** 108, 126
Travel Freedom Ranking
diversity of 162, 163, 165, 167–8, 170
ranking 162
weight of 162, 163, 166, 167–8, 170
trusts
Austria 210
Canada 241–2
inheritance tax 19
Monaco 318
New Zealand 329
real estate holding structures 44
Switzerland 370
United Kingdom 412
Turkey 83, 164
UK-Ireland Common Travel Area 108,
    110, 126–7
Channel Islands 126–7
Isle of Man 126–7
Jersey 279
UK Immigration Rules 126–7
visas 127
United Arab Emirates (UAE)/Dubai
    387–400

Abu Dhabi 389
advantages and disadvantages 398
Ajman 389
alcohol, taxes on 397
Branch or Representative Office
    392–3
business licensing 390, 392
children 391
citizenship 398
climate 400
corporations
    Branch or Representative Office
        392–3
    Free Trade Zone Company or
        Establishment 393–5
    Limited Liability Company (LLC)
        392
    residence permits, procedure for
        396
    tax 397
culture 390
dependents 391
documentation 396
Domestic Help Residence Permit 391
double tax treaties 389
dual citizenship 398
Dubai International Financial Centre
    (DIFC) 394–5
economy 389–90
education and schools 390–1
employment 390, 395–6
    Employee Residence Permit 390–1
    Free Zones 394
    residence permits, procedure for
        396
families
    children 391
    Domestic Help Residence Permit
        391
    family law 397
    Family Residence Permit 391
    parents and grandparents 391, 393
    Relative Residence Permit 391
    spouses and partners 391
financial services 394–5
Free Trade Zone Company or
    Establishment 393–5
Free Trade Zones 390, 393–7
Fujairah 389

general information 399
haram, tax on products which are 397
health 396
identity cards 396
inheritance and succession 397
international organizations,
    membership of 389
investments 389, 393
Jebel Ali Free Zone (JAFZ) 394
Jumeirah Lakes Towers (Dubai Multi
    Commodities Centre – DMCC/
    JLT) 395
languages 389, 396
legal advice 397
licensing 390, 392–3
Limited Liability Company (LLC)
    392
member states 389
Mohammed Bin Rashid City,
    development of 390
naturalization 398
parents and grandparents 391, 393
passports 396, 398
procedures 396–7
professional licences 392
Ras Al Khaimah 389
Real Estate Investor Residence Visa
    391
Relative Residence Permit 391
residence 178, 186, 390–7
    duration 395
    permits 390–1, 395–7
    procedures 396–7
    requirements/conditions 395–6
    time frames 396–7
sales tax 397
security 7
Shari'ah law 397
Sharjah 389
sponsorship 390–1, 395–6
spouses and partners 391
Student Residence Permit 391
tax 389, 391–3, 397
tenancy agreements 396
time frames 396–7
tourism 390
Umm Al Qaiwain 389
Visa Restrictions Index (Henley &
    Partners) 148

visas 148, 392, 394, 396
work permits 390
United Kingdom 401–20
advantages and disadvantages 417–18
aggressive fiscal and regulatory
environment 7
airports 403
ancestry/descent, citizenship by (*ius sanguinis*) 416
Antigua and Barbuda 468, 475
biometric cards 411
birth, citizenship by (*ius soli*) 416
Brexit 111, 403–4
British Overseas Territories (BOTs) 416
British Protected Person status 102
capital gains tax 411–12
children 409, 415
Chinese travellers 50
citizenship 416–17
climate 420
colonialism 403, 505
Common Travel Area with Ireland 108, 110, 126–7, 279
Commonwealth citizens 416
criminal records 409, 411
culture 404
day counting and time spent in country 409–10, 412–13, 416–17
dependents 409, 411
diplomatic posts, submission of applications at 410
divorce 18
domicile 10
change of 65
tax 412–15
Dominica 497, 500
double tax treaties 415
dual citizenship 417
economy 403
education and schools 15, 404–5, 408–9
EEA nationals 408
employment 405–8
England 403
entrepreneurs 405–6
exceptional talent 405–6
extension of stay 409, 411
EU

Brexit 111, 403–4
passports 65
families 409–12
children 409, 415
Family Home Allowance 412
family law 415–16
parents and grandparents 416
spouses and partners 410–12, 415
financial services 403
forced heirship in Scotland 415
general information 419
Grenada 505, 509
Guernsey 249, 252, 254–5, 257
health 404
Highly Skilled Migrants 406
highly-valued migrants (Tier 1) 405–8, 411
Hong Kong 6, 263
identity and brand of nations 83
immigration 404–10
income tax 65, 411–13
indefinite leave to remain (ILR) 408, 411
inheritance and succession 415–16
Inheritance (Provision for Family and Dependents) Act 1975 416
inheritance tax 34, 412–13
international organizations, membership of 403–4
intestacy 416
intra-company transfers 407
investments 405–10
Investor category (Tier 1) 406, 408–11
Jersey 279, 288
language 409, 410, 411, 417
Life in the UK test 410, 411, 417
London 403, 404
divorce capital, as 18
Mayor and Assembly 404
No 1 city in world, as 404
Malaysia 293
Malta 303, 515
matrimonial property regime 415
ministers of religion 407
mobility scheme (Tier 5) 405
National Health Service (NHS) 404
naturalization 56, 416
non-EU nationals 404–5

Northern Ireland 403
nuptial agreements 18, 415
parents and grandparents 416
passports 132, 409
permanent residence 405–6, 408–10, 416
points-based system of immigration 405
police, registration with the 411
post-study workers 406
procedures 409–10
quality of life/standard of living 403
real estate, acquisition of 20–1
  £2 mill, rules on dwellings over 44
  holding structures 44
  professional advice 44
remittance basis of taxation 414
residence 178, 187, 404–15, 437
  change of 65
  day counting and time spent in country 409–10, 412–13, 416–17
  permanent 405–6, 408–10, 416
  procedures 410–11
  tax 28, 33, 412–15
  time frames 410–11
same sex relationships 410
Schengen area 118
Scotland 403, 415, 417
secure base, as 7, 403
service sector 403
Singapore 349
skilled workers (Tier 2) 405, 407
sportspersons 405, 407
spouses and partners 410–12, 415
St Kitts and Nevis 525, 532
St Lucia 537, 538, 543
students (Tier 4) 405, 408
sufficient time test 413
Swiss nationals 408
tax 7, 28, 33, 403–4, 412–15
  domicile 412–15
  non-residents 404
  residence 28, 33, 412–15
temporary migration scheme (Tier 3) 405, 407–8
tiers 404–11
time frames 410–11
travel, as base for 403

trusts 412
UK Border Agency 409–10
Visa Restrictions Index (Henley & Partners) 148
visas 148, 408–9
Wales 403, 415–16, 417
wills and testament 416
Youth Mobility Scheme (Tier 5) 405
United Nations (UN) 109, 142, 161–2, 163, 170, 325, 335
United States 421–33 *see also* **United States citizenship or Green Card, giving up**
advantages and disadvantages 430–1
age 426, 430
aggressive fiscal and regulatory environment 7
American Revolution 103
ancestry/descent, citizenship by (*ius sanguinis*) 430
Antigua and Barbuda 469
APEC Business Travel Card (ABTC) scheme 123
asset protection 35
birth, citizenship by (*ius soli*) 48, 55, 104, 430
Brazil 171
Canada 233
children 67
China, applications from 427
citizenship 49, 104, 430
  ancestry/descent, citizenship by (*ius sanguinis*) 430
  birth, citizenship by (*ius soli*) 48, 55, 104, 430
  nationality, quality of 161, 163, 165, 169, 171
  taxation based on citizenship 16
climate 433
conditional permanent residence 427–8
Constitution 104
criminal records 426
culture 423
divorce 429
domicile of origin 10
double tax treaties 429
dual citizenship 430
EB-5 Program 16, 423–31

economy 423–5
education and schools 15
Electronic System for Travel
    Authorization (ESTA) 140
employment 72, 423, 424–9
estate tax 429–30
European ancestry 56
expatriation, complex rules on 16
families 428, 429–30
    children 67
    family law 429–30
    inherited or gifted funds 426
    parents and grandparents 67
    spouses and partners 65–6, 71
Form I-485 427
Form I-526 427
Form I-829 428
general information 432
Green Card (EB-5 Program) 423–31
    Basic Program 424, 427
    citizenship, taxation based on 16
    Regional Center Pilot Program
        424, 425–8
Grenada 443, 505, 509–10
health 426
Hong Kong, persons from 6
identity and brand of nations 83
immigration 423
income tax 428
inheritance and succession 426,
    429–30
intestacy 429
investment 424–7
Iran 171
job creation 425, 427–8
language 426, 430
Limited Partnerships 425
nationality, quality of 161, 163, 165,
    169, 171
naturalization 430
net worth tax 429
Oath of Allegiance 430
parents and grandparents 67
political system 423
privacy 8
procedures 427–8
professional advice 424, 429
quotas 425
real estate, acquisition of 20–1

Regional Center Pilot Program 424,
    425–8
residence 178, 187
    conditional permanent residence
        427–8
    duration 430
    permanent 16, 423–31
    permits 424
    procedures 427–8
    requirements/conditions 426–7
    tax 27, 424, 428
    temporary permits 424
    time frames 427–8
securities 19
September 11, 2001, terrorist attacks
    on US 50
Singapore 357
spouses and partners 65–6, 71
St Kitts and Nevis 525, 532
St Lucia 538
states 423, 428, 429
Switzerland 367
tax 7, 27, 50, 64-72, 428–30
    advice 424, 429
    residence 27, 424, 428
    non-residents 50
    states 428
    types, list of 429
time frames 427–8
visas 139–40, 423, 427
    Antigua and Barbuda 469
    Grenada 443, 505, 509–10
    Visa Waiver Program 140, 142,
        469
wills and testament 429
**United States citizenship or Green
    Card, giving up** 63–74
    abroad, acquisition of US citizen of
        people born 67
    ancestry/descent, citizenship by (*ius
        sanguinis*) 67
    another citizenship, acquisition of
        64, 67
    beneficiaries, status of 66
    birth, citizenship by (*ius soli*) 67
    capital gains, tax on 70, 72
    Certificate of Loss of Nationality
        (CLN) 71
    citizenship 64, 65, 67

citizenship-by-investment programs 67
community property rules 65
date of expatriation 71
day counting and time spent in country 64–5, 71
death taxes 65, 69, 71–2, 74
Department of Homeland Security Form I-407, date of filing of 71
dividends, tax on 65
domicile, termination of 65
double tax treaties 65, 70
dual citizenship 66–7
exemptions from taxation 71–2
exit taxes 64, 66, 68–74
    assets included 70
    certification with IRS 69
    calculation of amount 70
    Congress' Joint Committee on Taxation report 73–4
    day counting and time spent in country 71
    double tax treaties 70
    gains and allowable losses 70
    indexation 69
    individual retirement accounts (IRAs) 70
    IRS Form W-8CE 70
    monetary tests 69
    postponement 66, 70–1
    real estate 70
    security 71
    transitional provisions 68–9
    withholding tax 70
expatriates
    Census 2010 68
    covered 69, 71
    number of 64, 66
extraterritoriality 65–7
Foreign Bank Account Reporting (FBAR) requirements 72
Foreign Investment in Real Property Tax Act (FIRPTA) 70
gifts and bequests, tax on 64–5, 66, 69, 71–2
immigration law 71–2
income tax 65–9, 72–4
    extraterritoriality 65–7
    returns 68

Internal Revenue Service (IRS) 66, 69
location of assets 66
marriage, acquisition of another citizenship through 67
matrimonial property regime 65
New York City, income tax rate in 72
number of expatriates 64, 66
oaths 71
parents, physical presence in US of 67
professional advice 69, 71, 74
real estate 70
relinquishment of citizenship 68, 71, 73
    Certificate of Loss of Nationality (CLN) 71
    oaths 71
residence 65
source of income 65
state or local income tax, states without 72
substantial presence test 65, 68, 71
tax 64–72
    exemptions 71–2
    residence 65
timing 66
visas 64, 71–2
withholding tax 70
Universal Declaration of Human Rights (UDHR) 100, 103, 109
useful addresses and websites 547–60
vaccinations 143
VAT see sales and goods tax/VAT
violence 49, 52–3
visa-free travel see also Henley & Partners Visa Restrictions Index (HVRI)
    Antigua and Barbuda 440, 448, 469
        comparison table 454, 458, 460, 462, 464
        criminal records 471
    Austria 205, 440, 448, 454, 456, 458, 460, 462, 464
    biometric passports 135
    Canada 526
    citizenship planning 48, 50, 53, 60
    Cyprus 448, 454, 456, 458, 460, 462, 464
    Dominica 443, 448, 455, 457, 459, 461, 463, 465, 500

EU 171
Global Citizenship Program Index
    (GCPI) 466
Global Residence Program Index
    (GRPI) 2016 188
Grenada 443, 448, 505
Malta 445, 448, 517
    comparison table 454, 456, 458,
        460, 462, 464
    Global Citizenship Program Index
        (GCPI) 466
nationality, quality of 162, 171
Portugal 188
residence 14
Schengen area 531–2
Singapore 357
St Kitts and Nevis 448, 528–9
    Canada, withdrawal of access by
        526
    comparison table 455, 457, 459,
        461, 463, 465
    Schengen area 531–2
St Lucia 447–8
    comparison table 455, 457, 459,
        461, 463, 465
    Schengen area 543
visas 129–32, 138–43 *see also* **Henley
    & Partners Visa Restrictions Index
    (HVRI); visa-free travel**
    Antigua and Barbuda 475
    APEC 123
    applications 131–2, 140–1
    Australia 136, 193–6
    Austria 205–6, 209
    Belgium 220, 222, 223–4
    Brazil 171
    breach of conditions 142
    business visas 141
    Canada 235, 239
    citizenship planning 48–50, 53, 60
    definition 131, 138
    diplomats 139
    electronic attachment of passports 197
    Electronic System for Travel
        Authorization (ESTA) 140
    employment 139, 141
    EU 113, 139
    expediting services 140
    foreign policy 130

Guernsey 255
health 130, 142–3
Hong Kong 266–7
IATA Travel Centre 143
immigrant visas 130, 141
Iran 171
Israel, travel to 139
Malaysia 295
Monaco 315, 316
multiple entry visas 142
New Zealand 325–8
non-immigrant visas 130, 141
overstayers 142
passports 130, 131–3, 135–6, 139–40
    electronic attachment 197
    second 132, 140
Portugal 336
refusals 141
requirements/conditions 130, 141–2
residence 141
Schengen area 118–20, 138
short-stays 141
single-entry visas 142
St Kitts and Nevis 531
Switzerland 138–9, 368
Thailand 379–82
tourism 141, 142
transit visas 139–40
transit without visa permission 140
Trans-Tasman Travel Arrangement
    (TTTA) 126
types of visas 141–2
UK-Ireland Common Travel Area
    127
UN World Tourism Organization
    (UNWTO) 142
United Arab Emirates (UAE)/Dubai
    392, 394, 396
United Kingdom 408–9
United States 64, 71–2, 139–40, 423,
    427
    Antigua and Barbuda 469
    immigrant intent 139
    Visa Waiver Program 71, 140, 142,
        469
vaccinations 143
World Health Organization (WHO).
    International Travel and Health
    book 143

Wales 403, 415–16, 417
water pressure 41
water, properties located near 41
wealth tax
  Belgium 224
  Canada 241
  Cyprus 491
  residence 16
  Switzerland 368–70
wills and testaments
  Austria 211
  Belgium 226
  Hong Kong 271
  Malta 306
  Portugal 341
  United Kingdom 416
  United States 429
wind exposure 40–1
withholding tax
  Belgium 225
  Cyprus 488
  Grenada 509
  Monaco 317
  pensions 34
  Portugal 340
  St Kitts and Nevis 531
  United States 70
work permits
  Belgium 220, 221–2, 223
  Jersey 280–1
  Monaco 315–16
  Singapore 351
  Switzerland 364, 366
  Thailand 380, 382
  United Arab Emirates (UAE)/Dubai
    390
**World Economic Forum. Global
  Competitiveness Index 2015-16** 488
World Health Organization (WHO).
  International Travel and Health **book**
  143
World Trade Organization (WTO) 263